Guide to Planning

THE FARM ESTATE

with Checklists and Forms

SECOND EDITION

THE IBP SERIES IN ESTATE PLANNING AND ADMINISTRATION

Complete Book of Wills and Trusts
Albert M. Lehrman

Complete Guide to the Marital Deduction in Estate Planning
Joseph Erdman

Estate Planner's Kit
Jack Arthur Kirby

Income Taxation of Estates, Trusts, and Beneficiaries
Ted D. Englebrecht and Michael L. Moore

The Ten Best Ways to Save Estate Taxes
Gilbert M. Cantor and Robert L. Franklin

Guide to Planning the Farm Estate with Checklists and Forms, Second Edition
Paul Douglass

MAJOR TYPES OF FARMING IN THE UNITED STATES

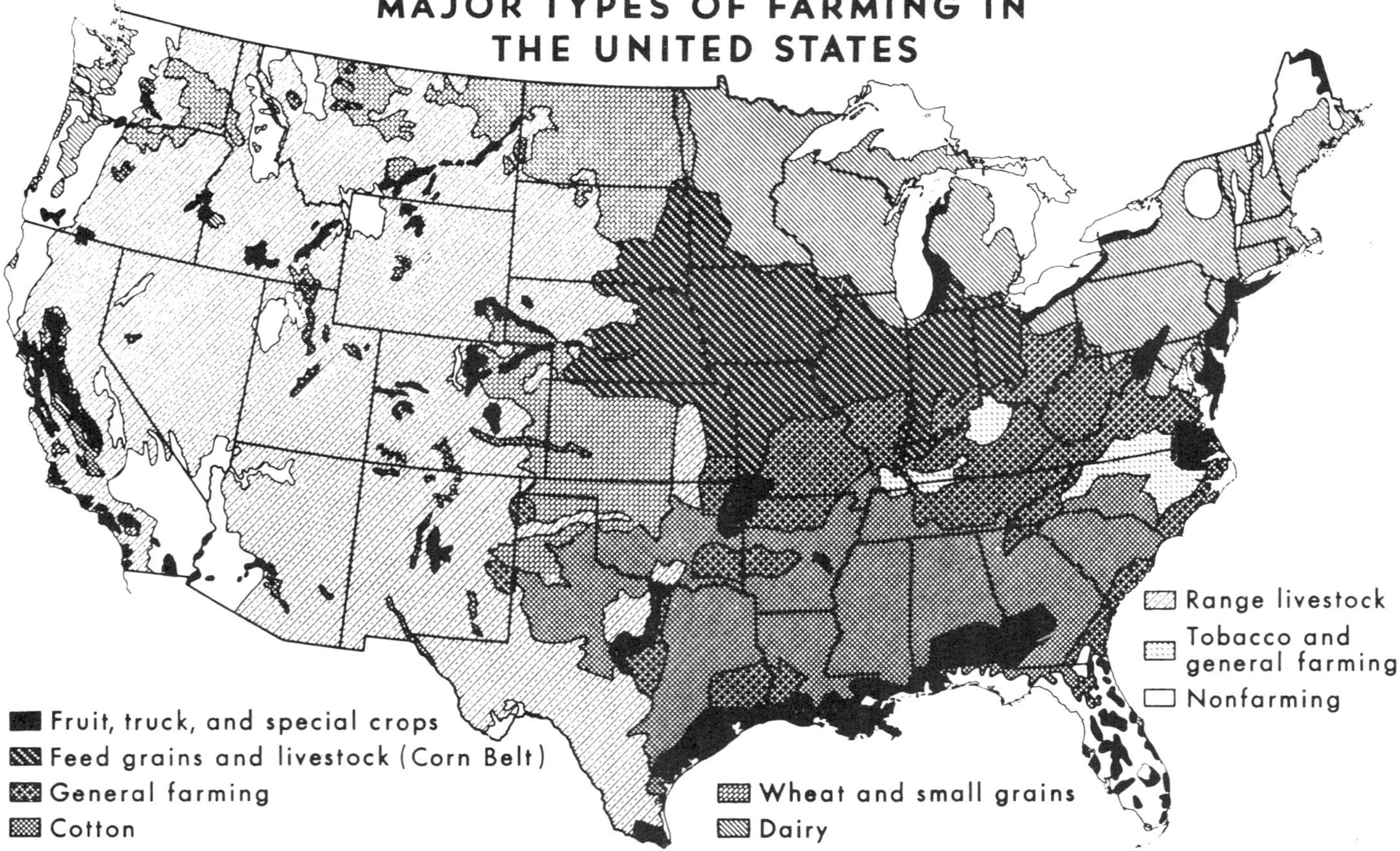

Guide to Planning THE FARM ESTATE with Checklists and Forms

SECOND EDITION

PAUL DOUGLASS
MEMBER OF THE BAR
DISTRICT OF COLUMBIA—STATE OF NEW YORK—STATE OF VERMONT
UNITED STATES SUPREME COURT

INSTITUTE FOR BUSINESS PLANNING, INC.
IBP PLAZA, ENGLEWOOD CLIFFS, N.J. 07632

Institute for Business Planning, Inc.
IBP Plaza, Englewood Cliffs, N.J. 07632

Library of Congress Cataloging in Publication Data

Douglass, Paul.
Guide to planning the farm estate, with checklists and forms.

(The IBP series in estate planning and administration)
Includes index.
1. Estate planning—United States. 2. Inheritance and transfer tax—United States. 3. Agriculture—Taxation—United States. 4. Farmers—United States.
I. Title. II. Series: Institute for Business Planning, inc. IBP series in estate planning and administration.
KF750.D68 1979 346'.73'052 79-17695
ISBN 0-87624-172-0

"This publication is designed to provide accurate and authoritative information in regard to the subject matter covered. It is sold with the understanding that the publisher is not engaged in rendering legal, accounting or other professional service. If legal advice is required, the services of a competent professional person should be sought."

—From a Declaration of Principles jointly adopted by a Committee of the American Bar Association and a Committee of Publishers and Associations.

Printed in the United States of America

ISBN 0-87624-172-0

ABOUT THE AUTHOR

Paul Douglass is a member of the bar in the District of Columbia, the State of New York, the State of Vermont, the United States Tax Court, and the United States Supreme Court. He is a member of the Committee on Trusts and Estates of the New York Bar Association.

Mr. Douglass lives in Washington County, New York, on a dairy farm which has been in his family since 1761.

WHAT THE SECOND EDITION OF THIS BOOK WILL DO FOR YOU

- PINPOINT the new and important changes of the REVENUE ACT OF 1978 as they apply to estate planning by agricultural families
- GUIDE you in the application of the complex provisions of the TAX REFORM ACT OF 1976, which had far-reaching impact on farm estate planning
- SHOW you how the most sweeping tax reform legislation since the enactment of the INTERNAL REVENUE CODE OF 1954 enables farmers to keep their farmsteads within their own family circles from generation to generation
- ANALYZE alternative forms of business organization to provide higher levels of income, better living conditions, and more family participation
- HELP you to manage money into agricultural wealth by the use of budgeting and credit
- EXPLAIN leasing as a tool in estate building
- SUGGEST ways by which a young man can buy a farm
- AID you in the orderly arrangement of your assets to achieve optimum financial security and enjoyment for yourself and your family through the whole life course
- DEMONSTRATE how agricultural decision making contributes to estate building and transfer
- INVENTORY the tools used in estate planning
- DISCUSS HOW TO MAKE A WILL, establish a trust, and probate an estate to settlement
- ADVISE on preparing and filing estate returns with the INTERNAL REVENUE SERVICE and state tax departments
- COUNSEL ways to minimize estate shrinkage and achieve the maximum transfer of estate worth
- SUPPLY step-by-step procedures together with filled-out forms that help make planning easier than ever
- PROVIDE convenient reference material for estate planners and their farm clients in five new and handy Appendixes

Preface

The major effect of the Revenue Act of 1978, from the standpoint of estate planning, has been to clarify and broaden provisions of previous legislation. This complex Act sought two major goals: (1) to reduce taxes, and (2) to generate new investment.

This new edition of *Guide to Planning the Farm Estate* is designed to show farmers and their advisers how they can benefit from these and other changes in the tax law. Since these statutes address themselves in some particulars to areas of the Tax Reform Act of 1976, this edition presents an updated analysis of the 1976 legislation—especially as it relates to farmers in their estate planning. Thus, *Guide to Planning the Farm Estate* is now a more valuable resource than ever.

Beyond its impact upon estate planning, the 1978 enactments contain important provisions relating to income taxes, credits, and capital gains. These are covered in this book, but farmers are strongly advised to discuss these provisions with their tax accountants. Further, it is recommended that farmers have at their elbows the *Tax Desk Book for Farming and Ranching* by Jon D. Wheeler (Institute for Business Planning, Inc., IBP Plaza, Englewood Cliffs, N.J. 07632).

Although *Guide to Planning the Farm Estate* has been updated to reflect recent legislative changes, its primary purpose remains the same: to help farmers develop a thought-through economic program that will provide an enjoyable and secure life for themselves and their families. This book is designed to show farmers how to transfer their wealth to succeeding generations with a minimum of estate shrinkage and a maximum of financial and personal security. The end result of careful estate planning is to promote family harmony and help farm families carry out their objectives for the future.

Paul Douglass

Contents

PART ONE

Introduction to Farm Planning

1

Differences in Planning the Farm Estate

[¶100] AGRICULTURAL ESTATE PLANNING IS DIFFERENT FOR FUNDAMENTAL REASONS

Thomas Jefferson held a life-long pride in just being called "a farmer." He bore this vocational classification with grace and distinction as one of America's first farmer-scientists. He said of himself that he would "never wear any other character than that of a farmer."

Like Jefferson, today's farmer must recognize several fundamental differences in the farm estate. First, the farmer deals with the God-given resource of land. The quantity of land is fixed and final. Second, the farmer works with nature to grow renewable products which vary with geography and the season. Third, like the products of the field and forest, the farmer breeds animals which grow and reproduce. Fourth, the human race for its survival depends upon the food and fibre produced on farms. For these and other basic reasons, a farm estate differs considerably from every other form of estate.

[¶101] A DYNAMIC GROWTH ENTERPRISE

The first step for the agricultural estate planner is to realize that he is dealing with a dynamic growth enterprise. He must be able to understand the magnitude of the economic unit and to project the mathematics of its growth.

As Adam Smith long ago observed, a farm is a complex entity. The farmer owns the land, often subject to a mortgage. By his labor he cultivates his acres and earns his living. By prudent management and savings he generates assets. He is landlord, capitalist, laborer, and manager with all the elements of proprietorship being bound together by his entrepreneurial activity.

[¶101.1] Why Farm Planning Is Unique

Every day a farmer's routine is studded with problems which demand answers. He has to make up his mind and weigh consequences of alternative courses of action. The farmer is always asking "What if?"—*What if* I cut my hay and it rains? *What if* I sell my steers today? Will I get the price I want? Or should I wait?

The farmer must take many factors into consideration as he plans his year. First of all, his work is governed by the clock, by the season, and by the rhythm of animal reproduction. Cato, the old Roman, used to say that if a farmer does one thing late, he will be late in all of his work. A farmer must be ready to get his crops in on time. A dairy farmer knows that the milk truck will be at the barn to collect his milk at a certain time. The farmer deals with weather—sunshine, snow, rain, warm days, and zero temperatures. He must know when to breed his cattle and compute on his calendar the date on which the new calf will probably be born. Keeping mathematical records is a continuing activity on the farmstead.

Once upon a time farmers took guidance from phases of the moon. The orb which shone over the barn supposedly gave signals to help the farmer in doing what might be right and timely in planting. Today, science provides more accurate guidance. Today's farmer, further, must reckon with massive change taking place in America and in world society. Population patterns are altering. Living standards and personal tastes are changing. Farm prices are volatile; they swing up and down. Prices paid by farmers, using 1967 = 100 as the base year, increased from 91 to 202, while prices received by farmers in the index moved from 96 to 183.* At much the same time, the number of farms has declined. Between 1963 and 1978 the number of farms dropped by some 893,050. There are fewer farms, but farms are larger. During the same years the value of farmland and buildings increased nearly 3½ times. The productive assets of the farm have grown. By 1978 the average farm assets reached $143,272 and the production assets per farm were $220,627.*

Farm real estate debt from 1963 to 1978 increased more than 68 times. Since 1956 credit to farmers has been rising about 9 percent a year on a compounded basis. By the end of 1977 the credit extended to farmers was some $118 billion. Extended to the year 2000, farmers' debt so projected by mathematics could reach $856 billion!

*Data from *Agricultural Statistics 1978,* U.S. Department of Agriculture.

[¶101.2] Good News for the Future

For the 1980s and 1990s, however, farm specialists predict good news. The family farm will continue to be the mainstay of United States agriculture. Management will continue to reside on the farm. Acreage will be larger. The legal unit will be broader with more partnerships and corporations. Farming will be intensified and integrated. Farmers, who over the years have been production-minded, will be concerned with producer discipline, i.e., supply at low cost to the food chains and the family.

No longer guided by the light of the moon, the farmer will study:

1. farm location in relation to good markets;
2. production control to achieve low costs;
3. financing to optimize returns.

[¶101.3] What Makes Farm Estate Planning Different

But today's farmer—and the farmer of the future—will find it crucial to study a fourth and equally important aspect of farm business: estate planning.

Since farming is a capital intensive industry, the per man investment is higher than that required by nonagricultural industries. Consider the profile of today's successful farmer. He is 35 years of age. After some 15 years of farming, he operates upward of 900 acres. He may have increased his net worth as much as twelve times already, and, in the remaining 30 years of his active life, he may increase his assets to exceed a million dollars.

Today's successful farmer is looking ahead to building, preserving, and protecting his wealth. By its very nature, his farm business is unique. Government legislation makes special provisions for it. He may hope to pass it on to his children—and their children. The forward-thinking farmer will study estate planning to maximize his assets in life and provide for passing the farmstead on to succeeding generations with the least shrinkage and taxation.

This book is designed as a basic guide for farmers through 2000 A.D. and beyond—into the third millennium.

2

How the Revenue Act of 1978 and the Tax Reform Act of 1976 Affect the Farm Estate Today

[¶200] ESTATE PLANNING AND TAX POLICY

Estate planning and tax policy are organically related. By two recent enactments, the Tax Reform Act of 1976 and the Revenue Act of 1978, the Congress of the United States opened new chapters in federal policy. The text of these laws, taken together with technical adjustments and the revised Internal Revenue Code, constitute the working library which every estate planner needs at his elbow.

This chapter analyzes these laws, ties them together, and relates them to estate planning. For clarity, the Tax Reform Act of 1976 is abbreviated as TRA 76 here, whereas references to the Revenue Act of 1978 are spelled out in full.

[¶201] TRA 76: GOOD NEWS FOR FARMERS

On October 4, 1976, the President of the United States signed the TAX REFORM ACT OF 1976 as PUBLIC LAW 94-455. After years of study, months of committee hearings, endless drafting of legislative bills, extended debates in the Senate and House, and conference committee recommendations, the final result, especially TITLE XX dealing with *estate and gift taxes,* stands as the most wide-ranging piece of tax legislation since Congress enacted the INTERNAL REVENUE CODE OF 1954.

TRA 76 brought good news to farmers, who lobbied actively on its behalf. Some of the special concerns of farmers in working for TRA 76 were these:

1. Soaring land values had forced farm estates up to unprecedented levels that made it difficult for farmers to pay estate tax liabilities.
2. Farm widows suffered under outdated exemption limits for interspousal transfers and rules governing the attribution of ownership of property held in joint tenancy. Wives often called the old estate tax a "tax on widows."
3. Farmers' wives contributed to the net worth of the farm estate to be sure, but unless they could demonstrate actual cash contributions they were frequently in the position of "inheriting" assets they felt were already theirs.

TRA 76 took into account the impact of inflation on land values, equipment costs, and other factors that had combined to impede intergenerational transfers within farm families. The law now enables agricultural families to transmit farmsteads more easily from generation to generation. TRA 76 established new rules for determining tax liabilities on gifts of property during life and at death. In its comprehensive reach it affects every taxpayer in the nation, and necessitates the review of wills and estate plans.

[¶202] THE REVENUE ACT OF 1978

On November 6, 1978, the President of the United States signed PUBLIC LAW 95-600, called the REVENUE ACT OF 1978. This law affects many areas of TRA 76, and its major effect on estate planning has been to clarify and broaden provisions of the previous legislation. Beyond estate planning, the 1978 law contains important provisions relating to income tax, credits, and capital gains.

[¶203] ESTATE PLANNING AND TAX STRATEGY

The mathematical hub around which estate planning revolves is the federal estate tax. The government takes the biggest slice from a decedent's assets. Moreover, the information required by the Internal Revenue Service pulls together and summarizes the elements that constitute the estate's worth. It is extremely important to estimate what the federal estate tax will be and what must be available in liquid assets to pay the levy. Therefore, it is necessary to understand the fundamentals of the federal estate tax process and to project the current situation into the years ahead.

You must try to answer the following questions: (1) What will the federal estate tax be? (2) What steps are needed to reduce that tax if the husband dies first; if the wife dies first? Because of the uncertainty of life, no one can be sure when one will die. Likewise, the size of the estate at any projected point in time is at best a guess. Nevertheless, since the assets of an estate are accumulated from the earliest days of family life, decisions on estate strategy have to be made early. Estate planning and tax strategy run side by side with the life course.

[¶204] LIQUIDITY IS A NECESSITY

In building an estate plan, every person needs to estimate the future tax and provide liquid funds for its payment. Liquidity, in this context, means having money enough to pay the estate taxes to the federal government and the various state jurisdictions.

Sometimes liquidity is provided by actual cash in the bank; sometimes by insurance. In any case, an essential duty of the personal representative is to have available liquid assets to pay the tax.

[¶205] PROGRESSIVE TAX

The federal estate tax is based on a rate schedule established by TRA 76 [Section 2001 (c)]. This tax schedule is progressive, increasing from a marginal rate of 18 percent to 70 percent on taxable transfers of more than $5,000,000. The federal estate tax rates established by TRA 76 are found in Figure 2-1. Farmers and their professional advisors would also be wise to refer to the unified schedule as actually spelled out in the text of the act.

[¶205.1] An Example of Tax Calculation

Here is an example to demonstrate the use of the tax rate schedule in calculating the federal estate tax liability.

A farmer dies in 1981 and has made no lifetime taxable gifts. He leaves an estate of $400,000 (after all debts and estate administrative fees are paid) to his wife. The estate is entitled to use the marital deduction which, under TRA 76, is $250,000. Thus the taxable estate is $150,000. Find this figure in column 1; the tax liability in the second column is $33,800.

However, if the man made no prior use of the tax credit established by TRA 76, the full credit of $47,000 may be deducted, leaving no tax liability. Under the provisions of the old laws prior to TRA 76, the tax liability for this estate would have been $32,700.

Figure 2-1 Federal Estate Tax Rate Schedule

If taxable estate value is at least 1/--	*Tax liability is--*	*Plus--*	*Of excess value over 2/--*
Dollars	Dollars	Percent	Dollars
0	0	18	0
10,000	1,800	20	10,000
20,000	3,800	22	20,000
40,000	8,200	24	40,000
60,000	13,000	26	60,000
80,000	18,200	28	80,000
100,000	23,800	30	100,000
150,000	38,800	32	150,000
250,000	70,800	34	250,000
500,000	155,800	37	500,000
750,000	248,300	39	750,000
1,000,000	345,800	41	1,000,000
1,250,000	448,300	43	1,250,000
1,500,000	555,800	45	1,500,000
2,000,000	780,800	49	2,000,000
2,500,000	1,025,800	53	2,500,000
3,000,000	1,290,800	57	3,000,000
3,500,000	1,575,800	61	3,500,000
4,000,000	1,880,800	65	4,000,000
4,500,000	2,205,800	69	4,500,000
5,000,000	2,550,800	70	5,000,000

[¶206] THE UNIFIED TAX SCHEDULE— A REVOLUTIONARY CONCEPT

The federal estate tax law imposes a tax on the transfer of the taxable estate of every decedent who is a citizen or resident of the United States. To determine the tax after 1976, Congress introduced a new fundamental concept known as *unified* estate and gift tax schedule. The unified schedule creates a single, graduated transfer tax levied at progressive rates on cumulative lifetime (gift) and deathtime (testamentary) transfers.

[¶206.1] Former Levies Combined

The hearings leading to the passage of TRA 76 made it clear that Congress was reluctant to favor lifetime transfers over transfers effective at death. Under the previous laws, the estate and gift taxes each had its own rate schedule. Because the gift tax was lower than the estate tax, an individual could substantially reduce the federal tax on intergenerational transfers by giving part of his property away during his lifetime.

TRA 76 eliminated this separation. It treats all transfers—whether given during one's lifetime or at death—in substantially the same way. Thus, the previous $60,000.00 exemption allowed in the federal estate tax process and a one-only lifetime gift tax exemption of $30,000.00 were superseded by a unified tax credit.

The determination of tax liability under TRA 76 relieves tens of thousands of farm estates from making a return at all. In fact, most estates worth less than $175,000 need not file once the unified credit reaches its maximum in 1981.

[¶206.2] How the Unified Tax Works

The amount of *estate tax* is determined by applying the unified rate schedule (Figure 2-1) to the cumulative lifetime and deathtime transfers, subtracting the *gift taxes* that have been paid on lifetime transfers, and then applying the unified credit against the tax.

The unified tax credit is more generous than were the old exemptions. Since the credit escalates each year until 1981, the credits will be even more generous when they reach the permanent level of $47,000.00 in 1981 and thereafter. By 1981, the credit will mean approximately that the first $175,625 of an estate's taxable value escapes taxation. The unified credit schedule is being phased in over a 5-year period as illustrated in Figure 2-2.

[¶207] THE MARITAL DEDUCTION: A MAJOR TOOL

[TRA 76: Section 2002 (1); Amended Code Section 2056 (c)(1)]

The marital deduction is the most important tool in the estate planner's kit. It is a social and historical concept based on the realistic sharing of property between husband and wife.

Back in 1948, the marital deduction was introduced to eliminate certain inequities in the tax treatment of estates in the community property states of California, New Mexico, Arizona, Texas, Idaho, Louisiana, Nevada, and Washington and the remaining states that are known as "common law" states. In community property states, each spouse owns half of the property earned and accumulated by either the husband or

[¶210] CLARIFICATION OF THE FRACTIONAL INTEREST RULE

[Code Section 2040 (b) and (d)]

In its policy to promote fairness and equality between the sexes, Congress has continued to recognize the monetary values produced by a spouse—and especially a wife—in increasing the value of a farm. By material participation, spouses working side by side enhance values.

As a matter of history, the title to many farms is a joint tenancy. A wife can slave on the farm. Unless enlightened estate planning has been done, however, the entire value of the property held in joint tenancy with the right of survivorship has been included in the gross estate of the spouse to die first except to the extent the surviving spouse could prove the amount he or she actually contributed to the acquisition of the property.

TRA 76 established the *fractional interest rule.* This rule provides that if a qualified joint interest was created between the spouses after December 31, 1976, one-half of the value of the joint interest was included in the gross estate of the first to die.

To trigger this fractional interest rule, certain qualifying conditions were necessary:

1. The interest must have been created by the decedent, his or her spouse, or both, after 1976.
2. The joint tenancy must consist exclusively of the decedent and his or her spouse.
3. The creation of the interest in personal property must have been a gift subject to the federal gift tax.
4. The donor, in the case of real property, must have elected to treat the creation of the joint tenancy as a gift for federal tax purposes.

A taxpayer could benefit from the fractional interest rule by severing the joint tenancy created before January 1, 1977, and recreating it if the transfer is subject to gift tax.

[¶210.1] Revenue Act of 1978 Simplifies Conversion [Revenue Act of 1978: Section 702 (k) Code Section 2040 (d) and (e)]

The Revenue Act of 1978 simplifies the conversion of pre-1977 joint tenancies into qualified joint interests.

Here are the steps to be taken:

1. The donor-spouse elects to report a gift of the property in a gift tax return filed with respect to any calendar quarter in 1977, 1978 or 1979.
2. The pre-1977 joint tenancy does not have to be severed and recreated.
3. The donor-spouse who chooses to make this election is considered to have made a gift at the close of the quarter for which the return is filed.
4. The amount of this gift is generally equal to the appreciation attributable to the gift portion of the consideration furnished by the donor-spouse at the time the joint tenancy was created.

[¶210.2] Surviving Spouse Credit for Material Participation in the Farm Enterprise [Revenue Act of 1978: Section 511 Code Section 2040 (c)]

In another step advancing equality of the sexes in the farm enterprise, the Revenue Act of 1978 provides a formula for giving a surviving spouse credit for participation in the family farm enterprise.

The Revenue Act permits the executor of an estate to elect to employ a *special rule* for excluding a portion of the value of a jointly owned property used in farming. This exclusion is based on material participation of the decedent's spouse in farm operation.

Here is the formula for computing the material participation of a surviving spouse to establish the sum excludable from the full value of the jointly held property. This sum is excluded only if an election under Section 2040 (c) is filed by an estate after 1978.

$$A - [B + C]$$

where A = value of such interest; B = Section 2040(c) value; and C = adjusted consideration furnished by the decedent's spouse.

The value of such interest (A) is determined without regard to Section 2040(c). Presumably, this means that the estate tax should be used.

To determine the Section 2040(c) value (B):

1. Calculate the number of taxable years in which the spouse materially participated in the operation of the farm or business. Multiply this number (which cannot exceed 25) by 2%.

2. Determine *adjusted consideration,* for *both* the decedent and the decedent's spouse, by adding together (a) the original consideration furnished by the tenant (disregarding any income or gain from the business) and (b) the amount of 6% simple interest which the original consideration would have earned if invested during the period of ownership of the business.

3. Multiply the percentage rate (found under item 1, above) by the

value of the property minus the adjusted consideration furnished by the decedent, decedent's spouse, or both (item 2, above).

The adjusted consideration furnished by the decedent's surviving spouse (C) is determined in the manner described in item 2, above.

There are two limitations that apply: The application of the formula cannot reduce the includable amount to less than 50% of the value of the eligible joint interest. The aggregate decrease in the value of the decedent's gross estate cannot exceed $500,000.

Example: Suppose Mary and Bill Johnson purchased a potato farm on eastern Long Island in 1963. Out of a purchase price of $400,000, Mary paid 20% and Bill paid 80%. They did not elect to treat the creation of their tenancy by the entirety as a gift. Although Mary holds a part-time sales job in a local department store, she materially participates in the operation of the farm by consulting with Bill as to growing and selecting crops.

Assume that Bill dies in 1983, when the farm is worth $1,000,000 (assuming no special use valuation under Code Section 2032A). The executor elects to treat Bill's interest in the farm as an "eligible joint interest" under Section 2040(c).

The value included in Bill's estate is calculated, using the same procedures outlined above, as follows:

A = $1,000,000 (estate tax value)
B = (1) 20 years × 2% = 40%
(2) Bill's adjusted consideration = $704,000 ($320,000 + $384,000)
Mary's adjusted consideration = $176,000 ($80,000 + $96,000)
Total adjusted consideration = $880,000
(3) 40% × [$1,000,000 − $880,000] = $48,000 = B
C = $176,000 (Mary's adjusted consideration)

Hence, $776,000 would be included in Bill's gross estate ($1,000,000 − [$48,000 + $176,000]).

[¶211] ORPHAN'S DEDUCTION

[TRA 76: Section 2007 Code Section 2057]

TRA 76 provided preferential estate tax treatment for dispositions to minor orphaned children. When a decedent is survived by no spouse but by a child under age 21—when such child has no known parents—TRA 76 allows a deduction from the gross estate in an amount equal to the value of any interest included in the gross estate that passes or has passed from the decedent to the child.

This deduction, however, is limited to $5,000.00 for each year the child is under age 21 at the decedent's death. If the child was age 12 at the time of the parent's death, the orphan's deduction would then be

$$\$5,000 \times 9 \text{ years} = \$45,000$$

The deduction is allowed for each child under age 21. If four minor children survive without known parents, for example, the aggregate maximum amount allowable as a deduction (assuming death as of January 1) would be as shown in the accompanying table.

Child No.	*Years below 21*	*Computation*	*Maximum allowable deduction*
1—age 7	14	14 × $5000	$70,000
2—age 14	7	7 × $5000	$35,000
3—age 17	4	4 × $5000	$20,000
4—age 20	1	1 × $5000	$5,000

As in the case of the marital deduction, an orphan's deduction is not generally allowed with respect to a terminable interest such as a life estate.

When there are several minors, the total orphan's deduction may be a large amount. For three orphaned children, 1, 5 and 12 years old, for instance, the total deduction would be $225,000. In such cases, the potential deduction for orphans may be larger than the possible marital deduction—a fact which has weight in planning an estate for a couple with young children.

[¶211.1] Changes under the Revenue Act of 1978

The Revenue Act of 1978 again addressed itself to the orphan's deduction. The Revenue Act of 1978 provides an exception to the terminable interest rule for certain trusts established for more than one minor child of the decedent, thereby alleviating the problems caused by the requirement under the 1976 law that any minor's trust have totally separate shares (such separate share trusts have much higher administrative costs). The requirements for a "qualified minor's trust," one which does not violate the terminable interest rule, are as follows:

1. All of the initial corpus of the trust must be property which passes or has passed to the trust from the decedent's estate (either before or after decedent's death). Post mortem additions by other persons are permitted.
2. All of the initial beneficiaries with present interests must be children of the decedent. Other beneficiaries may have future interests, as noted below.
3. All of the initial beneficiaries with present interests must be under 21 years of age at the date of the decedent's death.
4. All distributions to the decedent's children must be made either pro rata to all the beneficiaries or to individual beneficiaries under an ascertainable standard relating to health, education, support, or maintenance.
5. The trustee may be given discretion to accumulate income of the trust, subject only to the distribution rules noted above.
6. In the event one of the decedent's children dies, that child's share of the trust may be distributed to a person who is not a child of the decedent, vested in a separate share for such persons, or remain in the trust for the benefit of the remaining children of the decedent. This is the only situation in which the trust may make a nonterminating distribution to someone who is not one of the decedent's children.
7. The trust need not vest absolutely or terminate until the youngest of the decedent's children reaches age 23.
8. Upon termination of the trust, all of the corpus and accumulated income (other than that in separate shares because of the earlier death of one of the children) must be distributed to the remaining children pro rata.

This provides a useful mechanism by which a testamentary gift may be made to multiple orphaned children of the decedent, providing management of the funds by a responsible trustee until the children reach 23 years of age and still ensuring the estate of its orphans' exclusion.

This provision is effective for estates of decedents dying after December 31, 1976.

[¶212] GENERATION-SKIPPING TRANSFERS

[TRA 76: Section 2008 (b) 2001 (c)(1)(j);
Revenue Act of 1978: Section 702 (n)(1)]

The Code (Section 2611) defines a generation-skipping transfer as "any taxable distribution or taxable termination with respect to a generation-skipping trust or trust equivalent."

TRA 76 imposes a tax on generation-skipping transfers of property by trust or its equivalents such as life-estates and insurance annuity contracts that split the beneficial enjoyment of assets between generations.

Under the old law the termination of the interest of a trust beneficiary was not taxable unless the beneficiary had a general power of appointment or was also the grantor. Thus under the old law the grantor could make a transfer to his child and then to his grandchild for life with a remainder over to his great-grandchild. The transfer in such cases would be subject to tax neither in the child's nor the grandchild's estate.

TRA 76 removes the tax advantage of setting up this kind of trust. The result is about the same if the outright gift had been made to each successive generation.

A generation-skipping transfer under a trust or similar arrangement is one that provides for a splitting of benefits between two or more generations that are younger than the generation of the grantor of the trust. Under such trusts a grantor creates life interests with remainder interest reserved for members of subsequent generations.

[¶212.1] Exclusion for Grandchildren

TRA 76 provides an exclusion not to exceed $250,000.00 in the case of a generation-skipping transfer of trust property to the grantor's grandchildren. Since the exclusion is allowed to each deemed transferor, the maximum excludable amount is limited by the number of children, not by the number of grandchildren.

[¶212.2] Changes and Clarifications Made by the Revenue Act of 1978

The most important action with regard to generation-skipping transfers taken in the Revenue Act of 1978 is the extension of the effective date from April 30, 1976 to June 11, 1976. Thus, the generation-skipping transfer tax will not apply to transfers under irrevocable documents executed prior to June 11, 1976, or to transfers under revocable documents executed prior to that date if the decedent dies prior to January 1, 1982, without changing the will or trust to increase the generation-skipping share.

Powers Held by Independent Trustees. The Revenue Act of 1978 also prevents the imposition of a generation-skipping transfer tax on certain trusts for the benefit of persons other than the lineal descendants of the grantor. The Act creates an additional exception to the generation-skipping transfer tax rules for powers retained by certain independent trustees, avoiding the problem raised where a grantor vests in an unrelated trustee more than 12½ years younger than the grantor, the authority to make discretionary distributions of income or corpus among various of the grantor's nieces or nephews or the young children of the grantor's friends. The Revenue Act of 1978 provides that a trustee does not have a power, for generation-skipping transfer tax purposes, if:

1. the trustee does not have an interest in the trust;
2. the trustee has no present or future power over the trust income or corpus other than a power to allocate corpus or income to or for a beneficiary or class of beneficiaries designated in the trust; and
3. the trustee is independent of the grantor, to the extent that the trustee is not the spouse, parent, lineal descendant, brother, or sister of the grantor or any of the beneficiaries, an employee of a corporation in which the grantor's, the trust's or the beneficiaries' stockholdings are significant with regard to voting control, or in which the grantor or a beneficiary is an executive. See Code Section 2613(e).

Multiple Powers Held by the Same Beneficiary. One of the rules with which estate planners can plan around the generation-skipping transfer tax provides that where a beneficiary has more than one power or interest, the termination of one of them is not a taxable event. The Revenue Act of 1978, however, limits this rule by noting that if the remaining powers are solely future or contingent powers, the termination of the only present power is a taxable event. See Code Section 2613(b)(2).

Both generation-skipping tax amendments apply as if enacted as part of TRA 76.

[¶212.3] Computation of the Tax [Code Sections 2602 (a)(1)(A)(B)(C)]

In the event that the deemed transferor is deceased at the time when the distribution of the trust assets or intervening interests are terminated, the transfer tax is computed, in effect, by adding the deemed transfer back onto the deemed transferor's estate. To estimate this tax, then:

1. Take the fair market value of the transferred property.
2. Take the fair market value of prior generation-skipping from the same deemed transfer.
3. Take the deemed transferor's prior adjusted taxable gifts.
4. Take the deemed transferor's taxable estate.

With these data, compute a tentative tax on the sum of the amounts in items 1, 2, 3, and 4, above. Subtract the tax computed on the total of items 2, 3, and 4.

If the deemed transferor is not dead at the time of transfer, omit Step 4.

[¶213] CARRY-OVER BASIS

[TRA 76: Section 2005 Code Section 6039 (A), 6694]

One of the new provisions in TRA 76, and perhaps the most controversial, relates to assets acquired from or passing from a decedent. Under prior law, capital gain realized during an individual's lifetime was not taxed. Rather, the tax basis of inherited property was "stepped up" to its fair market value at the time of the decedent's death. When an individual inherited property later, taxes were paid on the difference between the selling price and the stepped-up value of the property. Any appreciation before the time of the inheritance, however, was never taxable income.

TRA 76 established new carry-over basis rules. However, the Revenue Act of 1978 imposed a 3-year moratorium on the application of these rules. Thus, the stepped-up basis rules have been revived for the estates of decedents dying after 1976 but before 1980. The following discussion presently applies only to estates of decedents dying after December 31, 1979.

The rules under TRA 76 apply to items of carry-over basis property, which is defined as any property "acquired from" or "passed from" a decedent. Basically, this definition includes the traditional concept of property that would be taxed at capital gain rates, with the following specific *exclusions:*

1. items considered "gross income in respect of a decedent" under Code Section 691;
2. proceeds of insurance on the decedent's life;
3. the survivor's taxable interest in a joint and survivor annuity;
4. payments under a deferred compensation plan to the extent taxable to the decedent's beneficiary;
5. property includable in the decedent's gross estate by virtue of being a transfer made within 3 years of death (Code Section 2035) or being a revocable transfer (Section 2038), or general power of appointment (Section 2041), if the property has been disposed of before the decedent's death in a transaction where gain or loss is recognizable;
6. certain types of stock or stock options;
7. foreign personal holding company stock.

In addition, a limited exclusion is allowed for personal and household effects.

The Personal and Household Effects Election. An executor is permitted to exclude from carry-over basis property up to $10,000 worth of the decedent's personal and household effects. The selected assets receive a basis equal to their value as of the date of death or the alternate valuation date. In enacting this exclusion, Congress recognized the difficulty of valuing this type of asset and the fact that, in most cases, the fair market value of the property would be lower than its adjusted basis.

A "personal or household effect" is defined as "a piece of property that was held by the decedent for personal use rather than for use in a trade or business or investment purposes." If the executor selects an asset that was transferred by the decedent, the date of the transfer is used in deciding whether it is a "personal or household effect."

Certain objects (such as the decedent's clothing and home furnishings) that were used in the decedent's everyday life clearly fall within the regulation's definition. Other objects, such as antique furniture, may be more difficult to label as personal or investment items, and the regulation's definition offers little guidance in this area.

Making the Election. The election is made by giving the recipient of each piece of property a written notice including the following information:

1. a description of the property;
2. the fair market value of the property as of the decedent's date of death (or alternate valuation date, if elected);
3. a statement that the property is not carry-over basis property; and
4. a statement that the distributee should keep this information as part of his or her permanent records.

Pieces of property, none of which have a fair market value greater than $100 at the applicable valuation date and all of which are related in function or use, may be listed together (e.g., furniture, $500; dishes, $250).

Since the executor's election and designation of the property is irrevocable, the selection must be made carefully. Only if a subsequent adjustment in value causes the value of the designated personal and household effects to exceed $10,000 will the executor be permitted to revise the election in order to bring the sum of the fair market values below $10,000. The revised designation is made among the properties chosen in the initial election; any property no longer so designated becomes carry-over basis property.

The executor must notify the recipients of any adjustments made to the fair market value of the property within 3 months of either a determination or an agreement following the examination of a return. The recipient should be provided with the information set forth in items 1–4, above, recomputed as necessary. If property previously excluded is now carry-over basis property, the recipient must be informed and given the information required under Code Section 6039 (A).

Example. The application of these provisions is illustrated by the following example, adapted from the Regulations.

A decedent dies on December 31, 1981, and the executor elects to exclude the following personal and household effects from carry-over basis property, as shown here.

Asset	*Fair Market Value*
Clothing	$2,000
Furniture	3,000
Automobile	4,000
Painting	1,000

After examining the estate tax return, it was determined that the painting had an actual fair market value of $3,000. As a result, the total value of the items initially designated by the election is now $12,000. The executor may continue to treat the painting as excluded from carry-over basis property. However, in order to remain below the $10,000 limitation, the executor must select, from among the initially designated assets, items aggregating at least $2,000 in value (for example, the clothing) and treat these items as carry-over basis property.

Adjustments. If the decedent dies owning property that is not specifically excluded, the recipient's basis for income tax purposes will be determined under Code Section 1023. The basis of carry-over basis property acquired from a decedent dying after December 31, 1976, is equal to the decedent's adjusted basis for the property immediately before his or her death, but increased (in the following order) by these adjustments:

1. the so-called fresh start adjustment to bring the basis of the property to its fair market value as of December 31, 1976 (this adjustment applies only for purposes of determining gain);
2. federal and state estate taxes paid by the estate attributable to the appreciation in value of the carry-over basis property;
3. a $60,000 minimum basis adjustment;
4. state succession taxes paid by the recipient of the property attributable to the appreciation in the property.

The procedures on carry-over values are technical and complex. They are a matter on which professional advice should be sought—especially since the whole area is subject to technical clarification and probable congressional legislation.

[¶214] SPECIAL VALUATION OF FARMS

[TRA 76: Section 2003 (a) New Code 2032 A]

TRA 76 provided a new procedure for the valuation of farms which helps farmers keep their farmsteads in the family. Superseding the highest and best use principle, TRA 76 provides a procedure for farm land valuation at its current use value. The total decrease in value resulting from the actual use rule, however, may not exceed $500,000.00.

Certain conditions must be met to qualify farm real estate for the actual use valuation:

1. The property must be actually devoted to bona fide farming at the date of death of the decedent.
2. The property must be located in the United States, and the decedent must have been a citizen or resident of the United States.
3. The farm must pass to a qualified heir, i.e., a member of the decedent's family, a lineal descendant, a lineal descendant of a grandparent of the decedent, the spouse of the decedent, or the spouse of a descendant.
4. The farm must have been used or held for use as a farm for 5 of the last 8 years prior to the decedent's death.
5. There must have been material participation in the operation of the farm by the decedent or a member of the family in 5 out of the 8 years immediately preceding the decedent's death.
6. Farm property must be at least 50 percent of the gross estate, less expenses.
7. Twenty-five percent of the gross estate value is qualified farm realty.

[¶214.1] Valuation Methods

Special use value of farm land is determined by dividing (a) the average annual gross cash rental for comparable land used for farming in the same locality, less the average annual state and local real estate taxes for the comparable land [Code Section 2032 A(e)(7)], by (b) the average annual effective interest rate for all new Federal Land Bank Loans [Code Section 2032 (A)(e)(7)].

Under certain conditions, when the usual farm value method cannot be applied, alternative methods of valuation can be used:

1. Capitalize the expected income yield for farming over a reasonable period of time under prudent management practices.
2. Capitalize the fair rental value of the land for farming purposes.
3. Take the assessed land values in a state that provides a differential or use value assessment law for farm lands.

4. Take the comparable sales of other farm lands in the same area far enough removed from metropolitan or resort areas to minimize nonagricultural use factors.
5. Employ any other factors that fairly value the property as a farm.

[¶214.2] Recapture

In the event that qualified farm land property is disposed of by a qualified heir to someone who is not a family member or the qualified heir ceases to use the property for the qualified use within 10 years of the decedent's death, the tax benefit from the reduced valuation is recaptured. If the property is disposed of or ceases to be used for farming purposes between the tenth and fifteenth year after the decedent's death and before the death of the qualified heir, the recapture amount is reduced by this fraction:

$$\frac{\text{full months after death in excess of 120}}{\text{60 months}}$$

In the event of a partial disposition or a partial cessation of the qualified use, the recapture amounts are determined on a pro rata basis.

The qualified use ceases when:

1. the property itself ceases to be used for the qualified use; or
2. during any 8-year period after the date of the decedent's death and before the death of the qualified heir, there exist 3 years or more during which there was no material participation in the farm operation by the decedent or a member of his family while the property was held by the decedent *and* there was no material participation in the operation by a qualified heir or any member of his family while the property was held by a qualifying heir.

It needs to be noted that the statute of limitations for imposing the recapture tax is 3 years after the Internal Revenue Service is notified of any disposition of qualified real property or cessation of its qualified use.

[¶214.3] Election of Special Valuation and Tax Lien

To enjoy the benefits of the special valuation, the personal representative must elect the valuation method by the due date, including extensions for filing the estate tax return. This election must be made on forms provided by the Internal Revenue Service.

Moreover, the election must be accompanied by a written agreement with respect to the qualifying farm lands. This agreement must be signed by all the persons having an interest in the property, whether in possession or not. By this agreement the heirs consent to the application of the recapture provisions.

When the special valuation method has been elected, a tax lien for the amount of the potential recapture tax is imposed on the property. This lien continues during the period of potential recapture or until the Internal Revenue Service is satisfied that no further tax liability exists.

Title searchers will find the lien recorded in the records of the Internal Revenue District Office.

[¶214.4] Revenue Act of 1978 Eases Lien Provisions [Revenue Act of 1978: Section 702 (d)(1) Code Section 6324B]

The Revenue Act of 1978 eases the special lien attached to farm lands imposed on the property as a potential recapture lien. The Revenue Act now empowers the Secretary of the Treasury at his discretion to subordinate the lien that is created by virtue of the special agricultural use value.

For example, I. M. Farmer needs to put up the farm as collateral for a loan. Since the Federal Land Bank system loans money only on first lien security on real estate, the amended act now steps in to help. If he feels justified, the Secretary of the Treasury has the power to issue a certificate of subordination of the property.

The 1978 act also permits the Secretary of the Treasury to discharge an individual heir from personal liability for the deferred taxes upon substitution of a bond.

[¶214.5] Pecuniary Bequests in Special Valuation [Revenue Act of 1978: Section 702 (d)(2)(3) Code Section 2032 (A)(e)(9)]

The Revenue Act of 1978 further clarifies the distribution of real property by an estate or trust in satisfaction of a pecuniary bequest. Such distribution will not bar the special use valuation. Why? Because the real property is considered to have passed from the decedent. Moreover, when a pecuniary bequest is satisfied with an appreciated carry-over basis, the appreciation is determined without regard to the special use valuation.

The benefits gained as a result of special use valuation are recaptured if the qualified heir disposes of the property to someone who is not a family member or it ceases to be used for farming within 15 years after the death of the decedent.

[¶214.6] New Rule Concerning Community Property [Revenue Act of 1978: Section 702 (d)(4) Code Section 2032 (A)(e)(10)]

Because the question of how the special use valuation rules applied to community property was not spelled out, the Revenue Act of 1978 provides simply that community and individually owned property are to be treated equally. Legislative history gives as an example the fact that all of the value of a farm held as community property is counted for the 50 and 25 percent tests.

[¶215] GET ACQUAINTED WITH FORM 706

The federal process which mobilizes all the data about an estate concerns itself with Form 706. This form puts into supportable figures a person's financial status as it stands at death. A careful estate builder will obtain a copy of Form 706 from his Internal Revenue Service office and from time to time estimate his own worth and taxable estate.

The conscientious entries on 706, updated and kept current, will be of enormous benefit to a personal representative in settling an estate. As a matter of fact, the information is easily transferred from the continuing updated estate record that the careful estate builder maintains.

Every person should have a copy of 706. It is as important to him as a road map to a motorist. It tells him where he is going at a precise moment—and where he is going toward his goals.

[¶215.1] Example to Help in Understanding the 706 Form

The 706 form is made up of 17 schedules and a recapitulation sheet of 16 items. These sheets, taken together, establish the gross estate less deductions, thus determining the taxable estate.

Figure 2-3 presents an example of the 706 form of the estate of a farmer. Its study helps to understand Form 706.

[¶216] DUE DATES FOR FILING RETURNS FOR ESTATE SETTLEMENT

The law establishes a sequence of dates providing deadlines for filing a series of forms. Both the personal representative and the attorney

Figure 2-3

Form **706** (Rev. June 1977) Department of the Treasury Internal Revenue Service

United States Estate Tax Return

Estate of citizen or resident of the United States (see separate instructions)
Date of death after December 31, 1976.

IRS use only
Date received

Decedent's first name and middle initial	Decedent's last name	Date of death
George A.	Harris	12-24-77
Domicile at time of death	**Year domicile established**	**Decedent's social security number**
Hartford, New York		000-00-0000

Deceased's personal representative or persons in possession of property

Name	Address (Number and street, city, State, and ZIP code)
Peter G. Harris	R. D. Fort Ann, New York 12827

Name and location of court where will was probated or estate administered	Case number
Washington County Probate	

If decedent died testate check here ► [X] and attach a certified copy of the will.

Authorization to receive confidential tax information under 26 C.F.R. 601.502(c)(3)(ii) if return prepared by an attorney on behalf of the deceased's personal representative:

I declare that I am the attorney of record for the deceased's personal representative before the above court, that I prepared this return on behalf of the deceased's personal representative, that I am not currently under suspension or disbarment from practice before the Internal Revenue Service, and that I am currently qualified to practice in the State of New York

Paul Douglass (Signature of attorney) — Box 199, Folger Building, West Pawlet, Vermont 05775 (Address (number and street, city, State, and ZIP code)) — (Date)

Computation of Tax

1	Total gross estate (from Recapitulation, page 3, line 10)	1	208,917
2	Total allowable deductions (from Recapitulation, page 3, line 29)	2	19,826
3	Taxable estate (subtract the amount on line 2 from the amount on line 1)	3	189,091
4	Adjusted taxable gifts (total amount of taxable gifts (within the meaning of section 2503) made by decedent after December 31, 1976, other than gifts which are includible in decedent's gross estate (section 2001(b)))	4	None
5	Add the amount on line 3 and the amount on line 4	5	189,091
6	Tentative tax on the amount on line 5 from Table A in the separate instructions	6	51,309
7	Aggregate gift taxes payable with respect to gifts by decedent after December 31, 1976, including gift taxes paid by decedent's spouse for split gifts (section 2513) if decedent was the donor of such gifts and they are includible in decedent's gross estate	7	None
8	Subtract the amount on line 7 from the amount on line 6	8	51,309
9	Unified credit against estate tax from Table B in the separate instructions	9	30,000
10	Adjustment to unified credit (20% of aggregate amount allowed as a specific exemption under section 2521 (as in effect before its repeal by the Tax Reform Act of 1976) with respect to gifts made by decedent after September 8, 1976)	10	None
11	Allowable unified credit (subtract the amount on line 10 from the amount on line 9)	11	30,000
12	Subtract the amount on line 11 from the amount on line 8 (but not less than zero)	12	21,309
13	Credit for State death taxes not to exceed the amount on line 12; see Table C in the separate instructions and attach credit evidence	13	1,025
14	Subtract the amount on line 13 from the amount on line 12	14	20,284
15	Credit for Federal gift taxes (see section 2012 and attach computation) — 15: None		
16	Credit for foreign death taxes (from Schedule P). (Form 706CE is required) — 16: None		
17	Credit for tax on prior transfers (from Schedule Q) — 17: None		
18	Total (add the amounts on lines 15, 16, and 17)	18	None
19	Subtract the amount on line 18 from the amount on line 14	19	20,284
20	Prior payments. Explain in attached statement; see instruction 5 — 20: None		
21	United States Treasury bonds redeemed in payment of estate tax — 21: None		
22	Total (add the amount on line 20 and the amount on line 21)	22	None
23	Balance due (subtract the amount on line 22 from the amount on line 19)	23	20,284

Note: *Please attach the necessary supplemental documents; see instruction 6.*

Under penalties of perjury, I declare that I have examined this return, including accompanying schedules and statements, and to the best of my knowledge and belief, it is true, correct, and complete. Declaration of preparer other than deceased's personal representative or person in possession of property is based on all information of which preparer has any knowledge.

Peter G. Harris — Signature of deceased's personal representative or person in possession of property — 6/8/78 Date

John Randolph, Jr. CPA — Signature of preparer other than deceased's personal representative, etc. — A. B. Smith & Company, C.P.A.'s, Box 000, Rutland VT 00-0000000 — Address (and ZIP code) — 7/6/78 Date

Figure 2-3 Cont.

Form 706 (Rev. 5-77)

Estate of: George A. Harris

General Information

1 Address of decedent at time of death (Number and street, city, State, and ZIP code)
Hartford, New York 12838

2 Place of death, if different than decedent's address (e.g., name of hospital)
Indian River Nursing Home Granville, New York

3 Cause of death
Coronary Artery Occlusion - Cardiac Arrest

4 Length of last illness
12 days

5 Decedent's physicians

Name	Address (Number and street, city, State, and ZIP code)

6 Date and place of birth
6-10-98 - Hartford, New York

7 Decedent's business or occupation. If retired check here ▶ ☐ and state decedent's former business or occupation ▶
Farmer

8 Marital status of decedent at time of death

☐ Married—Date of marriage to surviving spouse ▶
—Domicile at time of marriage ▶
☒ Widow or widower—Name and date of death of deceased spouse ▶
☐ Single
☐ Legally separated—Name of legally separated spouse ▶
☐ Divorced—Date divorce decree became final ▶

9 Did the deceased's personal representative or person in possession of property who is required to file the return make a diligent and careful search for property of every kind left by the decedent for whose estate this return is filed? . . . . XX Yes ☐ No

10 Individuals who receive benefits from the estate (do not include charitable beneficiaries shown in Schedule O or any heir receiving less than $1,000). For Privacy Act Notification, see the Instructions for Form 1040.

Name.—Enter the name of each individual who receives benefits from the estate directly as an heir, next-of-kin, devisee, or legatee or indirectly (for example, as beneficiary of a trust, annuity or insurance policy, shareholder of a corporation or partner of a partnership which is an heir, etc.).
Social Security Number.—If the individual has not been located or has no social security number, etc., enter such explanation.
Age.—On the date of the decedent's death.
Relationship.—Include relationships by blood, marriage, or adoption or indicate NONE.

Amount.—Value all interests on the date of death or the alternate valuation date, whichever is used, for estate tax purposes. The interest of each beneficiary should be valued in the same manner as it would be valued for estate or gift tax purposes. Where precise values cannot readily be determined (certain future interests, for example), a reasonable approximation should be entered. The sum of the values of the interests of all unborn or otherwise unascertainable beneficiaries should be shown on the last line (all unascertainable beneficiaries). Values should be stated without reduction for any estate or inheritance taxes.

Name	Social security number	Age	Relationship to decedent	Amount
Surviving spouse			x x x x x x x x x x	
None				
Others				
		67	Sister	81,764
		73	Brother	74,621
		44	None	6,000
			Niece	1,058
All unascertainable beneficiaries	x x x x x x x x x x	x x x x x	x x x x x x x x x x	

Alternate Valuation

(These instructions apply if alternate valuation is elected. For further information on this subject, see the separate instructions.)

11 An election to have the gross estate of the decedent valued as of the alternate date or dates is made by entering a checkmark in the box set forth below.
☐ The deceased's personal representative elects to have the gross estate of this decedent valued in accordance with values as of a date or dates subsequent to the decedent's death as authorized by section 2032 of the Code.

Page 2

Figure 2-3 Cont.

Form 706 (Rev. 6–77)

Estate of: George A. Harris

12 Is the special valuation authorized in section 2032A elected for certain farm, etc., real property? . . . . ☐ Yes ☒ No

If "Yes," the deceased's personal representative must attach a statement that includes the following information: (i) The items of real property which are to be valued pursuant to the election and the Form 706 schedule and item number where included in decedent's gross estate; (ii) The items of personal property that are used in a qualified use under section 2032A; (iii) The relevant qualified use; (iv) The fair market value of qualified real property determined without regard to section 2032A; (v) The method used to determine the special value based on use; (vi) Copies of any written appraisals; (vii) The date decedent acquired the property and the date decedent or a member of decedent's family commenced the qualified use (if different); (viii) Any periods following commencement of qualified use decedent or a member of decedent's family did not materially participate in the operation of the farm or other business within the meaning of section 2032A(e)(6); and (ix) The name and relationship to decedent of each person receiving an interest in each item of real or personal property used in a qualified use.

The deceased's personal representative must also attach an agreement in a form that is binding on all parties under applicable local law which is signed by all parties holding any interest in the property to express consent to personal liability under section 2032A(c) in the event of certain early dispositions of the property or early cessation of the qualified use.

Include the words "section 2032A valuation" in the "Description" column of any Form 706 schedule where section 2032A property is included in decedent's gross estate.

Recapitulation

Item number	Gross estate	Alternate value	Value at date of death
1	Schedule A—Real Estate		60,000
2	Schedule B—Stocks and Bonds		12,532
3	Schedule C—Mortgages, Notes, and Cash		127,498
4	Schedule D—Insurance on Decedent's Life		1,058
5	Schedule E—Jointly Owned Property		
6	Schedule F—Other Miscellaneous Property		7,829
7	Schedule G—Transfers During Decedent's Life		
8	Schedule H—Powers of Appointment		
9	Schedule I—Annuities		
10	Total gross estate		208,917

Item number	Deductions		Amount	
11	Schedule J—Funeral Expenses and Expenses Incurred in Administering Property Subject to Claims		19,826	
12	Schedule K—Debts of Decedent		None	
13	Schedule K—Mortgages and Liens		None	
14	Total of Items 11 through 13		19,826	
15	Allowable amount of deductions from item 14 (see note [1])		19,826	
16	Schedule L—Net Losses During Administration		None	
17	Schedule L—Expenses Incurred in Administering Property Not Subject to Claims		None	
18	Total of items 15 through 17			19,826
19	Schedule M—Bequests, etc., to Surviving Spouse		None	
20	Adjusted gross estate (see note [2])		189,091	
21	Greater of (i) $250,000 or (ii) one-half of amount on line 20 (see note [2])		250,000	
22	Aggregate of gift tax marital deduction allowed to decedent with respect to gifts made after December 31, 1976	None		
23	Aggregate of gift tax marital deduction which would have been allowable to decedent with respect to gifts made after December 31, 1976, if the amount deductible with respect to any gift were 50 percent of its value	None		
24	Balance (subtract the amount on line 23 from the amount on line 22)		None	
25	Balance (subtract the amount on line 24 from the amount on line 21 (but not less than zero))		250,000	
26	Amount of marital deduction (smaller of (i) amount on line 19 or (ii) amount on line 25)			None
27	Schedule N—Orphans' Deduction			None
28	Schedule O—Charitable, Public, and Similar Gifts and Bequests			None
29	Total allowable deductions (add amounts on lines 18, 26, 27, and 28)			19,826

[1] Note.—See paragraph 1 of the Instructions for the Recapitulation in the separate instructions.

[2] Note.—Enter at item 20 the excess of item 10, Total gross estate, over item 18, if the decedent and surviving spouse at no time held property as community property. If property was ever held as community property, compute item 20, Adjusted gross estate, and the reduced $250,000 limitation at item 21 in accordance with the separate Instructions for the Recapitulation and attach an additional sheet showing such computation.

Page 3

Figure 2-3 Cont.

Form 706 (Rev. 6–77)

Estate of: George A. Harris

SCHEDULE A—Real Estate

(For jointly owned property which must be disclosed on Schedule E, see the separate Instructions for Schedule E.)

Item number	Description	Alternate valuation date	Alternate value	Value at date of death
1	Farm - house, barns and 148± acres of land - located on Wright Road, County of Washington - town of Hartford, New York - price per offer from prospective buyer. Attached valuation is increased by $14,000			$60,000
	TOTAL (Also enter under the Recapitulation, page 3.)			$60,000

(If more space is needed, insert additional sheets of same size.)

Schedule A—Page 4

Figure 2-3 Cont.

Form 706 (Rev. 6–77)

Estate of: George A. Harris Date of Death - Dec. 24, 1977

SCHEDULE B—Stocks and Bonds

(For jointly owned property which must be disclosed on Schedule E, see the separate Instructions for Schedule E.)

Item number	Description including face amount of bonds or number of shares and par value where needed for identification, and stock CUSIP number if available	Unit value	Alternate valuation date	Alternate value	Value at date of death
1	159 Shares Capital Stock in American Telephone and Telegraph New York Stock Exchange.	$60.50			$9,619
	Dividend on item 1 of $1.05 per share payable on 1/3/78 to holders of record on 11/30/77.				167
2	120 Shares Common Stock in Bank of America - New York Exchange.	$22.88			2,746
	TOTAL (Also enter under the Recapitulation, page 3.)				$12,532

(If more space is needed, insert additional sheets of same size.)

Schedule B—Page 5

Figure 2-3 Cont.

Form 706 (Rev. 6–77)

Estate of: George A. Harris

SCHEDULE C—Mortgages, Notes, and Cash

(For jointly owned property which must be disclosed on Schedule E, see the separate Instructions for Schedule E.)

Item number	Description	Alternate valuation date	Alternate value	Value at date of death
1	First National Bank of Glens Falls, Hudson Falls, New York Checking Account No.			$21,498
2	The First National Bank of Glens Falls, Glens Falls, New York - Certificate of Deposit - #011123			10,000
	#011129			10,000
3	First Federal Savings & Loan, Glens Falls New York - Certificate of Deposit - #04-12-51			6,000
4	Albany Savings Bank, Glens Falls, New York Passbook accounts - #0461416			20,000
	#0464428			20,000
5	Home Savings Bank, Glens Falls, New York Savings #08003053			30,000
	#8681002			10,000
	TOTAL (Also enter under the Recapitulation, page 3.)			$127,498

(If more space is needed, insert additional sheets of same size.)

Schedule C—Page 6

Figure 2-3 Cont.

Form 706 (Rev. 6–77)

Estate of: George A. Harris

SCHEDULE D—Insurance on Decedent's Life

Was there any insurance on the decedent's life which is not included in the return as a part of the gross estate? ☐ Yes ☐ No
If "Yes," full details must be submitted under this schedule.

Item number	Description	Alternate valuation date	Alternate value	Value at date of death
1	Metropolitan Life Insurance Company, 420 Glen Street, Glens Falls, New York - Policy No. - Beneficiary is			$1,058
	TOTAL (Also enter under the Recapitulation, page 3.)			$1,058

(If more space is needed, insert additional sheets of same size.)

Schedule D—Page 7

Figure 2-3 Cont.

Form 706 (Rev. 6–77)

Estate of: George A. Harris

SCHEDULE E—Jointly Owned Property

1 Did the decedent, at the time of death, own any property as a joint tenant with right of survivorship or as a tenant by the entirety? . . . . ☐ Yes ☐ No
If "Yes," state the name and address of each surviving co-tenant.

	Name	Address (Number and street, city, State, and ZIP code)
A.		
B.		
C.		

2 If the answer to question 1 is "Yes," has the full value of the property been included in the gross estate? . . . ☐ Yes ☐ No
If "No," see the separate instructions for this schedule and submit the necessary proof.

Item number	Enter letter for co-tenant	Description and stock CUSIP number if available	Alternate valuation date	Alternate value	Value at date of death
1		None			
		TOTAL (Also enter under the Recapitulation, page 3.)			None

(If more space is needed, insert additional sheets of same size.)

Schedule E—Page 8

Figure 2-3 Cont.

Form 706 (Rev. 6–77)

Estate of: George A. Harris

SCHEDULE F—Other Miscellaneous Property

(For jointly owned property which must be disclosed on Schedule E, see the separate Instructions for Schedule E.)

	Yes	No
1 Did the decedent, at the time of death, own any interest in a partnership or unincorporated business? *If "Yes," state business name and address.*		X
2 Did the decedent, at the time of death, own any articles or collections having either artistic or intrinsic value, such as jewelry, furs, paintings, antiques, rare books, coins or stamps? *If "Yes," full details must be submitted under this schedule.*		X
3 Was there any insurance which the decedent owned on the life of another which is not included in the return as a part of the gross estate? *If "Yes," full details must be submitted under this schedule.*		X
4 Has the decedent's estate, spouse, or any other person, received (or will receive) any bonus or award as a result of the decedent's employment or death? *If "Yes," full details must be submitted under this schedule.*		X
5 Did the decedent at the time of death have a safe deposit box? *If "Yes," state location, and if held in joint names of decedent and another, state name and relationship of joint depositor.* First National Bank of Glens Falls, Hudson Falls, New York. If any of the contents of the safe deposit box are omitted from the schedules in this return, explain fully why omitted.	X	
6 Did the decedent, at the time of death, own any other miscellaneous property not reportable under any other schedule?		X

Item number	Description	Alternate valuation date	Alternate value	Value at date of death
1	Miscellaneous household furniture at the Hartford New York home listed as follows:			
	Dining room - dining room table, four chairs, chest of drawers and mirror			$ 225
	Living room - old settee and two stuffed chairs			110
	Den - desk and chair			50
	Bedrooms - three double beds - 1 single bed - 2 dressers - cedar chest - 6 odd chairs			340
	Stove, Refrigerator and miscellaneous household items.			200
2	One tractor and miscellaneous farm tools and machinery			5,000
3	Federal Income Tax Refund			479
4	1974 Chevy Chevelle			1,425
	TOTAL (Also enter under the Recapitulation, page 3.)			$7,829

(If more space is needed, insert additional sheets of same size.)

Schedule F—Page 9

Figure 2-3 Cont.

Form 706 (Rev. 6–77)

Estate of: George A. Harris

SCHEDULE G—Transfers During Decedent's Life

		Yes	No
1	Did the decedent make any transfer described in the first paragraph (including the six subparagraphs) of the separate instructions for this schedule?		X
2a	Did the decedent, at any time, make a transfer (other than an outright transfer not in trust) without an adequate and full consideration in money or money's worth, but not believed to be includible in the gross estate as indicated in the first paragraph (including the six subparagraphs) of the separate instructions for this schedule?		X
	If "Yes," furnish the following information:		
2b	Date / **2c** Amount or value / **2d** Character of transfer		
3a	Did the decedent, before January 1, 1977, and within 3 years immediately preceding death, make any transfer of property without an adequate and full consideration in money or money's worth?		X
	If "Yes," furnish the following information:		
3b	Date / **3c** Amount or value / **3d** Character of transfer		
3e	Motive which actuated decedent in making the transfer		
3f	Names and addresses of hospitals in which decedent was confined within 3 years of death		
4	Were there in existence at the time of the decedent's death any trusts created by decedent during decedent's lifetime?		X
5a	Have Federal gift tax returns ever been filed?		X
	If "Yes," furnish the following information:		
5b	Period(s) covered / **5c** Internal Revenue office(s) where filed		

Item number	Description and stock CUSIP number if available	Alternate valuation date	Alternate value	Value at date of death
	A. Transfers by decedent after December 31, 1976, and within 3 years of death unless excepted under section 2035(b):			
1	None			
	Gift tax paid by decedent or estate for above gifts made by decedent or spouse after December 31, 1976, and within 3 years of decedent's death	X X X X X	X X X X X	
	B. Other transfers:			
1	None			
	TOTAL (Also enter under the Recapitulation, page 3.)			None

(If more space is needed, insert additional sheets of same size.)

Schedule G—Page 10

Figure 2-3 Cont.

Form 706 (Rev. 6-77)

Estate of: George A. Harris

SCHEDULE H—Powers of Appointment

		Yes	No
1a	Did the decedent, at the time of death, possess a general power of appointment created after October 21, 1942?		X
1b	On or before such date?		X
2a	Did the decedent, at any time, by will or otherwise, exercise or release (to any extent) a general power of appointment created after October 21, 1942?		X
2b	On or before such date?		X
3	Were there in existence at the time of the decedent's death any trusts not created by decedent under which decedent possessed any power, beneficial interest, or trusteeship?		X

Item number	Description	Alternate valuation date	Alternate value	Value at date of death
1	None			
	TOTAL (Also enter under the Recapitulation, page 3.)			None

SCHEDULE I—Annuities

		Yes	No
1a	Was the decedent, immediately before death, receiving an annuity as described in paragraph 1 of the separate instructions for this schedule?		X
1b	If "Yes," was that annuity paid pursuant to an approved plan as described in paragraph 4 of the separate instructions for this schedule?		
1c	If the answer to "1b" is "Yes," state the ratio of the decedent's contribution to the total purchase price of the annuity.		
2a	If the decedent was employed at the time of death, did an annuity as described in paragraph 3(d) of the separate instructions for this schedule become payable to any beneficiary by reason of the beneficiary surviving the decedent?		X
2b	If "Yes," state the ratio of the decedent's contribution to the total purchase price of the annuity.		
3a	Did an annuity under an individual retirement account, annuity, or bond as described in section 2039(e) become payable to any beneficiary by reason of the beneficiary surviving the decedent?		X
3b	If "Yes," is the annuity payable to the beneficiary for life or for at least 36 months following decedent's death?		
3c	If the answer to 3a is "Yes," state the ratio of the amount paid for the individual retirement account, annuity, or bond which was allowable as an income tax deduction under section 219 (other than a rollover contribution) to the total amount paid for the account, annuity, or bond.		

Item number	Description	Alternate valuation date	Alternate value	Value at date of death
1	None			
	TOTAL (Also enter under the Recapitulation, page 3.)			None

(If more space is needed, insert additional sheets of same size.)

Schedules H and I—Page 11

Figure 2-3 Cont.

Form 706 (Rev. 6–77)

Estate of: George A. Harris

SCHEDULE J—Funeral Expenses and Expenses Incurred in Administering Property Subject to Claims

Note.—Do not list on this schedule expenses of administering property not subject to claims. In connection with such expenses, see the separate Instructions for Schedule L.

If deceased's personal representative commissions, attorney fees, etc., are claimed and allowed as a deduction for estate tax purposes, they are not allowable as a deduction in computing the taxable income of the estate for Federal income tax purposes.

Item number	Description		Amount
	A. Funeral expenses:		
1		$2,094	
	Total	x x x x x	$2,094
	B. Administration expenses:		
1	Deceased's personal representative commissions—amount estimated/agreed upon/paid. (Strike out words not applicable)	x x x x x	7,143
2	Attorney fees—amount estimated/agreed upon/paid. (Strike out words not applicable)	x x x x x	9,189
3	Miscellaneous expenses:		
		1,400	
	Total miscellaneous expenses	x x x x x	1,400
	TOTAL (Also enter under the Recapitulation, page 3.)		$19,826

(If more space is needed, insert additional sheets of same size.)

Schedule J—Page 12

Figure 2-3 Cont.

Form 706 (Rev. 6–77)

Estate of: George A. Harris

SCHEDULE K—Debts of Decedent and Mortgages and Liens

Item number	Debts of Decedent—Creditor and nature of claim, and allowable death taxes	Amount
1	None	
	TOTAL (Also enter under the Recapitulation, page 3.)	None

Item number	Mortgages and Liens—Description	Amount
1	None	
	TOTAL (Also enter under the Recapitulation, page 3.)	None

SCHEDULE L—Net Losses During Administration and Expenses Incurred in Administering Property Not Subject to Claims

Item number	Net losses during administration (Note: Do not deduct losses claimed in a Federal income tax return.)	Amount
1	None	
	TOTAL (Also enter under the Recapitulation, page 3.)	None

Item number	Expenses incurred in administering property not subject to claims (Indicate whether estimated, agreed upon, or paid.)	Amount
1	None	
	TOTAL (Also enter under the Recapitulation, page 3.)	None

(If more space is needed, insert additional sheets of same size.) **Schedules K and L—Page 13**

Figure 2-3 Cont.

Form 706 (Rev. 6–77)

Estate of: George A. Harris

SCHEDULE M—Bequests, etc., to Surviving Spouse

If the decedent died testate, the person or persons filing the return must answer the following questions. Only questions 1c, 3, and 5 need be answered if the decedent died intestate. If the answer to any question is "Yes," full details must be submitted under this schedule.	Yes	No
1a Has any action been instituted to contest the will or any provision thereof affecting any property interest listed on this schedule or for construction of the will or any such provision?		X
1b According to the information and belief of the person or persons filing the return, is any such action designed or contemplated?		X
1c According to the information and belief of such person or persons, has any person other than the surviving spouse asserted (or is any such assertion contemplated) a right to any property interest listed on this schedule, other than as indicated under question 1a or 1b?		X
2a Had the surviving spouse the right to declare an election between (i) the provisions made in favor of surviving spouse by the will and (ii) dower, curtesy, or a statutory interest?	N/	A
2b If the answer to question 2a is "Yes," has the surviving spouse renounced the will and elected to take dower, curtesy, or a statutory interest?	N/	A
2c Elected to take under the will?	N/	A
2d Does the surviving spouse contemplate renouncing the will and electing to take dower, curtesy, or a statutory interest?	N/	A
3 Did any property pass to the surviving spouse as the result of a qualified disclaimer? *If "Yes," attach a copy of the written disclaimer required by section 2518(b).*	N/	A
4 Was the amount of property passing to the surviving spouse determined under the "formula" rule in Public Law 94–455, section 2002(d)(1)(B) (Tax Reform Act of 1976)? *If "Yes," compute the marital deduction on an attached sheet, enter the amount on line 26 of the Recapitulation, and note line 26 "computation attached."*	N/	A
5 Was the marital deduction computed under section 2602(c)(5)(A) (generation-skipping transfer at same time or within 9 months after deemed transferor's death)? *If "Yes," compute the marital deduction on an attached sheet, enter the amount on line 26 of the Recapitulation, and note line 26 "computation attached."*	N/	A

Item number	Description of property interests passing to surviving spouse	Value
1	None	
	Total	None
	Less: (a) Federal estate tax payable out of above-listed property interests	
	(b) Other death taxes payable out of above-listed property interests	
	Total of items (a) and (b)	
	Net value of above-listed property interests (Also enter under the Recapitulation, page 3.)	None

(If more space is needed, insert additional sheets of same size.) **Schedule M—Page 14**

Figure 2-3 Cont.

Form 706 (Rev. 6–77)

Estate of: George A. Harris

SCHEDULE N—Orphans' Deduction

(Do Not complete this schedule if the answer to either question 1 or question 2 is "Yes." If there is more than one child, attach an additional schedule for each additional child.)

		Yes	No
1	Was the decedent survived by a spouse?		X
2	Does the child have a living parent?		X
3	Did any property pass to the child as the result of a qualified disclaimer? *If "Yes," attach a copy of the written disclaimer required by section 2518(b).*		X

4a Name of child | **4b** Date of birth

Item number	Description of property passing to child	Value
1	None	

(a) Total . . . . .

(b) Enter the amount obtained by multiplying $5,000 by the excess of 21 over the child's attained age (in years) at date of decedent's death . . . . .

(c) Enter the smaller of (i) the amount on line (a) or (ii) the amount on line (b). (Also enter this amount under the Recapitulation, page 3; if there is more than one child, enter the total of the respective line (c) amounts from all of the schedules.). . . . . None

SCHEDULE O—Charitable, Public, and Similar Gifts and Bequests

		Yes	No
1a	If the transfer was made by will, has any action been instituted to have interpreted or to contest the will or any provision thereof affecting the charitable deductions claimed in this schedule? *If "Yes," full details must be submitted under this schedule.*		X
1b	According to the information and belief of the person or persons filing the return, is any such action designed or contemplated? *If "Yes," full details must be submitted under this schedule.*		X
2	Did any property pass to charity as the result of a qualified disclaimer? *If "Yes," attach a copy of the written disclaimer required by section 2518(B).*		X

Item number	Name and address of beneficiary	Character of institution	Amount
1	None		

Total . . . . .

Less: (a) Federal estate tax payable out of above-listed property interests . . . . .

(b) Other death taxes payable out of above-listed property interests . . . . .

Total of items (a) and (b) . . . . .

Net value of above-listed property interests (Also enter under the Recapitulation, page 3.) . . . . . None

(If more space is needed, insert additional sheets of same size.) **Schedules N and O—Page 15**

Figure 2-3 Cont.

Form 706 (Rev. 6–77)

Estate of: George A. Harris

SCHEDULE P—Credit for Foreign Death Taxes

List all foreign countries to which death taxes have been paid and for which credit is claimed on this return.

If credit is claimed for death taxes paid to more than one foreign country, compute the credit for taxes paid to one country on this sheet and attach a separate copy of Schedule P for each of the other countries.

The credit computed on this sheet is for .... (Name of death tax or taxes)

.... imposed in .... (Name of country)

Credit is computed under the .... (Insert "treaty" or "statute")

Citizenship (Nationality) of decedent at time of death ....

(All amounts and values shown hereunder must be entered in United States money)

1 Amount of estate, inheritance, legacy and succession taxes imposed in the above country attributable to property situated in that country, and subjected to such taxes, and included in the gross estate (as defined by statute)	
2 Value of the gross estate (adjusted, if necessary, in accordance with the separate instructions for item 2)	
3 Value of property situated in that country, and subjected to death taxes imposed in that country, and included in the gross estate (adjusted, if necessary, in accordance with the separate instructions for item 3)	
4 Amount of tax imposed by section 2001 reduced by the total amount of the credits claimed under sections 2010, 2011, and 2012	
5 Amount of Federal estate tax attributable to property specified at item 3 (proportion of item 4 that item 3 bears to item 2)	
6 Credit for death taxes imposed in the above country (item 1 or item 5, whichever is the smaller)	None

SCHEDULE Q—Credit for Tax on Prior Transfers

Name of transferor	Date of transferor's death
None	
Internal Revenue Service office where prior return was filed	Transferor's soc. sec. no.

Check here ▶ ☐ if section 2013(f) (special valuation of farm, etc. real property) and/or section 2013(g) (generation-skipping transfers) adjustments are applicable to the computation of the credit and show the computation of the credit on an attached sheet.

PART I—Transferor's Tax on Prior Transfers	
1 Net value of transfers	
2 Value of transferor's estate (adjusted in accordance with the separate instructions for item 2)	
3 Tax on transferor's estate (adjusted in accordance with the separate instructions for item 3)	
4 Transferor's tax on prior transfers (proportion of item 3 which item 1 bears to item 2)	
PART II—Transferee's Tax on Prior Transfers	
5 Transferee's actual tax before allowance of credit for prior transfer tax	
6 Transferee's reduced gross estate	
7 Transferee's deductions (adjusted in accordance with the separate instructions for item 7)	
8 Transferee's reduced taxable estate (subtract amount on item 7 from amount on item 6)	
9 Enter amount of adjusted taxable gifts from line 4, page 1	
10 Add amount on item 8 and amount on item 9	
11 Tax on amount on item 10	
12 Enter amount from line 7, page 1	
13 Subtract amount on item 12 from amount on item 11	
14 Amount of unified credit plus credits for State death tax, gift tax, and foreign death tax	
15 Subtract amount on item 14 from amount on item 13	
16 Subtract amount on item 15 from amount on item 5	
PART III—Credit Allowable	
17 Maximum amount before application of percentage requirement (item 4 or item 16, whichever is smaller)	
18 Percent allowable is	
19 Credit allowable (multiply amount on item 17 by amount on item 18)	None

☆ U.S. GOVERNMENT PRINTING OFFICE: 1977-0-218-293 (38-1240-693) **Schedules P and Q—Page 16**

must perform the duties of estate settlement with care, diligence, and prudence.

[¶216.1] Form 56—Notice of Fiduciary Relationship

As soon as Letters Testamentary are issued by the court, the personal representative must file a notice of fiduciary relationship on Form 56 (see Figure 2-4) with the Internal Revenue Service. This notice must be filed by the personal representative within 30 days after his appointment or qualification.

This notice should be addressed as follows:

Chief of the Special Procedures Section
Form 56—Notice of Fiduciary Relationship
Internal Revenue Service Center
City, State, Zip

Upon termination of his fiduciary duty, the personal representative should dispatch a notice of the completion of his fiduciary relationship. There is no prescribed form for this notice; a simple letter is sufficient.

[¶216.2] The SS-4

Immediately upon qualification, the personal representative must obtain from the IRS an estate number. The request for this number is made on Form SS-4 (see Figure 2-5).

[¶216.3] Form 706

The 706 estate tax return must be filed with the Internal Revenue Service Center handling the taxes for the geographic place of legal residence of the decedent.

The estate tax return must be filed with the tax due by check or money order within 9 months after the date of death. In computing the due date for payment, the same numbered day of the month 9 months after the date of death is used, but if there is no similar numbered day in the ninth month, then the tax is due on the last day of that month. Thus, for example, if the date of death was December 31, 1979, then the tax would be due on September 30, 1980.

Figure 2-4

Form **56**
(Rev. Sept. 1976)
Department of the Treasury
Internal Revenue Service

Notice of Fiduciary Relationship

(Under section 6903 of the Internal Revenue Code)

PART I—In General. (All fiduciaries complete this part.)

Fiduciary's name
PETER G. HARRIS

Fiduciary's address (Number and street)
R. D.

City, State, and ZIP code
Fort Ann, New York 12827

Name of person for whom you are acting (as will be shown on the tax return)
GEORGE A. HARRIS

Identifying number (See Instr. D.)
00-0000000

Address of person for whom you are acting (Number and street)

City, State, and ZIP code
Hartford, New York 12838

If you are acting for a decedent, show date of death
12-24-77

Decedent's social security number
000-00-000

Description of evidence of authority to act as a fiduciary (Check the applicable boxes.)

- [X] Certified copy of will attached
- [X] Certified copy of court order appointing the fiduciary attached
- [ ] Certified copy of trust instrument attached
- [ ] Specimen form of "Illinois type" land trust agreement attached
- [ ] Specimen form of "Illinois type" land trust agreement filed previously with Internal Revenue Service (Specify location and date)
- [ ] Other (describe)

PART II—Nature of Liabilities. (All fiduciaries except "Illinois type" land trust fiduciaries complete this part.)

Specific liabilities of the person for whom you are acting known to you:

- [ ] Income tax for period(s) ►
- [ ] Gift tax for period(s) ►
- [X] Estate tax
- [ ] Other (specify) ►
- [ ] Liability of person for whom you are acting
- [ ] Transferee liability of person for whom you are acting
- [ ] Fiduciary liability of person for whom you are acting under section 3467 of the Revised Statutes as amended (31 U.S.C. 192) concerning payment of tax from a decedent's estate

PART III—"Illinois type" Land Trusts. ("Illinois type" land trusts fiduciaries complete this part.)

Beneficiary's name | Identifying number (See Instr. D.)

Beneficiary's address (Number and street) | Percentage (or fraction) owned

City, State, and ZIP code

Sign here ► I have examined this notice and to the best of my knowledge it is correct.

Peter G. Harris — Fiduciary's signature | Executor — Title | 3-30-78 — Date

[¶216.4] Form 1041: U.S. Fiduciary Income Tax Return

Early in the performance of his duties the personal representative should obtain a copy of Form 1041. This form includes specific instructions for preparation (see Figure 2-6).

[¶216.5] Request for Extension of Time

A personal representative may apply for an extension of time for the payment of an estate tax for a period not to exceed 12 months from the date fixed for payment of the estate tax if he is able to show that reasonable cause exists for granting such an extension. (See Form 4768 in Figure 2-7.)

Figure 2-5

☆ U. S. GOVERNMENT PRINTING OFFICE : 1976 627-200

For clear copy on both parts, please typewrite or print with ball point pen and press firmly
(See Instructions on pages 2 and 4)

Form SS–4 (Rev. 8–76)
Department of the Treasury
Internal Revenue Service

Application for Employer Identification Number
(For use by employers and others as explained in the Instructions)

1 Name (True name as distinguished from trade name. If partnership, see Instructions on page 4)

2 Trade name, if any (Enter name under which business is operated, if different from item 1)

3 Social security number, if sole proprietor

4 Address of principal place of business (Number and street)

5 Ending month of accounting year

6 City and State

7 ZIP code

8 County of business location

9 Type of organization
☐ Governmental (See Instr. on page 4)
☐ Individual
☐ Nonprofit organization (See Instr. on page 4)
☐ Partnership
☐ Corporation
☐ Other (specify)

10 Date you acquired or started this business (Mo., day, year)

11 Reason for applying
☐ Started new business
☐ Purchased going business
☐ Other (specify)

12 First date you paid or will pay wages for this business (Mo., day, year)

13 Nature of business (See Instructions on page 4)

14 Do you operate more than one place of business? ☐ Yes ☐ No

15 Peak number of employees expected in next 12 months (If none, enter "0") ▶ Nonagricultural | Agricultural | Household

16 If nature of business is manufacturing, state principal product and raw material used

17 To whom do you sell most of your products or services?
☐ Business establishments
☐ General public
☐ Other (specify)

18 Have you ever applied for an identification number for this or any other business? ☐ Yes ☐ No

If "Yes," enter name and trade name (if any). Also enter the approximate date, city, and State where you first applied and previous number if known. ▶

Date | Signature and title | Telephone number

Please leave blank ▶	Geo.	Ind.	Class	Size	Reas. for appl.	**Part I**

Figure 2-6

Form **1041** Department of the Treasury Internal Revenue Service

U.S. Fiduciary Income Tax Return **1978**

for the calendar year 1978 or fiscal year beginning ...., 1978, and ending ...., 19.....

Check applicable box(es):	Name of estate or trust ("Grantor type" trusts, see instruction J.)	Employer identification number
☐ Estate ($600 exemption)	PAUL M. DUNHAM ESTATE	00-0000000
☐ Testamentary trust ☐ Inter vivos trust ☐ Simple trust ($300)	Name and title of fiduciary ALBERT P. DUNHAM, EXECUTOR	Nonexempt charitable and split-interest trusts check applicable boxes (See instruction Q.):
☐ Complex trust ($100) ☐ Complex trust ($300)	Address of fiduciary (number and street) 47 ATWOOD DRIVE	☐ Described in section 4947(a)(1)
☐ Grantor type trust ☐ Family estate type trust ☐ Pooled income fund	City, State, and ZIP code ELKWOOD, NEW YORK 10789	☐ Not treated as a private foundation by reason of sec. 509(a) (1), (2) or (3)
Has the fiduciary's name and/or address changed? ☐ Yes ☐ No.	Final return? ☐ Yes ☐ No.	☐ Described in section 4947(a)(2)

Income	1 Dividends (Enter full amount before exclusion) **(Attach schedule if over $400)**	1			
	2 Interest (Attach schedule if over $400)	2	738		
	3 Income from partnerships and name and E.I. No.	3			
	4 Income from other estates and trusts and name and E.I. No.	4			
	5 Gross rents and royalties (Attach schedule if over $400)	5			
	6 Net business and farm income or (loss) **(Attach Schedules C and F (Form 1040))**	6			
	7 Capital gain or (loss) **(Attach Schedule D (Form 1041))**	7			
	8 Ordinary gain or (loss) **(Attach Form 4797)**	8			
	9 Other income (Attach schedule of income and list by payer if over $400)	9			
	10 Total income (add lines 1 to 9, inclusive)			10	738
Deductions	11 Interest	11			
	12 Taxes	12	20		
	13 Fiduciary's portion of depreciation (Schedule A) and depletion. Explain depletion	13			
	14 Charitable deduction (from line 56)	14			
	15 Fiduciary fees	15			
	16 Attorney, accountant, and return preparer fees	16			
	17 Other deductions (List on a separate sheet and attach)	17			
	18 Total (add lines 11 to 17, inclusive)			18	20
	19 Subtract line 18 from line 10 (Complex trusts and estates enter this amount on line 57; simple trusts, see instr. O.)			19	718
	20 Distributions deduction (from line 70) **(Attach Schedule K-1 (Form 1041))**	20			
	21 Adjustment of dividend exclusion	21			
	22 Estate tax deduction **(Attach computation)**	22			
	23 Long-term capital gain deduction from Schedule D (Form 1041)	23			
	24 Exemption (If final return, see instruction M.)	24	600		
	25 Total (add lines 20 to 24, inclusive)			25	600
	26 Taxable income of fiduciary (subtract line 25 from line 19)			26	118
Computation of Tax	27 Tax on amount on line 26 (See tax rate schedule)			27	17
	28 If alternative tax is applicable, enter the tax from Schedule D (Form 1041)			28	
	29 Fiduciary's share of foreign tax credit **(Attach Form 1116)**	29			
	30 Fiduciary's share of investment credit **(Attach Form 3468)**	30			
	31 a WIN credit ▶ ; b Jobs credit ▶ ; c Total ▶	31			
	32 Total (add lines 29 to 31, inclusive)			32	-0-
	33 Balance (subtract line 32 from 27 or 28, whichever is applicable)			33	17
	34 Tax from recomputing fiduciary's share of prior year investment credit **(Attach Form 4255)**			34	
	35 Minimum tax **(Attach Form 4626)**			35	
	36 Total (add lines 33 to 35, inclusive)			36	17
	37 Other credits; see instruction 37	37			
	38 Federal income tax: a Previously paid ▶ ; b Withheld ▶ ; c Total ▶	38			
	39 Total (add lines 37 and 38)			39	
	40 Balance of tax due (subtract line 39 from line 36) (See instruction H.)			40	21 *
	41 Overpayment (subtract line 36 from line 39)			41	

Please Sign Here

Under penalties of perjury, I declare that I have examined this return, including accompanying schedules and statements, and to the best of my knowledge and belief it is true, correct, and complete. Declaration of preparer (other than fiduciary) is based on all information of which preparer has any knowledge.

▶ Albert P. Dunham — Signature of fiduciary or officer representing fiduciary — Date 1/15/79

Paid Preparer's Information			
Preparer's signature ▶	James D. Miller C.P.A.	Preparer's social security no.	Check if self-employed ▶ ☐
Firm's name (or yours, if self-employed), address and ZIP code ▶	80 Main Street Mayfield, N.Y. 12575	E.I. No. ▶ 00 000000	Date ▶ 1/20/79

23-188-5979

Figure 2-6 Cont.

Schedule A.—DEPRECIATION—(See the Instructions for Schedule A for information on the depreciation methods)

a. Description of property	b. Date acquired	c. Cost or other basis	d. Depreciation allowed or allowable in prior years	e. Method of computing depreciation	f. Life or rate	g. Depreciation for this year
42 Total additional first-year depreciation—estates only (do not include in items below)						
43 Other depreciation:						
44 Totals						
45 Less amount of depreciation claimed elsewhere on return						
46 Balance (subtract line 45 from line 44)						
47 Fiduciary's portion of line 46. Enter here and on line 13						

Schedule B.—CHARITABLE DEDUCTION—(Attach statement giving name and address of charitable organization.)

48 Amounts paid or permanently set aside for charitable purposes from current year's income (See instructions.)

49 Tax-exempt interest allocable to charitable distribution (See instructions.)

(Complete lines 50 and 51 below only if gain on Schedule D (Form 1041) line 15, column 2, exceeds loss on Schedule D (Form 1041) line 14, column 2.)

50 a Long-term capital gain included on line 48 (See instructions.)

(Do not complete lines b and c if such amounts are greater than line a)

b Enter gain on Schedule D (Form 1041) line 15, column 2, minus loss on Schedule D (Form 1041) line 14, column 2

c Enter gain on Schedule D (Form 1041) line 15, column 3, minus loss on Schedule D (Form 1041) line 14, column 3

51 Enter the smallest of line 50a, 50b, or 50c adjusted for the section 1202 deduction

52 Add line 49 and line 51

53 Balance (subtract line 52 from line 48)

54 Enter the short-term capital gains and the long-term capital gains adjusted for the section 1202 deduction of the current taxable year allocable to corpus, paid or permanently set aside for charitable purposes

55 Amounts paid or permanently set aside for charitable purposes other than from income of the current year (See instructions.)

56 Total (add lines 53, 54 and 55). Enter here and on line 14

Schedule C.—DISTRIBUTIONS DEDUCTION

57 Enter amount from line 19 — 57

58 Add: a Tax-exempt interest (as adjusted—see instructions) — 58a

b Net gain shown on Schedule D (Form 1041) line 16, column 1. If net loss, enter zero — 58b

c Add lines 51 and 54 — 58c

d Short-term capital gain included on line 48 — 58d

e If amount on line 7 is a loss, enter amount here as a positive figure — 58e

59 Total (add lines 57 through 58e) — 59

60 If amount on line 7 is a gain, enter amount here — 60

61 Distributable net income (subtract line 60 from line 59) — 61

62 Amount of income required to be distributed currently (See instructions.) — 62

63 Other amounts paid, credited, or otherwise required to be distributed (See instructions.) — 63

64 Total (add lines 62 and 63). If a trust, was there undistributed net income at the beginning of the year? ☐ Yes ☐ No — 64

65 Enter the total of tax-exempt income included on lines 62 and 63 (as adjusted—see instructions) — 65

66 Balance (subtract line 65 from line 64) — 66

67 Enter distributable net income from line 61 — 67

68 Enter the amount from line 58a — 68

69 Balance (subtract line 68 from line 67) — 69

70 Distributions deduction. Enter here and on line 20, the lesser of line 66 or line 69 — 70

	Yes	No
71 Date trust was created or, if an estate, date of decedent's death. December 17, 1977		
72 Did the estate or trust receive tax-exempt income? If "Yes," did you deduct any expenses allocable to it? N/A		X
73 If the estate or trust received income from a nominee, state name, identifying number, and address of nominee ▶ N/A		
74 If a complex trust, is this a section 663(b) election? If "Yes," state amount ▶		X
75 If a trust, is any section 644 tax due? If "Yes," state amount ▶ and attach computation.		X
76 Does the estate or trust receive all or any part of the earnings (salary, wages, and other compensation) of any individual by reason of a contract assignment or similar arrangement?		X
77 Have you deducted on this return any amount paid directly or indirectly for the benefit of the grantor or spouse?		X
78 Did the estate or trust, at any time during the taxable year, have any interest in or signature or other authority over a bank, securities, or other financial account over $1,000 in a foreign country (except in a U.S. military banking facility operated by a U.S. financial institution)? If "Yes," see the instructions for question 78		X
79 Was the estate or trust the grantor of, or transferor to, a foreign trust during any taxable year, which foreign trust was in being during the current taxable year, whether or not the estate or trust has any beneficial interest in such trust? If "Yes," you may be required to file Forms 3520, 3520-A, or 926		X

☆ U.S. GOVERNMENT PRINTING OFFICE 1978—0-263-342

Figure 2-7

Form **4768** (Rev. Feb. 1978) Department of the Treasury Internal Revenue Service

Application for Extension of Time to File U.S. Estate Tax Return and/or Pay Estate Tax

(Sections 6081 and/or 6161 of the Internal Revenue Code)

Part I Identification

Decedent's first name and middle initial	Decedent's last name	Date of death
George A.	Harris	12-24-77
Name of application filer		Decedent's social security number
J. C. Agee & Company, C.P.A.		000-00-000
Address of application filer (Number and street)		Estate tax return due date
248 Elm Avenue		6-24-78
City, State and ZIP code		
Easton, New York 10052		

Part II Extension of Time to File (Sec. 6081)

You must attach your written statement to explain in detail why it is impossible or impractical to file a reasonably complete return within nine months after the date of the decedent's death.

Extension date requested 6-30-78

Part III Extension of Time to Pay (Sec. 6161)

You must attach your written statement to explain in detail why it is impossible or impractical to pay the full amount of the estate tax by the estate tax return due date.

Extension date requested 6-30-78

Amount of estate tax estimated to be due	$20,000.00
Amount of cash shortage claimed	10,000.00
Balance due (Pay with this application.)	10,000.00

Signature and Verification

If filed by personal representative—Under penalties of perjury, I declare that to the best of my knowledge and belief, the statements made herein and attached are true and correct.

Personal representative's signature .... Title .... Date ....

If filed by someone other than personal representative—Under penalties of perjury, I declare that to the best of my knowledge and belief, the statements made herein and attached are true and correct, that I am authorized by the personal representative to file this application, and that I am:

- ☐ A member in good standing of the bar of the highest court of (specify jurisdiction) ▶
- ☒ A certified public accountant duly qualified to practice in (specify jurisdiction) ▶ New York
- ☐ A person enrolled to practice before the Internal Revenue Service.
- ☐ A duly authorized agent holding a power of attorney. (The power of attorney need not be submitted unless requested.)

John Agee, Pres
J. C. Agee and Company, C.P.A. — 6-10-78

Filer's signature (other than personal representative) .... Date

Part IV Notice to Applicant—To be completed by Internal Revenue Service

1. The application for extension of time to file (Part II) is:
   - ☐ Approved
   - ☐ Not approved because ....
   - ☐ Other ....

2. The application for extension of time to pay (Part III) is:
   - ☐ Approved
   - ☐ Not approved because ....
   - ☐ Other ....

Internal Revenue Service official	Date	Internal Revenue Service official	Date

Form **4768** (Rev. 2-78)

Figure 2-8

Internal Revenue Service
District Director

Department of the Treasury

Date: December 19, 1978

Susanne Adams
39 Pierrepont Street
Brooklyn Heights, NY 11201

and

Jason W. Herkimer
15 Ebony Drive
Ames, NY 00211

Estate of:
Jason W. Herkimer
Decedent's Social Security Number:
000-00-0000
Date of Death:
June 5, 1977
Person to Contact:
BNH
Contact Telephone Number:
(914) 972-1403
Schoharie County

Estate Tax Closing letter
(This is not a bill for tax due)

Our computation of the Federal Tax liability for the above estate is shown below. It does not include any interest that may be charged. You should keep a copy of this letter as a permanent record because your attorney may need it to close the probate proceedings for the estate. This letter is evidence that the Federal tax return for the estate has either been accepted as filed, or has been accepted after an adjustment that you agreed to.

This is not a formal closing agreement under section 7121 of the Internal Revenue Code. We will not reopen this case, however, unless Revenue Procedure 74-5, reproduced on the back of this letter, applies.

If you have any questions, please contact the person whose name and telephone number are shown above. Thank you for your cooperation.

cc: Mr. P. Douglass
P.O. Box 199
West Pawlet, VT 05775

Sincerely yours,

R. A. Spellman

District Director

Tentative tax		$ 42,470.00
Less: Aggregate gift taxes payable (for gifts made after 12-31-76)	$ 0	
Unified credit	$ 30,000.00	
Credit for State death taxes	$ 583.00	
Credit for Federal gift taxes (on gifts prior to 1-1-77)	$ 0	
Credit for foreign death taxes	$ 0	
Credit for tax on prior transfers	$ 0	
Total subtractions		$ 30,583.00
Net estate tax		$ 11,887.00
Penalties, if any		$ 0

(over)

Clinton Avenue & North Pearl Street, Albany, N.Y. 12207

Letter 627(DO) (Rev. 2-78)

Figure 2-9 Douglas Estate (Refer to Figure 2-2)

WORKSHEET FOR COMPUTATION

RATE CLASS	BRACKET NO.	A ESTIMATED GROSS ESTATE	1 B ESTIMATED DEDUCTIONS	2 C (B MINUS A) ADJUSTED GROSS ESTATE	3 D MARITAL DEDUCTION (½C OR $250,000)	4 E (C MINUS D) TAXABLE ESTATE
	1					
	2					
	3					
	4					
	5					
	6					
	7					
	8					
	9					
	10					
	11					
	12					
	13					
	14					
	15					
	16					
	17					
	18					
	19					
	20					

ON TENTATIVE RATE SCHEDULE

5 F TENTATIVE TAX BRACKET	6 G OVERAGE ABOVE TAX BRACKET	7 H SURTAX %	8 I (G x H) TENTATIVE TAX	9 J UNIFIED CREDIT	10 K (I MINUS J) ESTIMATED FEDERAL TAX	11 L STATE DEATH TAX CREDIT	12 M (K MINUS L) FEDERAL ESTATE TAX DUE
0		.18					
$ 10000		.20					
20000		.22					
40000		.24					
60000		.26					
80000		.28					
100000		.30					
150000		.32					
250000		.34					
500000		.37					
750000		.39					
1000000		.41					
1250000		.43					
1500000		.45					
2000000		.49					
2500000		.53					
3000000		.57					
3500000		.61					
4000000		.65					
4500000		.69					
5000000		.70					
OVER 5000000							

[¶216.6] The Closing Letter

After reviewing the 706 form, the Internal Revenue Service issues a closing letter (see Figure 2-8).

The closing letter terminates the relationship of the personal representative with the Internal Revenue Service. It confirms that the federal tax levy has been satisfactorily paid.

[¶217] INSTALLMENT PAYMENT OF ESTATE TAX

Pursuant to the Tax Reform Act of 1976, an estate can elect to defer all payments of estate tax for 5 years by the payment of interest only. Thereafter, the estate tax is payable in equal installments over the next 10 years if more than 65 percent of the decedent's adjusted gross estate is an interest in a farm. Interest is payable at 4 percent on the estate tax attributable to the first million dollars of the farm interest.

To trigger the 65 percent rule a farm must have no more than 15 partners or 15 shareholders. Further, the partnership or corporation must hold 20 percent of the capital interest or at least 20 percent of the voting stock, includable in the decedent's gross estate.

The Revenue Act of 1978 liberalized the attribution rules for installment payment of estate tax. Thus, for estates of decedents dying after November 6, 1978, stock or partnership interests that were held by members of the decedent's family are treated as having been owned by the decedent. The decedent's "family," as defined by Code Section 267(c)(4), includes his or her spouse, siblings, ancestors, and lineal descendants. For purposes of the 20 percent requirement, any stock or partnership interest that is attributed to the decedent must be included in the gross estate [new Code Section 6166(b)(2)(D)].

Since an individual, his or her spouse, brothers, sisters, parents, and children will be treated as one person for purposes of determining eligibility for installment payment of the estate tax, up to 14 nonrelatives may be given interests in the business. However, if the benefits of the attribution rules are elected, the special 4 percent interest rate on the unpaid estate tax apparently is not available [new Code Section 6166(b)(7)].

[¶218] WORKSHEET FOR COMPUTING ESTATE TAX

The worksheet given in Figure 2-9 will enable you to compute your own estate tax. Here are step-by-step directions for making the computations:

A. Enter estimated gross estate
B. Subtract estimated deductions
C. Enter adjusted gross estate
D. Substract marital deduction
E. Taxable estate
F. Establish tentative tax bracket
G. Subtract tax bracket from taxable estate overage
H. Multiply overage by surtax
I. Estimate tentative tax
J. Apply unified credit
K. Federal estate tax
L. Credit for state death taxes
M. Federal estate tax due

THE LANGUAGE OF ESTATE AND GIFT TAX SETTLEMENT

Adjusted Gross Estate the gross estate less deductible costs.

Annual Exclusion gifts of present interests of not more than $3,000.00 in any calendar year by a donor to an unlimited number of donees.

Carry-over Basis the income tax basis of property acquired from or passing from a decedent—subject to certain post-death adjustments—as adjusted before the decedent's death; the carry-over basis rules are operative only with respect to decedents dying after December 31, 1979.

Current Use Value special procedure for valuing real estate devoted to operating farm value.

Death Tax the inheritance tax imposed by every state except Nevada.

Form 706 the form by which an estate is reported to the Internal Revenue Service.

Form 709 the quarterly report for reporting qualifying gifts to the Internal Revenue Service.

Fresh Start Rule a process of calculation of property values held by a decedent as of December 31, 1976, under which the appreciation in value is determined by an applicable fraction determined by the number of days in the holding period prior to January 1, 1977.

Generation Skipping favorable tax treatment up to $250,000.00 per child in a life estate arrangement that passes the trust corpus down to possible great-grandchildren.

Gifts shifts in property ownership that trigger tax consequences.

Gifts to Minor a legal arrangement established by law under which the custodianship of property is transferred to a custodian to manage until the minor comes of age.

Gross Estate everything owned in the name of the decedent.

Incidence of Ownership right especially in life insurance policies to change the beneficiary, borrow against the cash value, or to take paid-up additional insurance.

Liquidity resources adequate and available to pay taxes due the Internal Revenue Service.

Marital Deduction a deduction against federal estate tax due equal to the value of property passing (in certain ways) to the surviving spouse, up to a maximum of approximately one-half of the decedent spouse's estate.

Orphan's Exclusion an estate tax deduction granted to a minor when there is no surviving spouse of the decedent or other known parent.

Recapture repayment of tax benefits allowed in special use valuation when property ceases to be used for farming or closely held business purposes.

Taxable Estate the net estate on which the tax is assessed, i.e., the gross estate less deductions allowed by law as reported in item 3 of Part 1 of Form 706.

Trust a flexible estate planning tool by which an artificial being is created and in which the property (corpus) is placed in the custody of a trustee for the benefit of a beneficiary.

Trust, Clifford a short-term trust where the income is paid to or accumulated for a beneficiary other than the grantor: the trust may not be terminable within 10 years of its creation; however, the death of the grantor or beneficiary can terminate it.

Trust, Inter Vivos a living trust.

Trust, Irrevocable Living a trust in which the grantor surrenders all control and power over the trust and the trust property.

Trust, Living establishment of a trust during lifetime by the creator (grantor, settler).

Trust, Revocable Living a trust in which the grantor retains the power to amend, modify, or revoke the trust.

Trust, Testamentary a trust established by will or other instrument to take effect after the death of the decedent.

Unified Credit replaces the $30,000 specific lifetime gift exemption and the $60,000 specific federal tax exemption provided for prior to TRA 76; the unified credit is being phased in over a 5-year period, starting at $30,000 in 1977, increasing to a maximum of $47,000 in 1981, and remaining at that level thereafter.

OBTAIN FROM INTERNAL REVENUE SERVICE OFFICE

1. Instructions for Form 706: United States Estate Tax Return
2. Tax Tables and Instructions for Computing Interrelated Marital and Charitable Deductions
3. Instructions for Form 709: United States Quarterly Gift Tax Return

USEFUL TOOLS IN ESTATE TAX WORK

The following handy and authoritative books are useful in estate tax planning.

THE COMPLETE INTERNAL REVENUE CODE. Research Institute of America, 589 Fifth Avenue, New York, N.Y. 10017

PRENTICE-HALL ESTATE AND GIFT TAXES, REGULATIONS AND INTERNAL REVENUE CODE WITH 1976 TAX REFORM ACT CHANGES. Prentice-Hall, Inc., Englewood Cliffs, N.J. 07632.

OUTLINE OF THE TAX REFORM ACT OF 1976: PROVISIONS AFFECTING TRUSTS AND ESTATES. American Bankers Association, 1120 Connecticut Avenue, N.W., Washington, D.C. 20036

FEDERAL ESTATE AND GIFT TAXES. Commerce Clearing House, 4025 West Paterson Avenue, Chicago, Illinois 60646

MASTER FEDERAL TAX MANUAL. Research Institute of America, 589 Fifth Avenue, New York, N.Y. 10017

ESTATE PLANNING DESK BOOK, 4th Edition by William H. Behrenfeld, Institute for Business Planning, Inc., IBP Plaza, Englewood Cliffs, N.J. 07632.

TAX DESK BOOK FOR FARMING AND RANCHING by Jon D. Wheeler, Institute for Business Planning, Inc., IBP Plaza, Englewood Cliffs, N.J. 07632.

PRENTICE-HALL FEDERAL TAX COURSE. Prentice-Hall, Inc., Englewood Cliffs, N.J. 07632.

PARTNERSHIP DESK BOOK, by Burton J. DeFren, Institute for Business Planning, IBP Plaza, Englewood Cliffs, N.J. 07632.

ESTATE PLANNING. Institute for Business Planning, IBP Plaza, Englewood Cliffs, N.J. 07632.

ESTATE PLANNING STUDY COURSE. Institute for Business Planning, IBP Plaza, Englewood Cliffs, N.J. 07632.

PART TWO

The Fundamentals of Farm Estate Planning

Farm estate planning is a complex enterprise and requires a thorough knowledge of certain fundamental principles. Farmers should always be aware of the old adage they learned in 4-H: "Plan your work, and work your plan".

3

What Your Estate Plan Means to You

[¶300] YOUR ESTATE PLAN AS YOUR LIFETIME ECONOMIC MAP

This book provides the guidelines for drawing a lifetime economic map for agricultural families. With forms it describes in detail how income is budgeted to achieve a rewarding family life, how income is transformed into capital, and how economic worth is accumulated and passed on from generation to generation with the least shrinkage and taxation.

For our purposes in this book, we shall call agricultural families *farmers*. Farmers have one earmark which identifies their vocation and their economic activity: *farmers cultivate the soil to generate income and create wealth*. The volume describes the personal economics of farm families. It demonstrates how a family can optimize the benefits to be enjoyed by the accumulation of wealth, assure the integrity of principal and income, enhance financial and mental security, promote family harmony, and plan for an orderly transfer of property from one generation to the next so that the objectives of the owners are achieved smoothly and economically.

[¶301] YOUR ESTATE PLAN AS A BLUEPRINT TO ACHIEVE YOUR LIFE GOALS

An *Estate Plan* ought to be as much a part of the documentation of families throughout the life course as a birth certificate, a marriage license, a social security number, a bank account, an insurance policy, or a deed to real estate. It is a plan for living, rather than a hurried program made acute by approaching death. An *Estate Plan* should be projected and drafted early. The kaleidoscopic events of life make it necessary to review the plan regularly. Just as you visit the dentist twice a year and the physician for an examination once a year, your *Estate Plan* must be reviewed on a regular basis in order to reflect the dynamics of life.

[¶302] THE WORD "ESTATE" WITH MANY MEANINGS

The word *estate* is a term of many meanings.

In sociology it may refer to a position in the rank order of status in the social structure. It exhibits one's economic position and standing.

In history it refers to a traditional order within the state such as "the Commons" or "the Clergy" or "the Lords."

In constitutional law it refers to a class of human beings who have a separate voice in government. Thus in the thirteenth century when the feudal system was being broken up by the growth of towns, society was divided into three classes: the Nobility, the Clergy, and the Commons. The Commons were knights of the Third Estate. The sovereign would consult the several estates and consider grievances.

In public life the newspaper is often called "the fourth estate."

In legislation, the lobby that seeks to influence lawmaking, is sometimes designated as "the fifth estate."

In colonial record an estate describes a large landholding with a distinguished manor house—a place where the wealthy and powerful maintain life on a grand scale.

As a legal word, however, *estate describes the position in which a person stands in relation to the use, ownership, possession, and control of property.*

[¶303] PROPERTY IS A BUNDLE OF RIGHTS

Essentially, property is a bundle of rights. Its essence is the power over its exclusive and beneficial use and control. In the final analysis, property has no meaning aside from the power to control and to use. It means ownership. It represents the sum of all economic rights and powers that you possess.

[¶303.1] Property Has Several Classifications

In law, property is divided into classes. First of all, *Real Property* is the term that refers to three categories. *Land* is the basic term. It means the soil and everything attached to it. Trees, herbage, and water are real property as well as houses, barns, buildings, fixtures, and fences. *Tenements* is a more comprehensive term than "land." It denotes everything of a permanent nature that may be held or inherited. *Hereditments* is a third word of even more comprehensive meaning. It refers to everything which is capable of being inherited.

Second, *Personal Property* refers to everything that is the subject of ownership not coming within the realm of real property. Blackstone used to say that "things personal," that is, personal property, are objects that can be moved wherever the owner thinks he wants them.

Mixed Property is a sort of twilight term, sometimes used in testamentary documents. It refers to property that is not altogether real or altogether personal, but rather a combination of both. Some examples are keys to a house, fixtures, tombstones, and heirlooms.

Personal Property is further divided into two classes that are important in legal terminology. These two classes are *tangible* and *intangible*. *Tangible personal property* means property that can be possessed physically, such as goods, wares, and merchandise. *Intangible personal property* is ownership of anything that is not physical. It is a relationship between persons. Examples are bank accounts and shares of stock.

All personal property may be included under the general legal term *"Chattels." Personal chattels* are items of property that the owner may move and carry about with him from one part of the world to another. This category includes cows, sheep, money, grain, plows, tractors, and everything else that can be moved and transferred from place to place. *Real chattels* are property interests dependent upon the land. They describe all interests in real property less than an estate in fee simple. A lease of farm lands for less than a freehold is a "real chattel."

For agricultural families, the world "chattel" is commonly attached by an adjective to the phrase *"chattel mortgage."* A *Chattel mortgage* is an instrument by which a farmer transfers his title to, or creates a lien upon, his personal property as security for the performance of some act that is usually the payment of money. When a farmer pledges a cow as security for a bank loan, he has created a chattel mortgage.

[¶304] PLANNING PROJECTS YOUR LIFE GOALS

Your *ESTATE PLAN* is a method of projecting your life goals:

1. It puts down on paper where you want to be financially and when.
2. It thinks through how economic gains and benefits are to be shared in the family throughout the life course.

3. It optimizes the benefits and economic well-being shared by you and your family.
4. It guides you in distributing income to lay aside assets as capital.
5. It envisions a fund for comfortable retirement.
6. It provides for the simplest and most efficient transfer of the estate to meet the needs of ultimate beneficiaries.

An Estate Plan *is a testament to life rather than a psssport to death.*

[¶305] PLANNING MUST PROCEED WITHIN GOVERNMENTAL RULES

However personal an estate plan may be, however, it has to be developed with an eye to the federal tax that hovers over every person's assets. The Internal Revenue Service and the finance and taxation departments of the various states codify the tax rules by which a person must pay. They also open pathways to minimize the taxation bite.

As a general behavior pattern, few persons pay much attention to the way the government operates upon an estate. The executor in settling the estate may come face to face with the grim facts in making the estate returns. If a team of trust officer, accountant, insurance underwriter, and lawyer has been involved in drafting the estate plan, the ultimate costs of estate settlement may have lessened. For the estate owner himself, nevertheless, an understanding of the taxation process is a must.

Therefore in this book we proceed to get acquainted with the federal estate transfer process at the very beginning of the planning process rather than to recognize it belatedly at the end of the discussion.

Today order of presentation holds prime importance since the TAX REFORM ACT OF 1976 and the REVENUE ACT OF 1978 plot new ways through the labyrinth of laws, regulations, and court decisions.

[¶306] THIRTY QUESTIONS ABOUT THE FEASIBILITY OF CONTINUING THE FAMILY FARM

Whatever the laws may say, however, the farm family has certain decisions to make within its own circle. Thirty questions follow which relate to the feasibility of continuing the family farm and the legal status of the situation. The first fifteen questions provide a checklist as to family policy and outlook in continuing the farm within the family bloodstream. The second fifteen questions are more specifically directed to more technical subjects. Family policy determines the feasibility of continuing the family farm; technical detail sets the stage for implementing the state plan.

Family Policy

1. Does the family by family policy desire to continue the family farm?
2. By family arithmetic calculations is there assurance that the continuation of the family farm is economically feasible?
3. On what valuation would the continuation of the family farm be economically feasible?
4. Based on any recent sales of similar farm lands and properties in the area, what valuation as an operating farm might be anticipated?
5. How many head of cattle are supportable on the farm?
6. What is the estimated annual value of salable crops?
7. Can the cattle or crop productivity be increased and if so by what amount and at what cost?
8. What farm machines are owned and what is the condition of such machines?
9. If the farm operates a dairy, what is the condition of its equipment, i.e., stanchion barn, free-stall barn, automation implementation, etc.?
10. What has been the history of weather hazards as related to crop production?
11. Does the family have heirs who could and would work the farm?
12. Considering the realizable sum which might be obtained from the sale of the farm and alternative investment opportunities, what net return might be expected?
13. Are family farm heirs by historic sentiment and comparative family calculations ready to accept returns projected from continued farm operation?
14. Is there need for affordable modernization of machinery, farm buildings, and dwellings?
15. Has an operating plan for the continued operation of the farm been designed?

Technical Detail

16. Do you have a will?
17. Does your spouse have a will?
18. Does someone other than your spouse know where the wills are?
19. Do you keep a continuously updated lifetime record inventory of your assets and liabilities?
20. Does your will clearly specify who should be guardian of your children in the event that both parents should die?
21. Will your spouse have enough money to live on in the event of your death?
22. Will you and your spouse have enough money to live on during your retirement years?
23. Do you have enough cash or insurance (liquidity) to cover estate settlement costs and taxes?

24. Have you considered giving to minimize taxes?
25. Have you considered trusts in your estate plan?
26. Have you discussed your will generally with members of your immediate family?
27. Have you utilized the advice of your accountant, trust officer, insurance underwriter, and attorney?
28. Do you regularly review your will to keep it current?
29. Have you restudied your will in the light of the provisions of the Tax Reform Act of 1976 and the Revenue Act of 1978?
30. Have you taken counsel on ways to minimize estate shrinkage and achieve maximum transfer of estate worth?

THE LANGUAGE OF PROPERTY

Chattel Property which is moveable and not so connected with the ground as to become a part of the real estate.

Chattel Mortgage A formal security lien upon personal property to assure the performance of an act.

Co-ownership An estate held by more than one person.

Estate by the Entirety An estate predicated on the legal unity of husband and wife, being taken, created by a will or deed, to hold as a single person with right of survivorship.

Fee Simple The largest and most absolute estate known to the law.

Joint Tenancy An estate held by two or more persons with equal rights to share in its enjoyment with right of survivorship.

Life Estate A tenancy created by deed or will for the term of a particular life or lives.

Life Tenant A person who holds a life estate.

Personal Property Whatever is owned other than land.

Property The bundle of rights by which a person possesses, enjoys, and disposes of things.

Real Property Land and such things as are permanent, fixed, and immovable and cannot be annexed to a person.

Tenancy Possession under right or title.

Tenancy in Common Tenancy by two or more persons entitled to possession in such a manner that they have an undivided possession but several freeholds.

4

Establishing a Continuously Updated Estate Record System

[¶400] IMPORTANCE OF RECORDS

Every person needs to have a record describing the kinds of property owned and where each item is located. This information is necessary for mapping estate growth, for use in personal financial administration, and for the guidance of personal representatives in estate settlement.

A continuously updated lifetime estate record system, beginning with a person's first establishment of a bank account, insurance policy, and purchase of a home, provides a map of a person's financial development and present worth. The record, kept current throughout the life course, is as important as a travel map which guides the route toward a highway destination.

The forms given in this chapter are designed to assist any person in establishing and maintaining such a continuously updated estate plan. How shall one begin? The answer is simple: Pull records together, sit down, take your pen, and go to work. Once a person has made the beginning, the information in the record system must be kept current. The establishment of this kind of record system is a necessary first step. It is a personal record. It is an invaluable tool to every legal advisor and banker. It is a necessity for every personal representative in the settlement of estates. (See Figures 4-1 through 4-10.)

Figure 4-1 Family Tree

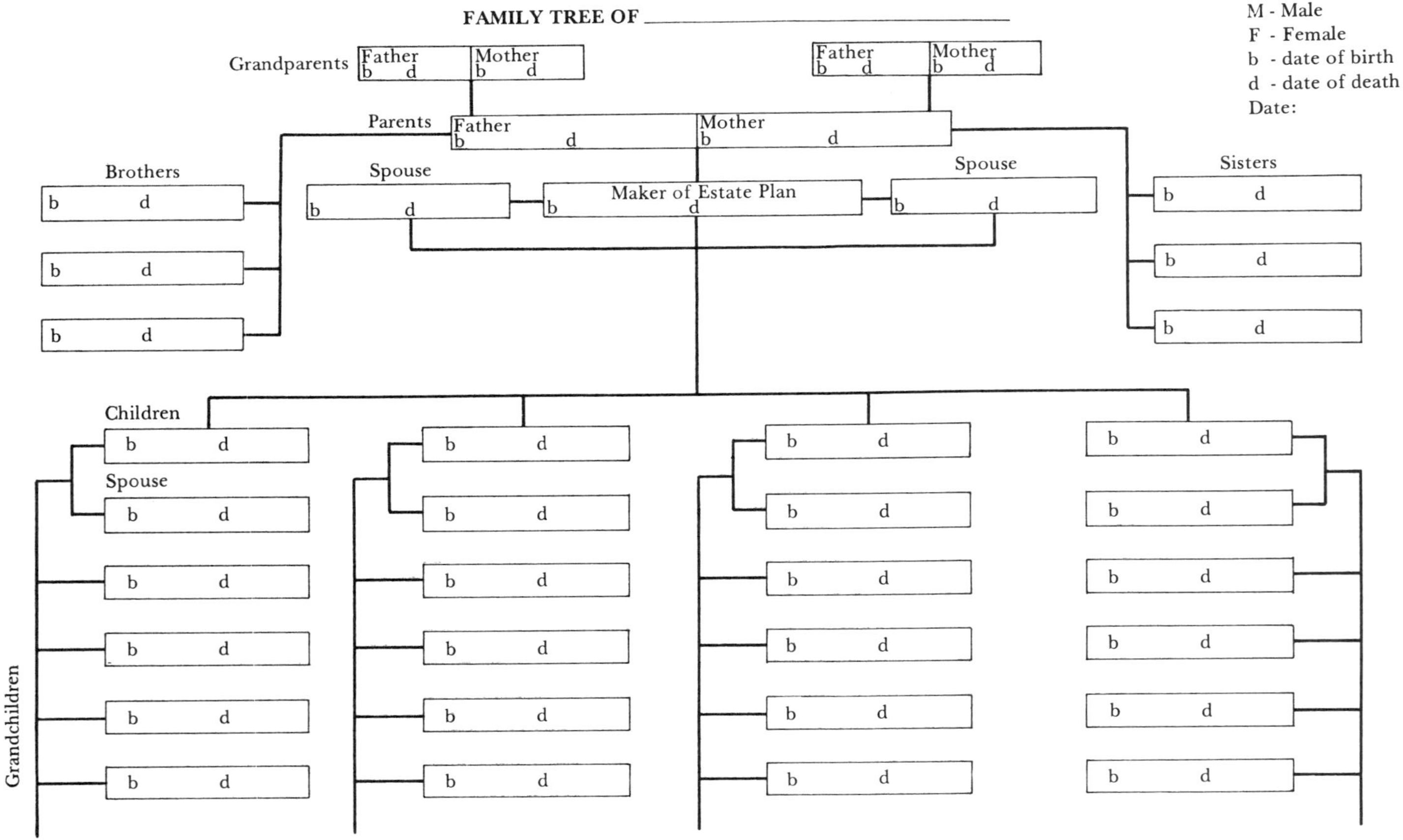

Figure 4-2 Persons With Whom I Transact My Affairs

Service	Institution	Street Address	City	State	Zip Code	Telephone with Area Code	Official with whom I deal	Position
ACCOUNTING								
BANKING								
Borrowing								
Checking								
Credit Union								
Savings								
EMPLOYMENT								
HEALTH								
Physician								
Dentist								
Hospital								

Figure 4-2 Cont.

Service	Institution	Street Address	City	State	Zip Code	Telephone with Area Code	Official with whom I deal	Position
INSURANCE								
Life								
Health								
Motor Vehicle								
General Liability								
Fire								
Other								
INVESTMENT								
RELIGION								
RETIREMENT PLAN								
VETERAN'S AFFAIRS								
MORTICIAN								

Figure 4-3 Details of the Agricultural Estate

Date: ______________________

HERE ARE THE DETAILS OF MY AGRICULTURAL ESTATE

PROPERTY OWNED			*DEBTS ON PROPERTY*
Real Estate Farms Owned	*Acres*	*Value* $	
Location			
Rented Location		*Rental* $	
Other Real Estate		$	
		$	
Total Real Estate		$	$
Livestock Heifers	*Number*	*Value* $	
Milking Cows		$	
Beef Cows		$	
Other Cattle		$	
Brood Sows and Gilts		$	
Other Hogs		$	
Ewes		$	
Other Sheep		$	
Poultry		$	
Horses		$	
Other Livestock		$	
Total Livestock		$	

Figure 4-3 Cont.

Machinery and Equipment	*Year*	*Make*	*Cost*	*Value* Present Value-Cost Less Depreciation
Tractors			$	$
				$
				$
				$
				$
Trucks			$	$
Major Items of Equipment			$	$
Other Farm Machinery			$	$
Total Machinery and Equipment				$

Total of cash on hand, crops and livestock held for immediate sale, + income to be received in immediate future $________

Total land debt $________

Total debts other than land $________

Net agricultural worth—total property owned minus all debts $________

Figure 4-4 Record of Bonds Owned

HERE ARE THE BONDS I OWN

M—Mortgage
D—Debenture
E—Equipment

Indicate Ownership (Husband—h (Wife—w (Joint—j

Governmental Unit or Company	Type	Face Value	Date of Purchase	Cost at Time of Purchase	Due Date	Market Price at Date	Interest Rate	Annual Income	Serial Number

Total $ ____________

+ Capital Gain $ ____________

− or Loss $ ____________

Figure 4-5 Record of Stocks Owned

HERE ARE THE STOCKS I OWN
(inclusive of mutual funds and investment trusts)

C—Common
P—Preferred
D—Stock Dividend

Ownership (Husband—h (Wife—w (Joint—j

Company	Type	Number Shares	Date of Purchase	Cost per Share Time of Purchase	Market Price at Date	Yield %	Annual Income	Serial Number	Date Sold
				$	$		$		

Total $ ______

+ Capital Gain $ ______

− Capital Loss $ ______

Figure 4-6 Record of Life Insurance Policies

HERE IS THE RECORD OF MY LIFE INSURANCE

Company	Policy Number	Face Value	Cash Value (date)	Type	Date Purchased	Maturity Date	Premium Date	Amount of Premium	Local Agent—Policy	Beneficiary
		$	$					$		

Total $______________

Figure 4-7 Record of Other Types of Insurance

HERE IS THE RECORD OF MY HEALTH, MEDICAL, HOSPITAL, DENTAL, ACCIDENT, AND LEGAL INSURANCE COVERAGE

Company	Address	Group Number	H.I.B. Number Claim Number	Plan	Number of Persons	Annual Premium	Benefits
						$	

Figure 4-8 Updated Statement of Five Year Net Worth

HERE IS MY NET WORTH FOR THE LAST FIVE YEARS—DECEMBER 31 OF EACH YEAR

WHAT I OWN	1 19___	2 19___	3 19___	4 19___	5 19___
Cash on Hand	$	$	$	$	$
Total Checking Balance					
Total Savings					
Bonds (market value)					
Stocks (market value)					
Insurance (cash value)					
Annuities and Retirement Plans (cash value)					
Amount Other People Owe Me					
Motor Vehicles (cash value)					
Home (fair market value)					
Other Real Estate (fair market value)					
Furniture and Appliances (fair market value)					
Heirlooms, Antiques, Jewelry, Art					
Miscellaneous (all other)					
TOTAL ASSETS	$______	$______	$______	$______	$______

Figure 4-9 Record of Debts

HERE IS THE RECORD OF MY DEBTS

WHAT I OWE	1 ___ 19___	2 ___ 19___	3 ___ 19___	4 ___ 19___	5 ___ 19___
Mortgage—Real Estate					
Mortgages—Chattel					
Liens					
Motor Vehicle Balance					
Installment Debts					
Credit Card Advances					
Unpaid Bills					
Other Indebtedness					

TOTAL DEBTS $______ $______ $______ $______ $______

NET WORTH $ ______________

(What I Own minus What I Owe)

Figure 4-10 Sample Chart to Plot Five Year History of Net Worth

HERE IS A CHART OF MY TOTAL NET WORTH FOR THE LAST FIVE YEARS

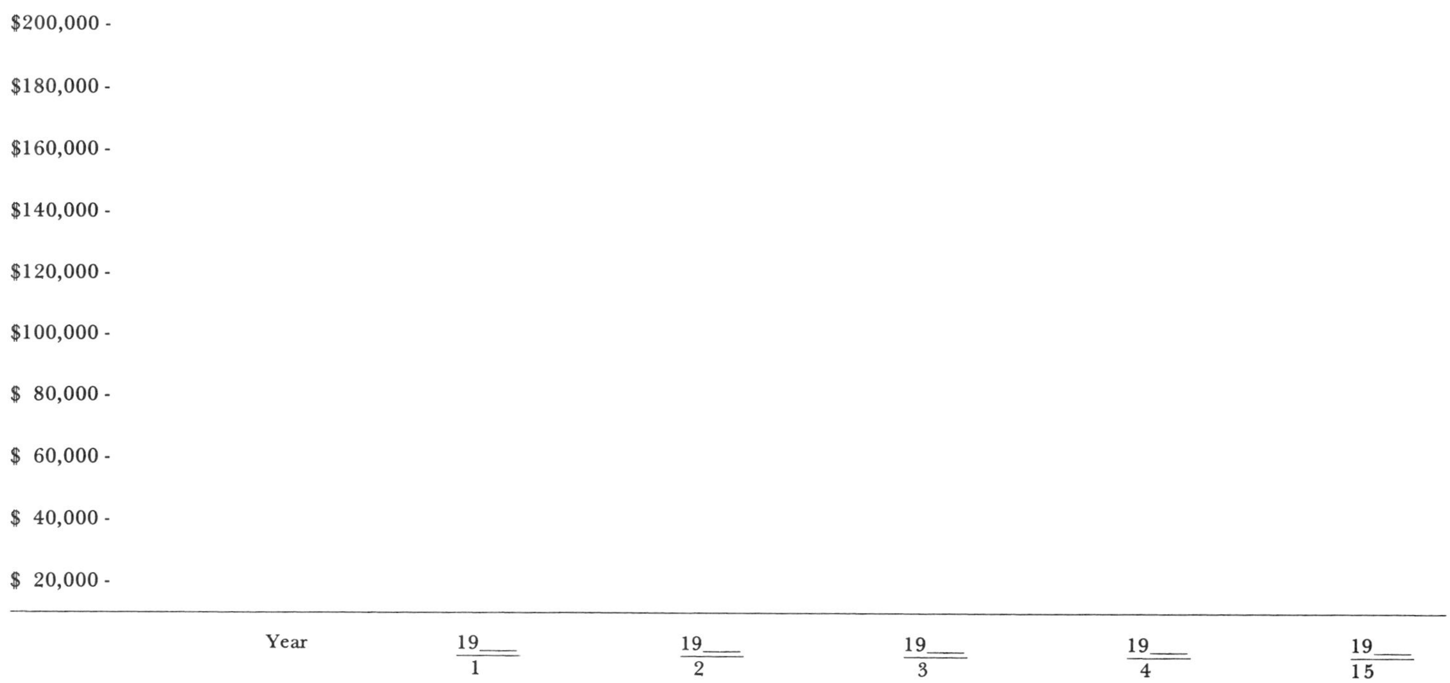

LOCATION OF RECORDS

You need also to keep a guide sheet that tells where your various documents are located (Figure 4-11). Such a continuously updated estate record with directions as to where the items can be located provides a quick reference for your own use and an indispensable guide for your personal representative in the event of your death.

Figure 4-11 Here Are The Places Where I Keep My Papers

(Keep a copy of this record in both your house file and your safe deposit box.)

Document	*House File*	*Safe Deposit Box*	*Billfold*
Abstracts of Title		x	
Account Book–income expenditure	x		
Adoption Papers		x	
Bank Statements	x		
Birth Certificates		x	
Bonds		x	
Citizenship Papers		x	
Check Books	x		
Contracts		x	
Credit Cards			x
Death Certificates		x	
Deeds		x	
Divorce Record		x	
Driver's License			x
Educational and Professional Records	x		
Guarantees and Warranties	x		
Employment Papers	x		
Health Insurance Card			x
Health Records	x		
Household Inventory	x		

Figure 4-11 Cont.

Document	*House File*	*Safe Deposit Box*	*Billfold*
Income History	x		
Insurance Policies	x		
Keys (duplicates in marked envelopes)	x	x	
List of Items in Billfold (duplicate in safe deposit box)	x	x	
List of Items in Safe Deposit Box	x		
Loans—what others owe you		x	
Marriage Certificates		x	
Medical Information			x
Membership Cards			x
Military Service Records		x	
Mortgage		x	
Motor Vehicle Insurance Card			x
Motor Vehicle License			x
Motor Vehicle Registration Card			x
Motor Vehicle Titles		x	
Passport		x	
Personal Representative (Executor)	x		
Person to be Notified in Emergency			x
Social Security Card		x	
Stocks		x	
Tax Records—at least 6 years	x		
U. S. Savings Bonds		x	
Will (unless filed with Court)	x Executed Copy	x Copy	

5

Building and Transferring an Estate Through Life's Course

[¶500] THE PROCESSION OF STAGES IN THE LIFE COURSE

Life is an experience in time. The farmer during the years of his life, like all other human beings, moves through a series of stages that relate to his biology, his family, his work cycle, his quest for security, and his ultimate years. The farmer, however, as those engaged in few other occupations, has an enterprise that can engage the efforts of his whole family at various ages, and provide a pattern by which he can move quietly into his latter years as he transfers his estate into the hands of the younger generations.

[¶501] THE FAMILY CYCLE

For purposes of estate building and planning, the family cycle may be divided into eight identifiable periods, as Figure 5-1 visualizes the forward movement. If the average life is taken as 72 years, then nearly two-thirds of the life span is contained in the years between 19 and 65. During this long period, estate building is more active and the transference of an estate to the younger generations is taking place.

[¶502] ADOLESCENCE: A CHAOTIC PERIOD IN THE LIFE CYCLE

It needs to be emphasized that the span of adolescence remains the shortest of all life periods, yet it is the most definitive. During the chaotic years of adolescence important choices are made concerning values,

Figure 5-1 Stages in the Life Course

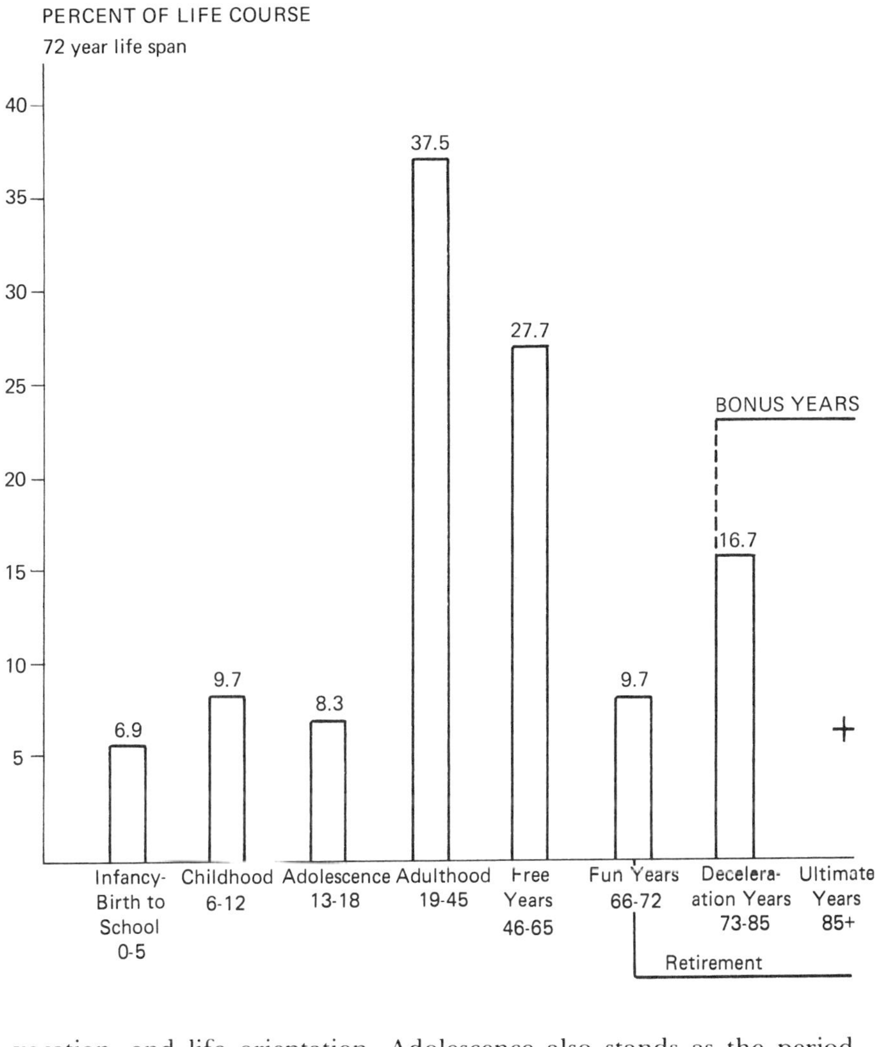

vocation, and life orientation. Adolescence also stands as the period during which a son and daughter can be of increasing usefulness in the farming enterprise.

[¶503] HIERARCHY OF VALUES IN THE LIFE COURSE

During all the stages, and hopefully with increasing awareness on into the ultimate years, the farmer is either consciously or unconsciously working out his own answers to five basic issues. These are:

1. *Values* What is worth working for as a good in life?
2. *Goals* What practical steps in life provide an agenda for realizing this projected good?
3. *Policies* What standards of life management will serve as guides to the achievement of the life goals?
4. *Procedures* What steps and modes of operation are necessary to accomplish goals and on what time schedule?
5. *Rules* What canons, standards of behavior, and ethics are to hold performance to criteria that say "yes" and "no" to certain practices?

In building his estate, the farmer is striving to attain his goals by equipping himself with the skills that will enable him to perform the roles required of those goals.

[¶504] THE FARMER IN THE RETIREMENT REVOLUTION

Whatever may be his goals as pursued in the successive life stages, the successful farmer is always concerned with estate building, with the enjoyment of his life, and with the disposition of what he has accumulated in his life.

Farmers in the last quarter of the 20th century live in a period that is witnessing what is called "the retirement revolution." While families that live on farms ease into retirement on a tempo that differs from that of assembly line and white-collar workers, they face certain life styles that are common to all. These common factors include (1) a tapering off of work in a work oriented society; (2) the reduction of purchasing power in a consumption oriented society; (3) the lessening of physical stamina and the increase in medical needs in an action oriented society; and (4) the approach of life's end in a time oriented society.

While mandatory retirement age is not inflexible in farming, the fact remains that the work and management load gradually shifts to a younger generation. Edward W. McGhee, director, Retirement Studies, Industrial Relations Center, University of Chicago, reviews retirement in three frameworks.

Framework One is descriptive. It identifies the number of people over 65. In 1975 this group numbered 19,000,000. McGhee classifies the people at age 65 or just under 65 as persons entering the *fun era*. They are for the most part healthy, vigorous men and women who engage in activities which they enjoy and can afford.

Framework Two includes people who, after about ten years of retirement, enter a cooling off period after the fun era has run its course. It is a period of deceleration.

Framework Three includes the seniors who are plagued by ill health and have great need of support in order to live—need for shelter, personal care, and medical attention. In these ultimate years those who are still living may experience certain plus years that may equal or exceed the total years of infancy, childhood, and adolescence. Estate planning must provide for security in these ultimate years. Because women live longer than men, the provision for the wife creates a special demand upon the estate plan (see Figure 5-2 for estimating retirement income).

Figure 5-2 Estimating Income in Retirement

I. Social Security		
Estimated average annual net farm profit, 1955 to retirement	$________	
Husband's retirement income	________	
Wife's retirement income	________	
Family retirement income from Social Security (monthly)		$________
II. Farm Property		
Estimated sum available from sale of farm property at retirement	$________	
A. Monthly *interest* dividend, or annuity income if farm is *sold*, and proceeds invested	________	
B. Monthly rental income if ownership of some or all farm property is retained	________	
Total monthly retirement income established from sale or rental of farm property		$________
III. Savings and Investments		
Life insurance cash value which can be used up in retirement	$________	
Cash value of stocks, bonds, or mutual funds at retirement	$________	
Amount of other savings at retirement	$________	
Total value of all savings and investment except farm property at retirement	$________	
Monthly retirement income estimated from all savings and investments except farm property		$________

Figure 5-2 Cont.

IV. Other Sources

Income from a retirement system, inheritance, etc. $________

V. Summary

A. Total estimated retirement income available from current or expected resources. ________

B. Estimated retirement income needed. If "B" exceeds "A" this amount must be made up from earnings during retirement or in some other way. $________

Prepared by the Cooperative Extension, New York State College of Agriculture, Cornell University.

[¶505] THE SUPPORT FRAMEWORK

Specialists in retirement speak of the "support framework" in four categories:

1. *Income* the retirees must have a basic floor of support.
2. *Medical Needs* they must have a physical floor of security.
3. *Housing* they must have shelter suited to their needs.
4. *Transportation* they must have the mobility to get around—and especially to the services they need.

[¶506] THE FAMILY PATTERNS

For many families, children will be in school by the time the mother is in her thirties. Qualification for social security benefits and pensions generally begin at an age something like 65+ or−.

[¶507] LIFE FULFILLMENT AND ESTATE PLANNING

Estate planning is an operation to be carried on actively through all the stages in the entire life course. It provides the financial and legal framework on which the fulfillment of life at any and all ages can be realized. Robert Browning once sang of *"That far land we dream about, Where every man is his own architect."*

Estate planning sees life whole—its responsibilities, its achievements, its transience. Beyond that, estate planning has a continuing and forward-looking purpose: to plant upon the days to come a vision of life described in dollars and safeguarded by law. The "architect" for this plan for the future is you, the estate builder—the person who has steered his life by his star.

6

Leasing in Farm Estate Building

Leasing provides a legal format by which farm operators may conduct agricultural operations. Because leasing is of such growing importance in both the expansion of family farms and investment enterprise, a comprehensive discussion of leasing with forms follows.

[¶600] INCREASING IMPORTANCE OF LEASING

In today's farming the leasing of land, livestock, and machinery bears a position of increasing importance as a tool in agricultural management and estate building. Leasing provides a way of meeting demands for larger scale farming with minimum investment.

In the State of Illinois, for example, some two-thirds of all farmers rent part or all of the land they cultivate and three-fifths of all farmlands are tenant operated.

To assure a profitable operation, the landlord and the tenant must calculate that the lease arrangement promises a fair and beneficial financial return for both of them.

[¶601] ELEMENTS OF A LEASE

A lease is a form of contract. By the terms of the document it grants the occupation, use, or holding of land, animals, or machines during a specified period of time in exchange for the payment of rent in money and/or kind.

The lease contract establishes the relationship between the parties. The party who owns the land is the *landlord* or *lessor*. The party who undertakes to operate under the terms of the lease is the *tenant* or *lessee*.

[¶602] CHARACTERISTICS OF A GOOD FARM LEASE

A good farm lease describes in writing how a landlord and a tenant may combine their resources to share an optimum net income over a period of years by the effective utilization of land, labor, and capital.

Farm leases generally relate to six broad areas:

1. property rights;
2. land use and livestock production;
3. improving, conserving, and maintaining the farm lands;
4. sharing costs and returns;
5. duration and termination; and
6. miscellaneous provisions such as denial of partnership, compliance with governmental programs, disclaimer for debts and accidents caused by the other party, legal remedies for willful neglect, and provision for arbitration of differences.*

[¶602.1] Checklist Helpful in Developing a Good Farm Lease

Over the years, the United States Department of Agriculture has developed guidelines helpful to the building of a sound relationship.† By studying these guidelines, by incorporating those that are relevant and by discarding those that are not applicable to a particular situation, a landlord and a tenant can lay the foundations for a good contract. The sections that follow should be of assistance in lease drafting.

[¶603] FINDING A GOOD FARM

The basic three elements in a good lease arrangement are (1) a good farm, (2) a good landlord, and (3) a good tenant. Each of these three elements needs careful attention. The first "must" is finding the best available site.

1. To locate a good farm:
   a. Determine the area where you want to locate;
   b. Consider all the farms that can be rented within this area;
   c. Discuss the general aspects of a possible lease with the owner of the land;
   d. Consider the accessibility of the farm;
   e. Inspect the farm buildings;

*The United States Department of Agriculture in Farmers' Bulletin No. 2164 discusses *Your Farm Lease Contract.* Page 20.

†See your FARM LEASE CHECKLIST, Farmers Bulletin No. 2163. Page 11. A valuable brochure entitled *Farm Leases for Illinois* by F. J. Reise is available from the Cooperative Extension Service, College of Agriculture, University of Illinois at Urbana 61801, Champaign (Circular 960). It discusses with forms (1) the cash lease, (2) the crop-share cash lease, (3) the livestock-share lease, (4) the labor-share lease, and (5) father-son agreements.

   f. Check the fences;
   g. Appraise the adequacy and quality of the water resources;
   h. Evaluate the kind and quality of the land.
2. To find a good landlord:
   a. Review operational objectives to see that those of landlord are in harmony with those of the tenant;
   b. Develop farm plans to achieve the common objectives of landlord and tenant; and
   c. Determine how landlord participation will contribute toward the realization of the plans.
3. To find a good tenant:
   a. Visualize plans for an entire year's operation;
   b. Formulate operating decisions that will effectively carry out long term plans; and
   c. Provide for adjustments in plans to meet changing situations.

[¶604] BASIC DATA FOR LEASE DRAFTING

It is necessary to make notes on the basic data that will be incorporated in the lease contract. Here are some of the elements to consider:

Obtain a farm plan map.
Describe accurately all property rights
Establish fair and equitable rental rates.
Provide for the fair sharing of expenses.
Encourage development and conservation of resources.
Provide for stable and secure occupancy.
Promote capable management practices.
Encourage the efficient use of all resources.
Know how farm leases are terminated by state law.
Understand what things are considered damages or waste at law.
Check the law for the rule on agricultural fixtures.
See how the law provides compensation for nonremovable or unexhausted improvements.
See how you can provide for arbitration.
Understand the nature of the landlord's lien for the collection of rent.
Determine the lease rights in relation to the sale of the farm real estate.

[¶605] DETERMINING RENT

While farmers are characteristically sharp bargainers, sharp bargaining has little place in the establishment of a productive relationship. A fair rental must provide financial benefits to landlord and tenant so that each obtains a fair share and is encouraged to engage in agricultural practices that enhance the productivity of the land and maintenance of the buildings.

On the facing page is a table developed by the United States Department of Agriculture which is helpful in estimating rent under the various forms of leases.

[¶606] PITFALLS IN LEASE DRAFTING

In drafting a lease that is mutually beneficial to landlord and tenant, particular attention needs to be given to avoid two pitfalls.

[¶606.1] Avoid Partnership Inference

The first pitfall is that the lease agreement should neither create nor imply a partnership or an employer-employee relationship. It should create *only the relationship of landlord and tenant.*

To be certain that the lease does not create a partnership:

1. Be cautious about a firm name. Do not have a firm name or the names of both parties on a truck, mailbox, barn or stationery.
2. Do not give both parties equal voice in the day-to-day management of the business.
3. Make certain that neither party can create a debt in the name of the firm.
4. Do not have a firm bank account.
5. Be careful about joint bank accounts.
6. Be cautious about carrying insurance on livestock, crops, and supplies in the names of both parties.
7. Do not carry out day-to-day operations as partners might.
8. Do nothing that would lead a third party to believe that landlord and tenant are partners.

[¶606.2] Assure Proper Lease Term

The second pitfall relates to the term of the lease. The term of a lease must give security to both landlord and tenant, and provide time enough for both parties to make the relationship work out profitably. In drafting the lease, the term needs careful consideration.

Leases may extend over any term agreed upon. The most common term is a one year agreement that terminates automatically. There is also an automatic renewable short term lease; a long term cancelable lease with provision for termination under specified circumstances; and a tenancy at suffrance or at will. This last form must be studied with particular reference to state law.

Figure 6-1 Table for Estimating Rent

Item of expense (1)	Estimated total value (2)	Estimated interest rate (3)	Estimated annual cost: Whole farm (4)	Estimated annual cost: Landlord's share (5)	Estimated annual cost: Tenant's share (6)
	Dollars	*Percent*	*Dollars*	*Dollars*	*Dollars*
I. Fixed expenses:					
A. Fixed investment expenses:					
1. Land					
2. Farm buildings					
3. Tractor, truck, and automobile					
4. Machinery and equipment					
5. Breeding stock					
6. Operating cash					
7.					
8.					
9.					
10. Total section *A*					
B. Fixed operating expenses:					
11. Labor					
a. Tenant's					
b. Unpaid family					
c. Landlord's					
d. Hired					
12. Depreciation					
a. Buildings, fences, and others					
b. Tractor, truck, and automobile					
c. Machinery and equipment					
13. Repairs					
a. Buildings, fences, and others					
b. Machinery and equipment					
14. Taxes*					
15. Insurance*					
16. Limestone					
17. Rock phosphate					
18. Conservation measures					
19. Management					
20.					
21.					
22.					
23. Total section *B*					
24. Total section I					
24a. Percent contributed by: Landlord					
Tenant					

*Include taxes and insurance only if they have been deducted from (or not included in) annual cost of property in column 4, section 4.

Figure 6-1 Cont.

Item of expense (1)	Estimated annual cost		
	Whole farm (4)	Landlord's share (5)	Tenant's share (6)
	Dollars	*Dollars*	*Dollars*
II. Variable expenses:			
25. Hired labor including board			
26. Tractor operating costs			
27. Truck operating costs			
28. Automobile, farm operating costs			
29. Machine work hired			
30. Seed			
31. Commercial fertilizer			
32. Pesticides, insecticides			
33. Other crop expenses			
34. Feed			
35. Veterinary and sanitation			
36. Other livestock expenses			
37. Electricity for the farm			
38. Telephone for the farm			
39. ________			
40. ________			
41. ________			
42. Total section II			
43. Grand total: Sections I and II			

Income to be divided $________

Cash rent on farm dwelling:

Estimated value $________ at

______ percent $________

Depreciation insurance, and
upkeep (add) $________

Total dwelling rent $________

The term of any lease should be fair, clear, and provide assurance to both landlord and tenant. It should allow time to develop maximum productive efficiency with, of course, provision for cancellation, and safeguards at termination.

[¶607] REPRESENTATIVE FORMS OF LEASE

As examples that demonstrate the kind of data to be incorporated into a lease contract, the following pages provide working forms.

[¶607.1] Types of Leases

A lease may be a simple handshake between neighbors or a short and simple document worked out between land owner and tenant. As a rule, however, leases should be in writing, and they should be painstakingly drafted.

[¶607.2] Know the Laws of Your State

Each state has certain laws that establish the legal framework of leasing. These laws differ from state to state. Among these laws are certain regulations with which you must become familiar.

1. Know the maximum and minimum length of lease terms permitted by the state.
2. Check the law to see under what circumstances a lease must be in writing. In all cases, however, it is best to have a written lease.
3. Review the state law to determine the length of termination notice required.

The next section of this book discusses and gives examples of the following farm lease forms.

I Cash Leases

1. Short Cash Memorandum: Definite Fields and/or Buildings
2. Cash Lease: Definite Fields and/or Buildings
3. Full Cash Farm Lease
4. Illinois Cash Farm Lease
5. Farm Rental Agreement
6. Cash Lease: Dairy Farm

II Share Leases

7. Crop-Share Farm Lease
8. Labor-Share Lease: Profit-Sharing Agreement
9. Livestock-Share Farm Lease
10. Share Operating Agreement: Dairy Farm
11. Income Sharing: Guaranteed Wage

III Maintenance Agreement

12. Dairy Cattle Maintenance Agreement

    Acknowledgement Form

[¶607.3] Dairy Cattle Maintenance Agreement

In a period of agricultural change, with farm units increasing in size as well as in capital intensity and rising land values, the dairy cattle maintenance agreement may be useful in farm estate building, especially when the farm lands and equipment are heavily mortgaged. By prudent management a farm operator with a herd of fifty cows can increase his cash flow something like $10,000 a year.

Under the terms of the agreement, the operator accepts the cows and all the costs of feeding and caring for them. The owners of the cows are primarily New York banks and high-income capitalists.

While the cattle maintenance agreement is a profitable investment for the owners and a high-cost arrangement on the part of the farm operator, the plan nevertheless provides a means by which a farm operator can build up a substantial equity, within 6 years come into full ownership of a complement of milking cows, and be on the way to building his estate.

The fully revised dairy cattle maintenance agreement, incorporating extensive experience, is presented in Figure 6-13.

[¶608] FARM RENTAL AND SOCIAL SECURITY

Landlord income from leasing must be carefully studied if it is to be counted for Social Security purposes. As a general rule, rental income does not count for social security purposes. Nevertheless, farm rental

Figure 6-2

SHORT CASH MEMORANDUM FOR DEFINITE
FIELDS AND/OR BUILDINGS*

This lease is entered into this ______ day of ________________, 19____,

between ________________________, the Landowner, and ______________________, Renter.

The Landowner hereby leases to the Renter to occupy and use for agricultural and related purposes the following described property, located in

the town of ________________________, ________________________ County, Vermont.

____

____

The terms of this lease shall be for ______ years from __________________,

19_____, to ______________, 19_____, and shall continue in effect upon the same terms and conditions as herein contained from year to year thereafter until written notice of termination is given by either party to the other on or before

the ___________ day of ___________, before expiration of this lease or any renewal.

The Renter shall pay to the Landowner the sum of $______ annual rent for the above described property. This annual rent shall be paid in two

installments due as follows: ______________ 1, and ______________ 1, of each contract year.

It is further agreed:

____

____

Signatures:

Date: __________________________ Landowner: ______________________________

Date: __________________________ Renter: _________________________________

*Compiled by Dwight K. Eddy, Extension Economist, University of Vermont. Adapted from "Farm Leases," New Hampshire Extension Service. Prepared by College of Agriculture and Life Services, University of Vermont.

Figure 6-3

CASH LEASE OF DEFINITE FIELDS AND BUILDINGS*

Section I. Date, Contracting Parties, Description of Property, and Term of Lease

1. This lease is made this ______ day of ______________, 19_____by and between __________________________, hereinafter called the Landowner, and __________________________, hereinafter called the Renter.

2. The Landowner, in consideration of the agreement with the Renter hereinafter set forth, hereby leases to the Renter, to occupy and to use for agricultural purposes only, the specific fields and buildings herein described on the ______________________________ farm, located in the town of ________________________, ________________________ County, Vermont.

Description of fields and buildings included in this lease:

A. Fields ____

____

____

B. Buildings ____

____

____

3. This lease shall become effective on the _____ day of ______________, 19_____, and shall continue in force until the ______ day of ________________, 19_____, and from year to year thereafter unless written notice of termination is given by either party to the other on or before the ______ day of ______________, which shall be not less than _____ months, immediately preceding the date of termination.

Section II. Land Use and Cropping Program

It is the intent of both parties that the land covered by this contract shall be improved and its yielding capacity increased by means of a good cropping program and good agricultural practices on a continuing long-term basis.

1. Fertilizer and lime used as soil test indicates need.
2. It is further agreed that:

____

____

____

____

*Compiled by Dwight K. Eddy, Extension Economist, Department of Resource Economics, The Extension Service, University of Vermont, Burlington, Vermont. Adapted from "Farm Leases," New Hampshire Extension Service. Revised 9/71.

Figure 6-3 Cont.

Section III. Amount of Rent and Time of Payment

1. The Renter shall pay to the Landowner the sum of $________ annual rent for the fields and buildings specified above and calculated as follows:

Field	____________________________	$__________
Barn	____________________________	$__________
House	____________________________	$__________
Pasture	____________________________	$__________
Total annual rent		$__________

2. The annual rent shall be paid in two equal installments due _________ 1, and __________ 1, of each contract year. Any unpaid rent shall bear interest at the rate of 6 percent per annum from the date due until paid.

Section IV. Liability for Accidents

1. Both parties agree that farm comprehensive liability insurance with a minimum coverage of $50,000 for liability and $500 for medical payments will be carried in the joint names of the Landowner and the Renter and covering the liability of either or both parties for accidents associated with the use of the above-described property. The Renter agrees to insure with a company or companies acceptable to the Landowner and to keep said insurance in force during the term of this lease or any renewal thereof. The policy shall be filed with the Landowner before this lease shall become effective.

Section V: The Landowner Agrees to:

1. Furnish the fields and the fixed improvements described above.
2. Pay all the taxes and assessments against the real estate and premiums for the insurance carried on the farm buildings.
3. Furnish materials and labor for such major permanent improvements on the fields and buildings as are mutually agreed upon.

Section VI. The Renter Agrees to:

1. Follow the farming practices mutually agreed upon including practices that are generally recommended for conserving and improving the land.
2. Furnish all labor, equipment, and supplies and all operational expenses.
3. Furnish all labor for minor repairs and minor improvements of the buildings described above. The buildings and fences are to be kept in as good repair and condition as they are at the beginning of the lease.
4. Cut the weeds and brush in the fields and around the buildings included in this lease.
5. Prevent the accumulation of fire hazards near buildings.
6. Neither assign this lease to any person or persons nor sublet any part of the real estate for any purpose without the written consent of the Landowner.
7. Seed down all land not in sod at the termination of the contract. By arrangement the seeding may be done after the termination date.

Figure 6-3 Cont.

Section VII. Rights and Privileges

1. The Landowner or anyone designated by him shall have the right of entry at any mutually convenient time to inspect his property and/or the farming methods being used.

2. The Renter shall have the right to erect, maintain, and remove at his expense, temporary fence and movable buildings on the farm, providing that such fences or buildings or their removal do not damage the Landowner's property in any way.

3. If the Renter, in view of the approaching termination of the lease, fails to plant crops in accordance with accepted farming practices, the Landowner or his designated agent shall have the right of entry to plant such crops.

Section VIII. Enforcement of Agreements and Arbitration

1.. Failure of either the Landowner or the Renter to comply with the agreements set forth in this lease shall make him liable for damages to the other party. Any claim by either party for such damages shall be presented, in writing to the other party, at least 10 days before the termination of this lease.

2. If either or both of the parties to this lease die during the term of the lease, the provisions of this lease shall be binding on the heirs, executors, administrators, and assigns of the party or parties involved.

3. Any disagreements between the Landowner and the Renter shall be referred to a board of three disinterested persons, one of whom shall be appointed by the Landowner, one by the Renter, and the third by the two thus appointed. The decision of these three shall be considered binding by the parties to this lease unless a sum exceeding $______ is involved. Any costs for such arbitration shall be shared equally between the two parties to this lease.

Section IX. Other Agreements

____

____

____

Section X. Signatures

______________________	______________________
(Date)	(Landowner)
______________________	______________________
(Date)	(Landowner)

Figure 6-4

AD 562 (Mar 1960)
U.S. DEPT. OF AGRICULTURE

CASH FARM LEASE

THIS LEASE is entered into this .... day of ...., 19........,

between ...., landlord, of ....
(Address)

and ...., tenant, of ....
(Address)

A. PROPERTY RIGHTS

The landlord hereby leases to the tenant, to occupy and use for agricultural and related purposes, the following-described property, hereinafter referred to as the "farm," located in .... County, State of ...., and commonly known as the .... farm:

....

....

....

....

....

....

....

....

and consisting of .... acres, more or less, together with all buildings and improvements thereon and all rights thereto except as specified below.

1. **Right of entry.**—The landlord reserves the right of himself, his agents, his employees, or his assigns to enter the farm at any reasonable time for purposes (a) of consultation with the tenant; (b) of making repairs, improvements, and inspections; (c) of developing mineral resources; and (d) after notice of termination of the lease is given, of plowing, seeding, fertilizing, and such customary seasonal work, none of which is to interfere with the tenant in carrying out regular farm operations.

2. **Transfer of farm.**—If the landlord should sell or otherwise transfer title to the farm, he will do so subject to the provisions of this lease.

3. **Heirs and successors.**—The terms of this lease shall be binding upon the heirs, executors, administrators, and successors of both landlord and tenant in like manner as upon the original parties. However, in the event the lease is for more than one year, the heirs or successors of the tenant shall have the option to give written notice of termination effective at the end of the lease year in which death occurs.

4. **Right to lease.**—The landlord warrants that he has the right to lease the farm, and will defend the tenant's possession against any and all persons whomsoever.

5. **Additional agreements regarding property rights:**

....

....

....

....

B. LAND USE AND LIVESTOCK PRODUCTION

1. **Land use and kind of livestock.**—Except when mutually agreed otherwise, the land use and cropping plan shall be as follows and the numbers of each kind of livestock shall not exceed those shown in the following table:

B. 1. Land Use and Livestock Production Table.

USE OF LAND	ACRES	FIELDS	KIND OF LIVESTOCK	MAXIMUM NUMBERS
TOTAL		xxxxxxxxxxx	xxxxxxxxxxxxxxxxxxxxxxxxxxxxxx	xxxxxxxxx

2. **Acres and numbers.**—The acres of crops and the fields on which grown and the numbers of livestock shown above are those planned for the first year of this lease. They may be adjusted within the year or from year to year by mutual agreement.

C. IMPROVING, CONSERVING, AND MAINTAINING THE FARM

To improve the farm, conserve its resources, and maintain it in a high state of cultivation, the two parties agree as follows:

1. **General maintenance.**—The tenant will maintain the farm during his tenancy in as good condition as at the beginning, normal wear and depreciation and damage from causes beyond the tenant's control excepted.

2. **Good husbandry.**—The tenant will operate the farm in an efficient and husbandlike way, will do the plowing, seeding, cultivating, and harvesting in a manner that will conserve the landlord's property.

3. **Cropping practices.**—The tenant will *not*, without oral consent of the landlord, (a) plow permanent pasture or meadowland, (b) cut live trees for sale or personal uses, but will take for fuel or use on the farm only dead or unmarketable timber designated by the landlord, (c) allow livestock other than his own on stalkfields or stubblefields, (d) burn or remove cornstalks, corncobs, straw, or other crop residues grown on the farm, (e) pasture new seedings of legumes or grasses in the year they are seeded, and (f) plant legumes on land not known to be thoroughly inoculated without first inoculating the seed.

4. **Manure and crop residue.**—The tenant will spread the manure straw, or other crop residues on the farm as soon as practicable on fields agreed upon by the two parties, except as follows:

....

....

....

....

5. **Pasturing.**—The tenant will prevent tramping of fields by stock and rooting by hogs when injury to the farm will be done.

6. **Waste.**—The tenant will not commit waste on, or damage to, the farm and will use due care to prevent others from so doing.

7. **Fire protection.**—The tenant will not, without written consent of the landlord, house automobiles, motortrucks, or tractors in barns, or otherwise violate restrictions in the landlord's insurance policy which restrictions the landlord shall make known to the tenant.

8. **Replace losses.**—The landlord will replace or repair as promptly as possible the dwelling or any other building that may be destroyed or damaged by fire, flood, or other cause beyond the control of the tenant or make rental adjustments in lieu of replacements.

Figure 6-4 Cont.

9. Noxious weeds.—The tenant will use diligence to prevent noxious weeds from going to seed on the farm and will destroy the same, and will keep the weeds and grass cut or destroyed on the fields, farmstead, roadside, and fence rows. Treatment of weed infestation and cost thereof shall be handled as follows:

....

....

....

....

....

10. Maintenance of improvements.—The tenant will keep the buildings, fences, and other improvements on the farm in as good repair and condition as they are when he takes possession, and in as good repair and condition as they may be put during the term of the lease, ordinary wear and tear, loss by fire, or unavoidable depreciation or destruction excepted.

11. Materials and labor.—The landlord will furnish materials and the tenant will perform labor for normal maintenance and repairs, except that skilled labor which the tenant himself is unable to perform satisfactorily will be furnished by the landlord. Additional agreements regarding materials and labor:

....

....

....

....

....

12. Purchase of materials.—The tenant may buy, without further authorization, materials for normal maintenance and repairs in a total amount not to exceed $.................. within each year, and the landlord will credit or reimburse the tenant for such expenditures as follows:

....

....

....

13. Add improvements.—The tenant will *not*, without written consent of the landlord, (a) erect or permit to be erected on the farm any nonremovable structure or building, or (b) incur any expense to the landlord for such purpose, or (c) add electrical wiring, plumbing, or heating to any buildings, and if consent is given, he will make such additions meet standards and requirements of power and insurance companies.

14. Conservation practices.—The tenant will control soil erosion as completely as practicable by stripcropping and contouring, and by filling in or otherwise controlling small washes or ditches that may form.

15. Conservation structures.—The tenant will keep in good repair all terraces, open ditches, and inlets and outlets of tile drains, preserve all established watercourses or ditches including grass waterways when seed and fertilizer are furnished by the landlord, and refrain from any operation or practice that will injure them.

16. Compensation for improvements.—The two parties will carry out new conservation practices and measures and make other improvements, and share contributions and costs necessary for completing such practices and improvements as set forth below. The tenant will be reimbursed by the landlord when the practice, measure or improvement is completed, or will be compensated for its unexhausted value when the tenant leaves the farm, according to the table below:

16. (Cont'd) Compensation for Improvements Table.

CONSERVATION PRACTICE, MEASURE, OR OTHER IMPROVEMENT	DATE TO BE COMPLETED	ESTIMATED COST (DOLLARS)	PERCENT TO BE FURNISHED BY LANDLORD AND BY TENANT						VALUE PLACED ON TENANT'S CONTRIBUTION (DOLLARS)	RATE OF ANNUAL DEPRECIATION (PERCENT)
			MATERIALS		LABOR		MACHINERY			
			L	T	L	T	L	T		

17. Additional agreements relative to conservation and improvements:

....

....

....

....

18. Review of conservation program.—A new schedule covering conservation practices and improvements will be prepared each year on an appropriate form, which will become a part of this lease when signed by the two parties.

19. Preparing or seeding land.—When the tenant leaves the farm, if the total acreages of prepared or seeded land are greater than at the beginning of his tenancy, he will be compensated by the landlord on the basis of the value of such excess acreages. If such total acreages are less than at the beginning of his tenancy, the tenant will compensate the landlord on the basis of the value of such deficiency, provided that the deficiency is not due to drought, flood, or other causes beyond the control of the tenant. The acreages at the beginning of this tenancy and the basis of payment are as follows:

19. (Cont'd) Preparing or Seeding Land Table.

PREPARED OR SEEDED	ACRES AT BEGINNING	RATE PER ACRE	PREPARED OR SEEDED	ACRES AT BEGINNING	RATE PER ACRE

20. Removable improvements.—Minor improvements of a temporary or removable nature, not provided for in item 16 of this section, which do not mar the condition or appearance of the farm may be made by the tenant at his own expense. The tenant may at any time this lease is in effect, or within a reasonable time thereafter, remove such improvements, provided he leaves in good condition that part of the farm from which they are removed.

21. Compensation for damages.—When the tenant leaves the farm he will pay the landlord reasonable compensation for any damages to the farm for which the tenant is responsible, except ordinary wear and depreciation and damages beyond the tenant's control.

Figure 6-4 Cont.

D. SHARING COSTS AND RETURNS

All costs and returns shall be divided between landlord and tenant as provided below, unless otherwise specifically stated elsewhere in this lease.

1. **Rental rates.**—The tenant agrees to pay as cash rent the amount as calculated below in either method 1 or 2 as completed:

METHOD 1—STRAIGHT CASH RENT				METHOD 2—FLEXIBLE CASH RENT				
KIND OF LAND (1)	ACRES (2)	RATE (3)	AMOUNT (4)	COMMODITY (5)	QUALITY (6)	QUANTITY (7)	PRICE (8)	AMOUNT (9)
INTERTILLED CROPS				CORN				
SMALL GRAINS				COTTON				
HAY				TOBACCO				
PASTURE				WHEAT				
FARM BUILDINGS	XXXXXXX	XXXXXXX		HOGS				
DWELLING	XXXXXXX	XXXXXXX		BEEF				
				MILK				
WOODLAND								
FARMSTEAD AND LOTS								
ENTIRE FARM				XXXXXXXXXXXXXXXXXX	XXXXXX	XXXXXXX	XXXXXX	

2. **Variations for price (for method 2).**—The prices to be used in column 8 will be determined as follows: ....

and the amount of column 9 will be the product of column 7 multiplied by column 8.

3. **Variations for production conditions.**—The total amount of rent for the entire farm as shown in either column 4 or as calculated for column 9 shall be adjusted for any year in which the yield of .... as reported by the State Crop Reporting Service is .... percent above or below the county average yield for the previous .... years, as follows: ....

....

4. **Rental payment.**—The annual rental due shall be paid as follows: $.................... on .... and $.................... on ...., and the payments shall be made at ....

5. **Additional agreements in regard to rental rates:** ....

6. **Expenses.**—Expenses shall be supplied by the tenant except as included in section C and except as follows:

EXPENSES	FURNISHED BY LANDLORD	EXPENSES	FURNISHED BY LANDLORD	EXPENSES	FURNISHED BY LANDLORD
LABOR		CROP EXPENSES		ELECTRICITY	
MAINTENANCE—BUILDINGS				TELEPHONE	
MAINTENANCE—FENCES		SEED		INSURANCE—BUILDINGS	
MACHINE REPAIRS				INSURANCE—CROPS	
FUEL—TRACTOR		INSECTICIDES			
FUEL—TRUCK		WEED CONTROL MATERIAL			
FUEL—OTHER		LIMING MATERIAL		TAXES—REAL ESTATE	
CUSTOM WORK AND HAULING		FERTILIZER		TAXES—PERSONAL	
FEED PURCHASED OR SUPPLIED					
LIVESTOCK EXPENSES					

Figure 6-4 Cont.

7. **Record of expenses.**—The tenant will keep a record of expenses furnished by the landlord, and settlement will be made by mutual agreement or at the time that final rent payment is due.

8. **Additional agreements relative to expenses:**

....

....

....

....

....

....

E. TERM OF LEASE

1. **Term.**—The term of this lease shall be .... year(s) from ...., 19....., to ...., 19......., and this lease shall continue in effect from year to year thereafter until written notice of termination is given by either party to the other at least .... months before expiration of this lease or any renewal.

2. **Continuous occupancy.**—The tenant agrees that he or his agent will possess and occupy the farm continuously during the term of the lease.

3. **Surrender of possession.**—The tenant agrees to surrender possession and occupancy of the premises peaceably at the termination of the lease.

4. **Review of lease.**—A request for general review of the lease may be made at least .... days prior to the final date for giving notice to terminate this lease. Amendments and alterations to this lease shall be made in writing.

F. MISCELLANEOUS PROVISIONS

1. **No partnership created.**—This lease shall not be deemed to give rise to a partnership relation, and neither party shall have authority to obligate the other without written consent, except as specifically provided in this lease.

2. **Government programs.**—The farm will be operated in compliance with Government programs as follows:

....

....

....

....

....

....

3. **Debts and accidents.**—Each party agrees that the other party shall in no way be responsible for the debts of, or liabilities for accidents or damages caused by, the other party.

4. **Willful neglect.**—Willful neglect, failure, or refusal by either party to carry out any substantial provision of this lease shall give the other party the benefits of any proceedings provided by law.

5. **Arbitration of differences.**—Any differences between the parties as to their several rights or obligations under this lease that are not settled by mutual agreement after thorough discussion, shall be submitted for arbitration to a committee of three disinterested persons, one selected by each party hereto and the third by the two thus selected; and the committee's decision shall be accepted by both parties.

6. **Additional agreements:**

....

....

....

....

....

....

....

....

....

IN WITNESS WHEREOF, the parties have signed this lease on the date first above written.

Witnesses:

....[SEAL]
(Landlord)

....[SEAL]

....[SEAL]
(Tenant)

(Acknowledgment in appropriate form to be attached.)

Figure 6-5

ILLINOIS CASH FARM LEASE

To use this lease form. Complete two identical copies — one for the Landlord, one for the Tenant. Cross out any provisions which are not to become a part of the contract. Write in any additional provisions that are desired. Use ink or typewriter. A leaflet on suggestions for completing and using this lease form has been enclosed for your information.

Date and names of parties

This lease is entered into on ...., 19..........., between ....,
.... Landlord, and..., Tenant.

Description of land

The Landlord rents and leases to the Tenant, to occupy and to use for agricultural purposes, the following real estate located in the County of .... and State of ....,
described as follows:...
....
commonly known as the .... farm and consisting of approximately .... acres, together with buildings and improvements on the property.

Length of tenure

The term of this lease shall be from ...., 19..........., to ...., 19..........., and the tenant shall surrender possession at the end of this term or at the end of any extension thereof. Extensions must be placed in writing on this lease, and both parties agree that failure to execute an extension at least .... months before the end of the current term shall be constructive notice of intent to allow the lease to expire.

Amendments and alterations

Amendments and alterations to this lease may be made in writing in the space provided on the back of this form at any time by mutual agreement. In the event of failure to agree on proposed alterations, the existing provisions of the lease shall control operations.

SECTION 1. AMOUNT OF RENT AND TIME OF PAYMENT

A. The Tenant agrees to pay the Landlord an annual cash rent for the above-described farm in the amount determined as follows: (Complete the desired method for determining the cash rent. Strike out the parts and other methods not desired. See the leaflet, "Suggestions for Completing and Using the Illinois Cash Farm Lease Form.")

Method 1. The annual cash rent shall be the sum of $....................... This represents .... acres of cropland at $...................... per acre, plus .... acres of .... at $...................... per acre, plus .... acres of .... at $...................... per acre, plus ....

Method 2. The cash rent shall be the amount stated in Method 1 above, but adjusted annually after the first year in proportion to changes in the USDA index of...
from a base index of .... for the first year of this lease.

Method 3. The cash rent shall be the current value of the standing amounts of commodities indicated below, calculated annually by applying the pricing methods specified. After the first year the standing amounts shall first be adjusted each year in proportion to changes in county average yields from the indicated base yields.

Commodity	*Standing amount*	*Base yield*	*Method of determining the price to be used each year*
Corn	..............................bu.	..............bu.	....
Soybeans	..............................bu.	..............bu.	....
Wheat.	..............................bu.	..............bu.	....
Milk	..............................lb.	XXXXX	....
Hogs.	..............................lb.	XXXXX	....
....	....	....	....

B. The cash rent shall be paid as follows:

Dollars or percent of rent due	*Date due each year*	*Dollars or percent of rent due*	*Date due each year*
....	....	....	....
....	....	....	....

Figure 6-5 Cont.

SECTION 2. LANDLORD'S INVESTMENT AND EXPENSES

The Landlord agrees to furnish the property and to pay the items of expense listed below:

A. The above-described farm, including fixed improvements.

B. Materials for necessary repairs and improvements to buildings and permanent fences except as agreed to in Sections 3D and amendments to this lease.

C. Skilled labor employed in making and repairing improvements and all labor for painting buildings.

D. Taxes on land, improvements, and personal property owned by the Landlord.

E. Fire and wind insurance, at a fair replacement value, on residence and all buildings owned by him and used by the Tenant in storing or housing grain, feed, livestock, and equipment.

F. Ground limestone and rock phosphate (state percentage or share of total cost, including hauling and spreading, furnished by Landlord):

Ground limestone: ....

Rock phosphate: ....

If the Tenant shares in the cost of limestone and rock phosphate, the Landlord agrees to reimburse the Tenant at the termination of the lease for his remaining cost, less government payments received by the Tenant. Depreciation is charged at annual rates as follows: limestone .... percent; rock phosphate .... percent.

G. Seeds (state percent or share furnished by Landlord):

alfalfa..........; red clover..........; sweet clover..........;

grass,..........; ....

H. A water supply adequate for household use and .... animal units of livestock.

I. Other items:..........

....

....

SECTION 3. TENANT'S INVESTMENT AND EXPENSES

The Tenant agrees to furnish the property and to pay the items of expense listed below:

A. All the machinery, equipment, labor, fuel, and power necessary to farm the premises properly.

B. The hauling to the farm, except when otherwise agreed, of all material which the Landlord furnishes for making repairs and minor improvements, and the performing of labor, except skilled, required for such repairing and improving.

C. All seed, inoculation, disease-treatment materials, and fertilizers, except that which the Landlord agrees to furnish in Section 2 above.

D. The following described items and all other items of expense not furnished by the Landlord as provided in Section 2:..........

....

....

....

....

....

SECTION 4. TENANT'S DUTIES IN OPERATING FARM

The Tenant further agrees that he will perform and carry out the stipulations below. (Strike out any not desired.)

A. Activities required:

1. To cultivate the farm faithfully and in a timely, thorough, and businesslike manner.

2. To inoculate all alfalfa and soybean seed sown on land not known to be thoroughly inoculated for the crop planted.

3. To prevent tramping of fields by stock and rooting by hogs when injury will be done.

4. To prevent noxious weeds from going to seed on said premises and to destroy the same and keep the weeds and grass cut.

5. To haul out and spread all manure as soon as practicable on appropriate fields.

6. To keep open ditches, tile drains, tile outlets, grass waterways, and terraces in good repair.

7. To preserve established watercourses or ditches, and to refrain from any operation that will injure them.

8. To keep the buildings, fences (including hedges), and other improvements on said premises in as good repair and condition as they are when he takes possession, or in as good repair and condition as they may be put by the Landlord during the term of the lease — ordinary wear, loss by fire, or unavoidable destruction excepted.

9. To take proper care of all trees, vines, and shrubs, and to prevent injury to the same.

10. To keep the farmstead neat and orderly.

11. To prevent all unnecessary waste, or loss, or damage to the property of the Landlord.

12. To comply with rules and regulations of the Illinois Pollution Control Board.

13. To practice fire prevention, follow safety rules, and abide by restrictions in the Landlord's insurance contracts.

B. Activities restricted:

1. The Tenant further agrees, unless he shall first have obtained the *written* consent of the Landlord:

a. Not to assign this lease to any person or persons or sublet any part of the premises.

b. Not to farm more than .... acres of additional land and not to enter into any other business, occupation, or sideline.

c. Not to erect or permit to be erected any structure or building or to incur any expense to the Landlord for such purpose.

d. Not to add electrical wiring, plumbing, or heating to any buildings and, if consent is given, to make such additions meet standards and requirements of power and insurance companies.

e. Not to permit, encourage, or invite other persons to use any part or all of this property for any purpose or activity not directly related to its use for agricultural production, except as specifically noted here:..........

....

....

2. The Tenant further agrees, unless he shall first have obtained the *oral* consent of the Landlord:

a. Not to plow permanent pasture or meadowland.

b. Not to cut live trees for sale purposes or personal uses.

c. Not to permit the erection of any commercial advertising signs on the farm.

C. Additional agreements:..........

....

....

....

Figure 6-5 Cont.

SECTION 5. MANAGEMENT AND BUSINESS PROCEDURES

The Landlord and Tenant agree that they will observe the following provisions. (Strike out any items not desired.)

A. Except when mutually decided otherwise, the land use and cropping system shall be approximately as follows:

.... acres to be used for rotated crops

.... acres to remain in permanent pasture

.... acres in nongrazed woodland

.... acres in buildings and lots

.... acres of tillable land planted to biennial or perennial legumes each year

.... acres of tillable land to be left in biennial or perennial legumes each year.

B. The Landlord agrees to reimburse the Tenant for the Tenant's cost of legume and grass seed in seedings made in the last year of this lease above .... acres. (Insert the acres in such seedings on the farm at the beginning of this lease.)

C. The Landlord agrees to reimburse the Tenant, at the end of this lease, for the Tenant's cost of readily soluble phosphate (P_2O_5) and potash (K_2O) applied as annual fertilizers on crops harvested for grain in the last year of this lease over and above the amount of these plant-food elements contained in such crops. (See "Suggestions.")

D. Other agreements: ....

....

....

....

....

....

....

....

....

SECTION 6. DEFAULT, YIELDING POSSESSION, RIGHT OF ENTRY

A. Termination upon default. If either party fails to carry out substanially the terms of this lease in due and proper time, the lease may be terminated by the other party by serving a written notice citing the instance(s) of default and specifying a termination date of .... days from the date of such notice. Settlement shall then be made in accordance with the provisions of Clause C of this section, the reimbursement agreements of Sections 2 and 5, and amendments.

B. Yielding possession. The Tenant agrees that at the expiration or termination of this lease he will yield possession of the premises to the Landlord without further demand or notice. If the Tenant fails to yield possession, he shall pay to the Landlord a penalty of $........................ per day, or if a penalty is not specified, the statutory double rent shall apply, for each day he remains in possession thereafter, in addition to any actual damages caused by the Tenant to the Landlord's land or improvements, and said payments shall not entitle said Tenant to any interest of any kind or character in or on the premises.

C. Landlord's lien for rent and performance. The Landlord's lien provided by law on crops grown or growing shall be the security for the rent herein specified and for the faithful performance of the terms of the lease. If the Tenant shall fail to pay the rent due or shall fail to keep any of the agreements of this lease, all costs and attorney fees of the Landlord in enforcing collection or performance shall be added to and become a part of the obligations payable by the Tenant hereunder.

D. Landlord's right of entry during term of lease. The Landlord reserves the right of himself, his agents, employees, or assigns to enter upon said premises at any reasonable time for the purpose of viewing the same, of working or making repairs or improvements thereon, of developing mineral resources as provided in Clause E below, or, after constructive notice has been given that the lease may not be extended, of plowing after severance of crops, of seeding, or of applying fertilizers and doing other field work.

E. Mineral rights. Nothing in this lease shall confer upon the Tenant any right to minerals underlying said land, but the same are hereby reserved by the Landlord together with the full right to enter upon the premises and to bore, search, and excavate for same, to work and remove same, and to deposit excavated rubbish, and with full liberty to pass over said premises with vehicles and lay down and work any railroad track or tracks, tanks, pipelines, powerlines, and structures as may be necessary or convenient for the above purpose. The Landlord agrees to reimburse the Tenant for any actual damage he may suffer for crops destroyed by these activities and to release the Tenant from obligation to continue farming this property when development of mineral resources interferes materially with the Tenant's farming operations.

F. Extent of agreement. The terms of this lease shall be binding on the heirs, executors, administrators, and assigns of both Landlord and Tenant in like manner as upon the original parties.

SECTION 7. ADDITIONAL AGREEMENTS

....

....

....

....

....

Signed ...., 19.........

....
Landlord

By ....
Agent

....
Tenant

Figure 6-5 Cont.

AMENDMENTS TO THE LEASE

A. Improvements made by the Tenant at his expense:

When the Landlord and Tenant agree that the Tenant may make all or part of an improvement (such as buildings, additions to buildings, major repairs, fences, bathrooms, water systems, etc.) to the farm at his own expense and that the Tenant is to be reimbursed for his remaining cost at the end of the lease (less any government payment received by the Tenant for the improvement), the necessary information shall be recorded in one of the following blanks, and after being duly signed by both parties, it shall become a part of the lease above and obligate the Landlord and his heirs and assigns to make such reimbursement. Such improvements become the Landlord's property upon completion of the form below. The Landlord thereby assumes the responsibility for insurance coverage and risk of loss.

Description and location of the improvement	Tenant's cost on completion less government payment	Annual rate of depreciation (percent)	Date depreciation begins	Date of signatures	Signatures
1..............................				....	..............................Lld.
....	....	....	....	....	..............................Ten.
2..............................				....	..............................Lld.
....	....	....	....	....	..............................Ten.
3..............................				....	..............................Lld.
....	....	....	....	....	..............................Ten.
4..............................				....	..............................Lld.
....	....	....	....	....	..............................Ten.

B. Landlord's written consent to Tenant's participation in items in Section 4, Clause B, Part 1.

1. Item:.............. Description and restrictions:..

....

.... Date:.............................. Landlord's signature:..

2. Item:.............. Description and restrictions:..

....

.... Date:.............................. Landlord's signature:..

C. Other amendments:..

....

....

....

....

This form prepared by the Department of Agricultural Economics, University of Illinois.

Figure 6-6

FARM RENTAL AGREEMENT*

Between Farmer and Non-Farmer

1. This agreement shall be made for a period of five (5) years. In the interests of both land owner and renter a shorter term is not advised.
2. The property considered under this agreement shall be used for both pasture and cropland.
3. All property considered in this agreement shall be farmed in conformity with good farm management practices.
4. When this contract expires, the land shall be left in sod.
5. This contract may be renewed by mutual consent of both parties at any time.
6. The purchase and application of lime and fertilizers shall be the responsibility of the renter. Costs may be shared if desired.
7. The renter shall lime, fertilize, plow and reseed ________ acres per year until at the end of five years the entire fillable acreage shall have been limed, fertilized and reseeded. In event the contract is not renewed, seeding expenses incurred the fifth year shall be adjusted as mutually agreed by both parties.
8. The renter shall erect and maintain fences in good condition at all times. However, the property owner shall supply fencing materials for permanent fences unless otherwise agreed.
9. Rental for the years 19_____ through 19_____ shall be $_________

   Rental for each year shall be paid on or before ___________________________

   Guides—1950 census records show the actual cash rent paid by Windham

   County farmers was $________________ per acre.

   The following rates are charged per cow per month in the Vermont Dairy Herd Improvement Associations under supervision of the Vermont Extension Service:

   > $7.00 per cow per month—Excellent Ladino clover and grass, winter rye or wheat, new seeded cover crops, Sudan grass, and Hungarian. Use this especially for irrigated pastures.
   >
   > $5.00 per cow per month—Well fertilized clover and grass sod.
   >
   > $3.00 per cow per month—Old sod with small amount of fertilizer, mostly White Dutch and bluegrass.
   >
   > $1.00 per cow per month—Old grass sod, no fertilizer, late in season. (Mostly an exercise lot.)

10. Any disagreement in connection with this contract that cannot be mutually settled by the two parties concerned shall be arbitrated. The farmer and the property owner shall each choose one person to represent

*Prepared by County Extension Agent, Brattleboro, Vermont.

Figure 6-6 Cont.

them and they in turn shall choose a third member. All decisions arrived at by this committee shall be binding upon the renter and property owner.

________________________ ________________________

Land Owner Renter

____

Date

Figure 6-7

CASH LEASE ON DAIRY FARM

Section I. Date, Contract Parties, Description of Property, and Term of Lease.

1. This lease is made this ______ day of ______________, 19_____, by and between ______________________, hereinafter called the Landowner, and ______________________, hereinafter called the Renter.

2. The Landowner, in consideration of the agreements with the Renter hereinafter set forth, hereby leases to the Renter, to occupy and to use for agricultural purposes only, the ______________ farm, containing ______ acres, located in the Town of ________________, ________________ County, Vermont, legally described as the ____________________, with all fixed improvements thereon except ______________________________________

____

____

3. This lease shall become effective on the ______ day of ______________ 19_____. It shall continue in force until the ______ day of ______________, 19_____, and from year to year thereafter unless written notice of termination is given by either party to the other on or before the ______ day of ___________, which shall be not less than six months immediately preceding the date of termination.

If the lease is for a five-year period with automatic year by year renewal thereafter, either party may terminate this agreement on ________ of the second, third, or fourth year by giving notice on or before __________________ preceding, of his purpose to do so and paying or forfeiting to the other party the sum of $______________.

Section II. Land Use and Cropping Program.

It is the intent of both parties that the land covered by this contract shall be improved and its yielding capacity increased by means of an aggressive cropping program and good cultural practices carried out on a continuing long-term basis. The farm will carry approximately ________ cows and accompanying stock at the beginning of this lease and it is the intent to have not less than this number. It is estimated that this farm should carry ________ cows at the end of five years and it is the intent of both parties to work toward that objective.

The farm contains approximately ________ acres of tillage land. The following land management practices for this tillage land are mutually agreed upon for the duration of this lease:

1. Not less than ________ acres of tillage land will be plowed, prepared and fertilized and reseeded during each crop year.

Figure 6-7 Cont

2. In seeding down the above-mentioned acreage, lime is to be applied where soil tests indicate need, and not less than 120 pounds of plant food shall be applied per acre.

3. The manure from the cow stable shall be protected from leaching as far as facilities permit and shall be spread first on corn land at the rate of

_______ to _________ tons per acre. The rest on hay land at the rate of _______ tons per acre.

4. It is further mutually agreed that_________________________________

____

____

____

____

____

Section III. Amount of Rent and Time of Payment

1. The Renter shall pay to the landowner the sum of $_________ annual rent for the entire farm, referred to in Section I.

2. The annual cash rent shall be paid in 12 equal installments, amounting

to $_________ each, due the first of each month during each contract year. Any unpaid rent shall bear interest at the rate of 6 percent per annum from the date due until paid. All rent due shall be paid in full before the Renter removes his personal property from the farm at the termination of this lease.

3. Provided always, that in case the premises or any part thereof shall, during said terms, be destroyed or damaged by fire or other unavoidable casualty, so that the same shall be thereby rendered unfit for use and habitation, then, and in such case, the rent hereinfore reserved, or a just and proportionate part thereof, according to the nature and extent of the injuries sustained, shall be suspended or abated, until the said premises shall have been put in proper condition for use and habitation by the Landowner.

Section IV. Liability for Accidents

Both parties agree that farm comprehensive liability insurance with a minimum coverage of $50,000 for liability and $500 for medical payments will be carried in the joint names of the Landowner and the Renter and covering the liability of either or both parties for accidents associated with the use of the above-described property. The Renter agrees to insure with a company or companies acceptable to the Landowner and to keep said insurance in force during the term of this lease or any renewal thereof. The policy shall be filled with the Landowner before this lease shall become effective.

Section V. The Landowner Agrees to:

1. Furnish the land and the fixed improvements referred to in Section I.

2. Pay all the taxes and the assessments against the real estate, all taxes on the Landowner's personal property on the farm, and the premiums for the fire insurance carried on the farm buildings.

Figure 6-7 Cont.

3. Make the following repairs or improvements on the farm by the dates specified or as near as practicable thereto.

Repair or Improvement:	To be completed by:
______________________	Date: ______________
______________________	Date: ______________
______________________	Date: ______________
______________________	Date: ______________
______________________	Date: ______________
______________________	Date: ______________

Section VI. The Renter Agrees to:

1. Follow the land management practices listed in Section II, including the furnishing and application of specified amounts of lime and fertilizer and carry out other farming practices that are generally recommended for and that are best adapted to this type of farm and for this locality unless other practices are mutually agreed upon.

2. Furnish all cattle, labor, power, machinery, and movable equipment and all operation and maintenance expenses involved thereto, to operate the farm, except the following items which will be furnished and/or maintained as follows:

Item	Furnished and/or maintained by:
______________________	______________________
______________________	______________________
______________________	______________________
______________________	______________________
______________________	______________________

3. Furnish all labor for the minor repair and the minor improvement of buildings, fences, and drains, and for constructing not more than ______ rods of new fence, the material to be furnished by the Landowner. The buildings, fences, and other improvements on the farm are to be kept in as good repair and condition as they are at the beginning of the lease, or in as good repair and condition as they may be put in by the Landowner during the term of the lease, ordinary wear, depreciation, or unavoidable destruction excepted.

4. Haul to the farm, except when other arrangements are agreed to with the Landowner, any material provided by the Landowner for the minor repair or minor improvement of buildings, fences, and drains.

5. Cut the weeds in lots, fence rows, and along roads whenever necessary to prevent reseeding.

6. Neither assign this lease to any person or persons nor sublet any part of the real estate for any purpose without the written consent of the Landowner.

7. Yield peaceable possession of the farm at the termination of this lease.

Figure 6-7 Cont.

8. Keep livestock out of the hay fields when the soil is soft and protect sod crops, especially new seedings, from too close grazing that might impair the following year's crop.

9. To prevent the accumulation of fire hazards near the buildings.

Section VII. Rights and Privileges.

1. The Landowner or anyone designated by him shall have the right of entry at any mutually convenient time to inspect his property and/or the farming methods being used.

2. The Renter shall have the right to use dead or fallen timber for fuel but he shall neither cut live trees nor market timber, gravel, or any other part of the real estate without the written consent of the Landowner.

3. The Renter shall have the right to erect, maintain and remove at his expense, temporary fence and movable buildings on the farm, provided that such fence or buildings or their removal do not damage the Landowner's property in any way.

4. If the Renter, in view of the approaching termination of the lease, fails to plow, fit, fertilize, and reseed the acreage agreed upon in Section II, Article 1, the landowner or his designated agent shall have the right of entry to plant such crops.

5. The Landowner shall have the right to sell standing timber or to cut and remove timber from the farm.

Section VIII. Enforcement of Agreements and Arbitration.

1. Failure of either the Landowner or the Renter to comply with the agreements set forth to this lease shall make him liable for damages to the other party. Any claim by either party for such damage shall be presented, in writing to the other party, at least ______ days before the termination of this lease.

2. If either or both of the parties of this lease die during the term of the lease, the provisions of this lease shall be binding on the heirs, executors, administrators, and assigns of the party or parties involved.

3. Any disagreements between the Landowner and the Renter shall be referred to a board of three disinterested persons, one of whom shall be appointed by the Landowner, one by the Renter, and the third by the two thus appointed. The decision of these three shall be considered binding by the parties to this lease unless a matter of law or a sum exceeding $________ is involved. Any costs for such arbitration shall be shared equally between the two parties to this lease.

Section IX. Other Agreements.

____

____

____

____

____

Figure 6-7 Cont.

Section X. Signatures.

______________________	______________________
Date	Landowner
______________________	______________________
Date	Renter

Compiled by Dwight K. Eddy, Extension Economist, Dept. of Resource Economics, University of Vermont. Adapted from "Farm Leases", New Hampshire Extension Service. Revised 10/71.

Figure 6-8

AD 561 (Oct. 1960)
U.S. DEPT. OF AGRICULTURE

CROP-SHARE-CASH FARM LEASE

THIS LEASE is entered into this .... day of ...., 19........,
between ...., landlord, of .... (Address)
and ...., tenant, of .... (Address)

A. PROPERTY RIGHTS.—The landlord hereby leases to the tenant, to occupy and use for agricultural and related purposes, the following-described property, hereinafter referred to as the "farm," located in .... County, State of ...., and commonly known as the .... farm.

....

....

....

....

....

....

....

....

and consisting of .... acres, more or less, together with all buildings and improvements thereon and all rights thereto except as specified below:

1. Reservation of land and buildings.—The landlord reserves the right to use the following land and buildings for the following purposes:

....

....

....

....

....

....

....

....

....

....

....

2. Right of entry.—The landlord reserves the right of himself, his agents, his employees, or his assigns to enter the farm at any reasonable time for purposes (a) of consultation with the tenant; (b) of making repairs, improvements, and inspections; (c) of developing mineral resources; and (d) after notice of termination of the lease is given, of plowing, seeding, fertilizing and such customary seasonal work, none of which is to interfere with the tenant in carrying out regular farm operations.

3. No right to sublease.—The landlord does not convey to the tenant the right to lease or sublet any part of the farm or to assign the lease to any person or persons whomsoever.

4. Transfer of farm.—If the landlord should sell or otherwise transfer title to the farm, he will do so subject to the provisions of this lease.

5. Heirs and successors.—The terms of this lease shall be binding upon the heirs, executors, administrators, and successors of both landlord and tenant in like manner as upon the original parties. However, in event the lease is for more than one year, the heirs or successors of the tenant shall have the option to give written notice of termination effective at the end of the lease year in which death occurs.

6. Right to lease.—The landlord warrants that he has the right to lease the farm, and will defend the tenant's possession against any and all persons whomsoever.

7. Rent additional land.—The tenant will not, unless he shall first have obtained written consent of the landlord, farm more than .... acres of additional land and will not enter into any other business, occupation, or sideline.

8. Additional agreements regarding property rights:

....

....

....

....

....

....

B. LAND USE AND LIVESTOCK PRODUCTION

1. Land use.—The agreed-upon use of the land is outlined in the following table:

USE OF LAND	ACRES	FIELDS	SEED VARIETY	KIND AND AMOUNT OF FERTILIZER PER ACRE
FOR FAMILY LIVING				
WOODLAND				
FARMSTEAD AND LOTS				
TOTAL		XXXXXXXXX	XXXXXXXXXXXXXXX	XXXXXXXXXXXXXXXXXXXXXXXXXXXXXXXXXXXXXX

2. Livestock production.—The tenant on his own may engage in the following production of livestock:

KIND OF LIVESTOCK	MAXIMUM NUMBERS	SPECIAL HEALTH, SANITATION, OR FEEDING PRACTICES

Figure 6-8 Cont.

3. **Acres and numbers.**—The acres of crops and the fields on which grown and numbers of livestock shown above are those planned for the first year of this lease. They may be adjusted within the year or from year to year by mutual agreement.

4. **Crop and livestock adjustments.**—If it is impracticable in any year, from causes beyond the tenant's control, to grow the crops and to keep within the number of livestock according to the plan shown, appropriate adjustments will be made by mutual agreement between the parties.

5. **Restriction on livestock.**—Neither the owner nor the tenant shall bring livestock that is not covered by this agreement on the farm during the period of the lease without express permission of the other party.

6. **Home use.**—The tenant and landlord may take for home use the following kinds and quantities of jointly owned crops:

----

7. **Buying and selling.**—The two parties will buy and sell jointly owned property according to the following agreement:

----

8. **Division of property.**—At the termination of this lease, all jointly owned property will be divided or disposed of as follows:

C. IMPROVING, CONSERVING, AND MAINTAINING THE FARM. To improve the farm, conserve its resources, and maintain it in a high state of cultivation, the two parties agree as follows:

1. **General maintenance.**—The tenant will maintain the farm during his tenancy in as good condition as at the beginning, normal wear and depreciation and damages from causes beyond the tenant's control excepted.

2. **Good husbandry.**—The tenant will operate the farm in an efficient and husbandlike way, will do the plowing, seeding, cultivating, and harvesting in a manner that will conserve the landlord's property.

3. **Cropping practices.**—The tenant will *not*, without oral consent of the landlord, (a) plow permanent pasture or meadowland, (b) cut live trees for sale or personal uses, but will take for fuel or use on the farm only dead or unmarketable timber designated by the landlord, (c) allow livestock other than his own on stalkfields or stubble-fields, (d) burn or remove cornstalks, corncobs, straw, or other crop residues grown on the farm, (e) pasture new seedings of legumes or grasses in the year they are seeded, and (f) plant legumes on land not known to be thoroughly inoculated without first inoculating the seed.

4. **Livestock practices.**—In caring for his livestock, the tenant will follow health and sanitation measures and guard against disease.

5. **Manure and crop residue.**—The tenant will spread the manure, straw, or other crop residues on the farm as soon as practicable on fields agreed upon by the two parties, except as follows:

----

6. **Pasturing.**—The tenant will prevent tramping of fields by stock and rooting by hogs when injury to the farm will be done.

7. **Waste.**—The tenant will not commit waste on or damage to the farm and will use due care to prevent others from so doing.

8. **Fire protection.**—The tenant will not, without written consent of the landlord, house automobiles, motortrucks, or tractors in barns, or otherwise violate restrictions in the landlord's insurance policy, which restrictions the landlord shall make known to the tenant.

9. **Replace losses.**—The landlord will replace or repair as promptly as possible the dwelling or any other building that may be destroyed or damaged by fire, flood, or other cause beyond the control of the tenant or make rental adjustments in lieu of replacements.

10. **Noxious weeds.**—The tenant will use diligence to prevent noxious weeds from going to seed on the farm and will destroy the same, and will keep the weeds and grass cut or destroyed on the fields, farmstead, roadside, and fence rows. Treatment of weed infestation and cost thereof shall be handled as follows:

----

11. **Maintenance of improvements.**—The tenant will keep the buildings, fences, and other improvements on the farm in as good repair and condition as they are when he takes possession, and in as good repair and condition as they may be put during the term of the lease, ordinary wear and tear, loss by fire, or unavoidable depreciation or destruction excepted.

12. **Materials and labor.**—The landlord will furnish materials and the tenant will perform labor for normal maintenance and repairs, except that skilled labor which the tenant himself is unable to perform satisfactorily will be furnished by the landlord. Additional agreements regarding materials and labor:

----

13. **Purchase of materials.**—The tenant may buy, without further authorization, materials for normal maintenance and repairs in a total amount not to exceed $.................... within each year, and the landlord will credit or reimburse the tenant for such expenditures, as follows:

----

14. **Add improvements.**—The tenant will *not*, without written consent of the landlord, (a) erect or permit to be erected on the farm any nonremovable structure or building, or (b) incur any expense to the landlord for such purpose, or (c) add electrical wiring, plumbing, or heating to any buildings, and, if consent is given, he will make such additions meet standards and requirements of power and insurance companies.

15. **Conservation practices.**—The tenant will control soil erosion as completely as practicable by stripcropping and contouring, and by filling in or otherwise controlling small washes or ditches that may form.

16. **Conservation structures.**—The tenant will keep in good repair all terraces, open ditches, and inlets and outlets of tile drains, preserve all established watercourses or ditches including grass waterways when seed and fertilizer are furnished by the landlord, and refrain from any operation or practice that will injure them.

17. **Compensation for improvements.**—The two parties will carry out new conservation practices and measures and make other improvements, and share contributions and costs necessary for completion of such practices and improvements as set forth below. The tenant will be reimbursed by the landlord when the practice, measure, or improvement is completed, or the tenant will be compensated for its unexhausted value when he leaves the farm, according to the table below:

Figure 6-8 Cont.

17 (Continued). Compensation for Improvements Table.

CONSERVATION PRACTICE, MEASURE, OR OTHER IMPROVEMENT	DATE TO BE COMPLETED	ESTIMATED COST (DOLLARS)	PERCENT TO BE FURNISHED BY LANDLORD AND BY TENANT						VALUE PLACED ON TENANT'S CONTRIBUTION (DOLLARS)	RATE OF ANNUAL DEPRECIATION (PERCENT)
			MATERIALS		LABOR		MACHINERY			
			L	T	L	T	L	T		

18. Additional agreements relative to conservation and improvements:

----

19. Review of conservation program.—A new schedule covering conservation practices and improvements will be prepared each year on an appropriate form which will become a part of this lease when signed by the two parties.

20. Preparing or seeding land.—When the tenant leaves the farm, if the total acreages of prepared or seeded land are greater than at the beginning of his tenancy, he will be compensated by the landlord on the basis of the value of such excess acreages. If such total acreages are less than at the beginning of his tenancy, the tenant will compensate the landlord on the basis of the value of such deficiency, provided that the deficiency is not due to drought, flood, or other causes beyond the control of the tenant. The acreages at the beginning of this tenancy and the basis of payment are as shown in the table at the right above:

20 (Continued). Preparing or Seeding Land Table.

PREPARED OR SEEDED	ACRES AT BEGINNING	RATE PER ACRE

21. Removable improvements.—Minor improvements of a temporary or removable nature, not provided for in item 17 of this section, which do not mar the condition or appearance of the farm may be made by the tenant at his own expense. The tenant may at any time this lease is in effect, or within a reasonable time thereafter, remove such improvements, provided he leaves in good condition that part of the farm from which they are removed.

22. Compensation for damages.—When the tenant leaves the farm he will pay the landlord reasonable compensation for any damage to the farm for which the tenant is responsible, except ordinary wear and depreciation and damages beyond the tenant's control.

D. SHARING COSTS AND RETURNS.—All costs and returns shall be divided between landlord and tenant as provided below, unless otherwise specifically stated elsewhere in this lease.

1. Rental rates.—The tenant agrees to pay as rent the shares or quantities of crops and cash as indicated below:

CROPS OR IMPROVEMENTS	ACRES	SHARE RENT	CASH RENT	PLACE OF SALE OR DELIVERY	DATE OF SALE, DELIVERY, OR PAYMENT
FARM BUILDINGS	xxxxxxx	xxxxxxx			
DWELLING	xxxxxxx	xxxxxxx			

2. Additional agreements in regard to rental rates:

----

3. Expenses.—Expenses, including investments in personal property, shall be supplied by the tenant, except as indicated in section C and except as follows:

INVESTMENTS IN PERSONAL PROPERTY	FURNISHED BY LANDLORD	EXPENSES	FURNISHED BY LANDLORD	EXPENSES	FURNISHED BY LANDLORD
TRACTOR		LABOR		LIMING MATERIAL	
MACHINERY AND EQUIPMENT		MAINTENANCE—BUILDINGS		FERTILIZER	
		MAINTENANCE—FENCES			
		MACHINE REPAIRS		SEED	
		FUEL—TRACTOR			
		FUEL—TRUCK			
		FUEL—OTHER		ELECTRICITY	
		CUSTOM WORK AND HAULING		TELEPHONE	
		WEED CONTROL MATERIAL		INSURANCE—BUILDINGS	
		INSECTICIDES		INSURANCE—CROPS	
		FEED PURCHASED OR SUPPLIED		TAXES—REAL ESTATE	
LIVESTOCK		LIVESTOCK EXPENSES		TAXES—PERSONAL	

Figure 6-8 Cont.

4. **Additional agreements relative to expenses:**

....

....

....

....

....

....

E. TERM OF LEASE

1. **Term.**—The term of this lease shall be........................year(s) from............................, 19....., to............................, 19....., and this lease shall continue in effect from year to year thereafter until written notice of termination is given by either party to the other at least .... months before expiration of this lease or any renewal.

2. **Continuous occupancy.**—The tenant agrees that he or his agent will possess and occupy the farm continuously during the term of the lease.

3. **Surrender of possession.**—The tenant agrees to surrender possession and occupancy of the premises peaceably at the termination of the lease.

4. **Review of lease.**—A request for general review of the lease may be made at least .... days prior to the final date for giving notice to terminate this lease. Amendments and alterations to this lease shall be made in writing.

F. MISCELLANEOUS PROVISIONS

1. **No partnership created.**—This lease shall not be deemed to give rise to a partnership relation, and neither party shall have authority to obligate the other without written consent, except as specifically provided in this lease.

2. **Government programs.**—The farm will be operated in compliance with Government programs as follows:

....

....

....

....

....

....

3. **Debts and accidents.**—Each party agrees that the other party shall in no way be responsible for the debts of, or liabilities for accidents or damages caused by, the other party.

4. **Willful neglect.**—Willful neglect, failure, or refusal by either party to carry out any substantial provision of this lease shall give the other party the benefits of any proceedings provided by law.

5. **Farm records.**—The tenant agrees to keep financial and production records of all income and expenses of mutual interest, which records shall be accessible to the landlord at all times, and to furnish an annual report to the landlord on or before the following date .... Accounts between the two parties shall be settled on or about ....

6. **Arbitration of differences.**—Any differences between the parties as to their several rights and obligations under this lease that are not settled by mutual agreement after thorough discussion, shall be submitted for arbitration to a committee of three disinterested persons, one selected by each party hereto and the third by the two thus selected, and the committee's decision shall be accepted by both parties.

7. **Additional agreements:**

....

....

....

....

....

....

....

....

....

....

....

....

....

....

....

....

IN WITNESS WHEREOF, the parties have signed this lease on the date first above written.

Witnesses:

[SEAL]

....
(Landlord)

.... [SEAL]

.... [SEAL]

....
(Tenant)

(Acknowledgment in appropriate form to be attached)

Figure 6-9

LABOR-SHARE LEASE (Farm Profit-Sharing Agreement)

(Provides for sharing returns to capital, unpaid labor, and management)

To use this agreement form. Complete two copies—one for the *senior operator* and one for the *junior operator*. Cross out *in ink* identically on both copies any provisions which are not to become a part of the contract. Write in, *in ink*, any additional provisions that are desired.

Date and names of parties

This agreement is entered into the____________________ day of____________, 19____ between ________________________________, the owner and/or senior operator and____________________________________ the junior operator.

Description of land

This agreement is entered into for the purpose of operating a farm business on the following described real estate:____

____

____

situated in the County of______________________________, in the State of________________ containing_________________ acres more or less.

Length of tenure

The term of this agreement shall be from the________ day of__________ ,19____ ,to the____________ day of______________ ,19____ and from year to year thereafter unless written notice to terminate is given by either party to the other at least ________________ months before the end of the agreement year.

Extent of agreement

The terms of this agreement shall be binding on the heirs, executors, administrators, and assigns of both parties in like manner as upon the original parties, except as shall be provided by mutual agreement otherwise.

No partnership created

This agreement shall not be construed as giving rise to a partnership; and neither party shall be liable for debts or obligations incurred by the other without written consent.

SECTION 1. DIVISION OF INCOME AND RELATED STIPULATIONS

A. Division of net farm returns

The net farm returns at the end of the contract year shall be divided on the basis of_______% to the senior operator and _______% to the junior operator. The basis for determing the net farm returns shall be a complete and accurate record of the farm business to be kept by ____________________________ with both parties responsible for contributing needed information. Both parties shall cooperate in setting up inventories and depreciation tables and in summarizing and interpreting the records. The farm account book shall be open for inspection by either party at any time.

B. Accounting methods and procedures

Only the operator's or tenant's share of the business shall be considered for purposes of determining the net farm returns to be divided. Therefore, all farm real estate owned by the senior operator and used in the farm business shall be treated as rented land for which he shall receive an appropriate cash or share rent and this amount shall come out of the gross farm income.

Complete inventories of feed, grain, livestock, and other products shall be made at the beginning and end of each year, together with appropriate values on these items.

A complete account shall be kept of all purchases, sales, depreciation, and remaining cost values on all operating capital items.

Figure 6-9 Cont.

A complete record shall be kept of all cash income and cash operating expenses, including cash rent paid, but not including interest and principal payments on indebtedness. The accounting system to be followed is the same as that required for income tax purposes. The form in Clause C of Section 1 is designed so that the information required can be taken from IRS Form 1040F.

C. Calculating net farm returns

Net farm returns shall be based on the operator's share of the business and, unless agreed otherwise, shall be calculated annually on the accrual basis. The calculation of net farm returns from totals in the farm account book or from IRS Form 1040F shall be as outlined below.

1. Summary of income to be divided:	*Lines on U.S. 1040F*	*Amounts*
a. End-of-year inventory of crops, livestock, etc.	Part V, Line 61	$________
b. Income from the sale of crops, livestock, and products	Part V, Line 62	________
c. Other farm income	Part V, add lines 63-67	________
Total income (add lines a, b and c)		$________

2. Summary of farm deductions (expenses) and depreciation:		
a. Beginning-of-year inventory of crops, livestock, etc.	Part V, Line 70	$________
b. Cost of livestock and products bought	Part V, Line 71	________
c. Depreciation on machinery, equipment, and livestock	Part III, Line 58	________
d. Additional first-year depreciation (enter amounts to be included)	Part III, Line 55	________
e. Farm deductions (operating expenses including rent paid on land owned by the senior operator)	Part II, Line 51; minus Lines 31, 32, 42, 46, 47	________
Total deductions (add lines 2a through 2e)		$________

3. Net farm returns (Total of 1 minus 2)	$________
4. Junior operator's share (____% of 3)	$________
5. Total of monthly advances to junior operator	$________
6. Balance due to junior operator (4 minus 5)	$________

D. In addition to the share of net farm returns above, the junior operator shall be permitted meat, milk, and eggs from the production on the farm for use in his household not to exceed the following amounts annually,____

____

He may also keep no more than the following numbers of livestock to be fed out of farm-grown feed for his own use:________________________________

____

E. Wage guarantee

The junior operator is guaranteed by the owner a cash income of $______ per month, the income for each month being due on or before the ______ day of the following month. Such compensation shall be considered advance payment against the junior operator's share of the net farm returns at the end of the year. If the junior operator's share of the net farm returns is not equal to the total amount paid above, he shall nevertheless be entitled to retain the above amount, and shall not be required to make any refund. The amount advanced to the junior operator shall not be considered a part of the cost of hired labor when determining farm expenses.

Figure 6-9 Cont.

SECTION 2. OTHER FARM BUSINESS CONSIDERATIONS

A. Receipts and disbursements

Since the senior operator owns all of the operating capital, he shall accept all income and pay all expenses except small expenses not exceeding $__________ each, which may be paid by the junior operator. For such expenses the senior operator shall reimburse the junior operator at the end of each month upon presentation of receipted statements.

All farm purchases and sales amounting to more than $__________ shall be made only with the knowledge and consent of both parties.

B. Management

General operating plans shall be discussed and agreed upon by both parties.

Investments in new capital items as replacements for old items or as capital additions shall be made by and at the discretion of the senior operator. However, the bookkeeping value of and depreciation charges on such new capital items shall be mutually decided.

C. Living arrangements

Unless otherwise agreed, each party shall provide his own living arrangements. If living arrangements are provided for either or both parties, those arrangements shall be as follows: __________

____

____

____

If either party boards the other, the party receiving board shall pay the party providing the board $________ a month for his laundry and his share of the cash cost of food and fuel.

D. Ownership

Inasmuch as the senior operator furnishes the investment in the farm business, ownership of farm property shall remain with him at the termination of this agreement, except as stipulated below: __________

____

____

____

E. Additional agreements

____

____

____

____

____

____

____

SECTION 3. ARBITRATION

The parties to this agreement agree that if a proper settlement cannot be reached between them at the close of the period of agreement, they will submit all matters of disagreement to an arbitration committee and will abide by the decision of that committee. Each party shall select one arbitrator; the two arbitrators so selected shall jointly select a third and the three shall determine the bases of settlement which to them seem equitable.

Dated____________________, 19______

____________________	____________________
(Senior Operator)	(Junior Operator)

Figure 6-9 Cont.

HOW TO FIGURE THE DIVISION OF NET FARM RETURNS

The general principle upon which a labor-share lease or profit-sharing agreement is based is that each party is to share in the net farm returns in proportion to the value of his contributions.[1]

Before the agreement is written. The two parties should place present-day values on the farm operating capital, interest, and labor. Since other items are charged against the farm account, they may be disregarded in the computation. Rented land does not enter into the calculations, but cash rent must be treated as a farm expense.

	Amount	Rate	Contributions for the year: Senior Operator	Junior Operator	Total
Operating capital	$______	_____%[2]	$______	$______	$______
Depreciation on operating capital	______	______	______	______	______
Labor and management . . .	______ (months)	$______ (per month)	______	______	______
Total value of contributions			$______	$______	$______
Percent contributed by each			______%	______%[3]	100 %

At the end of the year. After the farm account book has been summarized and the net farm income for the year has been determined, the following form may be used in figuring the cash settlement to the operator:

Total net farm returns from farm account	$______
Multiply by percent contributed by operator	______%
Operator's share	$______
Subtract total advance payments to operator	$______
Balance due operator at the end of the year	$______

[1] Since labor and management are closely associated, the word *labor* is used to describe either or both. In some instances, there may be a wide variation in the value of management as well as labor furnished by the two parties. If the owner has a reputation as a producer of seed, purebred livestock, or some other product, that fact may need to be considered as another item when figuring his contribution.

[2] Use the going interest rate on production loans.

[3] If the junior operator wants to grow into the business, he may want to leave some of his share of net farm returns invested in the business. This should be handled through a promissory note from the senior operator at a specified interest rate, or at zero interest but included as an operating capital contribution in succeeding years by the junior operator.

This form prepared by the Department of Agricultural Economics, University of Illinois.

Figure 6-10

AD 563 (Mar 1960)

U.S. DEPT. OF AGRICULTURE

LIVESTOCK-SHARE FARM LEASE

THIS LEASE is entered into this .... day of ...., 19........

between ...., landlord, of .... (Address)

and ...., tenant, of .... (Address)

A. PROPERTY RIGHTS.—The landlord hereby leases to the tenant, to occupy and use for agricultural and related purposes, the following-described property, hereinafter referred to as the "farm," located in .... County, State of ...., and commonly known as the .... farm:

....

....

....

....

....

and consisting of .... acres, more or less, together with all buildings and improvements thereon and all rights thereto except as specified below.

1. Right of entry.—The landlord reserves the right of himself, his agents, his employees, or his assigns to enter the farm at any reasonable time for purposes (a) of consultation with the tenant; (b) of making repairs, improvements, and inspections; (c) of developing mineral resources; and (d) after notice of termination of the lease is given, of plowing, seeding, fertilizing, and such customary seasonal work, none of which is to interfere with the tenant in carrying out regular farm operations.

2. No right to sublease.—The landlord does not convey to the tenant the right to lease or sublet any part of the farm or to assign the lease to any person or persons whomsoever.

3. Transfer of farm.—If the landlord should sell or otherwise transfer title to the farm, he will do so subject to the provisions of this lease.

4. Heirs and successors.—The terms of this lease shall be binding upon the heirs, executors, administrators, and successors, of both landlord and tenant in like manner as upon the original parties. However, in event the lease is for more than one year, the heirs or successors of either party shall have the option to give written notice of termination effective at the end of the lease year in which death occurs.

5. Right to lease.—The landlord warrants that he has the right to lease the farm, and will defend the tenant's possession against any and all persons whomsoever.

6. Rent additional land.—The tenant will not, unless he shall first have obtained written consent of the landlord, farm more than .... acres of additional land and will not enter into any other business, occupation, or sideline.

7. Additional agreements regarding property rights:

....

....

....

B. LAND USE AND LIVESTOCK PRODUCTION

1. Land use.—The agreed-upon use of the land is outlined in the following table:

USE OF LAND	ACRES	FIELDS	SEED VARIETY	KIND AND AMOUNT OF FERTILIZER PER ACRE
FOR FAMILY LIVING				
WOODLAND				
FARMSTEAD AND LOTS				
TOTAL		xxxxxxxxx	xxxxxxxxxxxxxxx	xxxxxxxxxxxxxxxxxxxxxxxxxxxxxxxxxxxxxxxxxx

2. Livestock production.—The two parties will engage in the following production of livestock:

KIND OF LIVESTOCK	NUMBER	BREED	SHARE OWNED BY LANDLORD	SPECIAL HEALTH, SANITATION, OR FEEDING PRACTICES

3. Acres and numbers.—The acres of crops and the fields on which grown and numbers of livestock shown above are those planned for the first year of this lease. They may be adjusted within the year or from year to year by mutual agreement.

4. Crop and livestock adjustments.—If it is impracticable in any year, from causes beyond the tenant's control, to grow the crops and to keep the livestock according to the plan shown, appropriate adjustments will be made by mutual agreement between the two parties.

5. Restriction on livestock.—Neither the owner nor the tenant shall bring livestock that is not covered by this agreement on the farm during the period of the lease without express permission of the other party.

6. Home use.—The tenant and landlord may take for home use the following kinds and quantities of jointly owned crops, livestock and/or livestock products:

....

....

....

Figure 6-10 Cont.

7. **Buying and selling.**—The tenant shall consult with the landlord regarding time, price, sales agency, and similar matters regarding the purchase and sale of livestock, feed, and crops whenever the transaction exceeds $.................................. in value. Additional agreements are as follows:

....

....

....

8. **Division of property.**—At the termination of this lease, all jointly owned livestock or other property will be divided or disposed of as follows:

....

....

....

C. **IMPROVING, CONSERVING, AND MAINTAINING THE FARM.**—To improve the farm, conserve its resources, and maintain it in a high state of cultivation, the two parties agree as follows:

1. **General maintenance.**—The tenant will maintain the farm during his tenancy in as good condition as at the beginning, normal wear and depreciation and damage from causes beyond the tenant's control excepted.

2. **Good husbandry.**—The tenant will operate the farm in an efficient and husbandlike way, will do the plowing, seeding, cultivating, and harvesting in a manner that will conserve the landlord's property.

3. **Cropping practices.**—The tenant will *not*, without oral consent of the landlord, (a) plow permanent pasture or meadowland, (b) cut live trees for sale or personal uses, but will take for fuel or use on the farm only dead or unmarketable timber designated by the landlord, (c) allow livestock other than his own or jointly owned on stalkfields or stubblefields, (d) burn or remove cornstalks, corncobs, straw, or other crop residues grown on the farm, (e) pasture new seedings of legumes or grasses in the year they are seeded, and (f) plant legumes on land not known to be thoroughly inoculated without first inoculating the seed.

4. **Livestock practices.**—The tenant will care for the livestock so as to maximize production, will do the breeding, feeding, and watering at the proper time and in the proper manner, and will follow health and sanitation measures and guard against disease.

5. **Manure and crop residue.**—The tenant will spread the manure, straw, or other crop residues on the farm as soon as practicable on fields agreed upon by the two parties, except as follows:

....

....

....

6. **Pasturing.**—The tenant will prevent tramping of fields by stock and rooting by hogs when injury to the farm will be done.

7. **Waste.**—The tenant will not commit waste on, or damage to, the farm and will use due care to prevent others from so doing.

8. **Fire protection.**—The tenant will not, without written consent of the landlord, house automobiles, motortrucks, or tractors in barns, or otherwise violate restrictions in the landlord's insurance policy, which restrictions the landlord shall make known to the tenant.

9. **Replace losses.**—The landlord will replace or repair as promptly as possible the dwelling or any other building that may be destroyed or damaged by fire, flood, or other cause beyond the control of the tenant or make rental adjustments in lieu of replacements.

10. **Noxious weeds.**—The tenant will use diligence to prevent noxious weeds from going to seed on the farm and will destroy the same, and will keep the weeds and grass cut or destroyed on the fields, farmstead, roadside, and fence rows. Treatment of weed infestation and cost thereof shall be handled as follows:

....

....

....

11. **Maintenance of improvements.**—The tenant will keep the buildings, fences, and other improvements on the farm in as good repair and condition as they are when he takes possession, and in as good repair and condition as they may be put during the term of the lease, ordinary wear and tear, loss by fire, or unavoidable depreciation or destruction excepted.

12. **Materials and labor.**—The landlord will furnish materials and the tenant will perform labor for normal maintenance and repairs, except that skilled labor which the tenant himself is unable to perform satisfactorily will be furnished by the landlord. Additional agreements regarding materials and labor:

....

....

....

13. **Purchase of materials.**—The tenant may buy, without further authorization, materials for normal maintenance and repairs in a total amount not to exceed $.......................... within each year, and the landlord will credit or reimburse the tenant for such expenditures as follows:

....

....

....

14. **Add improvements.**—The tenant will *not*, without written consent of the landlord, (a) erect or permit to be erected on the farm any nonremovable structure or building, or (b) incur any expense to the landlord for such purpose, or (c) add electrical wiring, plumbing, or heating to any buildings, and, if consent is given, he will make such additions meet standards and requirements of power and insurance companies.

15. **Conservation practices.**—The tenant will control soil erosion as completely as practicable by stripcropping and contouring, and by filling in or otherwise controlling small washes or ditches that may form.

16. **Conservation structures.**—The tenant will keep in good repair all terraces, open ditches, and inlets and outlets of tile drains, preserve all established watercourses or ditches, including grass waterways when seed and fertilizer are furnished by the landlord, and refrain from any operation or practice that will injure them.

17. **Compensation for improvements.**—The two parties will carry out new conservation practices and measures and make other improvements, and share contributions and costs necessary for completion of such practices and improvements as set forth below. The tenant will be reimbursed by the landlord when the practice, measure, or improvement is completed, or the tenant will be compensated for its unexhausted value when he leaves the farm, according to the schedule below:

17 (Cont'd). **Compensation for Improvements Table.**

CONSERVATION PRACTICE, MEASURE, OR OTHER IMPROVEMENT	DATE TO BE COMPLETED	ESTIMATED COST (DOLLARS)	PERCENT TO BE FURNISHED BY LANDLORD AND BY TENANT						VALUE PLACED ON TENANT'S CONTRIBUTION (DOLLARS)	RATE OF ANNUAL DEPRECIATION (PERCENT)
			MATERIALS		LABOR		MACHINERY			
			L	T	L	T	L	T		

18. **Additional agreements relative to conservation and improvements:**

....

....

19. **Review of conservation program.**—A new schedule covering conservation practices and improvements will be prepared each year on an appropriate form which will become a part of this lease when signed by the two parties.

Figure 6-10 Cont.

20. **Preparing or seeding land.**—When the tenant leaves the farm, if the total acreages of prepared or seeded land are greater than at the beginning of his tenancy, he will be compensated by the landlord on the basis of the value of such excess acreages. If such total acreages are less than at the beginning of his tenancy, the tenant will compensate the landlord on the basis of the value of such deficiency, provided that the deficiency is not due to drought, flood, or other causes beyond the control of the tenant. The acreages at the beginning of this tenancy and the basis of payment are as follows:

PREPARED OR SEEDED	ACRES AT BEGINNING	RATE PER ACRE	PREPARED OR SEEDED	ACRES AT BEGINNING	RATE PER ACRE

21. **Removable improvements.**—Minor improvements of a temporary or removable nature, not provided for in item 17 of this section, which do not mar the condition or appearance of the farm may be made by the tenant at his own expense. The tenant may at any time this lease is in effect, or within a reasonable time thereafter, remove such improvements, provided he leaves in good condition that part of the farm from which they are removed.

22. **Compensation for damages.**—When the tenant leaves the farm he will pay the landlord reasonable compensation for any damages to the farm for which the tenant is responsible, except ordinary wear and depreciation and damages beyond the tenant's control.

D. **SHARING COSTS AND RETURNS.**—All costs and returns shall be divided between landlord and tenant as provided below, unless otherwise specifically stated elsewhere in this lease.

1. **Rental rates.**—The tenant agrees to pay as rent the shares or quantities of crops and livestock as indicated below:

CROPS, LIVESTOCK, AND IMPROVEMENTS	SHARE OR AMOUNT PAID AS RENT				PLACE OF SALE OR DELIVERY	DATE OF SALE DELIVERY OR PAYMENT
	CROPS OR CASH	OFFSPRING OR INCREASE IN LIVESTOCK HERD	LIVESTOCK SALES	SALES OF LIVESTOCK PRODUCTS		
DWELLING		XXXXXXXXXXX	XXXXXXXXXXX	XXXXXXXXXXX		

2. **Additional agreements in regard to rental rates:**

----

3. **Expenses.**—Expenses, including investments in personal property, shall be supplied by the landlord and tenant as follows, except as indicated in section C:

INVESTMENTS IN PERSONAL PROPERTY	FURNISHED BY		EXPENSES	FURNISHED BY		EXPENSES	FURNISHED BY	
	L	T		L	T		L	T
TRACTOR			LABOR			LIMING MATERIAL		
WORKSTOCK			MAINTENANCE—BUILDINGS			FERTILIZER		
MACHINERY AND EQUIPMENT			MAINTENANCE—FENCES					
			MACHINE REPAIRS					
			FUEL—TRACTOR			SEED		
			FUEL—TRUCK					
			FUEL—OTHER					
			CUSTOM WORK AND HAULING					
			ELECTRICITY					
			TELEPHONE			INSURANCE—BUILDINGS		
			VETERINARY FEES			INSURANCE—CORPS		
			BREEDING FEES					
BEEF CATTLE						TAXES—REAL ESTATE		
FEEDER CATTLE			WEED CONTROL MATERIAL			TAXES—PERSONAL		
HOGS			INSECTICIDES					
SHEEP								
DAIRY			FEED PURCHASED OR SUPPLIED					

Figure 6-10 Cont.

4. Additional agreements relative to expenses:

....

....

....

....

....

....

E. TERM OF LEASE

1. **Term.**—The term of this lease shall be .... year(s) from ...., 19....., to ...., 19....., and this lease shall continue in effect from year to year thereafter until written notice of termination is given by either party to the other at least .... months before expiration of this lease or any renewal.

2. **Continuous occupancy.**—The tenant agrees that he or his agent will possess and occupy the farm continuously during the term of the lease.

3. **Surrender of possession.**—The tenant agrees to surrender possession and occupancy of the premises peaceably at the termination of the lease.

4. **Review of lease.**—A request for general review of the lease may be made at least .... days prior to the final date for giving notice to terminate this lease. Amendments and alterations to this lease shall be made in writing.

F. MISCELLANEOUS PROVISIONS

1. **No partnership created.**—This lease shall not be deemed to give rise to a partnership relation, and neither party shall have authority to obligate the other without written consent, except as specifically provided in this lease.

2. **Government programs.**—The farm will be operated in compliance with Government programs as follows:

....

....

....

....

....

....

3. **Debts and accidents.**—Each party agrees that the other party shall in no way be responsible for the debts of, or liabilities for accidents or damages caused by, the other party.

4. **Willful neglect.**—Willful neglect, failure, or refusal by either party to carry out any substantial provision of this lease shall give the other party the benefits of any proceedings provided by law.

5. **Farm records.**—The tenant shall keep a complete financial and production record of the entire farm business, which shall include a complete inventory of all property used in the farm business and a complete record of all purchases and sales related to the farm business. Such records are to be kept on mutually acceptable forms and shall be of such nature as to be usable by landlord and tenant in studying the farm business, in making financial and property settlements, and for purposes related to social security and income tax. Such records shall include appropriate sales statements, receipts, checks, and similar evidence and shall be accessible to the landlord at all times. Accounts between the two parties shall be settled on or about ....

6. **Arbitration of differences.**—Any differences between the parties as to their several rights and obligations under this lease that are not settled by mutual agreement after thorough discussion, shall be submitted for arbitration to a committee of three disinterested persons, one selected by each party hereto and the third by the two thus selected; and the committee's decision shall be accepted by both parties.

7. **Additional agreements:**

....

....

....

....

....

....

IN WITNESS WHEREOF, the parties have signed this lease on the date first above written.

Witnesses: .... [SEAL]
(Landlord)

.... [SEAL]

.... [SEAL]
(Tenant)

(Acknowledgment in appropriate form to be attached.)

Figure 6-11

SHARE OPERATING AGREEMENT ON A DAIRY FARM*

I. Purpose and Period Covered

A. This agreement is made this ______ day of ______________, 19_____,

between ________________________, hereinafter called the owner,

and ________________________, hereinafter called the oeprator.

B. The sole purpose of this agreement is to operate a farm business on

the following described real estate: ________________________________

____

C. This agreement shall become effective on the ______ day of

_______________, 19_____, and from year to year thereafter unless written notice of termination is given by either party to the other

on or before the ______ day of _______________, which shall be not less than six months, immediately preceding the date of termination.

II. Contributions

A. Owner to furnish all land, buildings, cattle, and machinery. It shall be his responsibility to make capital improvements as they are necessary.

B. Operator to furnish and be responsible for hiring, paying, and managing all labor for the operation of the farm.

C. It is agreed that supplies (especially roughage) shall be considered on an "as is" basis at the beginning and end of this agreement. No accounting for difference in quantity or quality will be made unless specified in this agreement.

III. Management

A. General operating plans shall be discussed and agreed upon at the beginning of each year. Adjustments that appear desirable during the year shall be made after being agreed upon by both parties.

B. All capital purchases involving more than _________ dollars shall be mutually agreed upon.

C. A current record of all operating farm receipts and expenses shall be kept by one of the parties to this agreement.

IV. Financial Settlement

A. Receipts

1. All receipts from sale of milk and bob calves shall be split 50-50.

*Complied by Dwight K. Eddy, Extension Economist, Department of Resource Economics, The Extension Service, University of Vermont, Burlington, Vermont. Revised 9/71.

Figure 6-11 Cont.

2. All receipts from sale of Capital items, such as cull beef, shall go to the farm owner.

B. Expenses

1. All operating expenses, with the exception of hired labor, shall be split 50-50 between owner and operator.
2. All labor costs shall be the sole responsibility of the operator.
3. All Capital Costs, including the purchase of one-half of the raised animals, shall be the sole responsibility of the owner. (This will normally be at the time of freshening but can be at any time mutually agreed upon.)

V. Living Arrangements

Living arrangements are to be provided for both owner and operator and their families. If an additional house is rented for either party, the rental cost shall be shared the same as other farm operating expenses. If either party furnishes the board of the other, the party so furnished shall pay

to the one providing the board ________ dollars per month as his share of the cash cost of such board.

VI. It is further agreed that liability insurance on the farm shall be carried in the name of both parties. Minimum coverage shall be $50,000 for liability and $500 for medical payments.

VII. Arbitration

If any matter pertaining to the farm business cannot be settled by mutual agreement, that matter shall be submitted to one disinterested person agreeable to both.

____

Owner and Wife

____

Operator and Wife

____

Date

Figure 6-12

INCOME-SHARING CONTRACT WITH GUARANTEED WAGE*

Section I. Date, Contracting Parties, Description of Property, and Term of the Contract.

1. This contract is made this ______ day of ______________, 19____, by and between ______________________, hereinafter called the Owner, and ______________________, hereinafter called the Operator.

2. The Owner, in consideration of the agreements with the Operator hereinafter set forth, hereby employs the Operator to occupy and to operate his farm containing ________ acres, located in ____________________ Township, ____________________ County, Vermont, legally described as the ____________________, ____________________Twp. ______________, Range ____________________, with all fixed improvements thereon except ____

____

3. This contract shall become effective on the ______ day of ______________, 19____, and shall continue in force for one year or until the ________________ day of ____________________, 19____, and from year to year thereafter unless written notice of termination is given by either party to the other on or before the ______________ day of ____________, which shall be not less than 90 days, immediately preceding the date of termination.

Section II. Land Use and Cropping Program

It is the intent of both parties that the land covered by this contract shall be improved and its yielding capacity increased by means of an aggressive cropping program and good cultural practices carried out on a continuing long-term basis. The farm will carry approximately ______________ cows and accompanying stock at the beginning of this lease and it is the intent to have not less than this number. It is estimated that this farm should carry ________ cows at the end of five years and it is the intent of both parties to work toward that objective.

It is the intent of both parties to operate the farm approxiamtely on the basis of ____________________ acres of corn silage, ____________________ acres of new seedings (in small grain or otherwise), ________ acres of hay in rotation, ________ acres of hay not in rotation, and ________ acrès of cash crops.

*Adapted from "Farm Leases", New Hampshire Extension Service.

Figure 6-12 Cont.

The Owner and the Operator shall mutually agree on the general plan of operations at the beginning of each year in the life of this contract.

In order to build up the land as rapidly as possible, the following land management practices will be observed by the tenant unless otherwise mutually agreed upon at the beginning of each year.

1. Not less than ________ acres of tillage land will be plowed, prepared and fertilized and reseeded to a legume mixture during each crop year.
2. In seeding down the above-mentioned acreage, sufficient lime shall be applied to bring the ph. up to ____, and not less than ____ pounds of 8-16-16 or its equivalent shall be applied per acre.
3. Acid phosphate shall be distributed in the gutters back of the cows in the stall-feeding season, at the approximate rate of ____ pounds daily per cow.
4. No crop other than hay shall be grown on the same land more than two years in succession without the consent of the owner.
5. The manure from the cow stable shall be protected from leaching as far as facilities permit and shall be spread on the land at the rate of not more than ____ tons for top dressing and not over ____ tons for corn in order to cover as large an acreage as possible each year.
6. The fields which are subject to heavy erosion shall be managed to reduce the loss of soil as far as practicable.
7. No hay shall be sold from the farm during the first two years of this lease without the consent of the owner. Not over __________ of hay are to be sold from the farm in subsequent years without the owner's consent except that at the termination of this lease, the tenant can sell his share of the jointly-owned hay and silage. However, the owner shall have the privilege of buying at appraised value such amounts of hay and silage as may be needed to carry the owner's livestock to the pasture season.
8. An area of pasture consisting of approxmately ________ acres shall be developed and maintained at a high level of production by application of fertilizer and lime in accordance with approved practices.
9. Both parties desire to expand the acreage of improved pasture in order to increase the capacity of the farm. The Owner and the Operator mutually agree that fertilizer and lime will be applied to this area as specified in subsection 8 above, providing the Owner clears, levels and prepares the land for improved pasture by application of ____ ton of lime and ____ pounds of 8-16-16 or its equivalent.

Section III. Liability for Accidents.

Both parties agree that farm comprehensive liability insurance with a minimum coverage of $10,000 for liability and $250 for medical payments will be carried in the joint names of the Owner and the Operator and covering the liability of either or both parties for accidents associated with the use of the above described property.

Section IV. The Owner Agrees to:

1. Furnish the land and the fixed improvements referred to in Section I.

Figure 6-12 Cont.

2. Furnish all machinery, equipment, livestock, feed, seed, and supplies and to pay all expenses incurred for the operation of the farm.

3. Provide the labor and the materials for making all major improvements and major repairs, and for the construction of new buildings, drains, and fences and provide the materials for the minor repair and minor improvement of buildings, fences, and drains on the farm.

4. Share the responsibility for the management of the farm with the Operator as follows: ____

____

5. Pay all taxes and assessments against the real estate, all taxes on the Owner's personal property, and all insurance on the improvements, crops, feed, equipment, and livestock owned by him.

Section V. The Operator Agrees to:

1. Furnish all of the labor required to operate the farm in a husbandlike manner, including labor for the minor repair of the buildings, fences, drains, and the machinery and equipment. If the Operator is unable to pay for the additional hired labor needed to operate the farm, the Owner shall advance to the Operator without interest the funds needed for the payment of his hired labor. The cost of labor employed on the farm, including the wage guaranteed to the Operator, shall not be included in the joint farm operating expenses.

2. Follow the land management practices listed in Section II.

3. Furnish all labor for the minor repair and the minor improvement of buildings, fences, and drains, and for constructing not more than ____________ rods of new fence, all materials for which shall be furnished by the Owner. The buildings, fences, and other improvements on the farm are to be kept in as good repair and condition as they are at the beginning of the contract or in as good repair and conditions as they may be put in by the Owner during the term of the contract; ordinary wear, depreciation, or unavoidable destruction excepted.

4. Haul to the farm, except when other arrangements are agreed to with the Owner, any material provided by the Owner for the minor repair or minor improvement of buildings, fences, and drains.

5. Keep livestock out of the fields when the soil is soft and protect sod crops, especially new seedings, from too close grazing that might impair the following year's crop.

6. Cut the weeds in lots, fence rows, and along roads whenever necessary to prevent reseeding.

7. Yield peaceable possession of the premises at the termination of this contract.

8. Cut no live trees, except by permission of the Owner. Leave all crop residues, including straw, on the land or spread them back on the land, and in no case remove such material from the farm without the consent of the Owner.

9. Pay all taxes and insurance on his personal property.

Section VI. Operator's Annual Compensation

1. The Owner guarantees the Operator an annual wage of $____________ for his labor, payable in twelve equal installments of $___________ each on the

Fig. 6-12 Cont.

________ day of each month or as follows: Jan. $________, Feb. $________,

Mar. $________, Apr. $________, May $________, June $________,

July $________, Aug. $________, Sept. $________, Oct. $________,

Nov. $________, Dec. $________. The guaranteed wage shall be considered as advances to the Operator for his labor against the total compensation due him at the end of the year.

2. At the end of the contract year the total compensation due the Operator for the year shall be calculated as hereinafter provided (Section VII) and the Owner shall pay the Operator, in cash, that amount minus the sum of the guaranteed wage advances, that were paid to the Operator during the year, the amount that was advanced to the Operator for the payment of the additional hired labor during the year, and the amount of any cash loans for personal use which may have been made by the Owner to the Operator during the year.

(a) If the Operator's total compensation for the year is less than the amount of his annual wage, the Operator nevertheless shall receive and retain his full guaranteed annual wage less any cash loans for personal use which may have been made by the Owner to the Operator during the year.

(b) When the total compensation due the Operator for the year exceeds the amount of his guaranteed annual wage, the Owner shall deduct the amount of the advance made to the Operator for the payment of the labor hired by the Operator during the year. If the Operator's compensation (above his guaranteed wage) is not sufficient to cover the advances made for the payment of his additional hired labor, the Operator shall not be required to pay the difference.

3. Each contract year shall begin with new account records without reference to gains or losses in the previous year.

Section VII. Calculating the Total Annual Compensation Due the Operator

The total compensation due the Operator for the year shall be ______ percent of the net farm income calculated as follows:

1. At the beginning and at the end of the contract year, the Owner and the Operator jointly shall list all working capital on the farm under the headings of livestock, equipment, supplies, This farm working capital shall include the Owner's property used or usable in the operation of the farm. Real estate shall not be included.

From this list a complete inventory shall be made up using as values

____________ dollars per cow, ____________ dollars per yearling heifer

over 10 months, ____________ per calf between 3 and 10 months, and

____________ per calf under 3, estimated sale values for supplies and sale values of equipment at beginning inventory minus an allowance of 8 percent for its depreciation for the ending inventory.

2. A complete and accurate record of the gross farm receipts and the joint farm operating expenses during the year shall be kept by the Owner and the Operator.

3. The gross farm receipts shall include the receipts from the sale of crops, livestock, livestock products, equipment and supplies, and the receipts

Figure 6-12 Cont.

from any custom work done by the Operator. If full-time employment is not available to the Operator on the farm and agreement has been made with the Owner for part-time work off the farm, the Operator's receipts from such work shall not be included with the farm receipts.

4. The farm expenses shall include all cash farm operating expenses with the exception of the following items: The annual wage guaranteed to the Operator and the wages paid for additional hired help; taxes, assessments, interest and principal paid on the real estate, insurance premiums paid on the fixed improvements on the land; the cost of materials and labor for the construction, major repair, or major improvement of buildings, fences, and drains.

5. The net farm income shall be determined by adding the sum of the gross farm receipts to the sum of the inventory at the end of the year and substracting therefrom the sum of the joint farm expenses and the sum of the inventory at the beginning of the year.

Section VIII. Management.

It is the intent of both parties that prior to the beginning of each new contract year, the general plans of management for the year will be discussed and mutually agreed upon and that from time to time during the year the parties will discuss adjustments to these plans. The owner agrees to advise with the Operator as to management practices and cooperating to make conditions most satisfactory for efficient operating practices. However, because the operator is furnishing labor, he will have the responsibility for handling labor and carrying on the farm operations.

Section IX. Provisions for Handling Receipts and Expenses.

1. All cash receipts, resulting from the operation of the farm, shall be deposited to the Owner's special farm account at the ______________________ Bank, located at ______________________.

2. Two types of checks can be drawn on this account by the Owner:
   (a) Operating expense checks: all farm operating expenses shall be paid from this account on checks marked "Operating Expense."
   (b) Advances to the Operator as installments on his guaranteed salary, advances to the Operator for the payment of the Operator's hired labor and personal withdrawal of funds by the Owner shall be marked "Personal."

Section X. Rights and Privileges.

1. While it is the intent, under the contract, that the Owner and the Operator shall share the management of the farm business, the Owner's decisions shall be binding on the Operator.

2. The Owner or anyone designated by him shall have the right of entry at any time and for any purpose not inconsistent with the rights of the Operator under this contract.

3. The Operator shall have the right to use the following without charge:
   (a) House

Figure 6-12 Cont.

(b) A plot of land not more than __________ acres for a family garden
(c) Milk for family use
(d) Dead or fallen timber for fuel

4. The Operator shall have the right to keep not more than ______ layers and grow ______ chickens and providing he pays for all supplies and feed consumed.

XI. Enforcement of Agreement and Arbitration.

1. Failure of either the Owner or the Operator to comply with the agreements in this contract shall make him liable for damages to the other party. Any claim by either party for such damages shall be presented in writing to the other party at least ______ days before the termination of this contract.

2. If satisfactory settlements cannot be made by the parties to this contract, they shall submit all matters of disagreement to a board of three disinterested persons, one of whom shall be appointed by the Owner, one by the Operator, and the third by the two thus appointed. The decision of this board shall be binding on both parties to this contract unless a matter of law or a sum exceeding $____________ is involved. Any costs for such arbitration shall be shared equally between the two parties.

3. If either or both parties to this contract die during the period of the contract, the terms of this contract shall be binding on the heirs, executors, administrators, and assigns of the party or parties involved.

4. This contract shall not be construed as giving rise to a partnership and neither party shall be liable for the debts or obligations incurred by the other without written consent.

5. ____

____

Section XII. Other Agreements.

____

____

Section XIII. Signatures.

______________________	______________________
(Date)	(Owner)
______________________	______________________
(Date)	(Operator)

Figure 6-13

DAIRY CATTLE MAINTENANCE CONTRACT

AGREEMENT made this __________ day of __________, 19___ by and between AGRICULTURAL ASSET MANAGEMENT CO. INC., a New York corporation having its principal office at Main Street, Salem, New York ("Agri-Asset"), as agent for the persons listed on Schedule "A" attached hereto and made a part hereof (the "Farmers"), and ____________________

____

residing at ____________________________________
(the "Operator").

WITNESSETH:

Whereas, Agri-Asset is the agent and attorney-in-fact for the Farmers who have purchased certain dairy cattle; and

Whereas, Agri-Asset manages such dairy cattle for the Farmers pursuant to one or more Dairy Cattle Management Contracts between Agri-Asset and the Farmers; and

Whereas, Agri-Asset wishes to engage the Operator to provide for the care and maintenance of said dairy cattle; and

Whereas, the Operator wishes to accept such engagement.

Now, Therefore, the parties hereto agree as follows:

1. *Engagement* On behalf of the Farmers, Agri-Asset hereby engages the Operator as an independent contractor to provide for the care and maintenance of certain cattle hereinafter described and defined, and the Operator hereby accepts such engagement as an independent contractor upon the terms and conditions hereinafter set forth.

2. *Term* Subject to the provisions for termination hereinafter provided, the term of this agreement shall be seven years, commencing with the date of the execution hereof.

3. *Delivery of Herd* The Operator hereby acknowledges delivery to him by Agri-Asset or its agent on behalf of the Farmer of _____ dairy cattle which are more specifically described and identified in Schedule B attached and made a part hereof. The dairy cattle delivered to the Operator, together with additions to and replacements of, hereinafter shall be collectively called the "Herd". All heifer calves to which Agri-Asset as agent for the Farmer shall be entitled hereunder, together with replacements thereof, if any, shall hereinafter be called the "Reserved Heifers".

4. *Condition of Herd* The Operator represents that he inspected the Herd prior to accepting delivery; that he was permitted to have it examined by a veterinarian of his selection prior to accepting delivery; that the Herd is in sound condition and free of disease or defect and suitable for use in accordance with this contract, and that neither Agri-Asset nor any person or entity has made any representation or warranty concerning the Herd except as specifically set forth herein.

5. *Duties* (a) The Operator shall maintain and care for the Herd and Reserved Heifers in a manner consistent with prudent dairy farming practices

Figure 6-13 Cont.

and shall bear the costs and expenses connected therewith, including assessments levied on the Herd or Reserved Heifers. Such care and maintenance shall include but not be limited to

(i) providing necessary feed, water, shelter, equipment and personnel;

(ii) maintaining a suitable health care program including necessary veterinary services and medication, if necessary;

(iii) breeding the Herd and Reserved Heifers to plus proven sires of the same breed;

(iv) maintaining the quality of the Herd by culling therefrom any animal or animals warranting such treatment in the normal course of the dairy business and replacing same with an animal or animals suitable for dairy purposes, it being understood that the Operator may keep the proceeds of the sale of any culled cow and apply same towards the purchase of a replacement cow which shall be the property of Agri-Asset as agent for the Farmers;

(v) milking the Herd on a regular and timely basis and selling the milk in the normal course of the dairy business on behalf of Agri-Asset, as agent for the Farmer; and

(vi) maintaining the size of the Herd and Reserved Heifers by replacing animals which die from whatever cause or become lost or stolen or in any other way missing from the Herd, it being understood that such replacement animals thereafter shall be the property of Agri-Asset as agent for the Farmers.

(b) If the Operator does not replace animals culled or which become lost, stolen or missing, Agri-Asset, on behalf of the Farmer, shall have the right to replace such animals at its own expense within twenty days. In such event, the milk proceeds payable to Agri-Asset pursuant to paragraph 8(b) hereof shall thereafter be increased to a sum equal to the purchase price of the replacement animal and the Operator shall have no further liability with respect to the replacement of the culled, lost, stolen or missing animal.

(c) Agri-Asset, on behalf of the Farmer, shall have the right to designate the sires to be used in the breeding of the Herd or Reserved Heifers. If such designation shall result in costs in excess of normal breeding fees, then Agri-Asset shall pay such cost differentials.

(d) Insurance proceeds, if any, paid to Agri-Asset as a result of the death or loss of an animal or animals shall be applied to the purchase of replacements.

(e) The Operator shall cull no more than ten per cent of the Herd during any thirty-day period without first obtaining the prior written consent of Agri-Asset.

6. *Reserved Heifers* (a) During each twelve-month period commencing with the date of the execution hereof, Agri-Asset, on behalf of the Farmers, shall be entitled to the number of first normal heifer calves born to the Herd which shall equal ten percent of the cows in the Herd at their original delivery to the Operator. If such computation shall result in a fraction, then the number of heifer calves due to Agri-Asset shall be increased or decreased to the nearest whole number. Such heifer calves to which Agri-Asset shall be entitled shall become its property and have been denominated "Reserved Heifers." All other calves born to the Herd during the term of this contract shall be the property of the Operator.

(b) The Reserved Heifers shall be maintained and cared for by the Operator in the manner described in paragraph 5 hereof, at Operator's cost and expense.

Figure 6-13 Cont.

Each Reserved Heifer shall be bred by the Operator to freshen between 25 and 32 months of age and each shall weigh no less than 650 lbs at 12 months of age, 1,050 lbs at 24 months of age and 1,200 lbs at freshening age. If a Reserved Heifer shall fail to achieve the prescribed minimum weight standards at any of the prescribed periods or shall fail to be bred to freshen between 25 and 32 months of age, then Agri-Asset shall have the right to reject it and to purchase in its stead, at the cost of the Operator, a Holstein–Friesian heifer meeting the prescribed standards. In such event, the newly purchased heifer shall be substituted for the rejected heifer and the rejected heifer shall become the property of the Operator.

(c) Upon freshening, the Operator shall sell the Reserved Heifer's offspring at the prevailing market price and shall remit the net proceeds thereof to Agri-Asset within thirty days of the sale.

(d) The Reserved Heifers shall be raised by the Operator at his own cost and expense at least until freshening, even if this should require their care and maintenance by him beyond the term of this contract. However, Agri-Asset may elect to remove all or a portion of the unfreshened Reserved Heifers upon the expiration of this contract, and as to those removed, the Operator shall have no further obligation. Upon freshening, the Reserved Heifer shall be added to the Herd unless Agri-Asset shall elect to withdraw it from the Herd. If the Reserved Heifer is added to the Herd, it shall be cared for and maintained by the Operator in the manner prescribed in paragraph 5 hereof. The Operator shall be entitled to all offspring of a Reserved Heifer added to the Herd except its first offspring which shall become the property of Agri-Asset in accordance with paragraph 6(c) hereof. If the Operator shall not have adequate facilities to properly care for and maintain the freshened Reserved Heifer, he may elect not to have such animal added to the Herd provided that he so notify Agri-Asset at least forty-five days prior to the estimated freshening date of the Reserved Heifer. In such event, Agri-Asset shall remove such Reserved Heifer from the Operator's care and control within a reasonable time prior to the animal's freshening.

7. *Extent of Services* The Operator shall devote all the time necessary to properly care for and maintain the Herd and Reserved Heifers. However, he shall not be required to devote all his time and energies exclusively to the care and maintenance of the Herd and Reserved Heifers and, if he so elects, may care for and maintain other dairy cattle of the same general quality on his premises. Regardless of whether the Operator shall maintain dairy cattle other than the Herd and Reserved Heifers, he shall use ear tags or other means of identification satisfactory to Agri-Asset so that at all times the Herd and Reserved Heifers in the possession, care or control of the Operator may be quickly and conclusively identified.

8. *Milk Proceeds* (a) In the regular course of business, the Operator shall sell the milk produced by the Herd. Such milk and the proceeds of its sale shall be the sole property of Agri-Asset as agent for the Farmer. The Operator shall have the privilege of receiving such proceeds as nominee for Agri-Asset, which privilege may be revoked by Agri-Asset at any time it considers the Operator to be in violation of any provision of this contract. The Operator specifically waives any rights he may have as a mechanic's or materialman's lienholder with respect to the milk produced by the Herd and the proceeds of its sale.

(b) Agri-Asset shall receive as agent for the Farmer $__________ per cow per month, or a total of $__________ per month for all cows in the Herd, and shall further receive $__________ per cow per month for each Reserved Heifer added

Figure 6-13 Cont.

to the Herd. All sums due hereunder shall be remitted monthly commencing ________________. However, it is agreed that the Operator will pay to Agri-Asset as agent for the Farmer twice the monthly sum due as and for the initial payment hereunder and shall not be required to remit anything with respect to the original Herd during the last month of the term hereof. All sums due hereunder shall be payable from the net proceeds of the sale of the milk produced by the Herd and the balance thereof shall be retained by the Operator. As used herein, the term "net proceeds" shall mean the gross proceeds from the sale of milk produced by the Herd, less direct operating costs exclusive of depreciation.

(c) The Operator agrees to take all action necessary or required of him by Agri-Asset so as to clearly indicate that the milk proceeds are the property of Agri-Asset as agent for the Farmers, including but not limited to noting on checks for milk proceeds remited to Agri-Asset on behalf of the Farmers that such payments are the Farmers' share of the milk proceeds. Furthermore, on tax returns and tax information forms prepared or filed by him, as well as on his own books and records, the Operator shall indicate that his share of the milk proceeds is only that portion provided for herein and not the whole thereof from which is subtracted Agri-Asset's share as agent for the Farmer.

(d) If during any period milk from cows other than those constituting the Herd shall be commingled with milk produced by the Herd in such manner that it is impossible to determine easily, quickly and conclusively the gross sales price of milk produced exclusively by the Herd, then the gross sales price for such period shall be determined by apportioning the gross sales price for all commingled milk for such period between the Herd and such other cows, taking into consideration the number of cows in the Herd and the number of such other cows during such period and the number of days in such period in which each cow produced milk.

9. *Books, Records and Reports* The Operator shall establish and maintain, to the satisfaction of Agri-Asset, books and records relating to the care and maintenance of the Herd and Reserved Heifers and the production and sale of milk. Within ten days after the close of each month, he shall report to Agri-Asset on the condition of the Herd and Reserved Heifers during such month, including relevant information concerning the culling and replacement of cows and the allocation of calves produced by the Herd and Reserved Heifers. He will also furnish Agri-Asset with an annual financial statement, including a balance sheet and statement of profit and loss. Such financial statement shall be furnished within sixty days of the close of the fiscal year of the Operator's farm or by March 1st if the fiscal year of the Operator's farm is on a calendar year basis.

10. *Inspection* Agri-Asset, by its designated agents or representatives, the Farmers or their designated agents or representatives and officials of The Chase Manhattan Bank, N.A., and any person who shall hold a security interest in any animal managed by Agri-Asset and maintained and cared for by the Operator pursuant to this contract, may inspect the Operator's premises and books and records periodically, at any time and from time to time between 6 A.M. and 6 P.M. during the term of this contract, to determine whether the Herd and Reserved Heifers are being maintained and cared for in all respects in accordance with this contract. Such rights of inspection shall include the right to inspect the Operator's milk receipts and breeding and veterinary records which relate to the Operator's responsibilities hereunder. The Operator hereby agrees to cooperate fully with Agri-Asset and the aforementioned persons having the rights of inspection

hereunder so that inspections may be conducted in an efficient and expeditious manner.

11. *Insurance* (a) At its own cost and expense, Agri-Asset agrees to obtain and maintain during the term of this contract named and optional peril insurance covering the full insurable value of the Herd and Reserved Heifers and public liability insurance on the Herd and Reserved Heifers in the sum of at least $300,000.

(b) At his sole cost and expense, the Operator agrees to obtain and maintain during the term hereof general liability insurance covering his farm in the sum of at least $300,000.

12. *Termination* (a) If the Operator shall at any time fail to remit to Agri-Asset the sums specified in paragraph 8(b) hereof, then Agri-Asset may terminate this contract immediately.

(b) If the Operator shall be deficient in any way in the fulfillment of his responsibilities hereunder, including the care and maintenance of the Herd and Reserved Heifers or the remittance of milk proceeds or other moneys due Agri-Asset (which evaluation shall be the sole and reasonable determination of Agri-Asset), and if such deficiency shall not constitute gross negligence, then the Operator shall be given a written statement of such deficiencies and shall be granted thirty days from the delivery of such statement to correct the deficiencies to the satisfaction of Agri-Asset.

(c) If the Operator shall be deficient in the fulfillment of his responsibilities hereunder in such a manner as to constitute gross negligence (which evaluation shall be the sole and reasonable determination of Agri-Asset), or if he shall fail to correct deficiencies not constituting gross negligence within the thirty days allowed, then Agri-Asset may terminate this contract immediately.

(d) For purposes of this contract, "gross negligence" shall mean such a substantial deficiency in the level of the Operator's care and maintenance of the Herd and Reserved Heifers that their health or safety are endangered or their general quality has declined significantly, or is likely to decline significantly, from the quality that existed at the time of their delivery to the Operator.

(e) This contract shall be terminated at the option of Agri-Asset if the Operator shall dissolve or become insolvent (however evidenced) or make a general assignment for the benefit of creditors, or if a proceeding under any bankruptcy or insolvency statute or law relating to the relief of debtors shall be commenced by or against the Operator, or if a receiver, trustee or liquidator shall be appointed of the Operator or of all or a substantial part of his assets, or if an order, judgment or decree shall be entered by a court of competent jurisdiction against the Operator and such order, judgment or decree shall continue unpaid and in effect for a period of sixty days without a stay of execution, or if an execution or writ or process shall be issued against the Operator whereby the Herd or Reserved Heifers, or any portion thereof, may be taken or restrained, or if the Operator in any way breached paragraph 13 hereof.

(f) Upon termination, Agri-Asset or its designated agents or representatives may enter upon the Operator's farm or other premises where the Herd or Reserved Heifers may be located, either by force, summary proceedings or otherwise, and remove the Herd and Reserved Heifers without further obligation or liability to the Operator. The Operator agrees to do nothing in any way to hinder or prevent the entry of Agri-Asset or the removal of the Herd and Reserved Heifers, and waives any right he may have to restrict such entry and

Figure 6-13 Cont.

removal. In addition, upon such termination, the Operator shall be entitled to no further payments under this contract and expressly waives any and all rights he may have to payments then or thereafter due him hereunder. Furthermore, upon termination, the Operator shall be liable to Agri-Asset for all losses, damages and expenses sustained or incurred by it personally or as agent for the Farmer arising from the Operator's breach of this contract or occasioned by the termination of this contract.

13. *Prohibition* The Operator represents and warrants that he is not the owner of the Herd or the Reserved Heifers and that his only rights with respect to them are contained in this contract. He further warrants and represents that except as herein specifically provided, he will not sell, secrete, mortgage, assign, transfer, lease, sublet, lend, part with possession of or encumber the Herd or Reserved Heifers or any portion thereof, or permit liens or charges to be effective thereon, or permit or attempt to do any of such acts.

14. *Right of First Refusal* (a) Upon the expiration of this contract, if Agri-Asset wishes to enter into a Dairy Cattle Maintenance Contract with another operator for the care and maintenance of all or a portion of the Herd and Reserved Heifers, it shall first offer the Operator the opportunity to enter into such a contract upon terms mutually satisfactory. If within thirty days after being offered such opportunity no contract is entered into between the parties, then Agri-Asset shall be free to enter into such a contract with another operator for the care and maintenance of all or a portion of the Herd and Reserved Heifers provided that the terms and conditions thereof are substantially the same as those offered to the Operator.

(b) If upon the expiration of this contract Agri-Asset wishes to sell all or a portion of the Herd, it shall first offer to sell to the Operator such portion thereof as it intends to sell. The purchase price to the Operator for the portion of the Herd to be sold shall be the lesser of 120% of the gross cost of such animals to Agri-Asset or the fair market value thereof. Upon notification of Agri-Asset's intention to sell the animals, the Operator shall have thirty days in which to consummate the purchase. If the purchase is not consummated within the specified time, then Agri-Asset shall be free to sell such animals to any other person on such terms and conditions as it wishes.

(c) The rights granted to the Operator by paragraphs 14(a) and 14(b) hereof are conditioned upon his having performed all his obligations under this contract in a manner completely satisfactory to Agri-Asset and upon his not having breached any of the terms and conditions hereof.

15. *General Security Interest and Financing Statements* The Operator's obligations and responsibilities hereunder shall be secured by a general security interest in all of his personal property, tangible and intangible, of whatever nature and wheresoever situated, including property presently owned or hereafter acquired and the products and proceeds therefrom, which interest the Operator hereby grants to Agri-Asset. At any time during the term of this contract and upon the request of Agri-Asset, the Operator agrees to execute and deliver to Agri-Asset a security agreement in the form approved by it which shall further reflect the general security interest granted hereby. The Operator authorizes and empowers Agri-Asset to prepare and file one or more UCC-1 Financing Statements naming him as debtor so as to enable Agri-Asset to perfect the security interest granted hereby.

Figure 6-13 Cont.

16. *Governing Law* The contract shall be governed by and construed in accordance with the laws of the State of New York.

17. *Independent Contractor* Nothing herein contained shall be construed to imply a partnership, agency, joint venture or lessor–lessee relationship between the Operator and Agri-Asset. In performing the services and responsibilities herein specified, the Operator shall act as an independent contractor and shall incur no obligation on behalf of Agri-Asset or hold himself out as having authority to incur obligations on behalf of Agri-Asset.

18. *Assignability* Agri-Asset may assign or delegate any or all rights and obligations hereunder upon prior written notice to the Operator. The Operator may not assign or delegate any or all of his rights or obligations hereunder without the prior written consent of Agri-Asset. This contract shall enure to the benefit of and be binding upon the heirs, executors, administrators, successors and assigns of the respective parties to the extent that assignment is authorized.

19. *Notices* Notices required or permitted to be given hereunder shall be sufficient if in writing and sent by registered or certified mail, return receipt requested, to the Operator at his residence and to Agri-Asset at its principal office. From time to time, either party may send to the other by such mail written notice of change of address. Delivery shall be deemed to have occurred two days after any notice is deposited in the mail.

20. *Entire Agreement* This contract contains the entire agreement and understanding of the parties concerning the subject matter hereof, and no representations, inducements, promises or agreements, oral or otherwise, between the parties with reference hereto not embodied herein shall be of any force or effect. None of the provisions of this contract may be changed, modified, waived, extended or abrogated except in writing signed by the parties hereto.

21. *Waiver of Breach* Neither the failure of either party to exercise any of its rights and options hereunder or to insist upon strict compliance by the other party, nor any custom or practice of the parties at variance with the terms of this contract, shall constitute a waiver of such party's right to demand strict compliance with the terms hereof. A waiver by either party of a specific default or right shall not affect or impair the right of such party with respect to a subsequent default or right.

22. *Invalidity* If a covenant or other provision of this contract is declared invalid, illegal or incapable of being enforced by reason of any rule of law or public policy, all other covenants and provisions hereof shall nevertheless remain in full force and effect, and no covenant or provision shall be deemed dependent upon any other covenant or provision.

23. *General* Whenever references are made herein to the Operator in the masculine gender and singular number, they shall be deemed to include the feminine and neuter genders and plural number as appropriate.

Figure 6-13 Cont.

IN WITNESS WHEREOF, the parties hereto have executed this contract as of the date hereinabove set forth.

AGRICULTURAL ASSET MANAGEMENT CO. INC.
as agent for the Farmers

By ____________________________________

____

Prepared by the Agricultural Asset Management Company, Inc., Main Street, Salem, New York 12865.

income will count if, under the rental arrangement, the farm landlord "materially participates" in the actual production of the farm commodities or in the management of production. In such event, the landlord must include the income in computing net-earnings from self-employment reported on the federal income tax return.

What does "materially participate" mean? Here is the answer. Farm rental income counts for social security if (1) The rental arrangement provides for the landlord or his agent—who can be any person or firm the landlord chooses to act for him or her—to take a significant part in the production or management activities involved in producing the farm commodities, and (2) The landlord or his agent or employee actually takes part in the production and management activities to the extent described in any one of the following four tests.*

TEST I

He must periodically *inspect production activities* from time to time to see if the farm work is being done properly, to observe that what should be done is actually being done, or to decide when various parts of the work should be finished. Inspection does not count if it is only a review of the farm property or improvements such as buildings, fences, and similar items. The number of qualifying inspections is *determined by the size and kind of the farm.* Inspections during the plowing, planting, cultivating, and harvesting seasons will count. The landlord must periodically consult with the tenant on efficient production such as the types of seeds to plant, the kind and timing of spraying and fertilizing, and what amount of the crop should be sold. Further, the landlord must furnish at least half of the tools, equipment, and livestock as well as making periodical consultation. The landlord is "materially participating" if he is responsible for paying at

*Social Security Administration SSI-66; Internal Revenue Service IRS Publication No. 363

least half of the production costs such as items directly related to production such as seeds, feed, plants, fertilizer, fuel, machinery repair, pesticides, and other supplies. Such factors as the living expenses of the tenant and his family, the value of work furnished by the tenant, or overhead expenses such as taxes and depreciation do not count.

Summary of Test I

Do three of the following:

a. *Inspect* Inspect the production activities periodically.

b. *Consult* Advise and consult with the tenant periodically.

c. *Furnish Equipment and Livestock* Furnish at least half the tools, equipment, and livestock used in producing the crop.

d. *Share Production Expenses* Advance, pay, or stand good for at least half the direct costs of producing the crop.

TEST II

The landlord is "materially participating" when, under the lease agreement, he can make decisions on a regular and frequent basis that significantly affect the success of the farm operation. Again, decisions that count include when to plant, cultivate, dust, spray, or harvest the crop; what goods to buy, sell, or rent; what farming practices are to be followed; what records are to be kept; when and how bills are to be paid; and like management practices.

The conditions of this test, however, are not met if the landlord merely decides what crops and livestock to raise, where to plant, and what land to leave idle.

Summary of Test II

Make Decisions Regularly and frequently make, or take an important part in making management decisions substantially contributing to or affecting the success of the enterprise.

TEST III

The landlord is "materially participating" if, under the lease arrangement, he works at least 100 hours spread over five or more weeks on activities connected with crop production. Work of less than 100 hours, or work in less than five weeks, may be "materially participating" if the landlord's efforts add up to a significant contribution to crop production. Kinds of qualifying work include cultivating, harvesting, purchasing, keeping records, caring for livestock, and repairing buildings, fences, and farm equipment used in connection with crop production. The qualifying work, it must be emphasized, must be called for in the lease agreement. Any agreement, for example, that provides for the landlord to work for the tenant part-time as his employee will not qualify.

Summary of Test III

Physical Work Work at least 100 hours spread over five or more weeks in activities connected with producing the crop.

TEST IV

The first three tests are based on the more common activities of farm landlords. When a landlord does not meet the conditions of Tests I, II, and III, he may under certain conditions qualify. In such cases the landlord should ask his social security officer or the Internal Revenue Office for a decision.

Summary of Test IV

Combination of Factors Do things which, considered in their total effect, show that you are materially and significantly involved in the production of the farm commodities. Any doubtful cases should be submitted to your social security office or to an Internal Revenue Service office for a decision.

[¶609] AGRICULTURAL PROGRAM PAYMENTS COUNT FOR SOCIAL SECURITY

Income from government payments received by the landlord who materially participates in production count for social security in the same way that such payments count for the tenants. In addition, to count for social security purposes, these program payments must be included as earnings for income tax purposes.

[¶610] SOCIAL SECURITY BENEFITS UNDER AGE 72

If the landlord gets cash social security benefits while under the age of 72, the farm rental income must be counted in the landlord's earnings if he is "materially participating."

[¶611] DREAMSTREET

One of the most exciting uses of individually tailored leases, partnerships, limited partnerships, and joint venture undertakings has developed in Walton, (Delaware County) New York 13856. As various investors have joined their farms and purebred cattle under what is known as W & J management, the operation has reached out to include twenty farms and 1,500 registered Holsteins. Each farm is owned by an individual or by a small group of acquainted persons who form a partnership. W & J as management provides managerial services, accounting and cropping services, relief milkers, heifer raising, bulk purchasing and merchandising of the thoroughbred cattle of the investors. The total value of land and purebred cattle under W & J management in 1977 exceeded $20,000,000.00.

The Dreamstreet model demonstrates the workability of imaginative management and the usefulness of the various forms of leasing discussed in this book.

7

Converting Farm Income into Wealth

[¶700] BUDGETING A MARGIN OF SAVINGS TO BUILD CAPITAL

Every farmer increases his wealth by budgeting his income to provide a margin of savings. Accumulated savings provide the nest egg for the down-payment in buying livestock, equipment, land, and a farm.

Charles Dickens stated the principle in *David Copperfield* like this: "Annual income twenty pounds, annual expenditures nineteen six, result happiness. Annual income twenty pounds, annual expenditures twenty pounds ought and six, result, misery."*

[¶700.1] Income Into Capital

The building of an agricultural estate proceeds by using income to build capital. This means that a farm family must decide early in its life how its members are to use their money.

How the family uses its money is a personal policy set to achieve its life goals. The family can fritter away its income on trivia. It can over-buy on credit, travel the weekend bar circuit, "get away" on flights to Bermuda. Or it can save to build a down-payment on the farm land the family wants to buy or the cow, or the machine that will make production more profitable.

*Any farm family will benefit by borrowing from the public library *Sylvia Porter's Money Book* (Garden City: Doubleday & Company, Inc.).

[¶700.2] The Family Sets Its Goals

These goals must be realistic, not idle and unrealizable fancies. The family decides what it wants to do with its money! The young farm family shapes its policy by writing down its goals (see Figure 7-1). These are of three types—(1) For the next year, (2) For the next five years, and (3) For age 50.

[¶701] CAPITAL GAINS AND THE MINIMUM TAX*

For many years, the Internal Revenue Code has provided favorable tax treatment to gains realized upon sales and exchanges of capital assets. Now, the Revenue Act of 1978 treats capital gains more favorably than ever before. The Revenue Act makes significant reduction in the capital gains tax for both sole proprietors and corporate farmers. These provisions are discussed below, but their impact on the farmer's pursuit of wealth should be carefully reviewed with his tax lawyer.

[¶701.1] Impact of the Revenue Act of 1978

The Revenue Act of 1978 effectively reduces the maximum tax rate on long-term capital gains to 28 percent by increasing the capital gains deduction from 50 percent to 60 percent of the net long-term capital gains occurring after October 31, 1978, and by excluding the deductible portion of long-term capital gains from the regular, add-on minimum tax (still applicable to the more exotic items of tax preference income) and terminating the poisoning of the maximum tax by items of tax preference income.

New Alternative Minimum Tax on Tax Preference Income. The deductible portion of long-term capital gains, no longer subject to the add-on minimum tax, is now subject to an alternative minimum tax which, though assuring at least a moderate income tax payment by taxpayers with significant capital gains, cannot result in an effective capital gains tax rate above 28 percent. An individual pays the alternative minimum tax only when it exceeds that person's regular taxes (including taxes on long-term capital gains and any add-on minimum tax liability). The alternative minimum tax is imposed on the individual's taxable income computed under normal rules, plus the taxpayer's adjusted itemized deductions and deductible portion of long-term capital gains, reduced by

*Portions of this section were adapted from *Summary and Explanation of the Revenue Act of 1978 and the Energy Tax Act of 1978*, published by the Institute for Business Planning, IBP Plaza, Englewood Cliffs, N.J. 07632.

Figure 7-1

FAMILY POLICY

Date: ________________

HERE ARE OUR GOALS:

Goals For This Year

19____.

1.

2.

3.

4.

Goals For The Next 5 Years

by 19____.

1.

2.

3.

4.

Long Range Goals

by Age 50 20___.

1.

2.

3.

4.

---

a $20,000 exemption. The result is subject to a flat rate of between 10 and 25 percent. As this tax is only imposed if it is higher than the taxpayer's ordinary income tax and regular minimum tax liability, it is impossible for the maximum rate on long-term capital gains to rise above 28 percent. The new alternative minimum tax is effective for all taxable years beginning after December 31, 1978.

Repeal of Alternate Tax on Capital Gains. The one exception to the general rule that the Revenue Act of 1978 reduces the tax rate on long-term capital gains is with respect to the first $50,000 of such gains incurred by very high bracket taxpayers. The 1978 law repeals the alternative tax on long-term capital gains, which permitted taxpayers to have the first $50,000 of long-term capital gains taxed at only 25 percent, rather than a maximum of 35 percent. However, since this change really adversely affects only those taxpayers for whom all capital gains are taxed at the maximum 28 percent rate, this should not prove a significant concern to estate planners. The repeal of the alternate computation of the tax on long-term capital gains is effective for taxable years ending after October 31, 1978.

[¶701.2] Election to Exclude Gain from Sale of Residence

Under prior law, an individual who reached the age of 65 could elect to exclude from gross income a portion of the gain realized on a sale of his principal residence. Under Section 121, this one-time election was available only if the taxpayer reached age 65 before the sale date and he owned and used the property as his principal residence for 5 or more years during the 8 years preceding the sale. The amount of gain excludable under Section 121 was determined by multiplying the entire gain by a fraction whose numerator was $35,000 and whose denominator was the sale price. For example, if the sale price was $100,000, then 35 percent ($35,000 ÷ 100,000) of the gain would be excluded from income.

The Revenue Act of 1978 amends Section 121 by lowering the age requirement, reducing the number of years of usage requirement and increasing the amount excludable from income.

Under the Revenue Act, the election is now available to taxpayers who have attained the age of 55 years. Exclusion of capital gain from home sale can only be used once in a lifetime. The taxpayer need only own and occupy the home as his principal residence for a total of 3 years out of the 5-year period immediately preceding the sale. (A special transitional rule is provided so that the Revenue Act does not disqualify individuals eligible under the old law.) All gain, but not more than $100,000 is excluded under the new Section 121.

The election does not apply separately to each spouse, and a married couple is permitted only one election. However, if each of two parties has made the election independently prior to becoming married, there is no recapture of taxes attributable to the gain excluded with respect to the sale of one of the residences. The Revenue Act applies to sales and exchanges after July 26, 1978. A special rule also provides that the holding period of a condemned or involuntarily converted residence may be tacked on to that of a replacement residence for purposes of qualifying for the Section 121 exclusion. The amount of gain excluded under Section 121 is not an item of tax preference. Capital gain from home sale is not an item of tax preference whether excluded under Section 121 or not.

[¶701.3] Rollover of Gain on Sale of Residence

Under Section 1034, an individual who sells his principal residence may elect to exclude the gain from the sale of income if he purchases a new residence within 18 months of the sale at a cost at least equal to the sale price of the former residence.

Under prior law, only the last principal residence purchased and used during this replacement period constituted a new residence for purposes of the rollover provision. Thus, taxpayers who needed to sell their residences within 18 months of a sale of a former residence were not eligible for more than one rollover.

Under the Revenue Act of 1978, a taxpayer who sells his principal residence within 18 months of a sale of a former principal residence may be eligible for a multiple rollover if his reason for making the sale is to relocate for employment purposes and the move satisfies the provisions of Section 217. Thus, if a taxpayer moves to a new locality with a reasonable expectation that he will be employed or remain at the new location for a substantial period of time, he may rollover gain from his previous residence to one purchased within 18 months of the sale. However, in order to qualify for this treatment, the sale must be made in connection with the commencement of work at a new principal place of work and the individual must satisfy both the geographic and length of employment requirements under Section 217.

The provision applies to sales and exchanges of principal residences after July 26, 1978.

[¶702] "GOLD MINE" PROVISIONS FOR INVESTMENT CREDIT UNDER THE REVENUE ACT OF 1978

For the farmer who is plowing income into capital, several provisions of the Revenue Act of 1978 have a gold mine value.

[¶702.1] Investment Credit

The first provision deals with investment credit. The 10 percent investment credit rate, scheduled by former legislation to drop to 7 percent in 1981, has been made permanent. The Revenue Act permanently sets the annual limit on used property eligible for the credit at $100,000. The Revenue Act, however, limits the amount of credit a farmer taxpayer may use to offset tax liability in any one year as equal to the first $25,000 of tax liability plus 90 percent of tax liability in excess of $25,000. The increase in the limit will be phased in by 10 percent a year starting with 60 percent in the year ending in 1979 and rising to 90 percent by 1982.

Further good news for farmers is investment credit for the rehabilitation expenditures on buildings in use over 20 years.

[¶702.2] Extension of the Law for Agricultural Structures

Another important provision is the extension of the law which makes investment credit available for single-purpose livestock and horticultural structures or enclosures. This extension is effective for tax years after August 15, 1971.

The structure for which investment credit is available must be designed, constructed, and used for housing, raising, and feeding livestock and their produce. The structure must include equipment to contain the livestock and to provide water, feed, and temperature control as necessary. The term "livestock" includes poultry and such buildings as used to breed chickens or hogs, to produce milk from dairy cattle, or to produce feeder cattle or pigs, broiler chickens, or eggs.

Investment credit is further extended to greenhouses specifically designed, constructed, and used for the commercial production of plants or mushrooms.

[¶702.3] Rehabilitation Expenditures

The investment credit is extended to certain expenditures for the rehabilitation of existing business and commercial properties, except those which are used for residential purposes.

Expenditures for which the credit may be claimed are those incurred to rehabilitate a building that has been in use for at least 20 years. The credit may be claimed only once on a given building during any 20-year period. The separate rehabilitation of a major portion of a building, however, may qualify as the rehabilitation of a separate building. The cost of renovation must be a capital expense for property with at least a 5-year useful life. In addition, 75% or more of the existing external walls of the building must remain in place. The qualified rehabilitation costs are treated as an investment in new property, so the $100,000 limit on used property does not apply. Qualifying expenditures incurred after October 31, 1978, are eligible for the credit.

Thus, for example, should a farmer in 1981 decide to rehabilitate a dairy barn built in 1960, the work would be eligible for investment credit, provided that not more than 25 percent of the exterior walls are replaced.

[¶702.4] Business Energy Credit

Farm businesses may claim an additional 10% investment credit for certain energy property acquired and placed in service after September 30, 1978, and before January 2, 1983, to the extent of basis attributable to this period. The useful life of the energy property must be at least 3 years. Energy property is property that comes within one of the six classifications of energy property discussed below.

1. *Alternative energy property* Within this classification are the following:
   a. a boiler that uses a substance other than oil, natural gas, or their products as its primary fuel;
   b. a burner for a combustor other than a boiler that uses a substance other than oil, natural gas, or their products as its primary fuel;
   c. equipment for converting a substance other than oil, natural gas, or their products into a synthetic liquid, gaseous, or solid fuel, other than coke or coke gas;
   d. equipment that modifies existing equipment which uses oil or natural gas as a fuel or as feedstock so that it will use some other substance alone or mixed with oil, if the other substance provides at least 25% of the fuel or feedstock;
   e. equipment that uses coal or lignite as a feedstock for the manufacture of chemicals or other products except coke or coke gas;
   f. pollution-control equipment that must be installed on or in connection with any of the equipment described above;
   g. equipment used for the unloading, transfer, storage, reclaiming from storage, and preparation at the point of use of a substance other than oil, natural gas, or their products for use in any of the equipment described above; and
   h. equipment used to produce, distribute, or use energy derived from a geothermal deposit, but only, in the case of electricity generated by geothermal power, up to the electrical transmission stage.
2. *Solar or wind energy property* Included is any equipment that uses solar or wind energy to generate electricity, heat or cool a structure, or provide hot water for use in a structure.

3. *Specially defined energy property* The property eligible for the additional credit under this classification is property that principally reduces the amount of energy consumed in any existing industrial or commercial process and is installed in connection with an existing industrial or commercial facility, including the following equipment:
   a. recuperator;
   b. heat wheel;
   c. regenerator;
   d. heat exchanger;
   e. waste heat boiler;
   f. heat pipe;
   g. automatic energy control system;
   h. turbulator;
   i. preheater;
   j. combustible gas recovery system;
   k. economizer; or
   l. other property specified by the Secretary of the Treasury by regulation.
4. *Recycling Equipment*
5. *Shale Oil Equipment*
6. *Equipment for producing natural gas from geopressured brine*

In general, oil and natural gas fueled boilers, portable air conditioners, and space heaters are no longer property eligible for the investment credit. Still eligible for the credit, however, are boilers used in a farm for farming purposes.

[¶703] DETERMINING CURRENT WORTH

From the beginning a farm family needs to know exactly where it stands financially. What is its current worth? What are the family's assets and liabilities? How does the family situation look on a balance sheet?

One of the most searching instruments for analyzing a farm family's financial position is the United States Department of Agriculture *Farm and Home Plan* (Figure 7-2). This form projects a complete farm operation by giving an overview of the items which need to be considered.

From the *Farm and Home Plan,* the farm family can extract basic data and visualize its net worth from Item A (4) like this:

Net Worth Statement

Date: ______________________________

Total Assets $______________________________

Minus Total Liabilities $ ______________________________

TOTAL NET WORTH $______________________________

(Subtract total liabilities from total assets to get net worth)

Figure 7-2

USDA–FHA
Form FHA 431–2
(Rev. 12–1–72)

Position 3

FORM APPROVED
OMB NO. 40–R1077

FARM AND HOME PLAN

COUNTY

NAME OF HUSBAND	NAME OF WIFE	ADDRESS

AGES OF PERSONS IN HOUSEHOLD	HUSBAND	WIFE	SONS	DAUGHTERS	OTHERS	TOTAL ACRES (OWNED) (RENTED)	CROP ACRES (OWNED) (RENTED)	OPERATED SAME FARM LAST YEAR? ☐ YES ☐ NO	WRITTEN LEASE? ☐ YES ☐ NO

TERMS OF LEASE	PERIOD OF LEASE
	, 19 TO , 19

A. FINANCIAL STATEMENT AS OF , 19

PROPERTY OWNED		
REAL ESTATE (LOCATION):	ACRES	VALUE
FARM		$
OTHER REAL ESTATE		
TOTAL REAL ESTATE		$
LIVESTOCK:	NO.	VALUE
LIVESTOCK HELD FOR SALE		$
DAIRY COWS		
BEEF COWS		
OTHER CATTLE		
BROOD SOWS AND GILTS		
OTHER HOGS		
EWES		
OTHER SHEEP		
POULTRY		
TOTAL LIVESTOCK		$
MACHINERY AND EQUIPMENT:		
TRUCK(S): YR. ____ MAKE ____		$
TRACTOR(S): YR. ____ MAKE ____		
MAJOR ITEMS OF EQUIPMENT		
OTHER FARM MACHINERY		
TOTAL MACHINERY AND EQUIPMENT		$
OTHER PERSONAL PROPERTY:	QUAN. OR NO.	VALUE
CROPS HELD FOR SALE		$
GROWING CROPS		
FEED		
SEED AND SUPPLIES		
AUTO: YR ____ MAKE ____		
HOUSEHOLD GOODS		
CASH ON HAND		
BONDS AND INVESTMENTS		
ACCTS. OWED US—COLLECTIBLE		
TOTAL OTHER PERSONAL PROP.		$
TOTAL PROPERTY OWNED		$

DEBTS OWED					
NAME AND ADDRESS OF CREDITOR	FINAL DUE DATE	INTEREST RATE	ANNUAL INSTAL.	AMOUNT DELINQ.	UNPAID BALANCE
LIENS ON REAL ESTATE:					
			$	$	$
TOTAL LIENS ON R. E.			$	$	$
LIENS ON CHATTELS AND CROPS:					
			$	$	$
TOTAL LIENS CHATTELS & CROPS			$	$	$
JUDGMENTS:					
TOTAL JUDGMENTS:			$	$	$

TAXES DUE: REAL ESTATE $ ________ PERSONAL $ ________

INCOME & SOCIAL SECURITY $ ________ TOTAL TAXES DUE $

ALL OTHER DEBTS (DOCTOR, STORE, ETC., DESCRIBE): $

TOTAL OTHER DEBTS $

TOTAL ALL DEBTS $

1. TOTAL OF CASH ON HAND, CROPS AND LIVESTOCK HELD FOR IMMEDIATE SALE, AND INCOME TO BE RECEIVED IN IMMEDIATE FUTURE	$
2. DEBTS AND EXPENSES WE WILL PAY FROM ABOVE CASH AND INCOME (Itemize)	$
3. CASH CARRY-OVER FOR NEXT YEAR'S OPERATIONS AFTER PAYING THESE DEBTS	$

	BEGINNING OF YEAR	END OF YEAR	INCREASE OR DECREASE
4. NET WORTH (TOTAL PROPERTY OWNED MINUS TOTAL ALL DEBTS)	$	$	$
5. TOTAL LAND DEBT			
6. TOTAL DEBTS OTHER THAN LAND	$	$	$

PERIOD COVERED BY PLAN: FROM ________ 19 ________ TO ________ 19

FHA 431–2 (Rev. 12–1–72)

Figure 7-2 Cont.

NOTE: All "actual" data to be completed by end of crop year

B. CROPS, PASTURE, ETC.—PRODUCTION AND SALES

	PLANNED						ACTUAL						
			OPERATOR'S SHARE						OPERATOR'S SHARE				
			UNITS FOR:						UNITS				
CROPS, PASTURE, SET-ASIDE PROGRAM PAYMENTS, ETC.	ACRES	YIELD PER ACRE	FARM USE	SALE	@	DOLLAR SALES	ACRES	YIELD PER ACRE	FARM USE	HELD FOR SALE	SOLD	@	CASH INCOME
1.					$	$						$	$
2.													
3.													
4.													
5.													
6.													
7.													
8.													
9.													
10.													
11.													
12.													
13.													
14. FARMSTEAD, GARDEN AND ROADS													
15. **TOTAL** (ENTER TABLE J, LINE 1)						$							$

C. LIVESTOCK AND PRODUCTS—PRODUCTION AND SALES

	PLANNED						ACTUAL						
			OPERATOR'S SHARE						OPERATOR'S SHARE				
			UNITS FOR:						UNITS				
LIVESTOCK AND PRODUCTS AND WOOL-MOHAIR PROGRAM PAYMENTS	NO.	PROD. PER ANIMAL	FARM USE	SALE	@	DOLLAR SALES	NO.	PROD. PER ANIMAL	FARM USE	HELD FOR SALE	SOLD	@	CASH INCOME
1.					$	$						$	$
2.													
3.													
4.													
5.													
6.													
7.													
8.													
9.													
10.													
11.													
12.													
13. MILK (LBS.)													
14. EGGS (DOZ.)													
15. **TOTAL** (ENTER TABLE J, LINE 2)						$							$

Figure 7-2 Cont.

D. IMPROVEMENTS AND KEY PRACTICES—FARM, HOME, AND FINANCIAL MANAGEMENT

CROPS; SOIL; LIVESTOCK; FINANCIAL MANAGEMENT; MAINTENANCE; REPAIRS; FOOD PRODUCTION AND CONSERVATION; HEALTH, HOME, ENVIRONMENTAL, COMMUNITY AND RURAL DEVELOPMENT ACTIVITIES; ETC.	WHEN TO DO IT	SOURCE OF FUNDS	ACTUAL ACCOMPLISHMENTS
TYPE OF ANALYSIS (____________________) MONTH			

E. FAMILY LIVING AND INSURANCE

WE PLAN TO PRODUCE, PROCESS, AND USE FOR OUR FAMILY:

ITEM	PLAN	ACTUAL	ITEM	PLAN	ACTUAL
MILK (GAL.)			GARDEN (SIZE)		
EGGS (DOZ.)			CANNED AND FROZEN:		
POULTRY (NO.)			VEGETABLES (QT.)		
PORK (LIVE WT. LB.)			FRUITS (QT.)		
BEEF (LIVE WT.-LB.)			DRY STORED VEGETABLES (BU.)		
OTHER MEATS (LIVE WT.-LB.)			DRY STORED FRUITS (BU.)		

TOTAL CASH VALUE OF FOOD ACTUALLY PRODUCED AND/OR PROCESSED FOR HOME USE $__________

TYPE OF INSURANCE	FACE VALUE			TYPE OF INSURANCE	FACE VALUE		
	PRESENT	PLAN	ACTUAL		PRESENT	PLAN	ACTUAL
DWELLING	$	$	$	LIFE	$	$	$
OTHER REAL ESTATE				HEALTH			
CHATTELS				HOUSEHOLD GOODS			
FARM LIABILITY				AUTO			

CHECK IF YOU HAVE					
	☐ RUNNING WATER	☐ REFRIGERATOR	☐ WASHING MACHINE	☐ TELEPHONE	☐ SEWING MACHINE
	☐ FULL BATH	☐ HOME FREEZER	☐ DRYER	☐ TELEVISION SET	☐ WATER HEATER

Figure 7-2 Cont.

F. CASH FAMILY LIVING EXPENSES	OTHER CREDIT NEEDED	FHA CREDIT NEEDED	PLANNED EXPENSES	ACTUAL EXPENSES
HOUSEHOLD OPNG.	$	$	$	$
FOOD INCL. LUNCHES				
CLOTH., PERS. CARE				
HEALTH				
HOUSE REPAIR AND SANITATION				
SCHOOL				
CHURCH, RECREATION				
PERS. INSURANCE				
TRANSPORTATION				
FURNITURE & OTHER				
TOTAL	$	$	$	$

G. CASH FARM OPERATING EXPENSES	OTHER CREDIT NEEDED	FHA CREDIT NEEDED	PLANNED EXPENSES	ACTUAL EXPENSES
HIRED LABOR	$	$	$	$
MACHINERY REPAIR				
FARM BUILDING & FENCE REPAIR				
INTEREST				
RENT				
FEED				
SEED				
FERTILIZER				
PESTICIDES & SPRAY MATERIALS				
OTHER SUPPLIES				
LIVESTOCK EXPENSE				
MACHINERY HIRE				
FUEL AND OIL				
PERSONAL PROP. TAX				
REAL ESTATE TAXES				
WATER CHARGES				
PROPERTY INSURANCE				
AUTO & TRUCK EXPENSE				
UTILITIES				
CURRENT OPNG. BILLS (TABLE A)				
TOTAL	$	$	$	$

H. CAPITAL EXPENDITURES	OTHER CREDIT NEEDED	FHA CREDIT NEEDED	PLANNED EXPENSES	ACTUAL EXPENSES
	$	$	$	$
DEBTS REFINANCED (TABLE A)				
TOTAL	$	$	$	$

I. CREDIT FOR:	OTHER	FHA	TOTAL	ACTUAL
FAMILY LIVING		$	$	$
FARM OPERATING				
CAPITAL EXPENDITURES				
TOTAL		$	$	$

J. SUMMARY OF YEAR'S BUSINESS	PLAN	ACTUAL
1. CROP INCOME (*Table B*)		
2. LIVESTOCK INCOME (*Table C*)	$	$
3. CONSERVATION PAYMENTS AND OTHER FARM INCOME		
4. TOTAL CASH FARM INCOME (*1, 2 and 3*)	$	$
5. CASH FARM OPERATING EXPENSES (*Table G*)		
6. NET CASH FARM INCOME (*4 Minus 5*)	$	$
7. NON-FARM INCOME		
8. TOTAL NET CASH FARM & NON-FARM INCOME (*6 Plus 7*)	$	$
9. CASH FAMILY LIVING EXPENSES (*Table F*)		
10. NET CASH INCOME (*8 Minus 9*)		
11. CASH CARRY-OVER (*Page 1, Line 3*)		
12. LOANS AND OTHER CREDIT (*Table I*)	$	$
13. INTEREST (*Table G*)		
14. TOTAL AVAILABLE (*10, 11, 12 and 13*)	$	$
15. CAPITAL EXPENDITURES (*Table H*)		
16. BALANCE AVAILABLE (*14 Minus 15*)	$	$
17. GROSS CASH INCOME (*4 Plus 7*)	$	$

K. DEBT REPAYMENT

TO WHOM OWED	AMOUNT DUE THIS YEAR (PRIN. AND INT.)	PLAN			ACTUAL AMOUNT PAID
		PRIN. AND INT. TO BE PAID	DATE	SOURCE OF FUNDS	
	$	$			$
INCOME AND SOCIAL SECURITY TAXES					
TOTAL	$	$			$

We agree to follow this plan and to discuss with the County Supervisor any important changes that may become necessary.

(DATE) (BORROWER) (WIFE)

(COUNTY SUPERVISOR)

☆ U. S. GPO: 1975-0-667-867

[¶704] BUDGETING AS ESSENTIAL IN ESTATE BUILDING

Four instruments help to visualize family policy in estate building. These are (A) the family budget; (B) the partial budget; (C) the cash flow schedule; and (D) the Pro-Ag Computerized Optimizing Plan.

A. THE FAMILY BUDGET

[¶705] THE FAMILY BUDGET AS A TOOL

The management of money in estate building begins with a family budget. This budget visualizes the farm family financial policy. It projects income and expenses for a period ahead—usually a calendar year (see Figure 7-3).

Figure 7-3 Farm Labor Family Budget Worksheet

Year 19____-Weekly Basis

Schedule I ESTIMATED OF TOTAL CASH INCOME

	Actual Previous Year	Estimated Next Year
A. Annual income-wage or salary	$9,100.00	$
B. All other anticipated earned income	$ 500.00	$
C. Income from interest on bank accounts, bonds, stocks, securities	$ 0	$
D. Less Social Security	$ 532.35	$
E. Total expected net income	$8,567.55	$
F. Weekly- excluding all other income	$ 164.76	$

Schedule II ESTIMATE OF FIXED OBLIGATIONS AND EXPENSES

A. Housing*	($25.00)	$
B. Heating-fuel*	($20.00)	$
C. Electricity*	($5.00)	$
D. Milk*	($5.00)	$
E. Telephone and long distance*	($5.00)	$
F. Food purchases*	($50.00)	$

*Prerequisites of farm labor for comparison with non-farm-workers. Garden, canning, assumed. 1977 estimate based on budget for farmer and wife, age 30, two children ages 10 and 5.

Figure 7-3 Cont.

Schedule III ESTIMATE OF WEEKLY HOUSEHOLD EXPENSES

A. Household supplies, soap, cleansing-items, toilet tissues, miscellaneous purchases	$4.00	$
B. Laundry and dry cleaning	$1.00	$
C. Transportation		
Family motor car	$7.00	$
Pick-up	$1.00	$
Tires & repairs	$3.00	$
D. Clothing	$5.00	$
E. Newspapers, magazines, books, birthday and Christmas gifts	$2.00	$
F. Baby-sitting	$2.00	$
G. Allowances to children	$1,00	$
H. Church	$1.00	$
I. Recreation, movies, county fairs, farm meetings, social, education	$5.00	$
J. Other weekly expenses	$2.00	$
K. Total- all weekly household expenses	$43.00	$

Schedule IV PROTECTION & HEALTH

A. Life insurance: whole life, endowment	$10.00	$
B. Health insurance	$8.00	$
C. Motor vehicle insurance	$4.00	$
D. Dental and other medical expenses	$2.00	$
E. Total- protection and health	$24.00	$

Schedule V TIME PAYMENTS

A. Installments	$12.00	$
B. Other payments	$ 3.00	$
C. Total time payments	$15.00	$

Schedule VI FEDERAL AND STATE INCOME TAXES

4 exemptions and standard deduction

A. Federal- 1040	$14.00	$
B. State- guesstimate average	$ 3.50	$
C. Total federal and state taxes	$17.50	$

Figure 7-3 Cont.

Schedule VII FINANCIAL LIQUIDITY AND CAPITAL GROWTH

A. Placed in emergency fund	$ 3.00	$
B. United States bonds	$ 4.32	$
C. Savings account	$ 7.00	$
D. Total financial liquidity and capital growth other than cash value of life insurance	$14.32	$

Schedule VIII WEEKLY BALANCE SHEET

Schedule I	$164.76			$
Schedule II			$50.00	$
Schedule III			$43.00	$
Schedule IV			$24.00	$
Schedule V			$15.00	$
Schedule VI			$17.50	$
Schedule VII			$14.32	$
Schedule VIII			$163.82	$
		+	.94	$

Net worth gain, excluding life insurance cash values and amortized values of installment purchases and excluding other income

Emergency	$156.00
U.S. Bonds	$224.64
Savings	$364.00
Total liquidity	$744.64

This budget chart is based on the analysis of actual family records of a young farmer prudently managing his money with a prudent farm wife- both husband and wife looking forward to farm ownership. His farm labor income is equivalent to a non-farm job paying $12,000 a year.

The experiences of life, however, are far from predictable. A budget is more than a mathematical formula and straight-jacket. It is closely related to the ups and downs of living and must always be subject to change as the life situation changes. The object of a good budget is to manage money to help the family reach its goals, not to compel the family household to conform to rigid rules. The budget may have to be revised from day to day, week to week, or month to month, but it always requires decisions in the allocation of income in terms of needs. Such decisions always take into consideration advancement toward defined goals.

[¶706] ESTABLISHING AN EMERGENCY FUND

No matter how carefully budgetary projections may be estimated, unforeseen circumstances may arise to make priority demands on money management. Every family needs to establish a reserve fund to which it may turn to tide its members over unanticipated and unforeseen occurrences. This fund can perhaps be best established in an interest bearing bank account, probably in the joint names of the husband and wife.

How much should the emergency fund be? The answer of course depends upon the size of the unexpected contingencies. As a rule of thumb, this emergency fund—to be carefully protected from routine invasions—should never be less than the equivalent of cash income for a two-month period. To this can be added a general savings account equivalent to a cash income of six months. This latter sum may seem like a sizeable amount, but it represents safety, and a substantial equity.

The first step in any budget-making process is to project *total cash income from every source* including interest, dividends, veteran's benefits, moonlighting, and the like. When this income is added up for the whole year, you will see how many dollars a family will probably handle. It is generally convenient to reduce this annual income to a weekly basis so that the family can see how much it will have available every seven days. Write this income sum in Section I of the Family Budget Chart.

[¶707] PROGRAMMED SAVINGS AS A FAMILY BUDGET CHARGE

To save, a family must decide a policy: How much is to be saved? One of the best tools for systematic saving is authority to the bank to transfer a specified sum to the savings account regularly.

[¶708] SYSTEMATIC BUDGETING BY U.S. SAVINGS BONDS

One of the ways by which a farmer can systematically build a part of his estate is by the purchase of United States Savings Bonds through a bond-of-the-month plan.

[¶708.1] Series E Bonds

Series E bonds will be sold at banks and other savings institutions until December 31, 1979. Final payroll sales of E bonds may continue until June 30, 1980.

The bond is automatically purchased from the farmer's checking account in denominations of $18.75 or $37.50, maturing respectively at $25.00 and $50.00. The bonds are purchased by an authorization filed with the local bank. The bonds themselves are delivered by mail to the farmer. Each bond must bear the social security number of the owner or owners. The bonds bear interest at the rate of 6 percent when held to maturity. They are exempt from state and local income and property taxes. They are safe. If a bond is lost, stolen, or destroyed, the government will replace it.

When redeemed, the difference between the price paid for the E bonds and the redemption value is subject to a federal income tax. At the election of the owner, however, the interest may be reported as it accrues.

The interest rate on new issues of U.S. Savings Bonds is subject to continuous review by the Treasury Department and may be increased or decreased in accordance with changes in economic and financial conditions.

Ownership registration depends on individual family circumstances. If the bond is registered in co-ownership, the surviving owners or beneficiaries become the immediate owners of the bond. Hence, the bonds do not have to be held in the estate of the decedent until the inheritance settlement is completed. While the value of the bonds is includable in the estate of the decedent for tax purposes, this does not affect the new owner's ability to cash the bonds or have them reissued.

Savings bonds, however, cannot be used as collateral. Moreover, they cannot be assigned, transferred, or sold. They may, nevertheless, be redeemed at most banks at any time after 2 months from the date of issue.

[¶708.2] Series H Bonds

Series H bonds are issued in denominations of $500, $1,000, $5,000, and $10,000 and have a maturity period of 10 years. Interest on Series H bonds is paid semiannually by the U.S. Treasury Department by check. Interest payments are on a graduated scale as follows: 4.2%, first 6 months; 5.8%, next 4½ years; 6.5%, final 5 years to yield 6% if held to maturity. Series H bonds are issuable on exchange from Series E bonds and savings notes in multiples of $500.

Series H bonds will be withdrawn from sale as of December 31, 1979, and replaced by Series HH bonds. The present E for H exchange offering will be terminated as of December 31, 1979.

[¶708.3] New Series EE and HH Bonds

Effective January 2, 1980, the Treasury Department replaces the current E and H U.S. Savings Bonds with EE and HH bonds.

The series EE bond—so named because it doubles in value between its purchase and maturity dates—has these features:

1. The purchase price is one-half the face value, e.g., $25 will buy a $50 (face value) bond.
2. The lowest available denomination is $50, face value. Other denominations are $75, $100, $200, $500, $1,000, $5,000, and $10,000.
3. The interest rate of 6 percent (for 5 or more years) remains, while the term to maturity is 11 years and 9 months.
4. The annual limitation on purchases increases from the present $7,500 (issue amount) to $15,000 (issue amount).
5. The new EE bonds are eligible for redemption 6 months after issue.
6. The requirement that a bond beneficiary must consent to a change in the bond has been eliminated.

The Series HH bond has these features:

1. Interest payments are a level 6 percent from day of issue.
2. Bonds purchased for cash (rather than through exchange of other savings bonds and notes) are subject to an interest penalty if redeemed before maturity.
3. The annual purchase limitation is $20,000 (face amount).

Series HH bonds can be bought for cash or obtained in exchange for the present Series E and Series EE bonds or savings notes, in multiples of $500. The HH bond has a 10-year maturity period and denominations ranging from $500 to $10,000.

B. CASH FLOW BUDGETING

[¶709] CASH FLOW BUDGETING

The cash flow budget is less common, but at the same time it has become more important because of the huge sums of money necessary to operate a modern farm. Rapid fluctuations in product prices, and general and persistent inflation contribute to the imperative use of cash flow budgeting.

Cash flow budgeting simply means estimating future values for all items that affect the cash position of the farm enterprise. It points out periods when cash will be short and thus when short-term debt or financing may be necessary. Most county extension agents make available various types of budget worksheets (for example, see Figure 7-4).

Because the cash flow budget is so important, interested farm families should obtain the basic manual from Cornell University and adapt it to their own enterprise.

While the manual and forms were designed for dairy farms, they can be adapted to any agricultural enterprise. Cornell periodically issues releases providing estimated prices for the next twelve months and expected annual inflation rates for most expense categories.

[¶710] CASH FLOW BUDGET TO IDENTIFY MONTHS WHEN CASH MAY BE SHORT

Farms need money to pay bills when they come due. Few other industries have such uneven balance of income and expenditures as agriculture. During what months will cash be short? During what months will the farm operate in the red? What short term financing may be necessary? What needs will crop and fruit farms have when expenses mount in the spring and income does not begin to flow until the fall? Over a period of a year, what do monthly worksheets show? As a matter of fact, some farmers have scheduled debt repayment schedules that bind against months when cash is short!

The worksheets developed at Cornell University cover a twelve-month period broken down by months. The worksheets collect basic data about the year to be budgeted. They provide space to estimate receipts, expenses, capital purchases and net cash flow. Here in Figure 7-5 is a suggestion for a cash flow program consisting of nineteen worksheets.* The information collected on the worksheets can then be gathered together and summarized as shown in Figures 7-6, 7-7, and 7-8.

*For a manual on *Monthly Cash Flow Budgeting: Worksheets and Instructions,* write Professor Robert A. Milligan, 113 Warren Hall, Department of Agricultural Economics, New York State College of Agriculture and Life Sciences, Cornell University, Ithaca, New York 14853.

Figure 7-4 Family Budget Projections
Estimate of Total Cash Income—Weekly

	JAN.	*FEB.*	*MAR.*	*APR.*	*MAY*	*JUN.*	*JUL.*	*AUG.*	*SEPT.*	*OCT.*	*NOV.*	*DEC.*	*Total 12 Months*	*Weekly*
I Income														
II Fixed Expenses and Obligations														
III Living Expenses														
IV Emergency Fund														
V Debts and Obligations														
VI Regular Savings														
VII Balance Sheet														

Figure 7-5 Cash Flow Worksheet Schedule

Worksheet 1.	Basic Data For Monthly Cash Flow Planning
Worksheet 2A.	Estimation of Cash Farm Receipts: Livestock Product and Livestock Sales
Worksheet 2B.	Estimation of Cash Farm Receipts: Crop and Other Income
Supplemental Worksheet 1.	Estimation of Receipts from Crop Sales
Worksheet 3A.	Estimation of Cash Farm Expenses: Labor and Feed
Worksheet 3B.	Estimation of Cash Farm Expenses: Machinery
Worksheet 3C.	Estimation of Cash Farm Expenses: Livestock
Worksheet 3D.	Estimation of Cash Farm Expenses: Crops
Worksheet 3E.	Estimation of Cash Farm Expenses: Real Estate Expenses
Worksheet 3F.	Estimation of Cash Farm Expenses: Utilities, Marketing, Misc.
Worksheet 4.	Summary of Cash Farm Expenses
Worksheet 5.	Capital Purchases Planned
Worksheet 6.	Cash Inflow and Outflow: Including Nonfarm: Excluding Credit
Supplemental Worksheet 2.	Family Living Expenses
Worksheet 7.	Projected Cash Flow
Supplemental Worksheet 3.	Scheduled Debt Payments
Adjustment Worksheet 1.	Changes in Cash Farm Expenses and Capital Purchases
Adjustment Worksheet 2.	Changes in Cash Farm Receipts
Adjustment Worksheet 3.	Adjusted Cash Flow

Figure 7-6 Annual Cash Outflow: Sunland Farms

					Cash Farm Operating Expenses		
Month	*Labor*	*Feed*	*Machine*	*Livestock*	*Crop*	*Rent*	*Insurance & Building*
Jan.	566	1,502	566	396	—	—	—
Feb.	387	1,443	1,496	534	1,594	650	533
Mar.	611	1,336	705	464	3,149	—	56
Apr.	464	1,245	213	613	560	—	375
May	807	1,527	269	288	61	—	658
Jun.	1,107	1,901	441	530	1,825	—	115
Jul.	1,050	1,878	504	304	2,879	—	10
Aug.	919	1,129	1,288	774	561	—	175
Sept.	660	1,953	695	601	224	—	—
Oct.	920	1,641	924	214	131	—	—
Nov.	652	1,674	681	468	1,215	—	284
Dec.	466	1,462	227	378	—	—	320
TOTAL	8,609	18,691	8,009	5,564	12,199	650	2,526

Taxes	*Utilities*	*Interest*	*Misc.*	*Total*	*Capital Purchases**	*Family Expense*	*Total Outflow Ex. Princ. Payments*
165	3	22	315	3,535	1,230	664	5,429
—	251	4	323	7,215	728	882	8,825
—	9	—	144	6,474	547	404	7,425
—	270	—	154	3,894	169	752	4,815
165	16	—	278	4,069	1,094	473	5,636
—	233	—	154	6,306	601	586	7,493
—	15	—	128	6,768	370	398	7,536
—	235	—	128	5,209	2,682	1,056	8,947
538	18	—	180	4,869	1,405	380	6,654
—	272	—	197	4,299	2,669	598	7,566
—	17	—	172	5,163	345	729	6,237
—	288	80	318	3,539	—	943	4,482
868	1,627	106	2,491	61,340	11,840	7,865	81,045

*Capital purchases include land, buildings, machinery, and livestock purchases for expansion.

Figure 7-7 Annual Cash Inflow: Sunland Farms

Month (produced)	*Number of cows*	*Production per cow*	*Total Production*	*Price per cut*	*Month (received)*	*Receipts*	*Livestock Sales: Last Year*	*Livestock Sales: Planned change*	*Livestock Sales: This Year*
Dec.	43	1,102	47,406	$9.50	Jan.	$ 4,504	$ 631	–200	$ 431
Jan.	41	1,176	48,225	9.40	Feb.	4,533	174	200	374
Feb.	43	1,030	44,274	9.30	Mar.	4,118	180	100	280
Mar.	44	1,244	54,740	9.10	Apr.	4,981	628	–300	328
Apr.	43	1,212	52,103	8.60	May	4,481	38	200	238
May	45	1,360	61,182	8.20	Jun.	5,017	—	200	200
Jun.	43	1,398	60,124	8.40	Jul.	5,050	2	200	202
Jul.	47	1,252	58,837	8.80	Aug.	5,178	978	–700	278
Aug.	47	1,136	53,381	9.20	Sept.	4,911	4	200	204
Sept.	47	1,153	54,203	9.40	Oct.	5,095	433	–100	333
Oct.	47	1,201	56,459	9.30	Nov.	5,364	118	100	218
Nov.	46	1,239	57,008	9.85	Dec.	5,615	207	—	207
TOTAL			647,942			$58,847	$3,393		$3,293

Figure 7-8 Cash Flow Summary: Sunland Farms

Month	Cash Inflow Less Outflow Excluding Credit Transactions	Scheduled Debt Payments	Capital Purchase Loans	Uncommitted Cash Flow	New Short Term Debt	Additional Debt Payments	Cash Flow This Month	Cash Flow Balance $1,200
Jan.	$ 657	$ –	$ –	$ 677	$ –	$ 300	$ 357	$1,557
Feb.	6,420	–	–	6,420	–	450	5,970	7,527
Mar.	(2,453)	–	–	(2,453)	–	2,100	(4,553)	2,974
Apr.	1,647	–	–	1,647	–	2,000	(353)	2,621
May	(380)	–	–	(380)	–	–	(380)	2,241
Jun.	(1,628)	–	–	(1,628)	–	–	(1,628)	613
Jul.	(2,904)	–	–	(2,904)	5,000	–	2,096	2,709
Aug.	(1,926)	–	–	(1,926)	–	–	(1,926)	783
Sept.	(994)	–	–	(994)	2,000	150	856	1,639
Oct.	(1,222)	–	–	(1,222)	–	–	(1,222)	417
Nov.	89	–	–	89	–	300	(211)	206
Dec.	8,171	–	–	8,171	–	7,300	871	1,077
TOTAL		$ –			$7,000	$12,600		

C. PARTIAL BUDGETING

[¶711] PARTIAL BUDGETING AS AN OPTIMIZING INSTRUMENT

Continually, the farmer must make decisions: What is best to do? At this point the farmer in partial budgeting has an instrument to guide him. The partial budget is a mathematical tool. The partial budget assembles and organizes information on prices, costs, technology and related factors to help a farm family arrive at sound financial decisions with respect to the profitable management of calculated farm resources.

On the basis of data in the partial budget, the farmer has guidance in answering three questions:

1. What products should be produced and in what quantity?
2. What are the most cost-efficient methods of production to be followed?
3. How will the products produced be marketed?

Each of these three questions require answers. All three relate decision-making to net returns.

A comprehensive farm budget projects costs and income for a period budgeted. The items are guesses as to what is expected to happen. A comprehensive farm budget schedule form may be obtained from any county extension agent. A partial budget, on the other hand, includes estimates of only the changes in costs and returns that may result from alterations in the form of the farm business organization, the allocation of farm resources, and the character of operations. Thus, partial budgeting does not show the net income of the whole farming system, but rather the probable difference in net income from pursuing alternative plans.

When the use of any resource is changed, four possible maximum effects may be estimated:

1. *increased costs* some items may go up.
2. *decreased receipts* income from some operations may decline.
3. *decreased costs* some items may go down.
4. *increased receipts* income from some operations may go up.

The partial budget is a tool to be used when farmers are considering changes in proposed uses of resources. Partial budgeting reduces guesswork in decision making.

A partial budget includes the four basic items discussed above. These factors may be put down on paper as a formula:

A		B	
Increased costs	$____	Increased Receipts	$____
Decreased Receipts	$____	Decreased Costs	$____
Total	$____	Total	$____
Total A		Total B	
(added costs)	$____	(added income)	$____
Total B		Minus Total A	
(added income)	$____	(added costs)	$____
		= net change in farm income	

If the total of B (added income) is greater than A (added costs) the farm management decision may be to make the change-over.

The value of exploring alternatives of farm budgeting depends upon four major acts. The farmer must:

1. explore the various alternatives open to him;
2. select the systems to be budgeted;
3. assemble all relevant information on resource requirements for each alternative allocation of resources to be included in the partial budget, including production or yield expectations; and
4. assemble information on prices of resources and products and estimated future prices for products.*

[¶712] THREE EXAMPLES OF PARTIAL BUDGETING

Here are three examples of partial budgeting:

Example 1

Problem: Shall we buy machinery or hire custom work? Is it more profitable to buy a machine or hire the work done?

Solution: By the use of the partial budget technique the farmer can determine the acreage necessary to break even as follows:

$$\frac{\text{Total Annual Overhead Costs}}{\text{Custom Rate per Acre less Operating Cost per Acre}} = \text{Break-even Acreage}$$

*Courtesy of Clifford Alston, University of Florida. See Circular 323, *Partial Budgeting,* (Gainesville: Florida Agricultural Extension Service).

Overhead (fixed) costs include such items as depreciation, interest on investment, taxes, insurance, non-operating repairs, and housing. The custom rate per acre can be obtained from the person performing the service.

Assume a farmer is considering whether to purchase a corn picker that costs $4,000. It has no salvage value, and is depreciated over 8 years, or $500 per year. Interest at 7 percent would be, $\frac{7\% \times \$4,000}{2}$, or $140 per year. Insurance, taxes, non-operating repairs, and housing amount to $60 per year, or total fixed costs of $700 per year. The custom rate is $12 per acre.

Operating (variable) costs include such items as labor, repairs, fuel, oil, and grease. Assume these amount to $4.00 per acre. Subtracting $4 from $12 for custom work leaves $8 per acre, the amount saved in cash costs per acre by owning a harvester rather than hiring the corn picked.

The above information, plus the formula, can be used to determine the number of acres needed to purchase a combine as follows:

$$\frac{\text{Overhead Costs} - \$700}{\text{Custom Rate at \$12 per Acre less Operating Costs per Acre at \$4}}$$

$$= \frac{\$700}{\$8} \text{ or 87.5 acres needed to break even.}$$

In justifying ownership the farmer should consider other alternatives such as:

1. loss in quality or quantity of crop if custom harvest is used;
2. greater return from investing limited capital elsewhere;
3. possibility of doing custom harvest for others; and
4. ownership of machine by two or more farmers.

Example 2

Problem: Shall we trade in a 5-year old 2-row tractor for a new 4-row tractor?

Solution: For simple figuring use a per-hour wage of $2.00 (which is considerable below the current legal minimum wage, but makes arithmetic easy to show the method) and these facts become basic:

The present tractor is used about 900 hours per year. The new tractor would be used 475 hours to accomplish the same amount of work, cost $5000, have a useful life of 8 years, fuel consumption at 38 cents per hour, repairs at 2 per cent of the cost, interest at 6 per cent, grease and oil at 7 cents per hour, and insurance and taxes at $40 per year.

The old tractor has been depreciated to $900 and needs an overhaul that will cost $400. The life of the tractor with the overhaul is estimated to be four years. Fuel consumption is 37 cents per hour, repairs at 10 per cent of present value plus overhaul, oil, and grease at 10 cents per hour, and insurance and taxes at $20 per year. It is estimated that crop income can be increased $300 per year with the new tractor because of timeliness of the work. Housing for the two tractors will be the same. Interest on investment is estimated at 6 per cent.

A Increased Costs		B Increased Receipts	
Labor—(475 hours X $2)	$950	Crops	$300
Depreciation—($5000 ÷ 8 yrs.)	$625		
Interest on Investment (6% X $5000) / (2)	$150		
Fuel—(475 hours X 6 cents)	$181		
Repairs—(2% X $5000)	$100		
Grease & Oil—(475 hours X 7 cents)	$ 33		
Insurance	$ 40		
Decreased Receipts		**Decreased Costs**	
None	$ 0	Labor—(900 hours X $2)	$1800
		Depreciation—($1300 ÷ 4 years)	$ 325
		Interest on Investment (6% X $1300) / (2)	$ 39
		Fuel—(900 hours X 37 cents)	$ 333
		Repairs—($1300 X 10%)	$ 130
		Grease & Oil—(900 hours X 10 cents)	$ 90
		Insurance	$ 20
Total A (Added Costs)	$2079	Total B (Added Income)	$3037

Total B, $3037 minus Total A, $2079 = $958 net change in farm income from buying a new tractor. The work data show the necessity for updating to make allowance for the escalation of costs.

Example 3

Problem: Shall a farmer drop his laying flock?

Solution: On a general farm the laying enterprise has 4,000 birds. During the past year total expenses have exceeded total income from the laying enterprise and the farmer is considering whether he should drop the enterprise. He has no alternative use for the laying houses or poultry equipment. The farmer would eliminate costs of machinery operation, but feels that all building costs would remain constant. With the following information on costs and returns we wish to determine if he should drop this enterprise. (The figures used below are intended only to demonstrate the decision-making process. Actual costs may vary.)

Expenses—Per Dozen Eggs

	cents
Feed	21.35
Hired Labor	
Machinery & Equipment	2.00
Operation	.60
Building Repairs	.40
Taxes (none on layers)	.33
Utilities	.47
Insurance—Buildings	.28
Supplies	1.04
Litter	.10
Medicine	.20
Other Cash Costs (none fixed)	.22
Depreciation on Machinery and Equipment	2.06
Depreciation on Buildings and Fences	1.65
Depreciation on Layers	8.01
Interest on Layers	.50
Interest on Other Investment	1.19
Total Expenses	40.40

Income—Per Dozen Eggs

	cents
Manure and Sacks	.79
Eggs	36.01
Total Income	36.80

Using this information, a simple comparison between continuing and dropping the layer enterprise now in production follows:

Increased Costs

	cents
None	.00

Increased Receipts

	cents
None	.00

Decreased Receipts

Sacks and Manure	.79
Value of Eggs	36.01

Decreased Costs

Feed	21.35
Hired Labor	2.00

Example 3 (Cont.)

TOTAL A (Added Costs)	36.80	Machinery and Equipment Operation	.60
		Utilities	.47
		Supplies	1.04
		Medicine	.20
		Litter	.10
		Other Cash Costs	.22
		Depreciation Layers	8.01
		Interest on Layers	.50
		TOTAL B (Added Income)	34.49

TOTAL – B, 34.49 cents minus TOTAL – A, 36.80 cents = 2.31 cents per dozen, net change in farm income.

D. TRIPLE COMPUTERIZED GUIDE IN DECISION-MAKING

[¶713] MATHEMATICS—MAXIMIZATION—MANAGEMENT

The size, complexity, and financial factors of today's farms make tools to aid accurate and comprehensive planning imperative. Such planning must take into consideration all the available resources of land, labor, equipment, and time, and allocate their factors stragetically to produce the maximum net return. The Triple M-3 process means: *Mathematics—Maximization—Management.*

During the 1960s, major land grant colleges joined together to program computers to provide scientific decision-making data for farmers. By 1974 farmers were turning to computers for help in optimum crop-planning. Farmers posed all kinds of questions to the computer such as these: What is the best crop mix to produce the optimum net income for my farm? What can I afford to pay hired help and still make a profit? What effect will renting 100 acres have on my profits? Should I invest in more grain-drying and storage facilities? Shall I increase the number of my milking cows? Would I be better off to buy custom work from a neighbor? At what point should I move up to a larger combine? What happens if you lease additional acreage? How can a son or son-in-law make the most significant contribution to your operation? Would a larger tractor, combine, or planter be a profitable investment?

[¶714] THE PRO-AG PROGRAM AS AN EXAMPLE

A number of programs are available and county extension agents and farmer cooperatives can provide guidance. For illustration in this book however, we will refer to the Pro-Ag program of International Harvester.

Pro-Ag computers are programmed for every major crop-producing area in the United States. Pro-Ag begins with a seminar. These seminars are usually held near one of the International Harvester's nine regional offices, each equipped with a Pro-Ag computer terminal. The farmer begins with a worksheet to describe his farm operation: his acreage, storage, labor supply, yield data for various crops, information about machinery and operating rates. By outlining his present resources he gives the computer the opportunity to explore all possible combinations in order to find the most advantageous use of each and every resource. Once the preliminary worksheets are completed, the farmer can go to work on his opportunities—his plan.

Then the computer goes to work. It gives the farmer a personalized printout comparing his plan with an "optimum plan" for his decision-making. The computer does not make decisions. It simply performs the arithmetic on the data the farmer feeds into it so that he can arrive at his own judgement.

The computer is programmed to observe *timeliness*, recognizing the fact that profits are influenced greatly by good or bad timing. While the computer digests the data, it searches for bottlenecks, that is, for areas in the farm operation that may prevent him from achieving substantially greater utilization of his resources—some of which he may not even be aware of.

Examples of two printouts (Figures 7-9a, b) will show how the Pro-Ag system provides information for farm management decision-making.

Figure 7-9a Pro-Ag System Computer Printout

Plan Identification 1L19B27

Table 1.	Present Plan	Optimal Plan
Net returns to mgt.	$6792.	$11387.
Acres corn	500.	270.
Acres silage	0.	0.
Acres soybeans	100.	330.
Acres wheat	0.	0.
Acres d.c. soybeans	0.	0.

Figure 7-9b Pro-Ag System Coumputer Printout

Resource	*Value Per Additional Unit ($/Unit)* Present Plan	*Optimum Plan*
Value of an additional hour of full-time labor		
1. Apr. 26-May 2	5.00	5.00
2. May 3-May 9	5.00	5.00
3. May 10-May 16	5.00	5.00
4. May 17-May 23	5.00	5.00
5. May 24-May 30	5.00	5.00
6. May 31-Jun. 6	0.0	5.00
7. Sep. 27-Oct. 17	5.00	5.00
8. Oct. 18-Nov. 7	5.00	5.00
9. Nov. 8-Nov. 28	5.00	5.00
10. Nov. 29-Dec. 12	5.00	5.00
Field hours-planting		
11. Apr. 26-May 2	184.11	155.62
12. May 3-May 9	176.35	146.73
13. May 10-May 16	129.23	99.64
14. May 17-May 23	51.10	49.04
Value of an additional acre of land		
15. Gross income	0.0	145.92
16. Rented in	0.0	55.92
Value of an additional crop acre		
17. Corn	132.73	0.0
18. Soybeans	157.04	0.0
19. Wheat	119.28	0.0
Field hours - harvesting		
Soybeans—corn —soybeans combine		
20. Sep. 27-Oct. 17	0.0	68.66
Corn —corn —soybeans combine		
21. Sep. 27-Oct. 17	17.12	0.0
22. Oct. 18-Nov. 7	18.14	0.42

8

Utilizing Credit in Farm Estate Building

[¶800] USING OTHER PEOPLE'S MONEY TO MAKE MORE MONEY FOR YOURSELF

Always, in years gone by as well as now, farmers borrowed money to buy farms, livestock, machinery, and buildings. For short-term money they went to local banks and private lenders. As farms have become larger and modern agriculture has demanded more capital, farmers have become a major customer for lending institutions.

Prudent use of credit can speed the ownership of a farm, make a farm more productive and efficient, and help increase income. It can provide conveniences for the family to make farm living more enjoyable and household work easier for wives. It can help in emergencies. By careful budgeting and cash flow projections a farmer and his wife can estimate how much credit they can afford, and what the borrowing will promise in increased income and enjoyment.

Use of other people's money can assist a farmer in making more money for himself, provided his calculations enable him to reduce his principal, pay his interest, and put himself month by month in a situation in which his assets increase.

[¶801] CREDIT FACTORS IN A SOUND LOAN

What factors help a lender decide to making a loan to a farmer? Five basic elements set as guidelines by the Federal Land Banks serve as the criteria by which most lenders determine the creditworthiness of a borrower. Here they are:

A. *Established integrity.* This factor outweighs all others. The evaluation includes (a) an examination of character, (b) experience, (c) demonstrated record of performance, (d) prospects of profitable operation, and (e) management track record in finance.

B. *Financial responsibility.* The factors that go into the analysis at this point are the applicant's ability to meet obligations, continue business operations, and protect the lender against undue risk. What are the applicant's total assets? What equity does he own? What are his contingent liabilities? What is the applicant's history of earnings?

C. *Repayment capacity.* Here the question is to determine that the cash flow will be sufficient to meet all obligations and provide a remainder for an acceptable standard of living and contingencies. The cash flow projection reflects cash generated both by the applicant's operation and all other sources. In short, is he going to have enough income to pay the loan without depriving his family of a decent standard of living.

D. *Constructive and practical purpose.* It is the obligation of the lender to determine that the purpose of the loan is constructive in amount and that the repayment terms are within the capability of the borrower. Loans may be conditioned by loan agreements, personal reliability, additional collateral, insurance, and other items as may be required.

E. *Collateral.* Collateral needs are dictated by the strengths and weaknesses of other credit factors. The collateral taken must reasonably protect the lender, provide the necessary control of equity and repayment, and leave the borrower in a position to constructively manage his business.

The prime purpose of these five credit factors is to assure loans that will be beneficial to the borrower and sound business for the lender.

Federal Land Banks are authorized to make only sound loans. In no case can the amount of the loan exceed 85 per cent of the appraised value of the real estate security, but the actual percentage loaned is dependent upon a consideration of all the credit factors.

[¶802] WHY CREDIT FAILS

Lending experience tells the story of why farmers get in trouble with their loans. In negotiating credit, these six principles should be borne in mind.

A. *Payment terms should be related to the periods of income generated by the investment.* While short repayment terms may express the ambition of the farmer, he should only consider a program that will not jeopardize the ratio of his current assets to his current liabilities (something like a two to one current ratio.)

B. *Projections of prices and yields should be conservative.* Sound financing requires a cushion to fall back on. While human nature makes some farmers overly optimistic, financial prudence dictates a level-headed outlook toward future markets and weather.

C. *During cash-deficit periods, payment schedules should be avoided.* In an expansion into a free-stall barn with milking parlor, for example, a lot of cash will be necessary before a dime in income is realized. The payment terms need to be planned in relation to an analysis of cash flow. Moreover, in the expansion there will be more expense in inventory, feed, breeding costs, and labor. These operational costs must be built into the capital costs to provide for loan repayment.

D. *Provision must be made from current assets for intermediate and long-term loans.* In computing repayment schedules, it is not unusual for a farmer to realize that his payment of principal and interest on intermediate and long-term loans must come from the same money he earns during the year. Thus, for example, a cattle feeder will need cash to pay off his cattle notes during the year. He will get that needed cash by selling current production such as grain and perhaps feeder cattle. But from these sources he may also have to derive money to pay on his long-term land loan. Thus, double claims stand as charges against his current income and assets. Neglect to compute all loan payments against current income means trouble.

E. *Farm expansion by borrowing may reduce liquid assets.* For example, the erection of a new barn for say, $50,000.00, may tie up assets because if the farmer should have to sell the barn to repay the loan, the banker might recover only a minor percentage of the investment. By capital investment in a facility that cannot be readily turned into cash, a farmer decreases his total available assets.

F. *Borrowing should be the result of hard-headed mathematics.* As farms grow in size and capital intensity, and neighborly competition pushes the family to go "all out," the wise farmer uses his hard-headed common sense together with his sharpened pencil to bring his expectations into focus. He asks three questions. First, do I need the loan? Second, "Will it pay me to go ahead?" And third, "At my age and situation over how many years shall I schedule repayment?"

[¶803] WHO LENDS MONEY TO FARMERS?

Here is a list of lending sources:

A. Private lenders
B. Federal Land Banks
C. Commercial banks
D. Farmers Home Administration
E. Production credit associations
F. Merchants and dealers
G. Sales Finance dealers
H. Insurance companies

A. *Operating Loans.* short term—for such purposes as seed, fertilizer, hired labor, and fuel. Operating loans usually run for a year less but under certain conditions may be renewed. They may or may not be secured by chattel mortgage.

B. *Working capital loans.* intermediate term—for such expenditures as equipment, breeding stock, improvements, major home appliances, and furnishings. Intermediate loans may run for up to seven years and are generally secured by chattel mortgage.

C. *Farm mortgage loans*—long term. Farm mortgage loans may have repayment terms which run for 30 years or more. Generally the loan terms include amortization—paying off the debt in regular annual, semi-annual, or monthly payments.

Figure 8-1 Amortization Schedule of Direct Reduction Loan

Annual % Rate	*Payment $*	*Loan $*	*Term: Years*	*Months*	*Periods*
8.50	196.95	20.000.00	15		180

Pay't No.	*Interest Payment*	*Principal Payment*	*Balance of Loan*
1	141.67	55.28	19,944.72
2	141.28	55.67	19,889.05
3	140.88	56.07	19,832.98
4	140.48	56.47	19,776.51
5	140.08	56.87	19,719.64
6	139.68	57.27	19,662.37
7	139.28	57.67	19,604.70
8	138.87	58.08	19,546.62
9	138.46	58.49	19,488.13

Figure 8-1 Cont.

Pay't No.	*Interest Payment*	*Principal Payment*	*Balance of Loan*
10	138.04	58.91	19,429.22
11	137.62	59.33	19,369.89
12	137.20	59.75	19,310.14
13	136.78	60.17	19,249.97
14	136.35	60.60	19,189.37
15	135.92	61.03	19,128.34
16	135.49	61.46	19,066.88
17	135.06	61.89	19,004.99
18	134.62	62.33	18,942.66
19	134.18	62.77	18,879.89
20	133.73	63.22	18,816.67
21	133.28	63.67	18,753.00
22	132.83	64.12	18,688.88
23	132.38	64.57	18,624.31
24	131.92	65.03	18,559.28
25	131.46	65.49	18,493.79
26	131.00	65.95	18,427.84
27	130.53	66.42	18,361.42
28	130.04	66.89	18.294.53
29	129.59	67.36	18,227.17
30	129.11	67.84	18,159.33
31	128.63	68.32	18,091.01
32	128.14	68.81	18,022.20
33	127.66	69.29	17,952.91
34	127.17	69.78	17,883.13
35	126.67	70.28	17,812.85
36	126.17	70.78	17,742.07
37	125.67	71.28	17,670.79
38	125.17	71.78	17,599.01
39	124,66	72.29	17,526.72
40	124.15	72.80	17,453.92
41	123.63	73.32	17,380.60
42	123.11	73.84	17,306.76
43	122.59	74.36	17,232.40
44	122.06	74.89	17,157.51
45	121.53	75.42	17,082.09
46	121.00	75.95	17,006.14
47	120.46	76.49	16,929.65
48	119.92	77.03	16,852.62
49	119.37	77.58	16,775.04
50	118.82	78.13	16,696.91
51	118.27	78.68	16,618.23
52	117.71	79.24	16,538.99
53	117.15	79.80	16,459.19
54	116.59	80.36	16,378.83
55	116.02	80.93	16,297.90

Figure 8-1 Cont.

Pay't No.	*Interest Payment*	*Principal Payment*	*Balance of Loan*
56	115.44	81.51	16,216.39
57	114.87	82.08	16,134.31
58	114.28	82.67	16,051.64
59	113.70	83.25	15,968.39
60	113.11	83.84	15,884.55
61	112.52	84.43	15,800.12
62	111.92	85.03	15.715.09
63	111.32	85.63	15,629.46
64	110.71	86.24	15,543.22
65	110.10	86.85	15,456.37
66	109.48	87.47	15,368.90
67	108.86	88.09	15,280.81
68	108.24	88.71	15,192.10
69	107.61	89.34	15,102.76
70	106.98	89.97	15,012.79
71	106.34	90.61	14,922.18
72	105.70	91.25	14,830.93
73	105.05	91.90	14,739.03
74	104.40	92.55	14,646.48
75	103.75	93.20	14,553.28
76	103.09	93.86	14,459.42
77	102.42	94.53	14,364.89
78	101.75	95.20	14,269.69
79	101.08	95.87	14,173.82
80	100.40	96.55	14,077.27
81	99.71	97.24	13,980.03
82	99.03	97.92	13,882.11
83	98.33	98.62	13,783.49
84	97.63	99.32	13,684.17
85	96.93	100.02	13,584.15
86	96.22	100.73	13,483.42
87	95.51	101.44	13,381.98
88	94.79	102.16	13,279.82
89	94.07	102.88	13,176.94
90	93,34	103.61	13,073.33
91	92.60	104.35	12,968.98
92	91.86	105.09	12,863.89
93	91.12	105.83	12,758.06
94	90.37	106.58	12,651.48
95	89.61	107.34	12,544.14
96	88.85	108.10	12,436.04
97	88.09	108.86	12,327.18
98	87.32	109.63	12,217.55
99	86.54	110.41	12,107.14
100	85.76	111.19	11,995.95
101	84.97	111.98	11,883.97
102	84.18	112.77	11,771.20

Figure 8-1 Cont.

Pay't No.	*Interest Payment*	*Principal Payment*	*Balance of Loan*
103	83.38	113.57	11,657.63
104	82.57	114.38	11,543.25
105	81.76	115.19	11,428.06
106	80.95	116.00	11,312.06
107	80.13	116.82	11,195.24
108	79.30	117.65	11,077.59
109	78.47	118.48	10,959.11
110	77.63	119.32	10,839.79
111	76.78	120.17	10,719.62
112	75.93	121.02	10,598.60
113	75.07	121.88	10,476.72
114	74.21	122.74	10,353.98
115	73.34	123.61	10,230.37
116	72.47	124.48	10,105.89
117	71.58	125.37	9,980.52
118	70.70	126.25	9,854.27
119	69.80	127.15	9,727.12
120	68.90	128.05	9,599.07
121	67.99	128.96	9,470.11
122	67.08	129.87	9,340.24
123	66.16	130.79	9,209.45
124	65.23	131.72	9,077.73
125	64.30	132.65	8,945.08
126	63.36	133.59	8,811.49
127	62.41	134.54	8,676.95
128	61.46	135.49	8,541.46
129	60.50	136.45	8,405.01
130	59.54	137.41	8,267.60
131	58.56	138.39	8,129.21
132	57.58	139.37	7,989.84
133	56.59	140.36	7,849.48
134	55.60	141.35	7,708.13
135	54.60	142.35	7,565.78
136	53.59	143.36	7,422.42
137	52.58	144.37	7,278.05
138	51.55	145.40	7,132.65
139	50.52	146.43	6,986.22
140	49.49	147.46	6,838.76
141	48.44	148.51	6,690.25
142	47.39	149.56	6,540.69
143	46.33	150.62	6,390.07
144	45.26	151.69	6,238.38
145	44.19	152.76	6,085.62
146	43.11	153.84	5,931.78
147	42.02	154.93	5,776.85
148	40.92	156.03	5,620.82
149	39.81	157.14	5,463.68

Figure 8-1 Cont.

Pay't No.	*Interest Payment*	*Principal Payment*	*Balance of Loan*
150	38.70	158.25	5,305.43
151	37.58	159.37	5,146.06
152	36.45	160.50	4,985.56
153	35.31	161.64	4,823.92
154	34.17	162.78	4,661.14
155	33.02	163.93	4,497.21
156	31.86	165.09	4,332.12
157	30.69	166.26	4,165.86
158	29.51	167.44	3,998.42
159	28.32	168.63	3,829.79
160	27.13	169.82	3,659.97
161	25.92	171.03	3,488.94
162	24.71	172.24	3,316.70
163	23.49	173.46	3,143.24
164	22.26	174.69	2,968.55
165	21.03	175.92	2,792.63
166	19.78	177.17	2,615.46
167	18.53	178.42	2,437.04
168	17.26	179.69	2,257.35
169	15.99	180.96	2,076.39
170	14.71	182.24	1,894.15
171	13.42	183.53	1,710.62
172	12.12	184.83	1,525.79
173	10.81	186.14	1,339.65
174	9.49	187.46	1,152.19
175	8.16	188.79	963.40
176	6.82	190.13	773.27
177	5.48	191.47	581.80
178	4.12	192.83	388.97
179	2.76	194.19	194.78
180	1.38	194.78	196.16*

The final payment is usually somewhat different from the regular payment, and is shown starred on the last line.

********** 15,450.21

As the farmer shops around for credit, he will find himself welcomed by lending experts. Lending to farmers is big business. Here for example is a track record of farm mortgage loans.

1960	$12,082,409,000.00
1965	$18,894,240,000.00
1970	$29,182,706,000.00

1973	$35,757,754,000.00
1974	$41,252,870,000.00*

Nearly three out of every five dollars loaned on farmlands comes from private lenders. That means that some farm owners take mortgages as they sell their lands. There are also private lenders who like farm mortgages. Next to private lenders, the Federal Land Banks are the biggest lenders—and are increasing in their loans.

Life insurance companies and local banks stand next with the Farmers Home Loan Administration at the bottom. Figure 8-2 shows the percentages.

Figure 8-2 Loans—By Percentage

Lender	*Per Cent*
Private Lenders–including of all other	38.5
Federal Land Banks	26.4
Life insurance companies	14.5
Commercial and savings banks	13.2
Farmers Home Loan Administration	8.6

It is interesting to catalog the first ten states on farm mortgages taken by legal reserve life insurance companies. Life insurance companies are the third largest lenders on farm mortgages in the United States. In 1975 farm mortgages made by legal reserve life insurance companies accounted for 7.5 per cent of all mortgages taken by the companies.

By states (1974) the first ten states in farm mortgages taken by legal reserve life insurance companies were:

		Per cent of Total
1. California	$884,500,000.00	14.04%
2. Texas	$654,300,000.00	10.39%
3. Iowa	$488,700,000.00	7.76%
4. Nebraska	$307,200,000.00	4.87%
5. Florida	$269,200,000.00	4.27%
6. Kansas	$263,900,000.00	4.19%
7. Washington	$221,300,000.00	3.51%
8. Colorado	$208,400,000.00	3.31%
9. Mississippi	$196,800,000.00	3.12%
10. Minnesota	$194,600,000.00	3.09%

Source: Institute of Life Insurance

*Agricultural Statistics 1975

[¶804] THE FEDERAL LAND BANKS

The Federal Land Banks were established by the Federal Farm Loan Act of 1916 to fill a need for a permanent and dependable source of borrowed capital at reasonable rates and on terms suited to agricultural needs.

[¶804.1] The Federal Land Banks Program

The Federal Land Banks programs provide a dependable source of long-term credit. Only through the use of increasingly large amounts of borrowed capital have agricultural producers been able to gain the necessary efficiency from enlarging operations and increasing income and equity. The Federal Land Banks have given to many farmers the credit by which American agriculture has become the most productive and efficient in the world. Born of necessity, these banks have financed agricultural producers through the transitional epoch from a subsistence endeavor of a man and his family to a highly developed and efficient profession providing the abundance of quality food and fiber (Fig. 8-3).

In historical retrospect it took 130 years (1790-1920) for American agriculture to shift from manpower and human muscles to animal power of the horse and mule. In thirty years (1920-1950) American agriculture with mechanical power and scientific farming doubled the output per man. Since 1950 the agricultural output has doubled every decade. Into the 21st century farmers must equip themselves to feed as many people as have been fed since the dawn of history, replacing crafts with science and machines for men. See Figure 8-4 for steps to take and forms to complete for obtaining a Federal Land Bank mortgage loan.

[¶805] THE FARM CREDIT ACT OF 1971

The Farm Credit Act of 1971 superseded all previous legislation. Today there are twelve Federal Land Banks in the United States, one in each of the twelve Farm Credit Districts (see Figure 8-3). These banks make long term loans secured by first liens on real estate in rural areas through more than five hundred local Federal Land Bank Associations. Loans are made to farmers, growers, ranchers, certain corporations engaged in agricultural production, rural residents, and selected farm related businesses. The local address can be found in almost any telephone book or can be obtained from the county agricultural extension agent.

Figure 8-3 Federal Land Banks and Territory Served By Each

Federal Land Banks	*Federal Intermediate Credit Banks*	*Farm Credit Banks*
The Federal Land Bank of Springfield P.O. Box 141 Springfield, Massachusetts 01101 Maine, New Hampshire, Vermont, Massachusetts, Rhode Island, Connecticut, New York, and New Jersey	**Federal Intermediate Credit Bank of Springfield** Farm Credit Building 310 State Street Box 141 Springfield, Massachusetts 01101 Maine, New Hampshire, Vermont, Massachusetts, Rhode Island, Connecticut, New York, and New Jersey	**The Farm Credit Banks of Springfield** Springfield, Massachusetts 01101 Maine, New Hampshire, Vermont, Massachusetts, Rhode Island, Connecticut, New York, and New Jersey
The Federal Land Bank of Baltimore P.O. Box 1555 Baltimore, Maryland 21203 Pennsylvania, Delaware, Maryland, Virginia, West Virginia, District of Columbia, and Puerto Rico	**Federal Intermediate Credit Bank of Baltimore** Farm Credit Building St. Paul and 24th Streets P.O. Box 1555 Baltimore, Maryland 21203 Pennsylvania, Delaware, Maryland, Virginia, West Virginia, District of Columbia, and Puerto Rico	**The Farm Credit Banks of Baltimore** Baltimore, Maryland 21203 Pennsylvania, Delaware, Maryland, Virginia, West Virginia, District of Columbia, and Puerto Rico
The Federal Land Bank of Columbia P.O. Box 1499 Columbia, South Carolina 29202 North Carolina, South Carolina, Georgia, and Florida	**Federal Intermediate Credit Bank of Columbia** Federal Land Bank Building 1401 Hampton Street Box 1060 Columbia, South Carolina 29202 North Carolina, South Carolina, Georgia, and Florida	**The Farm Credit Banks of Columbia** Columbia, South Carolina 29202 North Carolina, South Carolina, Georgia, and Florida
The Federal Land Bank of Louisville P.O. Box 239 Louisville, Kentucky, 40201 Ohio, Indiana, Kentucky, and Tennessee	**Federal Intermediate Credit Bank of Louisville** Farm Credit Building 224 East Broadway P.O. Box 1380 Louisville, Kentucky 40201 Ohio, Indiana, Kentucky, and Tennessee	**The Farm Credit Banks of Louisville** Louisville, Kentucky 40201 Ohio, Indiana, Kentucky, and Tennessee

Figure 8-3 Cont.

Federal Land Banks	*Federal Intermediate Credit Banks*	*Farm Credit Banks*
The Federal Land Bank of New Orleans P.O. Box 50590 New Orleans, Louisiana 70150 Alabama, Mississippi, and Louisiana	**Federal Intermediate Credit Bank of New Orleans** Farm Credit Building 860 St. Charles Avenue Box 50062 New Orleans, Louisiana 70150 Alabama, Mississippi, and Louisiana	**The Farm Credit Banks of New Orleans** New Orleans, Louisiana 70130 Alabama, Mississippi, and Louisiana
The Federal Land Bank of St. Louis Main P.O. Box 491 St. Louis, Missouri 63166 Illinois, Missouri, and Arkansas	**Federal Intermediate Credit Bank of St. Louis** 1415 Olive Street Main P.O. Box 431 St. Louis, Missouri 63166 Illinois, Missouri, and Arkansas	**The Farm Credit Banks of St. Louis** St. Louis, Missouri 63166 Illinois, Missouri, and Arkansas
The Federal Land Bank of St. Paul 375 Jackson Street St. Paul, Minnesota 55101 Michigan, Wisconsin, Minnesota, and North Dakota	**Federal Intermediate Credit Bank of St. Paul** 375 Jackson Street St. Paul, Minnesota 55101 Michigan, Wisconsin, Minnesota, and North Dakota	**The Farm Credit Banks of St. Paul** St. Paul, Minnesota 55101 Michigan, Wisconsin, Minnesota, and North Dakota
The Federal Land Bank of Omaha P.O. Box 1242 Omaha, Nebraska 68101 Iowa, Nebraska, South Dakota, and Wyoming	**Federal Intermediate Credit Bank of Omaha** Farm Credit Building 206 South 19th Street Omaha, Nebraska 68102 Iowa, Nebraska, South Dakota, and Wyoming	**The Farm Credit Banks of Omaha** Omaha, Nebraska 68101 Iowa, Nebraska, South Dakota, and Wyoming
The Federal Land Bank of Wichita 151 North Main Wichita, Kansas 67202 Oklahoma, Kansas, Colorado, and New Mexico	**Federal Intermediate Credit Bank of Wichita** 500 Farm Credit Banks Building 151 North Main Wichita, Kansas 67202 Oklahoma, Kansas, Colorado, and New Mexico	**The Farm Credit Banks of Wichita** Wichita, Kansas 67202 Oklahoma, Kansas, Colorado, and New Mexico

Figure 8-3 Cont.

Federal Land Banks	*Federal Intermediate Credit Banks*	*Farm Credit Banks*
The Federal Land Bank of Houston P.O. Box 2649 Houston, Texas 77001 Texas	**Federal Intermediate Credit Bank of Houston** Federal Land Bank Building 430 Lamar Avenue Box 2626 Houston, Texas 77001 Texas	**The Farm Credit Banks of Houston** Houston, Texas 77002 Texas
The Federal Land Bank of Berkeley P.O. Box 525 Berkeley, California 94701 California, Nevada, Utah, Arizona, and Hawaii	**Federal Intermediate Credit Bank of Berkeley** Farm Credit Building 2180 Milvia Street Box 771 Berkeley, California 94701 California, Nevada, Utah, Arizona, and Hawaii	**The Farm Credit Banks of Berkeley** Berkeley, California 94701 California, Nevada, Utah, Arizona, and Hawaii
The Federal Land Bank of Spokane W. 705 First Avenue Spokane, Washington 99204 Washington, Oregon, Montana, Idaho, and Alaska	**Federal Intermediate Credit Bank of Spokane** W. 705 First Avenue Spokane, Washington 99204 Washington, Oregon, Montana, Idaho, and Alaska	**The Farm Credit Banks of Spokane** Spokane, Washington 99204 Washington, Oregon, Montana, Idaho, and Alaska **Central Bank for Cooperatives** Denver, Colorado 80202 Serves District Banks for Cooperatives

Figure 8-4

STEPS IN OBTAINING A FEDERAL LAND BANK (FLB) MORTGAGE LOAN

1. Applicant calls or visits the Association office for an appointment.
2. An appointment is scheduled and the following transpires:
   (a) Introduction to the Farm Credit System and its operations, including System goals, purpose (sound credit to farmers), nature of cooperative, stock requirements and ownership, interest rates, methods of repayment, fees, availability of credit life insurance, etc.;
   (b) General discussion on borrower's experience, background, short and long-term goals, type of record keeping system, and specific loan request (evaluation of borrower's ability based on past experience is very important);
   (c) Feasibility of the request is discussed and whether the applicant meets the Federal Land Bank Association's standards for financing:
      (1) eligible for financing under the terms of the Farm Credit Administration and District guidelines,
      (2) has or will have necessary downpayment or equities,
      (3) adequate repayment ability and net worth reserves.
   (d) If the above are answered satisfactorily, then the following information is requested:
      (1) Membership Application listing personal information and request for membership in the FLB,
      (2) current and past two years' financial statements listing all assets and liabilities of the applicant,
      (3) past three years' actual earnings information reflecting income and expense from agricultural sources as well as nonagricultural sources,
      (4) an earnings projection reflecting anticipated income and expense after the loan has closed (if the purpose of the loan represents a new venture for which no previous earnings records exist, the applicant must show realistic potential to provide adequate income to service indebtedness, cover living expenses and have a suitable margin to cover adversity and capital purchases),
      (5) actual living costs for the last three years,
      (6) capital purchases information,
      (7) signed loan application covering the loan request, stock investment, and loan fees as well as the repayment program,
      (8) if applicable, information, required by the Real Estate Settlement and Procedures Act of the Department of Housing and Urban Development, is distributed to the applicant at this time.
3. Upon receipt, the above information is reviewed by the loan officer, and, if the request appears reasonable, a search of the County records is completed along with a check of the Credit Bureau records and/or a check with creditors to determine the applicant's past credit experience. If the applicant is not known personally by the loan officer, he must ask Directors, Advisory Committee members, or other good farmers in the community about the applicant's farming methods and ability. Farming ability, as well as credit reputation, must be checked out in order to form the correct opinion regarding the loan request.

Figure 8-4 Cont.

4. At this point, the applicant is contacted. If the credit search has been satisfactory, an appointment is scheduled to visit the property. An appraisal of the real estate offered as security is then completed.
5. This concludes the collection of source data. The loan officer analyzes the information collected and determines his recommendation as to approval of the application. If the loan request is within his loan approval delegation, a decision is made and conveyed to the applicant. If not within his delegation, the loan officer makes his recommendation to his superior.
6. If the loan request is rejected, the decision and reason is conveyed to the applicant.
7. If the loan request is approved, the applicant is notified of the loan decision. The loan packet is then forwarded to the Federal Land Bank of Springfield for loan processing, preparation of Truth-in-Lending documents and the loan closing information to the FLB attorney.
8. Upon completion, the closing information is returned to the local Association office for preparation of the closing documents and scheduling of a closing. If applicable, an appointment is scheduled for execution of the Truth-in-Lending documents.
9. The Association forwards the closing information to the Association attorney who completes a title search of the property in question. The attorney also completes the Bond and Mortgage, Closing Statement, and RESPA Settlement Statement, if applicable.
10. Once completed, a loan closing is scheduled where the closing documents can be signed, recorded in the County Clerk's Office and the loan proceeds distributed.

The time frame involved in reaching a decision greatly depends upon the applicant's submission of the information outlined above. As the Farm Credit Service's primary purpose is extension of credit to farmers and agribusinesses, the application is processed as quickly as possible, and, generally, a period of two to four weeks from receipt of the information is needed to reach a decision.

Forms and loan information supplied courtesy of the Farm Credit Banks of Springfield, Springfield, Mass. 01101.

Figure 8-4 Cont.

10365
05/78

FEDERAL LAND BANK
LOAN APPLICATION AND INFORMATION TO ATTORNEY

Association Office Number 300-4

Applicant(s') Names	PCA Member	Optional Credit Life Insurance	Will Principal Residence be Mortgaged Yes	No
1. John Farmer ☒ Married ☐ Unmarried (including single, divorced, and widowed) ☐ Separated RD #1 Hayside, N.Y. (Billing Address) 14321 (Zip Code) 421-364-9242 (Telephone Number) 018-42-3142 (Taxpayer Ident. No. (S.S.))	☒	☐	☒	☐
2. Mary Farmer ☒ Married ☐ Unmarried (including single, divorced, and widowed) ☐ Separated Address ______ Zip Code ______	☒	☐	☐	☐

Name(s) and Address(es) of Owners of Real Estate Collateral:

1. ______
2. ______

VOLUNTARY INFORMATION FOR GOVERNMENT MONITORING PURPOSES

If this loan is for purchase or construction of a home, the following information is requested by the Federal Government to monitor this lender's compliance with Equal Credit Opportunity and Fair Housing Laws. The law provides that a lender may neither discriminate on the basis of this information nor on whether or not it is furnished. Furnishing this information is optional. If you do not wish to furnish the following information, please initial below.

BORROWER: I do not wish to furnish this information (initials) ______	CO-BORROWER: I do not wish to furnish this information (initials) ______
Race/National Origin	Race/National Origin
☐ American Indian, Alaskan Native ☐ Asian, Pacific Islander ☐ Black ☐ Hispanic	☐ American Indian, Alaskan Native ☐ Asian, Pacific Islander ☐ Black ☐ Hispanic
☐ White ☐ Other (specify) ______	☐ White ☐ Other (specify) ______
Sex	Sex
☐ Female ☐ Male	☐ Female ☐ Male

LOAN APPLICATION ☒ FARM ☐ FARM HOME LOAN

I / we apply for:

Loan funds to refinance FLB loan(s) number	045-2787-0-0	$ 18,400.00
Loan funds to refinance PCA debts		$
Loan funds to refinance commercial Bank R/E loan(s)		$
Loan funds to refinance insurance company R/E loan(s)		$
Loan funds to refinance other R/E loan(s)		$
Loan funds to refinance Non R/E loan(s)		$
Loan funds to build dwelling on security		$
Loan funds to purchase residence only		$
Loan funds to purchase operating farm with residence		$
Loan funds to purchase operating farm without residence		$
Loan funds used for home improvements		$
Loan funds used for farm related improvements	Silo, baler	$ 18,520.00
Loan funds used for operating purposes		$
Other		$

TOTAL LOAN FUNDS REQUESTED .... $ 36,920.00

Stock required .... $ 1,900
Less stock presently owned 1,400
Stock required .... $ 500.00
Association Loan fee .... $ 173.00

TOTAL STOCK AND LOAN FEE .... $ 673.00

Estimated Filing fee $ 27.00 Estimated Title cost $ 380.00 for Total of .... $ 407.00

TOTAL LOAN REQUEST .... $ 38,000.00

Credit life insurance premium ☐ will ☐ will not be deducted from loan proceeds.

REPAYMENT PLAN

1. ☒ SPRINGFIELD PLAN ☐ Annual ☒ Semiannual Payments due month(s) of March and September

Preliminary Interest Payment 1 Number of Interest Only Payments 0 Number of Principal and Interest Payments 66

2. ☐ STANDARD MONTHLY PLAN .... Number of Years ______

Date: 1/2/79 Applicant(s) Signature(s) John Farmer

Mary Farmer

Figure 8-4 Cont.

Attorney's Name William Howard (Authorization to Attorney attached.)

NOTICE TO ATTORNEY: Please refer to the table of contents of the loan closing instructional pamphlet for those sections of pamphlet applicable to this loan.

Please prepare FLB Mortgage and Note/Bond to applicant(s) listed on reverse side for $ 38,000 to be repaid as detailed in the Federal Truth-in-Lending section below.

INFORMATION CONCERNING PROPERTY TO BE MORTGAGED TO THE LAND BANK

Acres	Purported Name of Present Record Owner	Year Of Deed	Location of Property (Town and County)
200	John and Mary Farmer	1970	Hayside, Baler

200 Total Acres

Appraiser's estimate is 200 acres, as per attached plat, with 3 % general shortage permitted to be waived. Special information from appraiser's report (such as parcels to be excluded, rights-of-way, fixture-type structures, e.g., harvestores appraised for value, mineral rights, water rights, etc.)

EXISTING LIENS ON PROPERTY TO BE MORTGAGED TO THE LAND BANK

The Association is aware of the following liens on this property. (If other liens are discovered, please contact the Association for instructions):

LIENHOLDER	AMOUNT (EST.)	DISPOSITION
FLB	18,400	To be refunded

ADDITIONAL CLOSING REQUIREMENTS AND / OR INFORMATION

1. Additional security required and value – $
2. Control $ none for
3. Unpaid property taxes $ – Disposition –
4. Title abstract held by: William Howard

   Former loan by FLB on ☒ all ☐ part of same security was closed in name(s) of John and Mary Farmer Date: 1970 Present acreage 200 (Attach Title Certificate.)
5. Insurance Required:

Dwelling	Barn	Other
$25,000	$10,000	

6. Additional information concerning partnerships, life estates, unrecorded deeds, etc., affecting title –
7. Other requirements –
8. Second mortgage to: ☐ Individual ☐ PCA ☐ FmHA - Joint Closing ☐ FmHA Subordination

FEDERAL TRUTH IN LENDING / RESPA / PAYMENT SCHEDULE

Estimated Loan Closing Date (Mo. / day / yr.) 2/9/79

Applicant's loan is (a) ☒ primarily for agricultural purpose (over $25,000)

OR Applicant purports to be (b) ☐ a corporation ☐ a partnership ☐ an estate ☐ a trust

The interest rate is variable and is currently billed at 8¼ %

Consequently, no disclosure has been made. (Please satisfy yourself that the declaration in (b), if applicable, is accurate.)

Loan may not be closed until after midnight

☐ RESPA does apply (See Land Bank manual, Related Legal Requirements section)

☒ RESPA does not apply. Explain refunding

PAYMENT SCHEDULE BASED ON ESTIMATED LOAN CLOSING DATE ABOVE (To be completed by the Bank)

1. Annual/Semi-Annual: First interest due September 1, 1979, first principal due March 1, 1980 with 65 principal pymnts. of $ 570.00 each, plus a final.
2. Monthly: The first installment shall consist of interest only and shall be payable on , 19 . Subsequent installments of principal and interest each in the amount of $ shall be payable on the 1st day of each consecutive month commencing , 19 until said principal sum is paid in full with interest.

FLBA LOAN ACTION

I ☒ do ☐ do not recommend this loan. Signed John Creditman

$ 38,000 Approved for Total Loan Request) ☐ Rejected ☐ Withdrawn

$ Other Direct FLB Loan # # #

$ Contingent FLB Loans # # #

$ 38,000 Total FLB Liability for

Approved under delegated authority by Loan Officer Date 1/5/79

Approved by loan committee by Date

BANK USE

FLB ACTION: ☐ Approved ☐ Rejected ☐ Withdrawn

By:

Date:

Figure 8-4 Cont.

10078
12/77

MEMBERSHIP APPLICATION

(A) ☐ PCA (B) ☒ FLBA

Assn. Office No. 300-4

Please indicate whether applying for individual or joint credit:

☐ Individual Credit - only your assets, liabilities and income will be considered in applying for credit.
☒ Joint Credit - your assets, liabilities and income and those of another joint applicant(s) will be considered in applying for credit.

Applicant's Full Name - Print John and Mary Farmer

Legal Business Entity: ☒ Individual ☐ Partnership ☐ Corporation ☐ Other Taxpayer Ident. No. (S.S.) 018-42-3142

Doing Business As: ☐ Same as above Other:

INDIVIDUALS OR PRINCIPALS

Name John Farmer Date of Birth 8/14/41	Name Mary Farmer Date of Birth 3/2/43
I have 2 children, ages 14, 12	I have children, ages
Address RD #1	Address
Town Hayside, N. Y.	Town
County Baler Zip Code 14321	County Zip Code
Years at above address 8 Telephone 421-364-9242	Years at above address Telephone
Have you filed bankruptcy within the past 14 years: ☐ Yes ☒ No	Have you filed bankruptcy within the past 14 years: ☐ Yes ☒ No

Directions for reaching my farm From Hayside, proceed north 3 miles. Turn right on County Road. Farm is 2nd on right.

I/we have ownership or other interests in the following real estate:

Acres	Township	County	Year Purchased	Price	I have Deed Contr. or Lease (specify which)	Title Is In The Name Of
200	Hayside	Baler	1970	$75,000	Deed	John and Mary Farmer

Title to all livestock, equipment and other personal property used in my farm operation is in the name of John and Mary Farmer

If anyone other than the above named title holders has any title, beneficial or other interest in any of the livestock, equipment and other personal property or real estate, give details -

If you have any involvement, interest or investment in any business other than the above farm operation, give details -

(COMPLETE APPROPRIATE SECTION)

I we hereby apply for membership in:

A

______ PRODUCTION CREDIT ASSOCIATION ______

and submit the above information as to my eligibility for membership to induce the Association to make any loans for which I may apply either individually or jointly with others. Unless I otherwise instruct you in writing, checks or drafts issued by the Association for proceeds of loans made to me individually or jointly with others may be made payable to

(Names) ______

Subject to the granting of any loans which may be made, I hereby subscribe to Class B stock in the Association in an amount necessary to meet the requirements of the Farm Credit Act of 1971 and I agree to be bound by the Articles of Incorporation and the By-Laws of the Association as they now exist or may be amended. (Borrowers must own, when loans are closed, Class B stock equal in fair book value, not to exceed par, to not less than $5 or more than $10 for each $100 or fraction thereof of their indebtedness to the Association.)
I agree to pay the uniform loan service fees established by the Association from time to time for which are applicable to the loans made to me by the Association.
I agree that the proceeds of any loan made to me may be advanced in installments and that the Association may withold such installments if, in its judgment, conditions do not justify further advances.
I agree that all payments on my indebtedness to the Association arising out of a loan or otherwise shall be applied to such indebtedness in such manner as the Association in its sole judgment and discretion shall elect.
I hereby authorize the Association to make direct disbursements out of the proceeds of loans made to me in payment for Class B stock, loan service fees, and charges for searching records, recording mortgages, and any other direct expenses incurred by the Association in making such loans, if not otherwise paid by me.
I also hereby authorize verification of any employment and/or financial information submitted to Association. I hereby request the Association, at its option, to retire all or part of my capital stock at any time and credit my account.

B

______ FEDERAL LAND BANK ASSOCIATION of Hayside

I HEREBY AUTHORIZE VERIFICATION OF ANY EMPLOYMENT AND/OR FINANCIAL INFORMATION SUBMITTED TO THE ASSOCIATION. Subject to the granting of any loans which may be made, I hereby subscribe to stock in the Association in an amount necessary to meet the requirements of the Farm Credit Act of 1971 and I agree to be bound by the Articles of Incorporation and the By-Laws of the Association as they now exist or may be amended.

UNLESS OTHERWISE INDICATED BELOW, ALL ASSOCIATION STOCK OWNED BY MEMBER BORROWERS WILL BE ISSUED TO THEM JOINTLY WITH RIGHT OF SURVIVORSHIP AND SO RECORDED ON THE STOCK RECORD OF THE ASSOCIATION.

APPLICANT(S) SIGNATURE(S)

John Farmer

Mary Farmer

I ACKNOWLEDGE THAT I HAVE READ THE ABOVE APPLICATION AND THAT I HAVE VERIFIED THE STATEMENTS WHICH IT CONTAINS AND I HEREBY CERTIFY THAT ALL INFORMATION GIVEN IS TRUE AND CORRECT.

Date 1/2/79

Figure 8-4 Cont.

MANAGEMENT EVALUATION REPORT

BORROWER'S BACKGROUND, HISTORY AND SOURCE OF ASSETS:

Operated rented farm in next county for 5 years. Purchased present farm in 1970, starting with 30 cows. Source of assets is earnings.

SHORT AND LONG TERM GOALS OF APPLICANT:

Short-term - increase herd size to maximum capacity of 60 cows.
Long -term - improve financial position; pass farm to two sons.

ELIGIBILITY GROUP: 1 EXPLAIN:

METHOD OF OPERATION: [X] Operator [ ] Landlord [ ] Combination

MANAGEMENT STRUCTURE (Roles of individuals):

John takes care of crops and oversees the milking of the cows. The two sons do most of the milking and Mary takes care of the yearling and calves.

PROPOSED CAPACITY OF FARMING OPERATION

Til. Acres Owned	Til. Acres Rented	Other Rented	Total Owned	Total Operated
140	-	-	200	200

Crop Corn No. of Acres 90 ; Crop Hay No. of Acres 50 ; Crop Pasture No. of Acres 40

Total facility capacity (poultry, cows, etc.):

Capacity for 60 cows. Well built stanchion barn. Good layout

QUALITY OF FARM (Soil type, structure, drainage, overall desirability):

Mostly Howard gravel soils. Level.

MANAGEMENT FACTORS:

Marketing Management (Co-op, retail, wholesale, broker, other):

Milk is marketed through local cooperative.

Financial Management (Record keeping program, financial decision maker):

On Agrifax. Mary Farmer keeps good records. Financial decisions made by both John & Mary Farmer.

Production Management (Agronomy practices, animal husbandry):

Excellent. Soil test; dairy and financial records; artificial breeding. 15,000 pound plus herd average. Crops always above average.

CREDIT SOURCES CHECKED	RESULTS
Present FLB and PCA members	Excellent in every respect

GENERAL COMMENTS:

1/5/79 — Date

Loan Officer — Completed by

Figure 8-4 Cont.

10080
12/77

STATEMENT OF FINANCIAL CONDITION

Of John and Mary Farmer as of 12/31/78 (Date) Assn. Office No. 300-4

Address RD #1 Hayside, N.Y. 14321

CURRENT ASSETS

Cash on hand and in Banks (Saving Account $ 3,000) (Checking Account $ 500)	$ 3,500
Accounts receivable	$ 6,900
Farm produce on hand to be sold (kind)	$
Feeder L/S # x $ # x $ # x $	$
Laying Hens # x $ Growing Replacements # x $ # x $	$
Feed $, Seed $, Fertilizer, chemicals $, Other $	$
Prepaid expenses 475 T CS - $225T Haylege 3500 bales	$ 12,500
Cash investment in growing crops	$
Collectible Notes	$
Other - describe IRA Account	$ 2,800
Total Current Assets	$ 25,700

INTERMEDIATE ASSETS

Cash value of life insurance (face amount $ 20,000) beneficiary ($10,000 on each)	$
Milk cows # 53 x $ 550 Bred heifers # 15 x $ 450 Other # x $	$ 35,900
Yearlings # 15 x $ 300 Calves # 15 x $ 100 # x $	$ 6,000
Cars (make and year) '77 Chevy '72 Olds	$ 7,000
Machinery/equipment/trucks (tractors # 4 $ 20,000)	$ 60,000
Stock: PCA $ 1,500 FLBA $ 1,400 Other 4,000	$ 6,900
Other - describe	$
Total Intermediate Assets	$ 115,800

FIXED ASSETS

Farm Real Estate	ACRES Total	ACRES Till.	Amount
	200	180	$ 140,000
			$
Other real estate (describe)			$
Other fixed assets (describe)			$
Equity in partnerships/corporations (attach Financial Statement when appropriate)			$
Total Fixed Assets			$ 140,000
TOTAL ASSETS			$ 281,500

CURRENT LIABILITIES

	Purpose	Secured By	Int. Rate	Paymt. Required	Freq.	Amount
Accounts Payable			%	$		$
Smith Feed Company	feed, fertilizer		12 %	$ 225	M	$ 2,500
			%	$		$
			%	$		$
			%	$		$
Taxes (real estate)						$
Income tax payable						$
PCA operating (demand note)			%	$		$
Notes payable			%	$		$
			%	$		$
Other			%	$		$
Total Current Liabilities						$ 2,500

INTERMEDIATE LIABILITIES

	Purpose	Secured By	Int. Rate	Paymt. Required	Freq.	Amount
PCA capital (demand note)	Unsecured		8.25 %	$ 530/mo.		$ 29,840
Loans secured by life insurance			%	$		$
Notes payable			%	$		$
			%	$		$
			%	$		$
			%	$		$
Total Intermediate Liabilities						$ 29,840

LONG TERM LIABILITIES

Real Estate Mtges. & Contracts	Property Covered	Int. Rate	Paymt. Required	Freq.	Amount
FLB	200 acres	8 %	$ 1,943 Prin.	S/A	$ 18,400
Other Father	200 acres	7 %	$ 3,725 Prin.	A	$ 63,560
Other		%	$		$
Total Long Term Liabilities					$ 81,960

TOTAL LIABILITIES	$ 114,300
59.4% NET WORTH	$ 167,200

Contingent Liabilities [X] No [ ] Yes (attach list)

Are there any judgments, liens, etc.? [X] No [ ] Yes Explain

I hereby certify that all information given above is true and correct.

Date 1/2/79 Signature John Farmer

Mary Farmer

Figure 8-4 Cont.

In my opinion, applicant's assets and liabilities as of financial statement dated 12/31/78 are substantially correct.
Yes x No ______ . Explain ______

______ Resulting in an adjusted net worth of $ ______

CROP INFORMATION

Crop	19 77 No. Acres	19 77 Yield	19 78 No. Acres	19 78 Yield	PROPOSED 19 79 No. Acres	PROPOSED 19 79 Yield
Ear corn	40	85 bu.	50	90 bu.	15	90 bu.
Corn Silage	30	15 ton	30	15 ton	55	15 ton
Hay	30	3.2	40	3.5	50	3.5
Pasture	80		60		40	

FOR LARGE CROP OPERATIONS, USE CROP WORKSHEET

PROPOSED CAPITAL EXPENDITURES

Silo	$ 19,420
Baler	$ 4,500
	$
FLB PCA Stock and Closing Costs	$ 1,080
Total Cost of Capital Expenditures	$ 25,000
Less Market Value of Proposed Capital Expenditures	$ 25,000
Equals Lost Capital	$ -

SOURCE OF FUNDS FOR CAPITAL EXPENDITURES

CASH & A/R	$ 6,480
PCA	$
FLB	$ 18,520
	$
	$
Total Source of Funds	$ 25,000

F S Reference Items and Comments:

John has made good progress over the years. Farm is well kept and total operation very efficient. His two sons and wife help a lot with the total operation and some part-time help is hired for the crops. Herd has averaged 48 cows for the last two years. He hopes to increase this to 60 during 1979. John raises his own replacements and herd average is close to 15,000 pounds per cow. With this application, he will construct a silo and purchase a new baler. John is active in the farming community. Good businessman. Net worth increase in 1978 due to earnings. Excess available after debt servicing and living is very adequate to cover emergencies. Projected debt/cow at $2,231 is high; however, operation has demonstrated it can handle this level of debt. It is John's intention to reduce debt as much as possible over the next few years.

1/2/79	Loan Officer
Date	Completed By

Figure 8-4 Cont.

10792
10/77

TREND ANALYSIS

Applicant's Name John and Mary Farmer Assoc. Office No. 300-4

For details and/or adjustments, attach schedule.

ADJUSTED FINANCIAL CONDITION	___ 19 ___ Mo. Yr.	___ 19 ___ Mo. Yr.	12/31 19 77 Mo. Yr.	12/31 19 78 Mo. Yr.	PROJECTED After loan closes ___ 19 ___ Mo. Yr.
Current Assets			22,425	25,700	19,220
Intermediate Assets			108,400	115,800	140,800
Fixed Assets			140,000	140,000	140,000
TOTAL ASSETS	$	$	$ 270,825	$ 281,500	$ 300,020
Current Liabilities			2,500	2,500	2,500
Intermediate Liabilities			33,145	29,840	29,840
Long-Term Liabilities			84,230	81,960	101,560
TOTAL LIABILITIES	$	$	$ 119,875	$ 114,300	$ 133,900
NET WORTH	$	$	$ 150,950	$ 167,200	$ 166,120
% Net Worth	%	%	55.7 %	59.4 %	55.4 %

I & E Farm	Date: ___ 19 ___ No. of Mos. ___ Mo.(s)	___ 19 ___ ___ Mo.(s)	12/31 19 77 12 Mo.(s)	12/31 19 78 12 Mo.(s)	12/31 19 79 PROPOSED BUDGET
Sales - Primary Product			65,774	73,308	89,540
Sales - Secondary Product			7,500	8,200	8,400
Other Farm Income			4,154	690	500
TOTAL FARM INCOME	$	$	$ 77,428	$ 82,198	$ 98,440
FARM EXPENSES			50,006	50,678	63,013
NET FARM INCOME			27,422	31,520	35,427
ADD: Interest			6,295	5,125	7,240
ADD: Depreciation					
TOTAL AVAILABLE - Farm	$	$	$ 33,717	$ 36,645	$ 42,667
ADD: Net Nonfarm Income					
ADD: Sale Capital Assets					
1 TOTAL FUNDS AVAILABLE	$	$	$ 33,717	$ 36,645	$ 42,667
Debt Repayment (Prin. & Int.) Omit operating principal					
PCA			5,490	6,360	6,360
Bank Loans					
Dealer Loans					
Other					
FLB			2,430	2,430	3,500
Other R/E Loans			4,500	4,500	4,500
2 TOTAL DEBT SERVICE REQUIREMENT	$	$	$ 12,420	$ 13,290	$ 14,360
3 Living Expense			12,000	13,000	14,000
4 Income & FICA Tax			960	1,040	1,120
5 Other					
6 TOTAL (3 + 4 + 5)	$	$	$ 12,960	$ 14,040	$ 15,120
7 TOTAL CASH REQUIRED (2 + 6)	$	$	$ 25,380	$ 27,330	$ 29,480
EXCESS (1 - 7)	$	$	$ 8,337	$ 9,315	$ 13,187
Present PCA Outstanding			$ 33,145	$ 29,840	
New PCA Commitment			$ 40,000	$ 40,000	$ 40,000
Present FLB Balance			$ 16,592	$ 18,400	$ 38,000
Credit Exam. Class PCA			1	1	
Credit Exam. Class FICB			1	1	

EVALUATION FACTORS	19 ___	19 ___	19 77	19 78	19 79
Number of cows			48	48	55
Herd average			14,200#	14,900#	14,800#
Price of milk/cwt			$9.65	$10.25	$11.00
Debt/cow			$2,497	$2,157	$2,231
Excess as % of total available			27.7%	25.4%	30.9%
Excess/cow			$174	$194	$240
Machinery investment/cow			$1,052	$1,132	$1,364

Completed By (initials):

Figure 8-4 Cont.

10789
12 77

DAIRY ANALYSIS WORKSHEET

Name John and Mary Farmer　　　Office No. 300-4

☒ CASH
☐ ADJUSTED

FARM RECEIPTS:	19 77 Total	19 77 Per Cow	19 78 Total	19 78 Per Cow	Benchmark Per Cow Comparison	Projection 19 79 Per Cow	Projection 19 79 Total
Calf Sales	2,100	44	2,200	46	30	44	2,400
Cow Sales	5,400	112	6,000	125	110	109	6,000
Grain Sales							
Hay Sales	1,726	36	-				
Milk Sales	65,774	1,370	73,308	1,527	1,460	1,628	89,540
Custom Work							
Other Farm Receipts	2,428	51	690	14		9	500
Total Cash Farm Receipts	77,428	1,613	82,198	1,712	1,600	1,790	98,440
OPERATING EXPENSES:							
Labor**	1,759	37	2,109	44	90	51	2,800
Repairs & Maint.	3,841	80	4,020	84	65	82	4,500
Interest**	6,295	131	5,125	107	127	132	7,240
Rent	-	-	-	-	30	-	-
Feed	16,443	343	16,127	336	365	358	19,699
Seed & Plants	980	20	940	20	25	27	1,500
Fert. - Lime - Chem.	4,200	87	4,523	94	110	105	5,775
Machine Hire	260	5	280	6	21	5	250
Supplies	4,245	88	5,301	110	40	101	5,600
Breeding Fees	842	18	1,210	25	10	27	1,500
Vet. & Medicine	315	7	245	5	6	7	400
Fuel & Oil	1,825	38	1,690	35	41	40	2,200
Taxes	3,420	71	3,650	76	65	73	4,000
Insurance	1,450	30	1,608	33	35	35	1,925
Farm Share Utilities	1,592	33	1,695	35	30	35	1,900
Freight & Truck	943	20	955	20	22	22	1,210
Other	1,596	33	1,200	25	15	46	2,514
Cow Replacements**	-	-	-		-		-
Total Cash Operating	50,006	1,042	50,670	1,056	1,097	1,146	63,013
Net Farm Income	27,422	571	31,520	657	503	644	35,427
** Cash Operating w/o Lab. Int. & Cow Replacements	41,952	874	43,444	905	880	963	52,973

EVALUATION FACTORS:	19 77	19 78	Benchmark	Projection 19 79
Avg. # of Cows	48	48	50	55
Lb. Milk Sold/Cow	14,200	14,900#	14,250#	14,800#
Price of milk/cwt.	$9.65	$10.25	$10.25	$11.00
Milk price - market av.	$9.70	$10.35		$11.25
Pounds of milk sold	681,600#	715,200#	712,500#	814,000#
Feed as % of milk	25%	22%	25%	22%
Man equivalent	1.2	1.2	1.5	1.25
(cows) - milk/man	(40) 568,000 lbs.	(40) 596,000 lbs.	(33) 475 M	(44) 651,200
Cull rate	25%	25%	22%	22%
Bred Heifers % of cows	31%	31%	25%	27%

Prepared by Loan Officer　　　Date 1/5/79

Figure 8-4 Cont.

CROP LOAN WORKSHEET

Name ______________________ Office No. ________

HISTORICAL CROP INFORMATION

Crop	19 ____ No. Acres	19 ____ Yield	19 ____ No. Acres	19 ____ Yield	19 ____ No. Acres	19 ____ Yield

PROPOSED CROP ANALYSIS

Crop	Number Of Acres	Yield/ Acre	Price/ Unit	Gross/ Acre	Cost/ Acre	Margin/ Acre	Total Gross	Total Cost	Margin
			$	$	$	$	$	$	$
						Sub Total			

SOURCE OF CROP FUNDS

Own Cash $__________

PCA __________

____

____

Total Funds Needed $__________

Other Farm Enterprises	Total Gross	Total Cost	Margin
Total for Yr.			

MARKETING: (Coop. - Retail - Wholesale - Broker - Other)

PRICES: (Discuss Member's Price Per Unit, Historically and for Area)

COSTS: (Discuss Member's Cost Per Unit, Historically and Projected)

YIELDS: (Discuss Member's Historical and Projected)

DATE ______________ PREPARED BY ______________

Figure 8-4 Cont.

10586
05/76

APPRAISER'S REPORT

Applicant's Name(s) John and Mary Farmer State New York

County Baler Town Hayside Road & House No RD #1

Location and Directions from nearest village from Hayside proceed north 3 miles. Turn right on County Road. Farm is 2nd on right.

Miles to major employment area 3 Is there significant non-agric. influence on property?
☐ none ☒ slight ☐ moderate ☐ great

PURCHASE DATA
Date applicant acquired property 1970 Property was acquired by Purchase
Along with personal property for $ 125,000 Net R/E $ 75,000
If acquired in parcels, list additional purchases

IMPROVEMENTS SINCE PURCHASE Remodeled kitchen. New vinyl siding. New heating system.

List zoning restrictions & easements Usual utility lines, buried tel. cable, Agric. District

Real Estate Taxes Year 1978 $ 3,650 Special Agric. Assessment? No

Water Supply 2 drilled wells Sewer Service - Septic Tank(s) yes

Dwelling #1
Style 2 story Age 70 Type of Construction wood frame Size 18 x 36, 16 x 16, 20 x 24 Sq. Ft. Living Area 2,400
No. Rooms 10 Bedrooms 5 Baths & Quality 2 up & down good Kitchen Quality Modern cabinet kitchen down, good semi-modern up
Heat Oil fired Bsbd hot water Fireplace yes Insulation yes Floors Hardwood Siding Vinyl
Roof & Condition Good - asphalt sh. Basement Full Garage Detached - 2 car
Describe General Condition Well kept and maintained. Quite attractive and comfortable. Open porch in front.

Contributory value of dwelling: (including min. size lot & improvements) $ 38,000

Dwelling #2
Style ___ Age ___ Type of Construction ___ Size ___ Sq. Ft. Living Area ___
No. Rooms ___ Bedrooms ___ Bath & Quality ___ Kitchen Quality ___
Heat ___ Fireplace ___ Insulation ___ Floors ___ Siding ___
Roof & Condition ___ Basement ___ Garage ___
Describe General Condition ___

Contributory value of dwelling: (including min. size lot & improvements) $

OTHER BUILDINGS - Give size & description. Indicate contributory value of major buildings and site. (combine major dairy barn, milking parlor, and silos in one figure.)

Barn #1 : 40 x 160 - 2 story gambel roof. 60 stalls arranged in 2 rows.	$ 17,000
Pipeline system Adequate storage above. Good milk house.	$
Barn #2 : 36 x 100 with 18 x 36 ell. Heifer facility with 30 ties	$ 5,000
Silos : 2 - 14 x 50 CS, 14 x 30 CS w/roof, new 20 x 64 CS	$ 12,000
Tool Shed : 30 x 60 quite good M/E storage, - metal sidewalls/roof	$
	$
Total value all buildings	$ 72,000

LAND - Type and Description

		Acres
Farmstead(s) (land included with buildings)		3
Tillage	Mapped as Howard gravelly silt loam. Well-drained soils in good state of fertility. Easily operated - convenient. Level	140
Pasture		40
Timber & Pulpwood	Second growth mixed hardwood and softwoods.	17
Other		
	Total Acres......	200

Capacity: No. Cows, etc. 60 Feeding Capacity (if different) ___ Principal & Secondary Products:
Classification of: Area 2 (1,2,3,4) Farm B (A,B,C,D) 1. Milk 2. ___

Figure 8-4 Cont.

SALES DATA OR BENCHMARK TO SUPPORT VALUES

1. Seller/Purchaser or Benchmark: A to B — Date: 3/78 — Price or PMV: $ 123,000 — County: Baler

Town: Hayside — Road & No.: County Rd. #2 — Acres: Total 225 — Till. 130

Dwellings: $ 30,000 $ ______ Barns: $ 25,000 $ ______ Capacity 80 cows

Harvestores: No. ______ $ ______ Other buildings $ ______ Total buildings $55,000

Value of remaining land $ 68,000 — Per Total acre $ 302 — Value of till./acre $ 450

Value of other land/acre $ 100

2. Seller/Purchaser: C to D — Date: 5/78 — Price: $ 155,000 — County: Baler

Town: Downing — Road & No.: R. #2 — Acres: Total 230 — Till. 200

Dwellings: $ 35,000 $ ______ Barns: $ 25,000 $ ______ Capacity 90 cows

Harvestores: No. ______ $ ______ Other buildings $ ______ Total buildings $60,000

Value of remaining land $ 91,000 — Per Total acre $ 395 — Value of till./acre $ 440

Value of other land/acre $ 100

3. Seller/Purchaser: E to F — Date: 8/78 — Price: $ 135,000 — County: Baler

Town: Fuller — Road & No.: North Rd. — Acres: Total 210 — Till. 150

Dwellings: $ 37,000 $ ______ Barns: $ 28,000 $ ______ Capacity 65 cows

Harvestores: No. ______ $ ______ Other buildings $ 3,000 — Total buildings $68,000

Value of remaining land $ 70,500 — Per Total acre $ 336 — Value of till./acre $ 430

Value of other land/acre $ 100

COMPARISON

Subject property compared to sales or benchmark <indicate (+) or(-) in dollars or (=)>
<If subject property greater value than sale **or** benchmark, use (+)>

Sale	Time Factor	Size	Quality of Land	Amount of Land	Location	Buildings	Indicated Value Subject Property
1	=	=	=	+$ 700	=	+$17,000	$ 140,700
2	=	=	=	- 23,700	=	+ 12,000	$ 143,300
3	=	=	=	- 4,600	=	+ 4,000	$ 134,400

REMARKS (Include any alternative valuation process)

#1 Land = $450 x 140 = $63,000 + $100 x 57 = $5,700 : $68,700 - $68,000 = +$700

#2 Land = $440 x 140 = $61,600 + $100 x 57 = $5,700 : $67,300 - $91,000 = -$23,700

#3 Land = $430 x 140 = $60,200 + $100 x 57 = $5,700 : $65,900 - $70,500 = -$4,600

A well-located, productive, one-man unit located north of the village of Hayside. Soils are productive, barn facilities are modern and convenient and the dwelling very comfortable and well maintained. There are adequate facilities for housing young and dry stock in Barn #2 along with ample storage. Property would be readily salable and attract an above average operator.

PMV of Property after improvements, if any, (AV if different $ ______) $ 140,000

Appraised value of all buildings (include min. size lot & site improvements) $ 72,000
Appraised value of remaining land $ 68,000
Value/remaining acre-per total acre $ 340 — Val. Til/acre $ 445 — Val. other land/acre $ 100

PMV of Property "AS IS" (AV if different $ ______) $ 140,000
List improvements required and cost ______

Plat of property indicating location of buildings, types of land, easements, photograph of principal dwellings and buildings of major significance attached.

Any general shortage of not more than 2 percent revealed by title examination which does not result from exclusion of any specific parcel will not affect my values.

1/3/79 — Date

Loan Officer — Appraiser's Signature

[¶806] FmHA AS A SOURCE OF FUNDS

Within the United States Department of Agriculture the Farmers Home Administration provides credit under certain circumstances for rural Americans unable to get credit from other sources at reasonable rates and terms. Operating principally under the Consolidated Farm and Rural Development Act (1921) and Title V of the Housing Act of 1949, FmHA provides financial and management assistance through operating and farm ownership loans. Applications for loans are made at over 1,750 FmHA offices located mostly in county seats throughout the nation. A county committee of three certifies or recommends eligibility of individual applicants, amounts of loans, and reviews borrowing. The whole thrust of FmHA is to encourage family-size farms. Of the more than a billion dollars in loans, FmHA has 58+ per cent of its funds in operating loans and 41+ per cent in farm ownerships.

[¶807] PCA LOANS UP TO SEVEN YEARS

The Production Credit Association can make loans to farmers up to seven years in length. A farmer applies to the PCA office serving his area. Together with the managers in the office, he outlines his needs, reviews repayment schedules, and provides a financial statement showing what he owns, and what he owes, and what he can pay. The whole discussion and application provide benefits to the farmer because the farmer gets an accurate picture of his operations. After the first loan is made, that farmer can use the telephone and work out his loans almost over the counter.

Moreover, PCA, recognizing the seasonal needs of farmers, provides a line-of-credit financing plans by which a farmer can arrange in advance for a loan that will adequately cover all his financial requirements for an entire season or agricultural cycle. He draws the money as he needs it and repays it according to a pre-arranged schedule, perhaps when he sells his product. There is no interest on a line-of-credit loan until the money is actually drawn. When any part of the loan is repaid, no further interest is charged on the portion repaid. This means that the farmer only pays interest on each dollar used for the number of days he uses the money.

[¶807.1] Investment in the PCA as a Cooperative

Since PCAs are credit cooperatives, each farmer who borrows must invest a certain sum to help capitalize the co-op. He buys stock in proportion to the amount of his loan. In actual practice, this investment is added to the amount of his loan so that he does not need to have the cash available. The control provided by stock ownership always remains in the hands of the active farmers who are present borrowers.

[¶808] USES OF CREDIT LIFE INSURANCE

Credit Life Insurance is term life insurance issued through a lender or lending agency to cover payment of a loan, installment purchase, or other obligation in case of death. It is generally limited to loans of ten years or less in duration. Ordinary life insurance may include credit life insurance on loans of more than ten year's duration. Beginning in 1900, credit insurance grew slowly but steadily, but since 1960 its growth has been phenomenal so that by the end of 1975 more than $112,032,000,000 credit insurance was in force which represented 5.3 per cent of the $2.1 trillion life insurance issued by legal reserve life insurance companies at the end of 1975.

Figure 8-5

Distribution Of Credit Life Insurance In Force By Geographic Division 1975

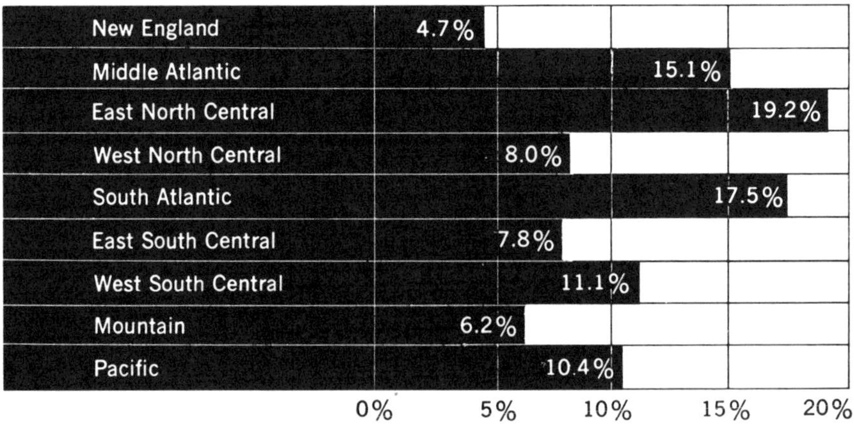

Credit Life Insurance, used to repay a debt in case the borrower should die, generally decreases in amount as a loan is repaid. It protects the farmer's family as well as the lender, against unpaid debt that may be left at death. Credit insurance is issued through such lenders as banks, finance companies, credit unions, and retailers who in turn make arrangements with the borrowers.

[¶809] RETAIL EQUIPMENT CREDIT

Most farmers buy machinery and equipment from their neighborhood implement dealer. The financing is arranged through the retail dealer through lending agencies of the manufacturer, through banks, or through financing companies. Figure 8-6 gives an example of an International Harvester Company retail installment contract. Figure 8-7 is a general form of credit application through a dealer to a local bank. Figure 8-8 gives a typical time sales application. Figure 8-9 gives a form generally used by a bank as a security agreement for the sale of consumer goods.

THE LANGUAGE OF CREDIT

Ability to Service Debt The amount of money and the time of year the sums will be available calculated by a formula:

1. Project the profit or loss from the farm operating statement.
\+ 2. Add projected outside income.
\+ 3. Depreciation charged against the farm enterprise.
\+ 4. Add inventory of some liquid assets such as surplus stored grain, cash in the bank, and other current liquid assets.
− 5. Subtract projected new investment in capital assets.
− 6. Subtract family living expenses.
− 7. Subtract cash reserve for emergencies.
= 8. Amount of cash available to service debt.

Plans for debt service must be scheduled to the available timing of the year when the debtor may be expected to have a surplus of cash.

Balance Sheet A listing of all assets and liabilities establishing net worth, i.e., assets minus liabilities equal net worth or equity, lenders using a gain in net worth as financial progress.

Cash Flow Statement As a historical statement the record provides a diary of the way the operating statement as compiled, shows how borrowed funds were used, how payment on debts were made, what withdrawals from savings were made, and what the expenditures for family living totaled. When projected, the statement charts the expected inflow of cash from all income sources and all cash outflows, including household expenses. The ability to repay debt is generally determined by examining the cash flow projection, ALONGSIDE THE CASH FLOW.

Current Assets Cash or other assets normally convertible into cash during the year, usually during an annual period, inclusive of the farm

Figure 8-6 Retail Instalment Contract

RETAIL INSTALMENT CONTRACT FOR AGRICULTURAL EQUIPMENT — IHCC® — DATE

SELLER	PURCHASER (LAST NAME FIRST)				
CITY AND STATE	ADDRESS	CITY	COUNTY	STATE	ZIP CODE

Purchaser hereby purchases and seller hereby sells subject to all terms, conditions and agreements contained herein, including the ADDITIONAL PROVISIONS printed on the REVERSE hereof the following described property, delivery, inspection and acceptance of which are hereby acknowledged by the purchaser:

QU.	N/U	MAKE / MODEL / DESCRIPTION (SHOW ALL SERIAL AND MOTOR NUMBERS)	PRICE

TRADE-IN		
MAKE		
DESCRIPTION		
YEAR—MODEL		
SERIAL NO.		
ALLOWANCE	$	$
AMOUNT OWING (IF ANY)		
NET TRADE-IN ALLOWANCE	$	$

1. SALES PRICE		
2. SALES TAX		
3. CASH PRICE PLUS TAX		
4. CASH DOWN PAYMENT		
TRADE-IN (NET ALLOWANCE)	X X X X X	X X
TOTAL DOWN PAYMENT		
5. UNPAID BALANCE OF CASH PRICE (3 LESS 4)		
6. OTHER CHARGES:		
a. Official Fees	X X X X X	X X
TOTAL OTHER CHARGES		
7. UNPAID BALANCE (Amount Financed) (TOTAL OF 5 and 6)		
8. **FINANCE CHARGE**		
ANNUAL PERCENTAGE RATE ____ %		
9. TOTAL OF PAYMENTS (TOTAL OF 7 and 8)		
10. DEFERRED PAYMENT PRICE (TOTAL OF 3, 6 and 8)		

SCHEDULE OF INSTALMENTS

	AMOUNT	DUE DATE		AMOUNT	DUE DATE
1			9		
2			10		
3			11		
4			12		
5			13		
6			14		
7			15		
8			16		

DATE FINANCE CHARGE BEGINS TO ACCRUE (IF DIFFERENT THAN CONTRACT DATE) / /

11. PAYMENT SCHEDULE: Purchaser agrees to pay seller, or if this contract is assigned, assignee of seller, the "TOTAL OF PAYMENTS" (Item 9 above) in ____ instalments of $____ each, and ____ instalments of $____ each, and ____ instalments of $____ each, payable on the same day of each successive month commencing ____, 19____, or as indicated in the Schedule of Instalments printed hereon. BALLOON PAYMENT(S): $____ on ___/___/___, $____ on ___/___/___, (insert date and amount of any payment more than twice the amount of an otherwise regularly scheduled equal payment). No such Balloon Payment will be refinanced if not paid when due, unless the parties hereto otherwise agree in writing on such due date.

NET CREDIT DUE	
UNPAID CASH BAL. (No. 5)	$
TOTAL OTHER CHARGES	
TOTAL TO BE APPLIED:	$

☐ SEND CHECK ☐ CREDIT ACCOUNT
☐ CREDIT FLOOR PLAN NOTE(S) AS INDICATED

REGIONAL OFFICE USE ONLY	
AMOUNT WAIVED	
CREDITED TO RESERVE	
FINANCE I.H.C.C.	

AMOUNT DUE

NOTE OR INVOICE NUMBER	PRINCIPAL	INTEREST	AMOUNT OWING
		TOTAL	
		LESS NET CREDIT DUE	
CHECK NO.	DATED	IS ATTACHED FOR	

Liability Insurance for bodily injury or property damage caused to others is NOT provided with this agreement. If you desire liability insurance coverage, you should obtain such coverage from an agent of your choice.

FOR DEALER USE ONLY

APPROVED for Seller and ASSIGNED to IHCC under the terms of Assignment #1 appearing on the reverse of this contract. (Initial (________ here if assigned under the terms of Assignment #2, Assignment and Guaranty).

AUTHORIZED SIGNATURE FOR SELLER

By ____________________
(Signature of Manager, Owner, Officer) (Title)

DEALER READ ASSIGNMENT ON REVERSE SIDE

RETAIL INSTALMENT CONTRACT
PURCHASER ACKNOWLEDGES RECEIPT OF AN EXACT COPY OF THIS CONTRACT

PURCHASER

BY ____ TITLE

CO-SIGNER

BY ____ TITLE

SALESMAN

APPROVED FOR INTERNATIONAL HARVESTER COMPANY (IN SALES ONLY)

BY: ____ MGR.

FH... For use in Minn., N.C., N.J., N.Mex. and N.Y. IHCC TRANSMITTAL COPY Form appr. 5-1-7?

Figure 8-7 Credit Application

CREDIT APPLICATION — **THE FIRST NATIONAL BANK OF GLENS FALLS, Glens Falls, New York 12801**

PERSONAL DATA — APPLICANT

DATE | AMOUNT REQUESTED | TERM | PAYMENT DATE | PROCEEDS OF LOAN TO BE USED FOR

NAME LAST | FIRST | MIDDLE | AGE | DEPENDENTS (IF ANY)

ADDRESS NO. & STREET | CITY | COUNTY | STATE | ZIP CODE | YEARS | SOCIAL SECURITY NO.

FORMER ADDRESS NO. & STREET | CITY | COUNTY | STATE | ZIP CODE | YEARS | RES. PHONE

NAME OF NEAREST RELATIVE OR FRIEND NOT LIVING WITH YOU | ADDRESS

PRESENT EMPLOYER | POSITION | INCOME | ☐ WEEKLY ☐ BI WEEKLY ☐ MONTHLY | NO. YRS. THERE

ADDRESS NO. & STREET | CITY | STATE | BADGE NO. | BUSINESS PHONE

FORMER EMPLOYER (IF LESS THAN 3 YEARS) | ADDRESS

ADDITIONAL INCOME ☐ MONTHLY ☐ QUARTERLY ☐ SEMI-ANNUALLY ☐ YEARLY — ALIMONY OR CHILD SUPPORT OR MAINTENANCE PAYMENTS ARE OPTIONAL INFORMATION AND NEED NOT BE REVEALED IF THE APPLICANT DOES NOT CHOOSE TO RELY ON SUCH INCOME IN APPLYING FOR CREDIT $ ________ SOURCE ________

CHECKING — BANK | BRANCH | SAVINGS ☐ BANK ☐ S & L | BRANCH

☐ RENT ☐ OWN | MONTHLY PAYMENT | TO WHOM PAID | MAKE OF AUTO | YEAR | HOLDER OF LIEN | BALANCE | PAYMENT

DEBTS — (BANKS, STORES, LOAN & FINANCE COMPANIES, CREDIT UNIONS AND OTHERS TO WHOM YOU ARE INDEBTED. INCLUDE ANY REVOLVING LINE OF CREDIT)	MONTHLY TERMS	PRESENT BALANCE

CREDIT REFERENCES

ARE YOU A CO-MAKER, ENDORSER OR GUARANTOR ON ANY LOAN OR CONTRACT? YES ☐ NO ☐ IF YES, FOR WHOM? | TO WHOM?

ARE THERE ANY UNSATISFIED JUDGMENTS AGAINST YOU? YES ☐ NO ☐ OMIT IF MORE THAN 7 YEARS AMOUNT $ | IF YES, TO WHOM OWED?

WERE YOU EVER BANKRUPT? YES ☐ NO ☐ OMIT IF MORE THAN 14 YEARS IF YES, WHERE? | YEAR

DEALER

DEALER | SALESMAN | CASH DOWN PAYMENT | CASH PRICE

ADDRESS | DATE | TRADE IN ALLOWANCE | SALES TAX

N/U | YR | CYL | MAKE — TRADE NAME — MODEL — SERIAL NUMBER | KEY NUMBER | LESS: LIEN OWING | TOTAL CASH PRICE

TOTAL DOWN PAYMENT | LESS: DOWN PAYMENT

EQUIPMENT ☐ A.T. ☐ A.C. ☐ P.B. ☐ P.S. ☐ P.W. ☐ AM FMR ☐ AM & FM STEREO ☐ TAPE DECK ☐ OTHER | CREDIT LIFE ☐ YES ☐ NO | CREDIT A & H ☐ YES ☐ NO | AUTO INS. FINANCED ☐ YES ☐ NO | CREDIT INS.

TRADE-IN DESCRIBE | LEIN HOLDER | AUTO INS.

DESCRIPTION OF GOODS & SERVICES OTHER THAN AUTOMOBILE | OFFICIAL FEES

TOTAL AMOUNT FINANCED

Will any other person become contractually liable by signing the instrument of indebtedness or a guaranty of this loan? YES ☐ NO ☐ If yes, OTHER PERSON MUST COMPLETE A SEPARATE APPLICATION.

I AUTHORIZE The Bank, to make whatever credit inquiries it deems necessary in connection with my credit application or in the course of review or collection of any credit extended in reliance on the application. I authorize and instruct any person or consumer reporting agency to compile and furnish The Bank any information it may have or obtain in response to such credit inquiries and agree that same shall remain your property whether or not credit is extended.

All information set forth in this application is declared to be a true representation of facts made for the purpose of obtaining an installment loan and any willful misrepresentation on this application could result in criminal action.

I acknowledge the receipt of the Equal Credit Opportunity Act Notice attached hereto.

APPLICANT'S SIGNATURE | APPLICANT'S SIGNATURE | DATE

BANCO CA1

Figure 8-8 Time Sales Application

TIME SALES APPLICATION — AGRICULTURAL EQUIPMENT

NAME	PHONE AREA CODE & NUMBER	AGE	U. S. CITIZEN ☐ YES ☐ NO	☐ SINGLE ☐ MARRIED	NO. OF DEPENDENTS

ADDRESS	CITY	COUNTY	STATE	ZIP CODE	YEARS IN BUSINESS	BUSINESS STRUCTURE ☐ INDIVIDUAL ☐ CORP. ☐ PARTNERSHIP	TIME DEVOTED TO BUSINESS ☐ FULL ☐ PART

SOCIAL SECURITY NUMBER	DRIVERS LICENSE NUMBER

FARM

NUMBER OF ACRES				MONTHLY INCOME	EMPLOYED BY (IF PART TIME FARMER)	YEARS	INCOME	OTHER INCOME	TOTAL OTHER INCOME
OWNED	RENTED	CULTIVATED	INCOME		AS				

SEASONAL INCOME

COMMODITY (LIVESTOCK, CROPS)	QUANTITY NUMBER OR ACRES	MARKET DATE	ANTICIPATED INCOME	PAYMENT AVAILABLE FROM THIS COMMODITY

PREVIOUS EQUIPMENT PURCHASES ARE (WERE) FINANCED BY:

EQUIPMENT	NAME AND ADDRESS	WHEN PURCHASED	BALANCE	PAYABLE

BANK WITH	TRADE REFERENCES

FINANCED WITH IHCC BEFORE ☐ YES ☐ NO	FINANCIAL STATEMENT, IF REQUIRED ☐ COMPLETED ON REVERSE SIDE ☐ ATTACHED	SIGNED - OWNER, PARTNER, OFFICER	DATE

DO NOT WRITE BELOW — DEALER TO COMPLETE

HAVE YOU SOLD OR LEASED TO CUSTOMER BEFORE?	YES ☐ NO ☐	DID HE PAY YOU PROMPTLY?	YES ☐ NO ☐
HAVE YOU CHECKED REFERENCES GIVEN YOU?	YES ☐ NO ☐	DID REFERENCES REPORT PROMPT PAYMENT?	YES ☐ NO ☐
IS CUSTOMER'S GENERAL HEALTH GOOD?	YES ☐ NO ☐	IS CUSTOMER AN FHA CLIENT?	YES ☐ NO ☐

FIRM NAME	BY	DATE

WORK SHEET FOR SEASONAL PAYMENTS

	DUE DATE	PRINCIPAL	NO. OF MONTHS	TOTAL PAYMENT	FINANCE CHARGE
1					
2					
3					
4					
5					
6					
7					
8					

WORK SHEET FOR LEVEL PAYMENTS

PAYMENT PLAN	PRINCIPAL	TOTAL DEFER. PAYMENT	LEVEL PAYMENT	FINANCE CHARGE

(FINANCE WAIVED TO ____________)

FH-15.1 PC. Page 1.

Figure 8-8 Cont.

FINANCIAL STATEMENT

HEREBY AFFIRM THAT THE FOLLOWING IS AN ACCURATE AND COMPLETE STATEMENT OF MY AFFAIRS AS OF THIS DATE.

ASSETS	AMOUNT	LIABILITIES	AMOUNT
CASH, STOCKS AND BONDS	$	OWE BANK UNSECURED (PLEDGE OF STOCK, BONDS)	$
ACCOUNTS, NOTES RECEIVABLE (AMOUNT PLEDGED $		ACCOUNTS PAYABLE — TRADE	
LIVESTOCK: ☐ CATTLE ☐ HOGS ☐ SHEEP		MTG. ON LIVESTOCK TO:	
HARVESTED CROPS		MTG. ON 19 CROPS TO	
		FUTURE EARNINGS ASSIGNED TO	
		WAGES, LICENSE AND TAXES PAYABLE	
MACHINERY AND EQUIPMENT		OWE ON MACHINERY & EQUIPMENT (FRONT SIDE)	
TRUCKS AND AUTOS		OWE ON TRUCKS & AUTOS TO	
LAND & BUILDINGS LOCATED		OWE ON LAND & BLDGS. TO	
OTHER ASSETS		OTHER INDEBTEDNESS	
TOTAL ASSETS	$	**TOTAL LIABILITIES**	$

SIGNED: ______________________ DATE ____________

REFERENCES: THE FOLLOWING CREDIT INFORMATION HAS BEEN OBTAINED ON THIS CUSTOMER:

CREDIT REFERENCES	YEARS YOU HAVE DONE BUS WITH CUSTOMER	BUSINESS RELATIONS SATISFACTORY (YES OR NO)	HIGHEST AMOUNT OF CREDIT EXTENDED	OWES NOW?	PAST DUE NOW	PROMPT OR SLOW PAYING HABITS?
1.			$	$	$	
2.						
3.						
4.						
5.						

NOTE: ABOVE REFERENCES SHOULD INCLUDE THE MAJOR SOURCE(S) OF FINANCING, BANKS OR OTHERWISE.

Figure 8-9 Retail Instalment Contract

RETAIL INSTALMENT CONTRACT (Security Agreement for Sale of Consumer Goods) Date____________, 19____

Buyer's Name
and Address____________

Seller's Name
and Place of Business ____________

Buyer has purchased from Seller and acknowledges delivery, examination and acceptance of the following described property in its present condition, subject to the terms and conditions of this contract.

DESCRIPTION OF GOODS SOLD

____

____

____

If a charge is made on lines 4 and/or 5 and Buyer signs below and checks coverage requested in box indicated, Buyer requests Seller to secure group credit life insurance and/or group credit accident and health insurance on the Buyer signing below in accordance with the notice of proposed group insurance on the back of Buyer's copy. The charges shall be the amounts stated on lines 4a and/or 5a as proposed charges. **SUCH INSURANCE IS NOT REQUIRED BY SELLER.** The term of such insurance is the period of repayment as specified herein. Buyer hereby requests the group insurance indicated below.

☐ (4a) Group Credit Life Insurance $ ______ (Proposed Charge)   ☐ (5a) Group Credit Accident & Health Insurance $ ______ (Proposed Charge)

______ Buyer To Be Insured   Date ______

No group insurance will be provided if Buyer has not checked coverage requested, signed above where indicated and a charge is made on lines 4 and/or 5.

Group Insurance Carrier: **John Hancock Mutual Life Insurance Company, Boston Massachusetts**

Maximum Life Insurance: **$20,000.00**

Total Down Payment (2)	
Trade-In	______
Allowance	$ ______
Less Lien	— ______
Net Trade-In	$ ______
Cash Down Payment	$ ______
Other Charges	$ ______
	$ ______

Cash Price incl. Sales Tax	$ 1
Total Down Payment	− 2
Unpaid Balance of Cash Price (1 - 2)	$ 3
Group Life Insurance	+ 4
Group A&H Insurance	+ 5
Other Charges	+ 6
Unpaid Balance & Amount Financed (3 + 4 + 5 + 6)	$ 7
FINANCE CHARGE	8
Total of Payments (7 + 8)	$ 9
Deferred Payment Price (2 + 9)	$ 10
ANNUAL PERCENTAGE RATE	%

Buyer agrees to pay Seller or assignee the foregoing Total of Payments (9) in ____ equal monthly instalments of $____________ each and a (first or final) instalment of $__________, the first instalment to be paid on ____________, 19______, and one instalment on the same day of each succeeding month thereafter until paid in full.

THE FIRST NATIONAL BANK
OF GLENS FALLS
Glens Falls, New York 12801

A security interest is granted to Seller on Goods described above. In the event of a default in payments, Buyer is required to pay a late payment charge of **5%** of any instalment past due for **10** days or **$5.00** whichever is less. In the event of prepayment, the **FINANCE CHARGE** will be prorated pursuant to the Rule of 78's method and the unearned portion refunded except that the Bank shall be entitled to retain a minimum **FINANCE CHARGE** of **$12.00** (or **$10.00** if the contract is repayable in 8 months or less) and also that no refund will be made if the unearned **FINANCE CHARGE** is less than **$1.00**. In the event of prepayment, the unearned portion of any group insurance premium will also be refunded pursuant to the Rule of 78's method.

THIS CONTRACT IS SUBJECT TO THE ABOVE TERMS AND CONDITIONS, AS CONTINUED ON THE REVERSE SIDE OF THIS PAGE.

(The following notice shall not apply to any sale for other than personal, family or household use.)

NOTICE — Any holder of this consumer credit contract is subject to all claims and defenses which the debtor could assert against the seller of goods or services obtained pursuant hereto or with the proceeds hereof. Recovery hereunder by the debtor shall not exceed amounts paid by the debtor hereunder.

NOTICE TO THE BUYER: 1. Do not sign this agreement before you read it or if it contains any blank space. 2. You are entitled to a completely filled in copy of this agreement. 3. Under the law, you have the right to pay off in advance the full amount due and under certain conditions to obtain a partial refund of the FINANCE CHARGE.

Seller agrees to this contract including the back and assigns it to the Bank named above pursuant to the assignment without recourse paragraph on the reverse hereof unless signed on the back.

BUYER ACKNOWLEDGES RECEIPT OF AN EXECUTED COPY OF THIS CONTRACT AND DISCLOSURE STATEMENT

RETAIL INSTALMENT CONTRACT

______________ (Seller)   ______________ (Buyer's Signature)

By ______________ (Title)   ______________ (Buyer's Signature)

NOTICE: SHADED AREA IS TRUTH IN LENDING AND OTHER DISCLOSURES REQUIRED BY FEDERAL LAW. SEE OTHER SIDE FOR IMPORTANT INFORMATION.

Banconsumer 210   BANK FILE COPY   1976 BANCONSUMER SERVICE, INC.

Figure 8-9 Cont.

Seller has retained title to and shall have a security interest in and a lien upon the goods sold until all amounts payable by Buyer hereunder are fully paid to Seller. "Seller" shall include Seller named herein and any holder who acquires this contract by purchase or assignment. If there is more than one Buyer, all obligations shall be joint and several and the term "Buyer" shall be read in the plural herein.

This contract is not binding upon Seller until accepted in writing by Seller's credit department. In the event that the credit of Buyer is not satisfactory to Seller, or the contract is not accepted by Seller or Seller is unable to deliver the goods for any reason whatsoever, this contract shall be cancelled and neither party shall be under any liability to the other, and all moneys paid by Buyer hereon shall be refunded. If delivery of the goods is not made at the time of the execution of this contract, the identifying numbers or marks of the goods and the due date of the first instalment may be left blank and later inserted by Seller in Seller's counterpart of this contract after it has been signed by Buyer.

Buyer agrees to insure goods against fire, and Buyer assumes entire risk of loss, or destruction of goods, and no such occurrence shall release Buyer.

Buyer shall choose person through whom insurance is to be obtained.

Buyer warrants and represents that the goods are bought for use primarily for personal, family or household purposes and that the residence address of Buyer is as set forth on the front hereof. The goods shall be and remain personal property for all purposes, and Buyer shall not affix them to any real estate so as to become a fixture or fixtures without the prior written consent of Seller. Buyer agrees to keep the goods safely, not to remove them from the address shown on the front hereof without the prior written consent of Seller and not to sell, transfer, create another security interest in or encumber the goods or any interest therein, or suffer the same to be encumbered, without the prior written consent of Seller. (If Buyer sells or transfers the goods, either in violation of this contract or with the written consent of Seller, Seller shall also have a security interest in the proceeds thereof.)

Buyer acknowledges notice of the intended assignment of this contract to the Bank named herein and agrees that after receiving notice of such assignment he will make no payments to Seller and will make no modification of this agreement with Seller without the consent of the assignee. Seller shall not be deemed to act as Agent of any assignee in the making of this contract or the collection of any moneys due hereunder, or for any other purpose.

The occurrence of any of the following shall be a default hereunder: (1) Buyer's failure to promptly perform any of his obligations hereunder; (2) the death, incompetency, bankruptcy or insolvency of Buyer; (3) any warranty or statement of Buyer proving to be materially incorrect; (4) if Seller shall with reasonable cause deem itself or the goods insecure. In the event of default, Seller shall have the right, without notice or demand, to (1) declare all unpaid instalments immediately due; (2) enter any premises where the goods are or may be supposed to be and take possession of the goods; (3) exercise any or all of the rights on default of a secured party under the Uniform Commercial Code. Seller may require Buyer to assemble the goods and make them available to Seller at a place to be designated by Seller which is reasonably convenient to Seller and Buyer. Any notice of sale, disposition or other intended action by Seller, sent to Buyer at the address specified herein or such other address of Buyer as may from time to time be shown on Seller's records, at least five days prior to such action, shall constitute reasonable notice to Buyer. Buyer will pay any deficiency that may remain after the exercise of such rights and will be entitled to any surplus. Buyer shall pay a delinquency and collection charge on each instalment in default for a period of not less than ten days at the rate of five per cent of such instalment or five dollars, whichever is less, subject to the limitations of such charge provided by law.

Buyer hereby authorizes Seller to file such financing statement or statements as Seller shall deem necessary or desirable under the Uniform Commercial Code, signed only by Seller. Buyer's obligation, if more than one, shall be joint and several.

UNLESS OTHERWISE AGREED BETWEEN THE PARTIES HERETO IN WRITING, THERE ARE NO WARRANTIES WHICH EXTEND BEYOND THE DESCRIPTION ON THE FACE HEREOF. NO WARRANTY OF MERCHANTIBILITY OR OF FITNESS FOR A PARTICULAR PURPOSE SHALL EXTEND BEYOND THE DURATION OF ANY SUCH WRITTEN WARRANTY.

NOTICE OF PROPOSED GROUP INSURANCE

NOTICE TO BUYER: Group credit life insurance coverage and/or group credit accident and health insurance coverage will be applicable to this contract if so marked on the front of this contract and will be written by the insurance company named.

No charge is or will be made to you for such insurance unless set forth in the space provided. If such insurance is declined by the insurer or otherwise does not become effective, any premium or identifiable charge to you will be refunded or credited pursuant to the provisions of Part 185 of the Regulations of the New York State Department of Insurance. The term of insurance will commence as of the date the indebtedness is incurred and will expire on the date the indebtedness on the contract is paid, or earlier in the event of default or other happenings as set forth in the group policy. Subject to acceptance by the insurer, and within 30 days, there will be delivered to the insured Buyer a certificate of insurance more fully describing the insurance.

and equipment, value of stocks and bonds, cash surrender value of life insurance, and artifacts easily sold.

Current Liabilities All debts, plus payments on debts due within a year, including principal payments on intermediate and long-term debts and notes and accounts payable within the next 12 months.

Fixed Assets Permanent elements such as land, land improvement, buildings, fences, irrigation wells, and building improvements.

Intermediate-Term Liabilities Notes, chattel mortgages, contracts, and other credit instruments that have terms of 1 to 8 years.

Leverage The use of a farmer's own money, which, when coupled with borrowed money, enables him to purchase more than he could with his own money alone. The more resources he can borrow from someone else in relation to his own, the greater his leverage.

Liquidity The degree of liquidity is the ability of the farm to service the debt. Three indexes are compiled often from the balance sheet:

1. $\text{Current Ratio} = \dfrac{\text{Total Current Assets}}{\text{Total Current Liabilities}}$

   Thus, a ratio greater than 1:1 would mean that a farmer is capable of paying off all current liabilities by selling or liquidating only his current assets.

2. $\text{Current Debt Ratio} = \dfrac{\text{Total Current Liabilities}}{\text{Total Liabilities}}$

   This index will show the proportion of the farm debt that will be due within a year. A high current debt ratio signals a drain on cash flow. It indicates that more risk will be involved in making debt payments on time.

3. $\text{Current Debt to Net Worth Ratio} = \dfrac{\text{Total Current Liabilities}}{\text{Net Worth}}$

   A farmer's ability to pay his current liabilities when due may depend on his equity in the farm.

Long-Term Liabilities Usually mortgages or contracts on real estate, less the current year's principal payment included in current liabilities.

Profit and Loss Statement This statement, often called the operating statement, shows how effectively a farmer uses assets to produce income. The statement lists all farm income and all farm expenses, including depreciation. The so-called bottom line describes how effectively the farmer has used his resources at his command in land, labor, capital, and management. The bottom line, further, is an index of the farmer's capacity to repay borrowed money. It shows how well the farmer has managed his operation.

Solvency This means simply that a farmer has the assets to pay all debts if he were to liquidate his farm enterprise.

Lenders use various formulas to measure the degree of solvency.

1. $\text{Net Capital Rates} = \dfrac{\text{Total Assets}}{\text{Total Liabilities}}$

   As long as the ratio is greater than 1:1, the farm is considered solvent.

2. $\text{Debt Equity Ratio} = \dfrac{\text{Total Debt}}{\text{Net Worth}}$

   A ratio of 1:1 means that for every dollar a farmer borrows, he has one dollar invested of his own.

Working Assets The assets of the farm that can be applied to its current productive operations, having a useful life of one to ten years and which cannot be converted into cash without seriously impairing the productive potential of the farm.

9

Insurance as a Tool in Estate Building and Settlement

[¶900] INCORPORATING INSURANCE IN THE ESTATE PLAN

In a comprehensive estate plan, life insurance plays a major role. It must be incorporated into the total scheme so that it dovetails to achieve the objectives of the plan. To define the optimum usefulness of life insurance in the estate plan, the counsel of an insurance underwriter is necessary—with this warning: an insurance agent may recommend maximum rather than optimum coverage at premium costs that may be too steep for the farmer's income to bear.

[¶901] INSURANCE AS RISK PROTECTION

What is the primary purpose of insurance? It is *protection against risk.* Insurance spreads risks over many people. By the payment of a premium, the farmer protects himself against the happening of events called "contingencies" that may affect his production of income and the security of his family.

"Insurance" is sometimes spelled "assurance." When it is spelled with an "I", the word describes protection against loss or death. When spelled with an "A", it means a positive declaration intended to give confidence. The Equitable Life Assurance Society of the United States calls itself an "assurance society" and the Metropolitan an "insurance" company. While both words are often interchangeable, it is good to think in terms of both spellings: one, the protection against loss and death; the other a declaration of confidence in the provision of needed income.

LIFE INSURANCE performs at least ten functions in estate planning. It can

1. provide liquidity for payment of federal and state death taxes
2. make money available for estate settlement costs
3. fund buy-sell agreements to assure continuity of the farm enterprise
4. produce cash to enable the on-the-farm heirs to acquire the farm asset by paying off their respective share to the off-the-farm heirs
5. assure retirement income, possibly with annuity
6. generate capital and create an estate where none might otherwise exist
7. protect wife and dependents against loss of income resulting from death of husband and father
8. deliver cash for the payment of mortgages and debts
9. provide a vehicle for systematic saving
10. generate cash value which can be used as equity or emergency fund.

[¶902] BASIC QUESTIONS

In determining the place of life insurance in an estate plan, the farmer asks himself four fundamental questions:

1. How much money do I need for the protection of my farm and the security of my family?
2. What alternative ways do I have to produce the money I need?
3. What is the most economical way I can meet the need?
4. How much premium payment can I afford at my stage in life and income level?

[¶903] CONCENTRATION ON INCOME GENERATOR

In answering these questions, the farmer needs to bear in mind—above all else—that his insurance protects his family from losing him as the producer of income. Hence, the foremost consideration in his decision is coverage to provide for the family's economic support.

[¶904] SPECIAL ROLE OF INSURANCE IN FARMER'S PLANNING

Farming presents a business occupation that differs in a number of ways from other vocational enterprises. The farmer must act on certain principles and practices that differ from those of corporate employees.

In the first place, the number of farm workers is relatively small as an economic unit. Second, the financing of a farm is distinguished by heavy capital requirements that cut heavily into cash flow. Third, as the farm family members grow up and grow older, the family living expenses escalate at the same time that the family has a substantial amount of non-liquid assets invested in the farm. Fourth, the continuing rise in farm values makes heavy demands for liquid cash to pay estate taxes.

[¶905] IMPORTANCE OF CONVERTIBLE TERM INSURANCE

These elements argue forcefully for a fairly heavy concentration on term insurance to protect the family in the asset-building years. This term insurance can be in convertible form for this reason: When the estate assets have been built up, they must be protected permanently so that when the farm family reaches retirement, that retirement may be funded by the assets of the farm. Further, in the event that the head-of-the-household should die, the survivors would probably need enough cash to protect the non-liquid values of the farm estate without being forced to sell the property to pay the federal and state death taxes.

[¶906] HOW MUCH INSURANCE IS ENOUGH?

In answering the question about "how much" insurance is enough, thinking can best begin with a concern for income necessary to meet the needs of the family if the father as the income producer dies or is disabled. Further, what does the farmer anticipate will be his needs upon retirement? The insurance question always is this: "How much income is needed under a variety of circumstances and different periods in the life cycle to replace income that theretofore has been assured from the earnings of the income producer?"

From their experience, insurance companies project income needs upon the death of the income producer.

Another rule of thumb runs like this: Most surviving families require from 50 to 75 per cent of the income they were receiving before the death of the breadwinner.

[¶907] ESTIMATED PREMIUM COSTS

Assuming that 5-year renewable and convertible term insurance is bought by a young farmer, here is an example of costs and benefits. If a young man for pure protection should take a $25,000.00 policy at age 24, his monthly premium would be something like $6.50. If at the age of 29,

Figure 9-1 Mortgages Owned by U.S. Life Insurance Companies by State

State	*Farm*	*State*	*Farm*
Alabama	$ 43,300	Nebraska	$ 307,200
Alaska	—	Nevada	37,800
Arizona	112,800	New Hampshire	3,000
Arkansas	262,000	New Jersey	4,400
California	884,500	New Mexico	74,800
Colorado	208,400	New York	9,000
Connecticut	1,000	North Carolina	35,100
Delaware	1,600	North Dakota	20,700
D.C.	—	Ohio	88,700
Florida	269,200	Oklahoma	166,700
Georgia	80,600	Oregon	114,700
Hawaii	4,200	Pennsylvania	19,500
Idaho	129,400	Rhode Island	—
Illinois	323,800	South Carolina	16,400
Indiana	172,700	South Dakota	76,000
Iowa	488,700	Tennessee	32,600
Kansas	263,900	Texas	654,300
Kentucky	70,700	Utah	13,000
Louisiana	155,900	Vermont	200
Maine	1,300	Virginia	33,200
Maryland	6,000	Washington	221,300
Massachusetts	1,400	West Virginia	2,200
Michigan	30,800	Wisconsin	55,700
Minnesota	194,600	Wyoming	77,000
Mississippi	196,800	Puerto Rico	—
Missouri	190,000	U.S. Territories and Possessions	—
Montana	138,300		
		TOTAL U.S.	$6,297,400

Institute of Life Insurance

he should convert his term policy into a $50,000.00 whole life policy, his monthly premium would be something like $75.00. By age 65, this farmer would have a guaranteed cash value of about $30,000.00 and dividend accumulations would add more than $30,000.00. Figure 9-2 summarizes the premium costs and settlement options.

[¶908] BUY-SELL AGREEMENTS TO AID FAMILY FARM CONTINUITY

Insurance provides an important tool in funding the continuity of family farmsteads. The buy-sell agreement is an instrument that defines the conditions upon which one person can acquire the farm and the conditions upon which another will sell. Thus, for example, a son could

Figure 9-2 Example of Term Converted To Whole Life: Premium and Options

5 Year Renewable & Convertible Term $25,000 Male

Ages	*Premium*	*Policy Fee*	
18	$73.25	$15.00	
24	74.75	10.00	renewed at lower than initial premium with lower fee.

Conversion to $50,000 Whole Life at age 29

Annual Premium	$ 887.50
Premiums paid to age 65	31,950.00
Guaranteed Cash Value at age 65	29,627.00
*Cash value of dividend additions—age 65	33,350.00
Difference between total cash value and total premiums at age 65	+$31,027.50

Settlement Options

1. Installments Certain—assuming 15 years

Guaranteed Cash	*w/dividends*
$210.16/month	$447.30/month

2&3. Life Income—Current guaranteed rates

		w/dividends
No refund	$252.19	$536.76
10 years certain	245.68	522.90
20 years certain	214.60	456.75
cash refund	240.94	512.82
installment refund	245.38	522.27

4. Proceeds held at interest

Guaranteed Cash	*w/dividends*
$84.95	$180.81

5. Fixed Income Option—assuming monthly income requirement of $300. Paid until proceeds are exhausted.

Guaranteed Cash	*w/dividends*
9 years 9 months	22 years 6 months

6. Joint & Survivor—assuming male 3 years older than spouse.

	Guaranteed Cash	*w/dividends*
No refund	$204.53	$435.33
2/3 to survivor	225.84	480.69
10 years certain	203.94	434.07

*Prepared by *Institute of Life* Insurance.

buy insurance on the life of his father, naming himself as beneficiary. With the proceeds paid upon the death of his father, the son has cash to buy the farm assets. Since the father had no incidence of ownership in the policy, and since the proceeds were payable directly to the son, the policy sum paid to the son is not included in the father's estate assets.

[¶909] TWO CLASSIC KINDS OF BUY-OUT PLANS

Two classic types of agreements for the sale of an interest in a closely-held business such as a partnerhsip or small family corporation exist. The first type is known as the "cross purchase agreement." The second type is the "entity purchase agreement." The "cross purchase agreement" provides for purchase of the farm interest from the estate of a deceased owner by the surviving farm associates. The "entity purchase agreement" provides for the purchase of the farm interest from the estate of the deceased owner by the farm entity.

Either type may be used, not only upon the death of a business associate, but quite as well upon the withdrawal of a partner or corporation stockholder from the farming enterprise or upon requirement.

[¶910] USE OF AGREEMENT IN SOLE PROPRIETORSHIPS

While "cross purchase" and "entity agreements" are commonly utilized in partnerships and closely-held corporations, the sole proprietor finds an insurance-funded agreement useful. In the case of an individual owner, the agreement for purchase and sale of the farm assets is comparable to a "cross purchase" arrangement. Why? Because the agreement provides for purchase of the farm assets from the estate of the deceased proprietor.

[¶911] USE OF A TRUSTEE

In some cases a trusteeship is established. The reason is that it is often more comforting to all concerned to know that the plan will be administered by an impartial stranger to the buy-out contract. Whether a trustee should be included in the agreement depends upon circumstances, especially in the "cross purchase agreement." The insurance underwriter can provide advice.

[¶912] DIAGRAM FLOW-CHART OF FORMS OF BUY-OUT PLANS

The patterns of "cross purchase" and "entity" agreements in partnerships and family corporations are visualized in Figures 9-3, 4, and 5.

In a corporate structure, the corporation applies for, owns, and is beneficiary of insurance policies on the life of each stockholder.

[¶913] PARTNERSHIP ENTITY PURCHASE PLAN: FORM

Here is a form for study and use in drafting partnership entity purchase plans.

*AGREEMENT made this ______ day of ____________________ 19___, by and between ____________________, ____________________ and ____________________, (hereinafter called "partners") and ____________________, (hereinafter called "the partnership").

WITNESSETH:

WHEREAS, ____________, ____________________ and ____________________ are co-partners in the business of ____________, and

WHEREAS, the interest of each partner in the partnership is as follows:

____________________ .... $____________%
____________________ .... $____________%
____________________ .... $____________%

WHEREAS, the primary purpose of this agreement is (1) to provide for the purchase by the partnership of the interest of any partner in the partnership in the event of the death or disability of a partner, (2) to provide for the purchase by the remaining partners of the interest of a partner withdrawing from the partnership during his lifetime, (3) to provide further for the uninterrupted continuance of the partnership business upon the death or disability of a partner, and (4) to provide the funds necessary to carry out such purchase and sale,

NOW, THEREFORE, in consideration of the mutual agreements and covenants contained herein and for other valuable consideration, receipt of which is hereby acknowledged, it is mutually agreed and covenanted by

*This specimen agreement is presented by courtesy and permission of the National Life Insurance Company, Montpelier, Vermont, copyright proprietor, from *Business-Partnership Purchase Agreements*.

Figure 9-3 Partnership Entity-Purchase Plan

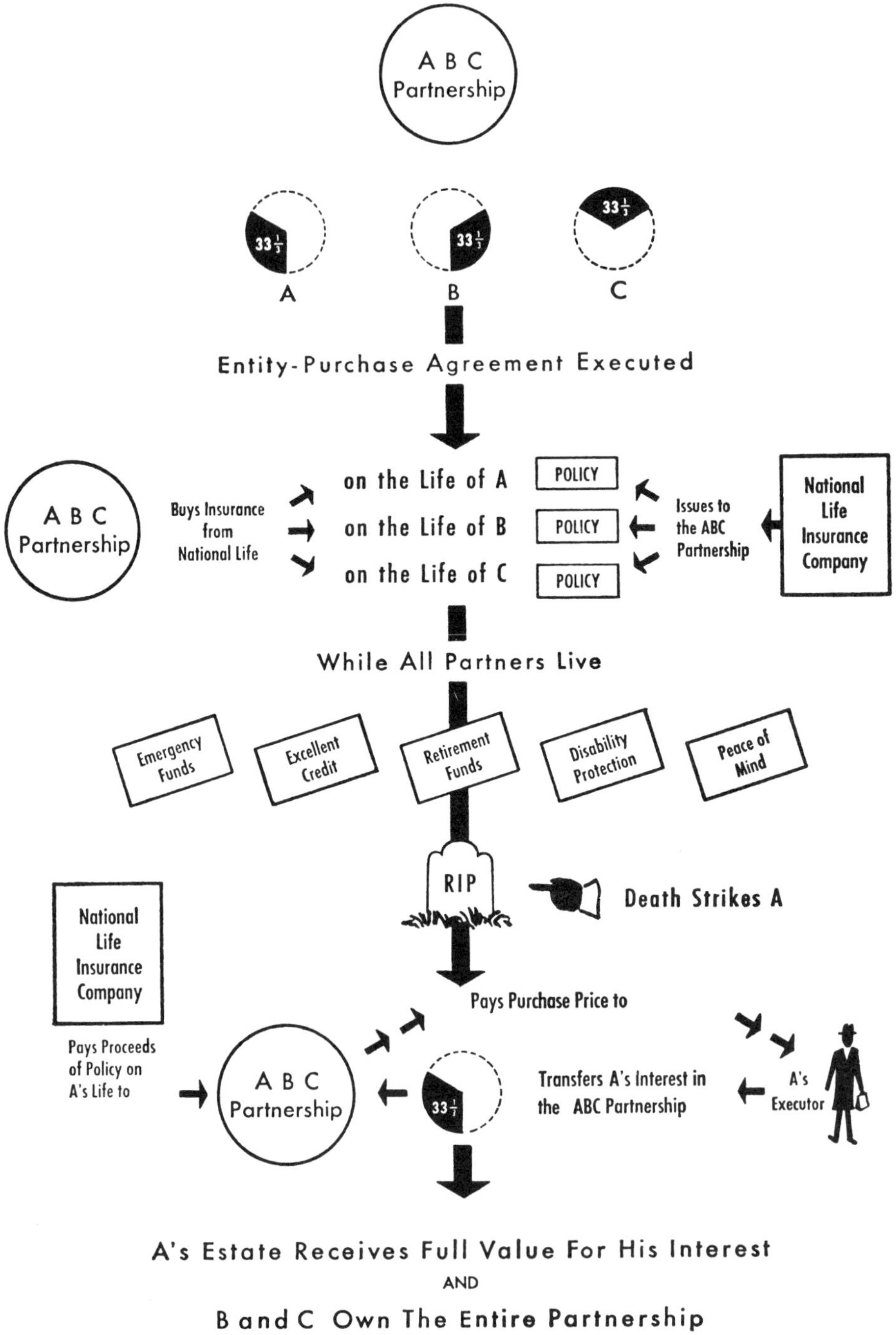

By permission, courtesy of the copyright proprietor, National Life Insurance Company, Montpelier, Vermont, from *Business-Partnership Purchase Agreements.*

Figure 9-4 Partnership Cross-Purchase Plan

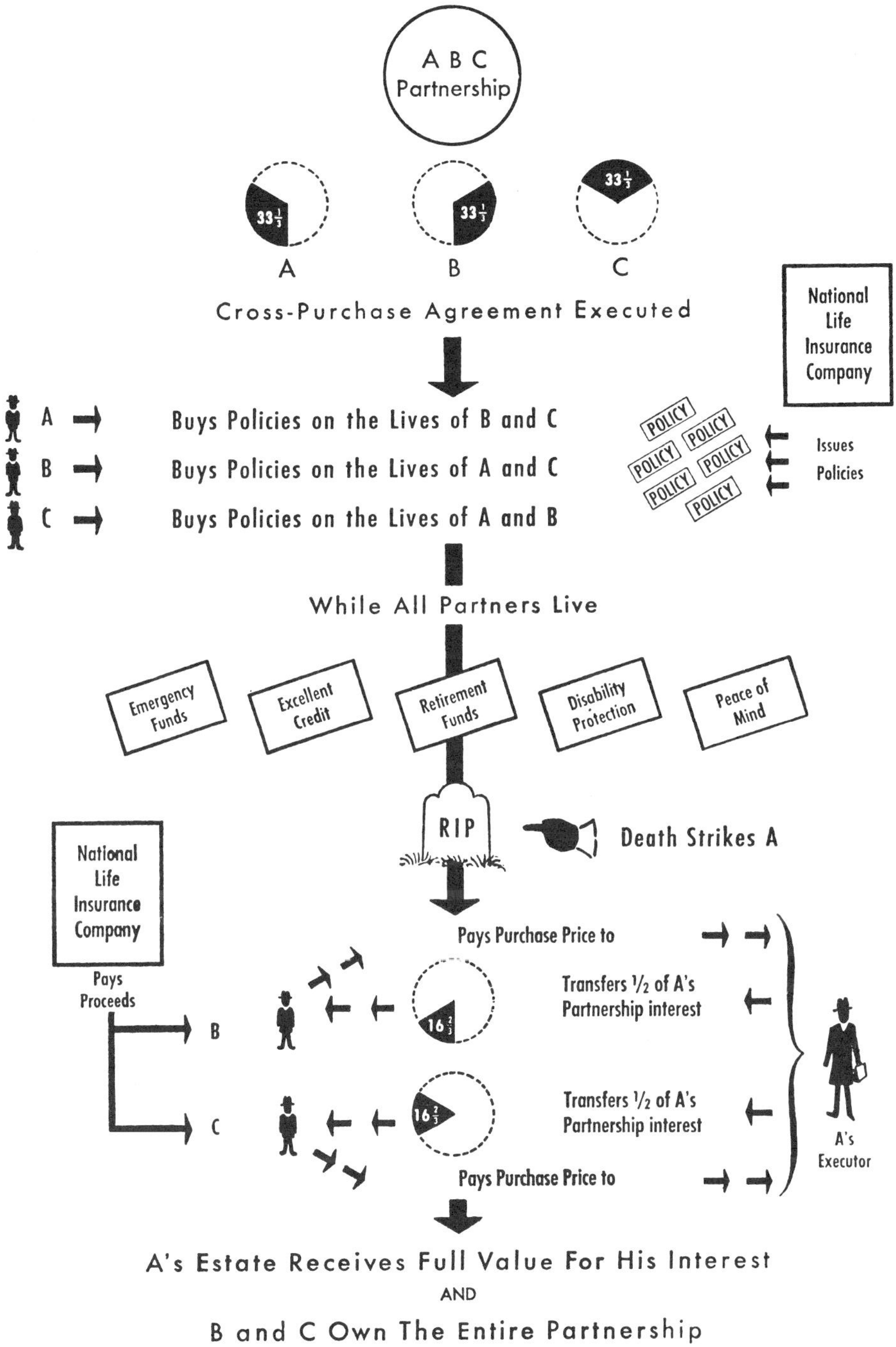

By permission, courtesy of the copyright proprietor, National Life Insurance Company, Montpelier, Vermont, from *Business-Partnership Purchase Agreements*. Upon request the National Life Insurance Company will provide a copy of this volume to estate-practicing attorneys.

Figure 9-5 Corporate Cross-Purchase Plan

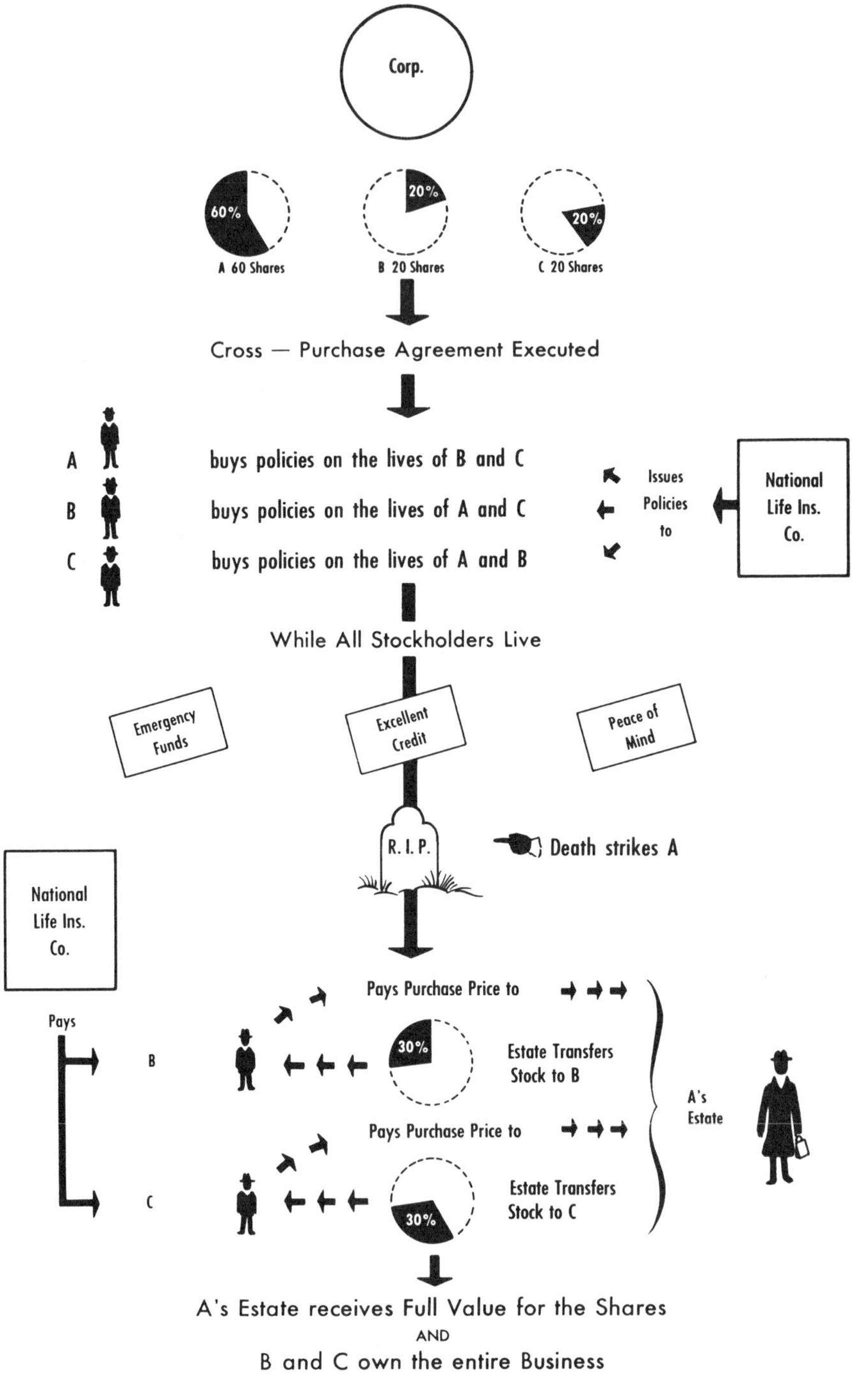

By permission, courtesy of the copyright proprietor, National Life Insurance Company, Montpelier, Vermont, from *Stock-Purchase Agreements and the Close Corporation.*

the partners, each for himself, his heirs, assigns and personal representatives, and by the partnership, for itself as an entity, its successors and assigns, as follows:

Article 1. No partner shall during his lifetime assign, encumber or otherwise dispose of his interest or any part thereof in the partnership, except as provided below:

(1) If a partner should desire to dispose voluntarily of his interest during his lifetime, then he shall first offer in writing to sell his interest to the partnership at the price determined in accordance with the provisions of Article 2 below, provided, however, that such price shall be paid in cash, fully on the date of sale, and that the selling partner shall not participate in future profits of the partnership. If the interest is not purchased by the partnership within ____ days of the receipt of the offer to it, then the selling partner may sell it to any other person but shall not sell it without first offering it to the partnership in accordance with the method established above at the price and on the terms offered to such other person if the price is less than the price established by Article 2. If, however, the partnership agreement forming this partnership further restricts, limits or prevents a lifetime sale or transfer by a partner of his interest in the partnership, then such partnership agreement shall prevail notwithstanding the provisions of this Article.

(2) In the event a partner party to this agreement becomes totally and permanently disabled before reaching age 55, and remains so for a period of ____ months from the onset of such disability, then the partnership shall purchase and the disabled partner shall sell, as of the end of such period, such disabled partner's interest in the partnership. "Disability" or "total and permanent disability" for purposes of this agreement shall be considered that disability of a particular insured partner which is described and determined by the insurer as total and permanent disability in the insurance policies on such insured partner listed in Article 3 below and/or Schedule B attached hereto, provided, however, that no insurer shall be subject to any liability other than its obligations in its policies of insurance. The purchase price shall be that which is established in Article 2 below, provided, however, that such purchase price shall not be paid in a lump sum but instead shall be paid in installments of $________ per month until the total purchase price shall have been paid plus an amount equal to ____% per year of the declining balance of such purchase price. If a disabled partner ceases to be so totally and permanently disabled at some time after such installment payments have commenced but before they have been completed, then such installments shall be spread out further, namely, at the rate of $________ per month until the balance of said purchase price and interest on the

declining balance at the rate of ____% per year shall be wholly paid and satisfied.

Alternative Article 2. (This Article contemplates a payment in lieu of good will as an income item, *not* as a payment for good will as mentioned in Section 736(b)(2)(B) of the 1954 Internal Revenue Code. This Article contemplates the payment in lieu of good will to be treated as an income payment under Section 736(a) of the 1954 Internal Revenue Code.) Upon the death or disability of a partner, the partnership shall purchase and the estate of the deceased partner or the disabled partner shall sell his entire interest in the partnership for a price as determined below. It is agreed that the current fair value of the partnership's capital assets, as defined in Section 736(b) of the 1954 Internal Revenue Code, excluding good will, is $________, that the fair value of the unrealized receivables is $________, that the fair market value of the inventory is $________, and that, therefore, the value of each partner's interest is as follows:

________________________ .... $________________
________________________ .... $________________
________________________ .... $________________

The partners agree to redetermine these values within ______ days following the end of each (fiscal) (calendar) year, such redetermined values to be endorsed on Schedule A attached hereto and made a part of this agreement. If the partners fail to make such a redetermination of values for a particular year, the last previously stipulated values shall control, except that if the partners fail to make such a redetermination within the ______ months immediately preceding the death or onset of disability of a partner, then the values shall be agreed upon by the personal representative of the deceased partner or the disabled partner on the one hand and the remaining partners on behalf of the partnership on the other. If they do not agree to a valuation within ______ days after the death or onset of disability of the partner, the value of the deceased or disabled partner's interest shall be determined by arbitration as follows: The remaining partners on behalf of the partnership on the one hand and the representative of the deceased partner or the disabled partner on the other shall each name one arbitrator; if the two arbitrators cannot agree upon the values, then the two arbitrators shall appoint a third arbitrator and the decision of the majority shall be binding upon all parties. In determining values by arbitration, the arbitrators (must) (must not) take into account (the value of the life insurance proceeds accruing from the policy on the deceased partner's life) (the cash surrender value of the life insurance policy on the disabled partner's life).

The parties hereto agree and covenant that upon the death or disability of a partner the remaining partners shall continue the partnership business without interruption. Payment of the total purchase price as determined above shall be made with respect to a deceased partner's interest in the partnership in _____ equal annual installments, the first such payment to be made within _____ months from the date of the decedent partner's death, the intent of the parties being that the first payments shall represent payment for the capital assets (Section 736(b) payments), the latter payments for the balance. Payment of the total purchase price as determined above shall be made with respect to a disabled partner's interest in the partnership in accordance with the provisions of Article 1 above.

Upon the death or disability of a partner, the surviving partners shall continue the partnership business without interruption and the estate of the deceased partner or the disabled partner, as the case may be, shall participate in the net profits of the partnership business starting on the first day of the month following the date of his death or the onset of his disability and continuing for a period of _____ years; the particular share shall equal _____% of the net profits of the partnership as determined by the partnership's regular accountants. This additional payment has been agreed upon by the partners to represent a payment under and in accordance with Section 736(a) (1) of the 1954 Internal Revenue Code.

Alternative Article 2. (This provision contemplates payment for good will as a capital asset or "interest in the partnership" in accordance with Section 736(b) (2) (B) of the 1954 Internal Revenue Code, *not* as an income payment under Section 736(a) (2) of the 1954 Internal Revenue Code.) Upon the death or disability of a partner, the partnership shall purchase and the estate of the deceased partner or the disabled partner shall sell his entire interest in the partnership for a price as determined below. It is agreed that the current fair value of the partnership's capital assets as defined in Section 736(b) of the 1954 Internal Revenue Code, including good will, is $_______, that the fair value of the unrealized receivables is $_______, and that the fair market value of the inventory is $_______ and that, therefore, the value of each partner's interest is as follows:

_________________________ .... $_________________
_________________________ .... $_________________
_________________________ .... $_________________

The partners agree to redetermine these values within _____ days following the end of each (fiscal) (calendar) year, such redetermined values to be endorsed on Schedule A attached hereto and made a part of this agreement. If the partners fail to make such a redetermination of values for a particular year, the last previously stipulated values shall control, except that if the partners fail to make such a redetermination within the ______ months immediately preceding the death or onset of disability of a partner, then the values shall be agreed upon by the personal representative of the deceased partner or the disabled partner on the one hand and the remaining partners on behalf of the partnership on the other. If they do not agree to a valuation within ______ days after the death or onset of disability of the partner, the value of the deceased or disabled partner's interest shall be determined by arbitration as follows: The remaining partners on behalf of the partnership on the one hand and the representative of the deceased partner or the disabled partner on the other shall each name one arbitrator; if the two arbitrators cannot agree upon the values, then the two arbitrators shall appoint a third arbitrator and the decision of the majority shall be binding upon all parties. In determining values by arbitration, (the life insurance proceeds accruing from the policy on the deceased partner's life) (the cash surrender value of the policies of insurance on the life of the disabled partner) (must) (must not) be taken into account; further, an amount for the addition to the good will of the partnership by the deceased of not less than $________ shall be used.

The parties hereto agree and covenant that upon the death or disability of a partner the remaining partners shall continue the partnership business without interruption. Payment of the total purchase price as determined above shall be made with respect to a deceased partner's interest in the partnership in ______ equal annual installments, the first such payment to be made ______ months from the date of the decedent partner's death. Payment of the total purchase price as determined above shall be made with respect to a disabled partner's interest in the partnership in accordance with the provisions in Article 1 above.

Article 3. The partnership is the applicant, owner and beneficiary of the following life insurance policies issued by National Life Insurance Company:

Policy # ________ insuring the life of ______________________
in the amount of $____________.
Policy # ________ insuring the life of ______________________
in the amount of $____________.
Policy # ________ insuring the life of ______________________
in the amount of $____________.

The partnership agrees to pay all premiums on the insurance policies taken out pursuant to this agreement and shall give proof of payment of premiums to the partners whenever any one of them shall so request such proof. If a premium is not paid within 20 days after its due date, the insured shall have the right to pay such premium and be reimbursed therefor by the partnership. The partnership shall have the right to purchase additional insurance on the life of any of the partners; such additional policies shall be listed in Schedule B attached hereto and made a part of this agreement, along with any substitution or withdrawal of life insurance policies subject to this agreement. In the event that the partnership decides to purchase additional insurance, each partner hereby agrees to co-operate fully by performing all the requisites of the life insurer which are necessary conditions precedent to the issuance of life insurance policies. Payment of premiums by the partnership shall be accounted for as an ordinary business expense.

Article 4. Upon the death or disability of a partner the partnership shall pay the purchase price and make the payments as established by this agreement. The executor or administrator of the estate of the deceased partner or the disabled partner shall execute a bill of sale of his interest in the partnership to the partnership and a waiver of any right of accounting on the part of the remaining partners. At the same time the remaining partners shall execute and deliver to the estate of the deceased partner or to the disabled partner an agreement indemnifying the estate of the deceased partner or the disabled partner against all liabilities of the partnership. With respect to a deceased's interest in the partnership, the sale shall take effect as of the close of business on the day of death of the deceased partner and the unpaid balance of the purchase price, except for participation, if any, in profits, shall be evidenced by a series of promissory notes made by the surviving partners on behalf of the partnership to the order of the estate of the deceased; these notes shall provide for the acceleration of the due date of all unpaid notes in default in the payment of any note.

Article 5. Any partner who disposes of his interest in the partnership during his lifetime shall have the right to purchase the policy or policies of insurance on his life owned by the partnership by paying an amount equal to the interpolated terminal reserve as of the date of transfer, plus the proportionate part of the gross premium last paid before the date of transfer which covers the period extending beyond that date, less any existing indebtedness charged against the policy or policies. This right shall lapse if not exercised within _____ days after such disposal.

Article 6. The partners, the partnership and the personal representative of any deceased partner shall make, execute and deliver any documents necessary or desirable to carry out this agreement.

Article 7. This agreement may be altered, amended or terminated by a writing signed by all of the partners. In the event of a termination of this agreement before the death of a partner, each partner shall be entitled to purchase from the partnership the policy or policies on his life upon payment of an amount equal to the interpolated terminal reserve as of the date of transfer, plus the proportionate part of the gross premium last paid before the date of transfer which covers the period extending beyond that date, less any existing indebtedness charged against the policy.

Article 8. This agreement shall terminate upon the occurrence of any of the following events:

(a) Bankruptcy of any partner,
(b) Bankruptcy, receivership or dissolution of the partnership, or
(c) Cessation of the partnership business.

In addition, this agreement shall be null and void if all the partners parties hereto die within a period of 30 days.*

Article 9. Notwithstanding the provisions of this agreement, any life insurance company whose policies are listed herein or in Schedule B attached hereto is hereby authorized to act in accordance with the terms of any policies issued by it as if this agreement did not exist, and payment or other performance of its contractual obligations by the insurer in accordance with the terms of any such policy shall completely discharge the insurer from all claims and demands of all persons whomsoever. Any insurer is further authorized to provide to an insured partner any information with respect to the policy or policies on his life owned by the partnership. No insurer shall be deemed or considered to be a party to this agreement for any purpose.

Article 10. This agreement shall be governed by the law of the State of ______________________.

*Counsel may feel that it would be desirable to treat simultaneous or rapidly successive deaths differently. The close deaths of even two of the three partners raise problems. Let us take an example. If A and B die simultaneously, then under the entity agreement C ends up with ownership of the entire partnership. If the partnership was worth $90,000 while all were alive and the agreement was *fully* funded ($45,000 of insurance on each life), then A's and B's estates, assuming all were equal partners, would each receive $45,000. But because of ballooning (see discussion above), i.e., maturation of *two* partnership-owned policies, the value of the partnership upon *two* deaths would be $180,000. One-third of $180,000 is $60,000, quite a substantial difference from the one-third value ($45,000) of the partnership if only one partner had died ($135,000). If A and B do not die sumultaneously but rather B dies a few moments later, then the problem is similar although the inequity is limited to B's estate only.

IN WITNESS WHEREOF the parties hereto have executed this agreement at ______________________________, in the County of __________, State of ______________________________, on the day and the year above written.

______________________ ______________________

By ______________________

______________________ ______________________

______________________ ______________________

______________________ ______________________

[¶914] FORM OF CORPORATION CROSS-PURCHASE AGREEMENT

Here is a form for study and use in drafting a corporation cross-purchase agreement.

AGREEMENT by and between ______________________, residing at ______________________, ______________________ residing at ______________________, and ______________________ residing at ______________________.

WHEREAS ____________, ______________________ and ____________ are the sole stockholders of the ______________________ Company, a corporation with its principal place of business at ______ (hereinafter referred to as the Company), ____________ owning ______ shares, ______________________ owning ______ shares, and ______________________ owning ______ shares of the Company, and

WHEREAS it is the desire of the aforesaid stockholders (1) to provide for the purchase by the survivors of a decedent stockholder's interest in the Company, (2) to provide for by the other stockholders the purchase of one stockholder's stock during his lifetime if any stockholder should desire to withdraw from the Company, and (3) to provide the funds necessary to carry out such purchase.

WITNESSETH:

NOW, THEREFORE, in consideration of the mutual agreements and covenants contained herein and for other valuable consideration, receipt of which is hereby acknowledged, it is mutually agreed and covenanted by and between the parties to this agreement as follows:

Article 1. Neither ______________________, nor ______________________, nor ______________________ shall, while all of them are living, transfer or encumber all or any part of their respective stockholdings in the Company by sale or otherwise except as provided below.

Article 2. Upon the death of a stockholder the survivors shall purchase and the estate of the decedent shall sell the stock interest now owned or hereafter acquired by the stockholder who is first to die. The purchase or sale price of such stock shall be determined in accordance with the provisions of Article 7 of this agreement. A surviving stockholder shall purchase that portion of stock owned by the deceased represented by the ratio of the number of shares owned by such survivor to those owned by all the survivors.

Article 3. In order to ensure funds to pay for the stock, insurance on the life of each stockholder has been obtained from the ____________ Insurance Company, of Montpelier, Vermont, by his associates, as follows:

On the life of ______________________________, ______________ dollars, applied for by and payable to ________________ or his estate, and ________ dollars applied for by and payable to ________________ or his estate.

On the life of ______________________________, ______________ dollars, applied for by and payable to ________________ or his estate, and ________ dollars applied for by and payable to ________________ or his estate.

On the life of ______________________________, ______________ dollars, applied for by and payable to ________________ or his estate, and ________ dollars applied for by and payable to ________________ or his estate.

Each applicant agrees to pay the premiums as they become due, and each policy shall be the sole and absolute property of the applicant, provided, however, that each such owner hereby collaterally assigns each policy owned by him to the insured therein as security only for the performance by each such owner of the obligations on his part to be performed under this agreement. Any dividends payable upon the policies prior to maturity by the death of the insured shall be paid to the owner in cash or disposed of as such owner may choose to direct. This agreement shall extend to and include all additional life insurance policies issued pursuant to this agreement, such additional policies to be listed in Schedule A attached hereto and made a part hereof.

Article 4. Each stockholder has assigned his stock in blank and has deposited the certificate with the Secretary of the corporation who is authorized and directed to write on the face of each stock certificate the following:

"This certificate is held subject to Stock-Purchase Agreement dated ____________"

Such assignment and deposit shall not affect the right of the stockholder to vote the stock and receive the dividends thereon until such time as the purchase price has been received by him or his executor or administrator under the terms of this agreement. The Secretary shall hold and deliver the stock in accordance with this agreement. A schedule of the stock included in this agreement is attached hereto as Schedule B. No certificate of stock subject to this agreement shall be assigned, encumbered or otherwise disposed of during the continuance of this agreement except as provided herein.

Article 5. If a stockholder desires to sell his stock during his lifetime, he shall give his associate stockholders and the Secretary of the corporation written notice of such desire, and the associate stockholders shall have the right to purchase such stock at any time within ______ days after such notice at the price determined by Article 7. Each such associate stockholder shall have the right to purchase a proportion of such stock equal to the ratio of the number of shares owned by him to the total shares owned by the remaining associate stockholders excluding the seller, and if a stockholder is unable or unwilling to buy the proportion of stock alloted to him, the other stockholders shall have the right to buy the balance in similar ratio. Upon the consummation of purchase and payment therefor, the Secretary of the corporation shall deliver the certificates to the purchasers.

Article 6. On payment of the purchase price by a survivor, the Secretary shall issue to the purchaser new certificates for as much stock as he is entitled to, which certificates shall not bear any reference to the Stock-Purchase Agreement, and the executor or administrator of the deceased shall execute such transfers, receipts, and releases as shall be required by the purchasing stockholder or the Secretary of the corporation for the protection of all parties concerned and to carry out the intent of this agreement.

Article 7. Unless and until changed as hereinafter provided, the value of each share of stock of the Company held by each stockholder shall be ____________________ dollars. Within thirty days following the end of each (fiscal/calendar) year ________________, ________________ and ________________ shall redetermine the value of each share of stock and shall indicate such value by endorsement on Schedule C attached hereto and made a part hereof. Such endorsement shall take the following form:

"The undersigned mutually agree on this ________________day of ____________, A.D. 19___, that for the purposes of this Stock-Purchase

Agreement each share of the Company has a value of ____________ dollars. Signed ____________________, ____________________ and ____________________."

If for any reason ____________________, ____________________ and ____________________ fail to redetermine the value for a particular year, the last previously stipulated value shall control, provided, however, that if no value is agreed upon within the twenty-four months following the end of the (fiscal/calendar) year, the value of a deceased stockholder's stock shall be agreed upon by the representative of the decedent and the surviving stockholders. If the representative of the decedent and the surviving stockholders do not agree upon the value within ______ days after the death of a stockholder, the value of the deceased stockholder's stock shall be determined by arbitration as follows: the surviving stockholders shall name one arbitrator and the representative of the estate shall name one arbitrator. If the two arbitrators do not agree upon the value of the stock of the deceased stockholder within ______ days of their appointment, they shall appoint a third arbitrator and the decision of the majority shall be binding.

For the purpose of this agreement the price at which the stock shall be sold and purchased during the life of a stockholder shall be the same as the price established immediately above.

Article 8. If a stockholder during his life sells all of his stock pursuant to the provisions of Articles 5 and 7 above, the stockholder or stockholders so purchasing such stock may purchase the policies of life insurance on his own life but owned by the withdrawing stockholder for a price not to exceed (the cash surrender value as of the date of the sale/the sum of the net premium payments made on each policy/etc.). On payment of the price by the purchaser, the seller shall assign the policy to the purchaser and shall execute such assignments or releases as may reasonably be required to effectuate a complete transfer of the title to the policy to the purchaser. On payment by the seller of the (cash surrender value as of the date of the sale/sum of the net premium payments made on each policy/etc.) of the policy on the seller's life, the seller may purchase from the other stockholder or stockholders the policy or policies on his life owned by the stockholder or stockholders so purchasing said stock, and the purchaser shall assign the policy to the seller and shall execute such assignments or releases as may reasonably be required to effectuate a complete transfer of the title to said policy or policies to the seller.

Upon the death of a stockholder each surviving stockholder shall have the right to purchase from the estate of the deceased stockholder, and the executor or administrator of the estate of the deceased stockholder shall have the duty to sell, any policies or policy of insurance upon the life of such surviving stockholders, for a price not to exceed (the cash surrender value as of the date of the termination of this agreement/the sum of the net premium payments made on each policy/etc.). Upon payment of the price the executor or administrator shall execute such assignments or releases as may reasonably be required to effectuate a complete transfer of the title to said policy or policies to the purchaser. If the insured does not, within 30 days from the sale of such stock, purchase the policy on his life, the seller or the executor or administrator may surrender the policy for its cash value and the other stockholders agree to execute such releases as may be necessary.

Article 9. If the purchase price exceeds the proceeds of the life insurance, the balance of the purchase price shall be paid in __ consecutive (monthly) (annual) (etc.) payments beginning ____ (days) (months) (etc.) after the date of the decedent's death. The unpaid balance of the purchase price shall be evidenced by a series of negotiable promissory notes made by the surviving stockholders to the order of the estate of the deceased stockholder with interest at ____% per annum. These notes shall provide for the acceleration of the due date of all unpaid notes in the series in the event of any default in the payment of any note or interest thereon, and they shall also give the makers thereof the option of prepayment in whole or in part at any time.

Article 10. The agreement shall terminate on

(1) The written agreement of the stockholders, or
(2) The dissolution, bankruptcy or insolvency of the Company, or
(3) The death of all stockholders simultaneously or within a period of ____ days, or
(4) The transfer of the stock of a deceased stockholder to the surviving stockholders or by the sale by a stockholder during his life of all of his stock to someone other than existing stockholders as herein provided. Upon the termination of this agreement, each stockholder may at his option within ____ days purchase the policies of life insurance on his own life but owned by the other stockholders for a price not to exceed (the cash surrender value as of the date of the termination of this agreement/the sum of the net premium payments made on each policy/etc.).

Article 11. The executor, administrator, or personal representative of a deceased stockholder shall execute and deliver any documents or legal instruments necessary or desirable to carry out the provisions of this agreement. This agreement shall be binding upon the stockholders, their heirs, legal representatives, successors and assigns.

Article 12. This agreement may be amended or altered in any provision and such change shall become effective when reduced to writing and signed by the stockholders who are parties hereto.

Article 13. Notwithstanding the provisions of this agreement, any life insurance company which has issued a policy of life insurance subject to the provisions of this agreement is hereby authorized to act in accordance with the terms of such policies as if this agreement did not exist, and the payment or other performance of its contractual obligations by any such insurance company in accordance with the terms of any such policy shall completely discharge such company from all claims, suits and demands of all persons whatsoever.

IN WITNESS WHEREOF the parties hereto have executed this agreement by subscribing their names and affixing their seals at ____________________, County of ____________________, State of ______________________________, on this __day of ________, A.D. 19__.

WITNESS ____________________ ____________________

WITNESS ____________________ ____________________

WITNESS ____________________ ____________________

THE LANGUAGE OF INSURANCE

Accidental Death Benefit An additional sum to be paid to your beneficiary if you die as a result of an accident. It is often referred to as double indemnity because it generally doubles the face amount of the policy.

Accrue The increase in value on dividends left on deposit with the company.

Allot Distribution of death proceeds according to a plan or formula.

Age The date of birth from which your premiums is calculated. This date may be your age on your last birthday before you brought your policy or your age on your nearest birthday.

Age Clause The right of the company to adjust the policy to your correct birthdate. The death proceeds to your beneficiary will be corrected as to whether you are younger or older than you said you were in the application.

Agent The representative of the company who sells you the policy and probably services it. The agent is sometimes called an underwriter which is a term which designated an agent who assesses the risk of insuring you as an applicant for coverage by a policy.

Annuity The payment provided for in a policy which specifies income for a specified period of time, such as for a number of years or for life.

Application The statement of information which you make in applying for insurance and which is used by the company to determine your acceptability as a risk.

Assignment You can transfer some or all of your policy right to someone else.

Authority The officers designated by the company legally to act in its behalf.

Automatic Premium Loan The authorization you give to the company to charge any premiums you fail to pay against the cash value of your policy.

Beneficiary The person named in your policy to receive the money from your policy when you die.

Cash Surrender Value—The amount of dollars to which you are entitled at any moment of time and to which you are entitled upon the voluntary termination of your policy before it becomes payable at maturity or upon your death.

Cash Value The amount of money which the company owes you and to which you are entitled if you completely surrender your policy. You can borrow on it, use it for collateral, or take it in payment. Generally, your policy tells you how much your cash value is for each $1,000.00 at each anniversary date of your policy.

Claim Your notice to the company that payment of an amount is due under the terms of the policy.

Contingent Beneficiary The person you name to receive the death proceeds if your named beneficiary should pre-decease you. Likewise, you can split the proceeds among two or more beneficiaries.

Convertible Term Insurance Term insurance which you can exchange at your option and without evidence of insurability, for another plan of insurance.

Death Proceeds The sum of money payable to your beneficiary. Such sum is usually the face value of the policy plus any dividends used to buy additional insurance left with the company on deposit or from the face value as reduced by the amount of any unpaid loans and unpaid interest.

Decreasing Term The amount of money your policy is worth as it shrinks each year, but the premium remaining the same.

Default Neglect to pay premiums on the due date except as it may be extended by the grace period or protective clauses in the contract.

Dividend Addition The amount of paid-up insurance which you purchase with the dividends on your policy and which is added to the face amount of your policy.

Dividend Options The choice which you make to take dividends in cash, to use them to cut your premiums, to leave them with the company in an interest bearing account, or to buy more insurance with them.

Due Date The calendar day on which the company bills you for the payment of your premiums.

Election of Settlement Choice of the method of taking the proceeds as you determine or as the beneficiary decides after your death if you give your beneficiary the privilege of such choice.

Endowment A policy which will pay you its face amount after a stated period of time and will pay the face amount to the beneficiary if you should die before the policy matures. An endowment combines whole life and a saving amount.

Extended Term A nonforfeiture value which provides for the continuation of your insurance for a limited period of time. It is usually automatic and is specified on a table in your policy. The premiums are deducted from the cash value of your policy. During the extended term your policy will not be cancelled for your failure to pay the premium due on time.

Face Amount The dollar amount stated in your insurance policy that the company will pay to you upon the maturity of your policy or to your beneficiary upon your death.

Family Income Policy A contract which combines whole life and decreasing term insurance under which the beneficiary receives income payments to the end of a specified period if you die prior to the end of the period.

Grace Period The days during which your policy remains in force during which an overdue premium may be paid without penalty. The period varies from company to company but is usually 30 or 31 days.

Guaranteed Cost The premium which the company computes as the cost of your policy over the life of the policy. You should find this figure somewhere on the front page of your policy. Your premium has been figured either on a guaranteed basis or on a participating basis.

Incontestability The calendar period after the policy has been in force for a stated period, usually two years, after which the company loses the right to challenge statements made in the application.

Insurance A contract (policy) between a person (insured) and a company (insurer) that guarantees to a named individual (beneficiary) the payment of a sum of money upon your death out of a fund to which many individuals exposed to the same risk (death) have contributed a payment or payments (premium) determined by the operation of the law of averages calculated by statisticians who compute risks and premiums (actuaries). To the cost of insurance (term) there may be added a sum which represents the accumulation of savings (limited payment life) or a savings fund (endowment).

Insured The person who is covered by the insurance contract—*you*.

Lapse The date on which your insurance expires if you have not paid your premium on the due date or during the grace period. A policy, however, may have some cash value after it lapses.

Legal Reserve Life Insurance Company A life insurance company that operates under state insurance laws which determine the minimum standards which the company must maintain for the protection of its policy holders.

Level Premium Insurance A policy which distributes the cost evenly over the period during which the premiums are payable. While the premium remains the same from year to year and is more than the actual cost of protection in the earlier years of the policy, it is less than the actual cost in latter years. The excess paid in the early years builds up the reserve.

Loan Value The amount of money you can borrow on your policy at a rate of interest provided for in the insurance contract.

Maturity Date The date at which an endowment policy begins to pay benefits to you as the policy holder.

Modified Whole Life A policy which adjusts the premium to accommodate your budget, being usually a lower premium during the first five or ten years and higher later in life as your income increases.

Mutual Life Insurance Company A company without stockholders whose management is directed by a board elected by the policyholders. Mutual companies generally issue participating insurance.

Nonforfeiture The right that you have—if you discontinue the required premium payments—and the values that you cannot lose even if the policy lapses. Whole life, endowments, and their variations have such values. Term policies as a rule do not include such rights.

Nonparticipating Insurance A policy on which your premium is calculated to cover as closely as possible the anticipated cost of the insurance protection and on which no dividends are payable.

Paid Up Whole Life A policy on which you can stop paying premiums at some date in the future, at a certain age or after a certain number of years.

Participating The description of a company that builds some leeway into its costs to cover unexpected events and hence has an extra margin included in your premium. At the end of the year the company computes its actual costs and refunds whatever portion of the premium exceeds costs.

Participating Insurance A policy which entitles you to receive dividends that reflect the difference between the premiums charged and actual experience, since the premium is calculated to provide some margin over the anticipated cost of the insurance protection.

Policy The printed document that describes the terms of the contract under which you are insured as issued to you by the company. The policy is divided into three parts. The *summary*—first page—visualizes the basic terms of the contract. The *details* in the following pages spell out the conditions of the agreement. The *application* reproduces the information that you gave the company about yourself.

Policy Date The calendar date on which your insurance goes into effect and from which date premium payments are calculated.

Policy Dividend A refund of part of your premium on a participating life insurance policy. It reflects the difference between the premium that you have contracted to pay and the actual experience of the company.

Policy Rights Your legal rights as the insured under the policy contract. They belong to you alone and you alone can make changes or amendments unless you sign away these rights to someone else. You can change the beneficiary. In agreement with the company you can alter the frequency of premium payments. You may borrow money on the policy, direct how the death proceeds are to be paid, and decide how the dividends are to be handled.

Premiums The amount of money you agree to pay periodically for your insurance coverage as specified in your insurance policy, either annually, semi-annually, quarterly, monthly, weekly or otherwise.

Premium Class The actuarial group of persons who pay the same premium as all other policyholders of the same age and sex. This is called the *standard class.* If because of your hazardous occupation or sport, or health, a special group of persons provides your criteria. Such a special class is called *substandard* or just *special class.*

Reduced Paid Up This is the amount of insurance your cash value will buy for the rest of your life if you pay no more premiums. It is a nonforfeiture provision.

Renewable Term A term policy which you renew for a higher premium cost after your term policy expires and at standard premium rates regardless of a change in your health.

Reinstatement The act of putting your insurance back into force, if you are in reasonably good health, by paying overdue premiums with interest. Generally policies can be reinstated up to five years after they lapse.

Risks Not Assumed The cause of death specified by the company in an accidental death rider by which the company says that it will not pay the additional accidental death benefit.

Settlement Option The choice that you as a policyholder or your beneficiary may elect for the payment of the proceeds of the policy. Among the settlement options are these choices:

1. Regular payment of the total in a lump sum;
2. Interest income that the company pays on the money you prefer it hold for you;
3. Income for a specified period that is regular income to your beneficiary by authorizing the company to draw on both principal and interest over a chosen period of time, a table on your policy demonstrating how it works;
4. Income of specified amount—a specified amount of income that the company will pay for as long as the principal and interest last, a table on your policy demonstrating how it works;
5. Income for life—an income based on the amount of the proceeds and the age of the beneficiary for as long as the beneficiary lives.

Stock Life Insurance Company One owned by stockholders who elect a board to direct the company's management. Stock companies generally issue nonparticipating insurance, but may also issue participating insurance.

Suicide The intentional killing of one's self if it occurs within a specified period, usually two years, within which the company will return to your beneficiary only the premiums paid in. If the suicide occurs after the specified period, the company must pay the death proceeds.

Summary The first page of your policy presenting the concise condensation of the contents of your policy.

Supplemental Contract The agreement with the company that spells out the settlement option.

Term Insurance A policy payable to your beneficiary upon your death provided the death occurs within a specified period, such as five or ten years, or before a specified age. It becomes void and without cash value when the conditions expire.

Term Rider An additional coverage that you may buy when a permanent policy is purchased, both types of insurance being included in a single policy contract.

Waiver of Premium A provision in your policy under which the company picks up your payments for you if illness or accident prevent you from working. Such a provision usually goes into effect six months after a policyholder is totally disabled.

Whole Life Insurance A contract payable to your beneficiary upon your death. The policy continues in effect as long as you pay the premium and the premium never changes.

WORKING TOOLS

1. BUSINESS INSURANCE AGREEMENTS
   Springfield, Massachusetts: Massachusetts Mutual Life Insurance Company
2. BUSINESS PARTNERSHIP AGREEMENTS
   Montpelier, Vermont: National Life Insurance Company
3. STOCK-PURCHASE AGREEMENTS AND THE CLOSE CORPORATION
   Montpelier, Vermont: National Life Insurance Company

10

Sixteen Ways to Own a Farm

[¶1000] REALIZING THE DREAM OF FARM OWNERSHIP

The goal of owning one's own farm has been the dream of thousands of Americans—whether they were born on these shores or migrated to them. To agricultural families who love and respect the soil, ownership provides a vocation that assures steady work, produces a flow of income that can be built into capital, and promises an enjoyable family life. Agriculture gives to a family the satisfaction of managing its own business. It rewards hard work. It encourages financial prudence. It rewards sound management judgments. It generates a safe and appreciating investment. It provides an equity that produces income during senior years. Above all other considerations, farm ownership offers a rewarding life style.

Because the active productive life cycle of a farmer covers hardly four decades at best, a young man who aspires to farm ownership must plan, save, work, and invest from his early employment years.

[¶1001] STATISTICS OF CHANGING OWNERSHIP

Statistically, the number of farmsteads declines, but the size of operating farms increases. The value of farms escalates, and the indebtedness of farmers soars. In the years between 1959 and 1975, the number of farms dropped, but the average acreage grew from 288 to 375. In 1975 the average value of an acre of land (1967 = 100) stood at an index figure of 214 compared with the index of 66 in 1959. Farm mortgages skyrocketed from $571,712,000 in 1959 to $2,487,227,000 in

1975. As farms have grown larger, they have utilized more and more credit. Operating expenses have jumped upward. Taxes per acre rose from an index number of 61 in 1959 (1967 = 100) to 150 in 1974.

[¶1002] CONVEYANCES OF FARM LANDS

There is a constant turnover in farm lands. The encroachment of urban life gobbles up thousands of acres. Farmers die, sell out, retire, and shift ownership patterns.

In 1978, conveyances of farmsteads totaled something like 4.8 per cent of all farms. A good part of the purchasers of farm lands were nearby neighboring farmers.

As farms change hands, the young farmer who aspires to own his own farm must be alert to find a property that can be financed at a price that will bring an adequate return.

[¶1003] CHARACTERISTICS OF A FARM PROPRIETOR

A young man who moves to buy a farm has certain qualities that identify him as a proprietor. He has the earmarks of an entrepreneur. He has vision, ambition, readiness to take calculated risks, agricultural competence, the ability "to get things done", and financial discipline.

[¶1004] INVENTORY OF WAYS TO OWN A FARM

Moving up to farm ownership takes planning. How does a young man proceed?

1. First of all, he needs to prepare himself by agricultural studies and hard work on the farm. He starts on the home farm or on a farm nearby.
2. The second step is to build an agricultural reputation. The young farmer becomes a competent, professional workman. He undertakes a systematic plan for saving. His cash equity provides leverage for his future activities. Once he is recognized as a first-class farmer, he has laid the foundations for his success.
3. The third step is to hire out, work for a while as a farm hand, and watch for opportunities.
4. The fourth step is to watch for increasing opportunities as they emerge. A young farmer can rent and lease according to the various forms of agreements discussed in Chapter 6. With family, friends, and neighbors, he can hire or do custom work, rent machinery. By renting, a young farmer needs less capital and takes less risk. He exchanges work with neighbors during the

several seasons. Characteristically, the successful young farmer buys some land and rents some more. By leasing, he meets today's demand for larger operating units with limited capital investment on his part. By his own work and frugal living he lays the basis for success.

5. The fifth step—and this might go first—a young farmer profits from being born right! It goes without saying that when a father and mother take their children into partnership and ultimately devise or sell their farm to a son or daughter, the family tradition carries on. Ownership by inheritance is, however, only the good fortune of those who are born on the farmstead.
6. The sixth way to own a farm is for an ambitious young man to marry a farm daughter who is in line to inherit the farmstead. Agricultural records are replete with examples of how a young man has wisely married a farm girl to whom her parents ultimately devise the farm. Once again, the family tradition is carried on by the young farm family that competently moves up to manage and inherit the farm.
7. The seventh way to own a farm is by purchase of the interests of off-farm heirs. By diplomacy, a young man can show how the acres rented to him or mortgaged provide a good investment to the heirs who otherwise might sell their inherited farm assets and place them in a city bank, or invest such assets on Wall Street. Sometimes the off-the-farm heirs will take their share in mortgages—and they are wise to do so.
8. The eighth way to own a farm is to branch out from the home farm and obtain help from the respective families in finances, livestock, machinery, work-sharing, and joint ventures.
9. The ninth way to own a farm is to hire out to a childless farm family with the prospect of inheriting the farmstead. Situations exist in which childless couples develop an affection as well as a need for a young farm family. In consideration of operating the farm and providing personal care, the owners sometime devise the farmstead to the young farmers.
10. The tenth way to own a farm is to move upward through the leasing process. This rental entrepreneurship can begin with land, rental of machines and livestock, and custom work.
11. An eleventh way to own a farm is to enter into a partnership with a farmstead owner in which labor and management are shared to produce income. Likewise, livestock increases may be shared, thus generating equity.
12. A twelfth way to own a farm is to find a limited partner who wants to invest in a farming enterprise. Many examples exist, especially among medical doctors who like the quiet of the farm and want a competent young farm family to run the farm.
13. The thirteenth way to own a farm is to buy it with the mortgage being held by the seller of the farmstead or by a lending institution. It is at this point that a young farmer's reputation for agricultural competence and financial realiability count for most. From his own work and savings he has generated leverage.
14. A young man moves toward farm ownership by associating himself with good farmers, by taking part in farm organizations, and by letting his light shine as a productive farmer.
15. Purchase on a long term installment contract is another way to buy a farm. Two brothers owned a farm as tenants in common. One brother had a son

who remained on the farm and operated it. The other brother had five children—all of whom ultimately settled in the city. The two brothers put their heads together, sold the farm to the son who was operating the farm, and banked the installments—less living expenses—for later distribution as legacies to the other children. Another farmer sold his farm to a young professional neighboring farmer on a fifteen year contract. The arrangement was beneficial to both.

16. The sixteenth way to own a farm is by means of a Confidence Contract: purchase of a farm on percentage productivity. The retiring farmer and the upward moving young farmer, who has demonstrated his professional capability, can benefit each other by the sale and purchase of a farm under a confidence agreement. What this kind of agreement means is that the owner has faith in the young man to run the farm. The sale enables the young man to take ownership and management by the reasonable payments from what the farm produces. The young man produces a flow of income for the old farmer.

When a farm is incorporated, it is possible for the young farmer-operator to buy shares of stock. Often, a young farmer can arrange to rent a farm with payments including purchase money.

[¶1005] TESTIMONY OF A SUCCESSFUL FARMER

Marvin R. Morrison, co-partner in Morrison Bros. Ranch, Higley, Arizona, had this question put to him, "Can a young man at today's costs buy a farm?" Morrison knows. He answers with a firm "Yes!" In three decades, he and his brother have built an enterprise that farms 3,000 acres of irrigated cropland. Three times a day they milk 2,800 cows. The ranch has 1,200 acres of cotton, and 1,500 acres of alfalfa with seven cuttings a year. The Morrisons grow 20 acres of wheat and are developing a citrus grove. The Morrisons have substantial life insurance, buy-and-sell agreements, and continually updated wills. By a process of transfer, they are in the process of giving parts of the ranch to their total of six children according to values established by careful appraisals. The Morrisons are as careful in their legal affairs as they are in their professional farming operations.

Over the years the growth of the Morrison Bros. Ranch has been paced by borrowings from local banks and from the Equitable Life Assurance Society. When the Morrison brothers began to buy land in 1947, they were paying $250.00 an acre. Subsequent purchases cost much more: $300.00, $480.00, $750.00, $1,255.00, and $3,000.00 per acre. To establish appraised land values in 1975, the Morrisons bought an additional 100 acres for $3,000.00 an acre. A neighboring farm, with little in the way of improvements, sold for $3,300.00.

Here are some suggestions of Marvin Morrison to young farmers.

1. Be active in getting to know people in the ranch and agribusiness.
2. Build a reputation as a ranch hand for good hard work.
3. Get experience as a ranch foreman.
4. Branch out on some sharecropping on your own.
5. Build a reputation for creditworthiness.
6. Borrow wisely. Morrisons have borrowed over $2,000,000.00 from the Federal Land Bank, regularly from the Production Credit Association, from insurance companies, and from local banks.

PART THREE

Forms of Agricultural Business Organization

Farmers choose to conduct their operations under one of several vehicles. The selection of the form of business organization bears a relationship to personal and family goals, the size and complexity of the operation, the duration of the enterprise through time, and optimum financial returns.

11

The Forms of Business Organization

[¶1100] CHOICE OF FORM

In determining the most satisfactory form of organization under which to carry on his agricultural enterprise, the farmer has several forms from which to choose. What legal vehicle promises best to serve his purpose at a particular time in the life cycle, and in relation to the size and complexity of his operation? What form is most desirable in terms of himself and his family?

The forms from which the farmer can choose are:

A. sole proprietorship
B. father and son operation
C. general partnership
D. limited partnership
E. joint venture
F. sub-chapter C corporation
G. sub-chapter S corporation

[¶1100.1] A Search for Optimum Form

Once upon a time, the man owned the farm. His farm was generally a subsistence enterprise with emphasis on the muscle power of man and animal. Land was cheap and the need for costly equipment was small. As farms grew larger and technology mechanized agricultural operations, the farm size, like the farm debt, increased. Management became more complex and exacting. In the context of this agricultural transformation, optimum forms of business organization developed.

Figure 11-1 Alternative Forms of Business Organization For Farmers: Advantages and Disadvantages

SOLE PROPRIETORSHIP

ADVANTAGES

1. This is the simplest and most common form of farm operation.
2. The owner can buy, sell, mortgage.
3. Profits and losses accrue to the proprietor alone.
4. One man makes decisions

DISADVANTAGES

1. The form is fragile in relation to continuity upon death.
2. Farmer may possibly bear heavier Federal and State taxes.
3. Owner cannot enjoy fringe benefits of employee.

PARTNERSHIP

ADVANTAGES

1. This is the most intimate vehicle—a sort of family affair.
2. A partnership is easy to create and less costly than a corporation.
3. Income tax is paid by partners.

DISADVANTAGES

1. More than one person is involved in planning the operations.
2. Farm continuity may not survive the death of a partner.
3. Partnership has difficulty in involving off-the-farm heirs.

CORPORATION

ADVANTAGES

1. The corporate form limits personal liability.
2. It encourages family involvement.
3. Its flexible ownership may be transferred by shares.
4. It simplifies estate settlement.
5. It provides a way of involving off-the-farm heirs.
6. It necessitates decision-making by family stockholders as a group.
7. It simplifies farm continuity from one generation to the next.
8. It encourages orderly habits of record keeping.
9. It makes fringe benefits possible with shareowners as employees.
10. It provides for farm growth.
11. It makes for possible income tax savings.
12. It enables parents to divest ownership and retain majority control while son takes over step-by-step.

DISADVANTAGES

1. Some believe that the corporate form creates red tape, delay, too many reports and too much bookkeeping.
2. The legal establishment of a corporation is expensive.
3. The corporation form may entail increases in self-employment and workman's compensation taxes.
4. It may subject shareholders to double taxation, unless Sub-Chapter S is elected.
5. It may require the burdens of franchise taxes.
6. It may establish a rigid framework for planning, accounting, and record keeping.

12

Sole Proprietorship

[¶1200] THE ELEMENTARY FORM

Sole proprietorship means individual ownership. It is the elementary form of agricultural business organization. The man owns and operates the establishment. The deeds run in his name—or perhaps in the name of the farmer and his wife, but it almost always continues to be a man's world. The wife could slave in the kitchen, help in the barns, ride a tractor on the fields, and keep the books, but she rarely accumulated an estate of her own—and the law condoned the practice.

True, the husband and wife around the kitchen table discussed farm affairs. Influential as she might be—and however sound her common sense the fact remained that it was the man who was the farmer—the boss. The tax bills came in his name. The rural mail carrier for the most part found correspondence and invoices addressed to the farmer. His name was on the mail box. He belonged to the Farm Bureau, he was the one who served on cooperative committees.

[¶1200.1] Sole Proprietorship as the Simplest Form

Not only was the sole proprietorship historically the commonest form of agricultural bsuiness organization, it was the simplest. There were no complicated relationships. All the farmer needed was to have a social security number and a business identification number.

[¶1200.2] Death and Sole Proprietorship

The efficiency of a farmer's performance, however, tends to move with the life cycle. It rises to a peak in the middle years and declines thereafter. With death, the sole proprietorship ends. Who will carry on? What will happen to the farm? Where will the wife live?

The sole proprietorship, which began as a one-man's world, terminates with the demise of that man—unless careful estate planning had been done.

In the 1970s, a New York State census reported that 87.3 per cent of the farms in the state were owned and operated by sole proprietors, 10.7 per cent by partnerships, and 1.5 per cent by Sub-Chapter S Corporations. As a matter of record, seven out of eight farms with sales volume of products valued at $2,500 or more were operated by individual owners.

[¶1200.3] Search For Optimum Form

In the wake of agricultural transformation, economic, legal and political issues developed to force the farmer to search for optimum forms of business organization.

Nevertheless, in overwhelming proportion, farms continue to be owned by the male. He holds the title to acres. He bears the risk—whether for profit or loss. He makes the decisions. He does what he wants to do on a time schedule that is his own. Except as state law gives his spouse certain limited rights, he can buy, sell, and mortgage his lands.

In the beginning, as the Bible says, God made man. Farming was pretty much a one-man business—his business. Thus it was for generations since the creation. Toward the twenty-first century A.D., law and custom have begun to recognize the wife as a farm partner.

As time and technology place a heavy burden on the one-man's shoulder, sole proprietorship is being rethought. The simple and uncomplicated form dependent upon the life span of the farmer, plus the strain of the increasingly complex and more sophisticated world, are no longer the unquestioned option for agricultural business organization.

13

Father and Son Operation

[¶1300] FATHER AND SON OPERATION AS A FORM

In the general natural history of farm business organization, a father and son operation is a step in the life cycle. It develops as naturally as a cow gives birth to a calf. It is a biological succession.

[¶1301] ADVANTAGES FOR THE SON

The son moves into the farm operation quite often without any formal understanding except that he "works with his father."

The monetary advantages for the son are several. He can enjoy farming without the burden of heavy debt. At the start of his career he is a part of a "going enterprise." As he proves his competence, he can "grow in" on the operation. He enjoys the advice and counsel of his father—the experienced farmer. He shares the work load. The father gets the opportunity to take it a little easier, and to take a little time off. Further, the son enjoys a good and steady job and involvement in the business. For his father, the son provides a steady, reliable, and interested worker. The son injects new ideas and enthusiasm into the farm enterprise. He can enjoy the shared relationship. Meanwhile the father gradually shifts responsibilities and has the satisfaction that the farm is "going on." This is the dream of a father with a capable son.

[¶1302] FATHER AND SON OPERATION AS DYNAMIC

A Father and Son operation involves two generations and two stages in the life cycle. The younger member is in the process of getting started and getting on with his life. The older member is in process of disengaging step-by-step, with an eye toward an enjoyable and financially secure retirement. Father is on the downswing of the life cycle. Son is on the upbeat.

As a result of this movement in the life cycle, a successful father and son operation is dynamic and not static. It looks forward, not back. As the younger member assumes more responsibility and gains more ownership, the older partner disengages and moves toward retirement with certain questions in his mind:

1. When shall he actually retire?
2. Where will he live?
3. What will he do with his time?
4. How will his plans affect others?
5. What will he do with his money—if he seeks liquidity?
6. With what projected income will he finance his retirement?

This process of disengagement is quite as important for the father as for the son.

[¶1303] WHY FATHER AND SON PARTNERSHIPS GO SOUR

Despite the naturalness and the frequency of father and son operations, all too frequently things go sour. Why? Sometimes the understanding is oral and vague. The father fails to make it clear how the son is going to grow into the enterprise, and how he and father are to team up in the operation. How is the son to engage and the father to disengage? The relationship between father and son may deteriorate, and finally terminate in hard feelings.

A durable and satisfactory father and son arrangement must be thought through, written down, and performed in such mutual good faith that the father can lessen his work burden and increase his enjoyment, and the son can increase his responsibility. The relationship must be clear; it must be honestly and fairly carried out.

[¶1303.1] Off-the-Cuff Arrangement

Often—and quite understandably—the early relationships of father and son are casual and off-the-cuff. The farm just goes on as it always has done—except that the son is older, probably married, and perhaps is forming his family. In the absence of clear-cut understandings, trouble is ahead.

[¶1304] SIX BASIC TYPES OF FATHER AND SON OPERATIONS

Within agricultural experience, six basic types of father and son agreements are common as the men work together into full partnership.

[¶1304.1] Junior Profit Sharing Plan

Under this arrangement, the father retains all ownership but the son receives a share of the net income as his compensation for his work. The son, under this plan, is the junior member of the operation. He never gains an ownership of anything—land or chattels.This arrangement is common during a trial period, since no joint ownership is involved and the relationships can be terminated easily. It is an experimental plan to test out the boy.

[¶1304.2] Growing-In Arrangement

Under this pattern, the son or daughter—both called juniors—gradually acquire a share in the ownership of the personal property. The junior acquires a share in all animals raised and all animals and machinery purchased after the "growing-in" arrangement beings.

Although this arrangement seems simple and easy on the surface, problems develop that have to be worked through. One of these is depreciation costs.

The plan needs careful arrangement to establish a policy that makes relationships clear. Policy and practices need to be spelled out in a written memorandum.

[¶1304.3] The "Buying-In" Plan

Here the son buys a share in the ownership of property. The son agrees to buy a half-interest in all the personal property from the father at the very beginning. The father often finances the purchase, taking a promisory note. Under this clear-cut and business-like transaction, all ownership of livestock, machinery, feed, supplies, and crops are joint, and all increases or decreases are shared in proportion to ownership.

[¶1304.4] Formal Partnership Plan

Once the juniors have demonstrated their interest in farming and have proved their capability, the father and junior can perhaps best enter into a straight-forward and fully spelled-out partnership agreement.

[¶1304.5] Outright Sale With Mortgage Held by the Father

One of the least common but clear-cut types of agreement is the outright sale with father holding the mortgage. Under this plan, the junior is the sole manager of the farm and the senior receives the income according to the established purchase price.

[¶1304.6] Incorporation

As one generation passes the farming operation to the next, incorporation may prove to be the most convenient and fairest to all members of the family.

[¶1305] THINKING THROUGH THE FATHER AND SON BUSINESS AGREEMENT

Once the father and son sit down to work out a mutually satisfactory agreement, they are on the pathway to success. Figure 13-1 provides an outline for drafting such an understanding.

Figure 13-1 Outline for Father and Son Farm Business Agreement

SECTION I. Parties to the Agreement

This agreement made this ____________ day of ____________________,

19_____, by and between the following parties: ______________________________

__________________________ __________________________ ____________________

SECTION II. Purpose of the Agreement

The above parties form this agreement for the sole purpose of operating a farm business on the following described real estate __________________________

____

____

____

SECTION III. Period Covered

This agreement is to start (Mo.) __________________ (Day) ____________

19_____, and to continue from year to year on the terms herein stated until this agreement is dissolved or until it is replaced by another written agreement. The agreement may be dissolved by either party serving notice on the other at least

Figure 13-1 Cont.

__________ months prior to the end of the year on which dissolution is desired.

SECTION IV. Contributions

A. *Labor*
Each party shall contribute his entire labor and management to the farm business.

B. *Real Estate*
The father is to furnish the land and buildings as described in SECTION II and all material and labor for any capital improvements to land and buildings.

C. *Personal Property*
Livestock
Machinery and equipment
Feed and Supplies

SECTION V. Management

A. General operating plans shall be discussed and agreed upon at the beginning of each year. Adjustments that appear desirable during the year shall be made after being agreed upon by both parties.

B. All purchases involving more than __________ dollars shall be mutually agreed upon.

C. A joint checking account shall be carried with __________________________ __________________________ bank. Checks shall be signed by either party.

D. The following financial records are to be kept:
   1. A complete inventory showing ownership and value of all property used in the farm business shall be made at the time the agreement starts and at the end of each year thereafter. All values shall be agreed upon by both parties.
   2. A current record of all farm receipts and expenses, including allowances made to each party, shall be kept.

SECTION VI. Receipts and Expenses

Profits for the year shall be calculated as indicated in the following table:

Receipts		*Expenses*	
Cash receipts	$________	Cash expenses	$________
		Son's wage allowance	________
		Father's wage allowance	________
	________	Interest on the value of property not jointly owned	________
Total receipts	$________	Total expenses	$________

Total receipts $________ less total expenses $________ = $________ Profit

Figure 13-1 Cont.

Explanation of Items

A. Cash receipts shall include all income from the sale of crops, livestock, and livestock products. Also all income from work off the farm by either party. Also any miscellaneous cash income of the farm business.

B. Cash expenses of the farm business shall include fertilizer and lime; seed; purchased feed; spray materials; wages and cash cost of board for hired labor; taxes; insurance; rent for additional land; purchases of livestock; purchases of new equipment; operating expenses of all equipment and tools; repairs and replacements necessary to keep buildings, fences, wells, and drains in good condition; machine hire; electric lights and power; debt payments on debts of the partnership; and other such expenses mutually agreed necessary for the operation of the farm business.

C. The wage allowance for each party shall be paid ________________________ (weekly or monthly). The amount of these wage allowances shall be agreed upon at the beginning of each year.

D. Each party shall receive interest at ________ per cent on his investment in property which is not jointly owned, but which is used by the partnership. This interest payment includes interest on debts secured by such property, and interest on the value of the property above the debts.

E. If the inventory of property not jointly owned has increased or decreased, an adjustment must be made in the final settlement. If the property has increased in value, the partner who owns it owes the amount of the increase to the partnership. If the property has decreased in value, the partnership owes the owner the amount of the decrease. Increases or decreases in inventory of livestock and equipment should not include changes in value due to general changes in prices. Include only changes due to more or less livestock and equipment, or better or poorer livestock and equipment.

SECTION VII. Financial Settlement

Each party is to have one-half of the profits as calculated in SECTION VI. A complete financial settlement shall be made at the end of each year.

SECTION VIII. Living Arrangements

Living arrangements are to be provided for both father and son and their families. If an additional house is rented for either party, the rental cost shall be shared the same as other farm operating expenses. If either party furnishes the board of the other, the party so furnished shall pay to the one providing the board __________ dollars per month as his share of the cash cost of such board.

SECTION IX. Death of Either Party

At the death of either partner, this partnership agreement shall terminate. Dissolution of the partnership shall be effected in the following manner:

____

____

____

____

Figure 13-1 Cont.

SECTION X.

It is further agreed that ____

____

____

SECTION XI. Arbitration

If any matter pertaining to the farm business cannot be settled by mutual agreement, that matter shall be submitted to one disinterested person agreeable to both.

[¶1305.1] Making Agreements Simple

The relationship of father and son in a farming enterprise should be one of mutual profitability. Otherwise, the working arrangement may deteriorate to the disappointment of all concerned.

A durable and satisfactory father and son understanding must be thought through in detail, written down, and performed in mutual good faith in such a way as to enable the father as well as the son to feel at ease. Father and son must be frank and honest with each other at all times.

Often the father and son get bogged down in an understanding that is too formal and too complicated. What is needed is a simple, clear, and unambiguous projection. Figure 13-2 suggests a simple form of father and son agreement that is a legal document, but written in every -day, easy to understand language.

While a father and son agreement of this type does not generally need to be witnessed and acknowledged, the understanding has more importance if it is witnessed and acknowledged.

The father and son operating agreement, if successful, moves into formal partnership.

Figure 13-2 Father & Son Agreement

THIS IS THE AGREEMENT BETWEEN ME,
John Eks, Father and
John Eks, Jr., Son

entered into by us on _______________, 19_____.

FIRST: OUR PURPOSE

By this written agreement John and I undertake the operation of the family farm located on ________________ acres in the County of ________________ in the State of ________________ and on any other land that John and I agree to buy or rent to farm.

Figure 13-2 Cont.

It is our common purpose to continue the family farm, to provide the opportunity for John to grow into the management and ownership of the farm establishment, to work side by side with each other in labor and decision-making. Step-by-step I intend to disengage myself as I grow older so that I can enjoy the fruits of a more leisurely life.

SECOND: OUR TIMETABLE

John and I begin our association under this agreement on

_______________, 197___. Our relationship shall continue from year to year on terms that we describe in this agreement or amend or until this agreement is replaced by another agreement or is dissolved.

Either John or I may dissolve our relationship under this agreement after conference by serving notice on the other at lease three months prior to the end of the year in which dissolution is desired.

THIRD: OUR RESPECTIVE CONTRIBUTIONS

Here is a specific inventory of the contributions that John and I make to this understanding.

A. *Labor* Both John and I will contribute our labor and management fulltime, to the farming enterprise.

B. *Real Estate* I as father will furnish the land and buildings on the operating farm. Further, I as father will provide all material and labor for any capital improvements.

C. *Personal Property* I as father will furnish all livestock, power equipment, machinery, and tools used in conducting the farming enterprise.

When this agreement becomes effective, John, shall purchase a half interest in all feeds and supplies on hand that will be used in the operation. If necessary, I will accept his promissory note to enable my son to perform this requirement.

FOURTH: MANAGEMENT

John and I will discuss together our general operating plans and agree upon them at the beginning of each year. As adjustments may be desirable as the year wears on, we will discuss what needs to be altered and agree upon the course of action.

John and I will agree on all purchases involving the expenditure of more than $200. We will maintain a joint checking account in the

_______________ Bank. Checks may be signed by either John or me.

John and I will set up a financial record system and include a complete inventory of our financial records.

These records shall include the ownership and value of all property used in the farming enterprise with values established as of the date

Figure 13-2 Cont.

time this agreement begins and thereafter at the end of each year. All values shall be agreed upon by us.

John and I shall keep a current record of all farm purchases, receipts, and expenses, including allowances made to either of us.

The financial record books shall be kept as arranged between us, but shall be open for a review.

FIFTH: RECEIPTS AND EXPENSES

John and I will calculate the profits for the year according to the following table:

RECEPITS		*EXPENSES*	
Cash Receipts	$______	Cash expenses	$________________
Increase in inventory value or property not jointly owned	$______	My wage allowance	$____________
		John's wage allowance	$__________
		Interest on value of property not jointly owned	$____________
		Decrease in inventory value or property not jointly owned	$____________
Total Receipts	$______________	Total Expenses	$______________

Total Receipts = $_____________ less total expense $_______ = $_______ Profit

In establishing this formula, John and I agree that

(a) Cash receipts shall include all cash income derived from the farm operation inclusive livestock, livestock products, and crops plus miscellaneous cash income derived from all other farm operations.

(b) Cash expenses include fertilizer and lime, seed, purchased feed, spray materials and custom spray work, wages and cash cost of board for hired labor, taxes, insurance, rent for additional land, purchases of livestock, purchases of new equipment, operating expenses of equipment and tools, repairs and replacements necessary to keep buildings, fences, water systems and drains in good condition, machine hire and custom work, electric lights and power, payment of debts incurred by the partnership and other expenses mutually agreed upon by John and me as necessary for the profitable operation of the farm enterprise.

(c) The wage allowance for both me and John shall be paid weekly (or monthly). The amount of these wages allowances shall be agreed upon by us at the beginning of each year.

Figure 13-2 Cont.

(d) Both John and I shall receive interest at ________ per cent on our respective investments in property which is not jointly owned, but is used in the farming enterprise under this agreement.

(e) If the inventory of property not jointly owned has increased or decreased, John and I will make an adjustment in the final settlement. If this the property has increased in value, then the one of us who owns it owes the amount of the increase to this partnership. If the property has decreased in value, then the partnership owes to us respectively the amount of the decrease. Increase in inventory of livestock and equipment shall not include changes in value resulting from general changes in prices. Only such changes as result from livestock and equipment or better or poorer livestock and equipment shall be included.

SIXTH: ANNUAL SETTLEMENT

At the end of each year, John and I will review our account and make a complete financial settlement to share one-half of the profits as calculated by the formula in the preceding paragraph.

SEVENTH: LIVING ARRANGEMENTS

By agreement between us, living arrangements are to be provided for both me and John and for our respective families. If an additional house is rented for either of us, the rental cost shall be shared in the same manner as other farm operating expenses. If either John or I furnish board to the other, the one of us boarded shall pay to the other providing the board $__________ a week as his share of the cash cost of such board.

EIGHTH: TERMINATION

Upon the death of either of us, this agreement shall terminate.

NINTH: MISCELLANEOUS

John and I further agree that

TENTH: SETTLEMENT OF DIFFERENCES

In the event that any of our problems cannot be resolved by mutual agreement, then the question in dispute shall be submitted to one disinterested person agreed upon by us.

____

John Eks, Father

____

John Eks, Jr. Son

Figure 13-2 Cont.

WITNESSES

____

____

Sworn to and subscribed in my presence

DATE ____________________ ________________________________

Notary Public

14

The Partnership

[¶1400] PARTNERSHIP AS A COMMON FORM OF ASSOCIATION

Next to sole proprietorship, the partnership is the most common form of farm business organization. A partnership, as defined by the Uniform Partnership Act, is an association of two or more persons to do business for profit.

It is the most intimate form of business organization—much like a family in business together.

[¶1401] NECESSARY PERSONAL CHARACTERISTICS FOR A SUCCESSFUL PARTNERSHIP

A successful partnership requires certain guarantees. Here are seven of them:

1. The partners must have confidence in the partnership as a form of business organizaton.
2. The partners must have confidence in each other.
3. The partners must have informed and interested wives.
4. The partners must have farming competence and demonstrated sound judgment.
5. The partners must have dependable work habits.
6. The partners must be willing to "give and take."
7. The partners must have the ability to work with other people.

[¶1402] NECESSARY ECONOMIC FACTORS

Certain necessary economic conditions must exist to lay the foundations for a successful partnership. Here are six of these economic considerations stated as questions:

1. Is the farm enterprise big enough to provide adequate income for two families?
2. Are there adequate living quarters for two families?
3. Is income to be shared on the basis of what each contributes?
4. Is there a workable plan for handling records and finances?
5. Is management shared by both parties with mutual respect?
6. Is there a definite written agreement?

Here is an iron-clad rule: *Partnership relationships should always be spelled out in a written agreement.*

[¶1403] PARTNERSHIP CHECKLIST

The shaping of a partnership agreement is made more precise by the use of the 100 question schedule provided in the following worksheet.

Step one in establishing a sound partnership is to assemble all the facts that are necessary for use in drafting the partnership agreement.

I. Definition of Farm Enterprise

1. What is the scope of the farming business to be carried on? (Describe the range and type of activity).
2. What are the full legal names and addresses of the proposed partners? (Name the partners)

NAMES	ADDRESSES
______________________	______________________
______________________	______________________
______________________	______________________

3. Under what name is the partnership to operate (If the name of the partnership differs from the names of the partners, it must be registered in most states).
4. What lands and equipment does the proposed partnership require to carry out the scope of the enterprise as defined in (1) above? (Specify lands, buildings, machinery, livestock, tools, and other items).
5. What specific part of (4) do the proposed partners as individuals own?
6. How much cash will be needed to buy what parts of (4) which the partners do not now own? $________

7. What special skills or experience do each of the partners bring to the enterprise?
8. What are the financial resources of each partner?
9. What are the family circumstances of each partner?
10. Do the proposed partners plan to expand the farm enterprise?
11. Approximately how much money will be required for such expansion?

II. Definition of Existing Operations?

12. What—if the partnership is to carry on an existing farm operation—are the properties in kind to be transferred to the proposed partnership?
13. Are all the licenses, insurance policies, certificates of ownership, and the like to be assigned to the new partnership?
14. Will the new partnership assume all liabilities of the old farming operation?
15. Will the new partnership follow the same farming policies and practices as of old?
16. What will be the accounting method?
17. What will be the fiscal year?
18. What provisions have been made to dissolve and terminate the previous form of farm business organization?

III. Specific Details

19. What will be the legal and principal place of business of the farming operation?
20. For how long a term is the partnership to exist and on what date will its existence begin and on what date will it end?
21. What contributions in money will be made by each partner?
22. What contributions in property will be made by each partner?
23. When is the money to be paid in?
24. What is the agreed value of each property contribution?
25. What was the cost of each item in (24)?
26. Is a partner to have the right to make additional contributions?
27. Is a partner to have the right to withdraw part of his contribution?
28. Is any property being loaned by a partner such as a truck, machinery, tools, or the like?
29. What percentage of the total property does each partner own?
30. What percentage of money contributions does each partner own?
31. To what extent is each partner to leave part of his profits in the farming enterprise as additional capital?

IV. Distribution of Partnership Income

32. Is each partner to receive interest on his contributions?
33. What salary or wage is each partner to receive?

34. May a partner withdraw profits in advance of the annual accounting?
35. Is any partner to be guaranteed a specified minimum return?
36. Are profits to be shared according to capital contributions?
37. How is depreciation to be shared on property contributed at a value different from its tax cost?
38. Who is to pay the tax on precontribution gain, or to receive the benefit of precontribution loss in the contributed property?
39. What expense and entertainment accounts are the respective partners to have?

V. Accounting Policy

40. What is the accounting and tax year of each partner?
41. What is the fiscal year of the partnership to be?
42. Are the books to be kept on a cash or accural basis?
43. Are financial statements to be issued to partners montly, semi-annually, or annually?
44. Is provision made for periodic auditing by an accounting firm?
45. Are all partners to have access to all books at reasonable times?
46. On what date is the annual profit or loss of the partnership to be determined?
47. Are current or drawing and capital accounts to be established for each partner?
48. Are reserves for the payment of claims to be created?

VI. Management Policy

49. Is each partner to have an equal voice in farm management policy and practice?
50. How—if partners are not to have equal voice—are the voices of each partner to be determined, such as senior and junior, managing or non-managing, active and silent?
51. Is management to be vested in the partners acting together or by one of the partners so designated?
52. What is the description of the duty of the managing partner or partners?
53. In what instance are the managing partners to secure the approval of the non-managing partners?
54. Is a bond to be required of any partner?
55. How are salary changes of the partners to be made?
56. How are checks to be signed?
57. Are meetings of the partners to be scheduled at regular times?
58. Are the partners each to devote full time to the farm business?
59. To what extent may partners engage in other activities?
60. How are disputes arising under the partnership agreement to be settled? (For example, by a majority of the partners, each having one vote? By

partners entitled to more than fifty per cent of the profits? By a designated partner? By arbitration?)

61. Should any or all of the partners be prohibited from performing certain acts without the consent of all partners?
62. Should parnters—as individuals—be restricted in their power or right to act as accommodation parties and from going into debit except for household and current expenses?
63. Should partners be restricted in their power to lend money to the farm, to mortgage, or to pledge the partnership property?
64. Should a partner have the right to discharge an employee?
65. Should a partner have the power to close a transaction involving more than a certain sum of money?
66. Should one or all the partners be prohibited from mortgaging or disposing of any or all of their interests in the partnership?
67. What provision is to be made for the expulsion of a partner?
68. Can a partner be expelled for disability and if so how shall such disability continue before action is taken?
69. What advance notice shall a partner give of his intention to withdraw from the farming operation?
70. Is a withdrawing partner to be prohibited from engaging in a competing business such as a dairy route and from using the firm name?
71. Is provision to be made for the continuance of the business upon the death, disability, bankruptcy, expulsion, or withdrawal of a partner?
72. Is notice to be given of the exercise of the option specified in (74).
73. How is a partner who wrongfully withdraws to be penalized?
74. Are the partners jointly or individually to have the right or option to purchase the interest of a deceased or retiring partner?
75. How is the value of such interest referred to in (74) to be determined such as by book value, or by a certified public accountant?
76. Is good will to be considered and if so, on what basis?
77. How are payments to be made if partners are to purchase and continue the farming business? By cash within what periods? By promissory notes? By mortgage? By liens or charges on the assets of the partnership?
78. Is the partnership to incorporate upon the death of a partner so that stock may be given to the estate of the deceased partner for settlement?
79. Is the estate of the deceased partner to continue to participate in profits and for how long?
80. What provision is to be made to make certain that the deceased or withdrawing partner bears his equitable share of losses?
81. Is a fund to be withheld or created for payment of contingent claims?
82. In what proportions are the remaining partners to divide the interest of the deceased or retiring partner upon purchase?
83. Do the partners desire to purchase life insurance on each other's life with which to purchase the interest of a deceased partner?
84. If (83) is answered by "Yes," then how much insurance is each to maintain on the life of the other or others?

85. If there are more than two partners, do the partners desire a trustee to monitor the arrangement and who shall be the trustee?
86. What provision is to be made for a partner whose life is not insurable?
87. How are new partners to be admitted during the existence of the agreement? With the consent of all partners? Upon what conditions?
88. What acts other than the expiration of the term of the partnership agreement shall result in the discontinuance of the partnership?.
89. What shall be the power of the continuing partners when a partner dies or is adjudicated incompetent or is incapacitated so as to be unable to discharge his duties?
90. What policy is to be followed when a partner assigns for the benefit of creditors, or withdraws, or is expelled?
91. Are all partners to act as liquidators or are managing partners to select the liquidators? And what salaries shall liquidators receive?
92. Are partnership assets to be distributed in whole or partly in kind?
93. Does any partner wish the return of the specific items of property which he contributed?
94. What shall be the order of distribution of the assets?

VIII Characteristics of Successful Partnership

95. Do the proposed partners have reason to believe that they can work profitably with one another?
96. Do the proposed partners have a record of good business judgement?
97. Do the proposed partners have good work habits?
98. Are the wives of all partners informed and interested?
99. Will there be adequate income to support the families of the respective partners?
100. Have the proposed partners reviewed all the foregoing questions? Do they understand the ramifications of their partnership form of farming business organization?

[¶1404] NAME OF PARTNERSHIP

The name of a farming enterprise has some bearing upon its success. The commonest pattern is to pair the names, such as John Doe & Son, or John & Michael Doe. If the partners are not related in the same family, the partnership may be given a name such as Bailey and Thompson.

When a descriptive name is selected, it must generally be registered with the state under provisions of state law. Thus Sunnyside Farms, as a name of a partnership, would require registration.

[¶1405] WORKING MODEL OF PARTNERSHIP AGREEMENT

To assist the draftsman, a general farm partnership agreement follows.

THIS AGREEMENT, entered into on the ______ day of ______ 19__, establishes a partnership by and between ______John EX______, residing State Highway 130, and ______George WX______, residing State Highway 130, both of the County of Sunland, State of ANYWHERE.

ARTICLE I

Purposes of This Partnership

THE PARTNERS associate themselves together for the purpose of general farming, and such related to agricultural activities as may be agreed upon by the partners.

ARTICLE II

Place

The primary farm is located at Blossom's Corner, State Highway 130, situated in the County of Sunland, State of Anywhere. The partnership may be extended to lands and facilities as the partners may agree to buy or rent for the purpose of their association.

ARTICLE III

Name

The name of the partnership shall be E X (if the operating name differs from that of the partners, it must be registered by the State.)

ARTICLE IV

Term

This partnership shall begin on the ______ day of ______ 19__ and shall continue from year to year on terms as stated in this agreement or until this agreement is dissolved or is replaced by another written agreement. This partnership may be terminated by either partner by serving written notice on the other partner at least 120 days prior to the end of the year in which dissolution is desired.

ARTICLE V

Contributions, Accounts, and Withdrawals

1. The capital of this partnership shall consist of the amount shown on the balance sheet attached to this agreement and by this reference incorporated herein. The capital contributions of each partner shall consist of the capital invested by each partner as shown in the aforementioned balance sheet.

2. An individual capital account shall be maintained for each partner.

3. Except by unanimous agreement of the partners, or upon dissolution, the capital contributions of the partners shall not be subject to withdrawal.

4. Each party shall contribute his entire labor and management to the farm business.

5. Land and buildings, as appraised at the date of this agreement shall be accepted to be their values. Any increase in these values shall be considered and owned by the partnership.

6. Chattels as contributed by either partner as owners at the time this agreement begins shall be inventoried, valued, and listed on a schedule attached to this agreement and incorporated by this reference into this agreement. Each partner shall share equally in the increase in livestock raised or purchased after this agreement begins.

ARTICLE VI

Profits and Losses

1. The net profits or net losses of the partnership shall be distributable or chargeable, as the case may be, to each of the partners in equal proportions.

2. An individual income account shall be maintained for each partner. Profits and losses shall be credited or debited to the individual income accounts as soon as practicable after the close of each fiscal year.

3. If there be no balance in the individual income accounts, net losses shall be debited to the individual capital accounts. If the capital account of a partner shall have been depleted by the debiting of losses

under this paragraph, future profits of that partner shall not be credited to his income account until the depletion shall have been made good, but shall be credited to his capital account. After the depletion in his capital account shall have been made good, his share of the profit thereafter shall be credited to his income account.

ARTICLE VII

Management; Salaries

1. Each of the partners shall have an equal voice in the management and conduct of the partnership business. All decisions shall be unanimous, except that if and when other partners are added, all decisions shall be a majority vote and each partner shall be entitled to one vote.

2. Each partner shall devote his full time and attention to the partnership business.

3. Each partner shall receive such salary as shall from time to time be agreed upon, but the payment of salaries shall be an obligation of the partnership only to the extent that there are assets available for them, and shall not be an obligation of the partners individually.

4. Salaries shall be treated as expenses of the partnership in determining net profits or net losses.

5. General operating plans shall be discussed and agreed upon at the beginning of each year. Adjustments that appear desirable during the year shall be made after being agreed upon by both partners.

6. All capital purchasing involving more than $200 shall be mutually agreed upon.

7. A joint checking account shall be carried with the __________ bank. Checks may be signed by either party.

ARTICLE VIII

Dissolution Because of the Retirement, Death or Insanity of a Partner

1. Retirement, death or insanity of a partner shall work an immediate dissolution of the partnership.

2. In the event of a dissolution of the partnership by the retirement, death, or insanity of a partner, a proper accounting shall be made of the capital and income accounts of each partner and of the net profit or loss of the partnership from the date of the last previous accounting to the date of dissolution.

3. In the event of the retirement, death, or insanity of a partner, the remaining partners shall have the right to continue the business of the partnership under the present name by themselves, or in conjunction with any other person or persons they may select, but they shall pay to the retiring partner, or to the legal representative of the deceased or insane partner, as the case may be, the value of his interest in the partnership as provided in the following paragraphs of this Article. If the remaining partner shall desire to continue the business, but not altogether, the partnership shall be liquidated in accordance with the provisions of Paragraph 1 of Article IX.

4. The value of the interest if a retiring, deceased, or insane partner as of the date of dissolution shall be the sum of:

a. his capital account
b. his income account
c. any earned and unpaid salary due him; and
d. his proportionate share of accrued net profits.

If a net loss has been incurred to the date of dissolution, his share of such loss shall be deducted.

5. Inventory for purposes of this article shall be valued at cost or market value—whichever is lower. Other assets shall be valued at book value.

6. No value for good will or firm name shall be included in any computations of a partner's interest under this Article.

ARTICLE IX

Voluntary Dissolution

1. Unless dissolved by the retirements, death or insanity of a partner, the partnership shall continue until dissolved by agreement of the partners. Upon any such voluntary dissolution by agreement, the affairs of the partnership shall be liquidated forthwith. The assets of the partnership shall first be used to pay or provide for all debts of the partnership. Thereafter, all moneys in the income accounts of the partnership and all amounts due for earned or unpaid salaries of the partners shall be paid to the partners respectively entitled thereto. Then the remaining assets shall be divided according to the proportionate interests of the partners on the basis of their respective capital accounts as they stood upon the date of such dissolution, after crediting or debiting to them the net profits or net losses accrued or incurred, as the case may be, from the date of the last accounting to the date of dissolution.

2. Upon termination of the partnership by agreement of the partners, any two partners—if there be more than two—shall have the right, in lieu of liquidation provided for in the preceding paragraph of this Article, to continue the business of the partnership under its present name, by themselves or in conjunction with any person or persons they may select, upon paying in cash forthwith to the withdrawing partner the amounts to which he would be entitled under Paragraph 5 of Article VI, in case of a dissolution under Article VI. If more than one of the partners desires to take advantage of this paragraph, but they do not desire to continue the business of the partnership together, then the affairs of the partnership shall be liquidated in accordance with the preceding paragraph of this Article.

ARTICLE X

Partners' Powers and Limitations

1. Checks shall be drawn on the partnership bank account for partnership purposes only. Either partner may sign such checks, but if there are more than two partners, then checks shall be signed by any two partners.

2. No partner may without the consent of the other partner:

a. borrow money in the firm name for firm purposes or utilize collateral owned by the partnership as security for such loans;
b. assign, transfer, pledge, compromise, or release any of the claims of or debts due the partnership except upon payment in full, or arbitrate or consent to the arbitration of any of the disputes or controversies of the partnership;
c. make, execute, or deliver any assignment for the benefit of creditors, or any bond, confession of judgment, chattel mortgage, deed, guarantee, indemnity bond, surety bond, or contract to sell or contract of sale of all or substantially all of the property of the partnership;
d. lease or mortgage any partnership real estate or any interest therein or enter upon any contract for any such purpose;
e. pledge or hypothecate or in any manner transfer his interest in the partnership, except to another party to this agreement;
f. become a surety, guarantor, or accommodation party to any obligation.

ARTICLE XI

Miscellaneous

1. The partnership shall maintain a bank account or bank accounts in such bank or banks as may be agreed upon by the partners.

2. All notices provided for under this agreement shall be in writing and shall be sufficient if sent registered mail to the last known address of the party to which such notice is to be given.

3. Proper and complete books of account shall be kept at all times and shall be open to inspection by any partner or his accredited representative at any reasonable time during farm hours. The books shall be examined and reviewed as of the close of each fiscal year by an independent certified public accountant agreeable to the partners. He shall make a report of his examination.

4. The parties hereto consent and agree that they will execute any further instruments and that they will perform any acts which are or may become necessary to effectuate and to carry on the partnership created by this agreement.

ARTICLE XII

If any matters pertaining to this partnership agreement cannot be settled by mutual agreement, that matter shall be submitted to one disinterested person agreeable to both.

PARTNERSHIP

IN WITNESS WHEREOF, the parties hereto have hereunto set their hands and seals the day and year first written above.

__________________________ L.S.

__________________________ L.S.

WITNESSES:

____

____

15

The Limited Partnership

[¶1500] USEFULNESS OF LIMITED PARTNERSHIP

As farming becomes increasingly capital-intensive, requiring the injection of large sums of money, and as investors search for investment opportunities in soil-based economic entities, the limited partnership becomes an advantageous form of business organization. It provides one of the ways an owner-farmer may expand, and the legal vehicle by which a young man may build his own highway in career farming.

Thus for example, a physician, who has funds to invest and who may also love the land, may become a limited partner with the young man who professionally knows how to run a farm. Farm lenders exist who seek limited partnership opportunities. Sometimes within farm families, a father, a father-in-law, or an uncle may emerge as a limited partner. In estate settlements, a limited partnership may provide a means of keeping the family interest together.

[¶1501] HISTORY OF THE UNIFORM LIMITED PARTNERSHIP ACT

In 1916, the National Conference of Commissioners of Uniform State Laws promulgated a Uniform Limited Partnership Act. In the years since the first draft was published, legislation has been enacted by all the states.

A limited partnership is a partnership formed by two or more persons, having as members one or more general partners and one or more limited partners. The limited partners are not bound by the obligations of the partnership beyond the amount of their investment.

[¶1502] THE NATURE OF A LIMITED PARTNERSHIP

The manual issued by the Joint Committee on Continuing Legal Education of the American Law Institute and the American Bar Association states the nature of a limited partnership in a classic definition:

> "A limited partnership is a hybrid, somewhat of a cross between a general partnership and a corporation . . . General partners in a limited partnership are subject to all the risks involved in a general partnership, while the risks of limited partners are restricted to their rights to participate in management of the business."
>
> "In short, a general partner in a limited partnership is much the same as a general partner in a general partnership. On the other hand, a limited partner more closely resembles a stockholder in a corporation."*

[¶1503] UNIFORM LIMITED PARTNERSHIP ACT

Throughout the United States and outlying territories, with few exceptions, limited partnerships are governed by the *UNIFORM LIMITED PARTNERSHIP ACT*. In each jurisdiction, however, it is essential to study the state legislation on the subject. Compliance with the local statutes is mandatory. These state statutes commonly require the filing of a certificate which describes the rights and duties of members among themselves.

Unless the statutory procedures are carefully followed, the limited partnership may fail, and limited partners may be held to the same liability as general partners.

[¶1503.1] Description of a Limited Partnership

A limited partnership is constructed from one or more general partners and one or more limited partners. As generally established, the general partner runs the farm and has the same liability for losses as he would in a general partnership. Limited partners, on the other hand, share profits like general partners or receive other compensation by way of income.

The liability of limited partners for losses, however, is limited by the amount of their capital investment.

**The Drafting of Partnership Agreements* (Philadelphia: ALI-ABA Committee on Professional Education) 1976 6th edition (1976).

[¶1503.2] Restrictions of Name

By provisions of the Limited Partnership Act, the name of the limited partnership must not contain the surname (family name) of a limited partner unless it is also the surname of a general partner. If it does so appear in the name, the limited partner is liable as a general partner to creditors who rely on the representation.

[¶1503.3] Contributions

The capital contributions of a limited partner are restricted to cash or other property. The property must be specifically described and given an agreed valuation.

[¶1503.4] Rights

A limited partner is liable to the partnership and to any creditors who rely on the filed certificate for the unpaid portion of his contribution. Moreover, a limited partner may (1) not contribute services, nor (2) take part in management nor (3) take part in the control of the farming operation. If he does so, he forfeits his limited liability and is clothed with the unlimited liability of a general partner.

[¶1503.5] Taxation

For income tax purposes, a limited partnership is treated either as an ordinary partnership or an association taxable as a corporation. Generally, the limited partnership qualifies as an ordinary partnership. Whenever the limited partnership exhibits certain corporate characteristics such as limited liability, centralization of management, unlimited duration, transferability of interests, taxation as a corporation may then result.

As a general rule, the Internal Revenue Service will not issue a ruling on the classification of a partnership *if there is a question whether tax avoidance may be a principal purpose of the arrangement.*

[¶1503.6] Transferability of Interest and Dissolution

A limited partnership dissolves at the expiration of the term stated in the certificate or for reasons that would cause the dissolution of a general partnership.

[¶1503.7] Death of Limited Partner

The death of a limited partner does not dissolve the business entity. The personal representative of the decedent acceeds to the rights of the deceased limited partner and exercises the rights of a limited partner for probate purposes. Further, the articles may expressly empower the limited partner to substitute a new limited partner in his own place. In such case the estate or assignee becomes a member of the limited partnership and the certificate must be amended to show the new interest.

[¶1503.8] Formation of a Limited Partnership

In the formation of a limited partnership, there are two steps to take. The first step is the execution and filing of a *Certificate of Limited Partnership* for public record. The second step is the *Agreement of Limited Partnership*. This second and more detailed agreement does not need to be placed in the public record.

The Certificate. The blank certificate form in most jurisdictions will be supplied by the corporate division of the office of the Secretary of State.

Here is an example:

Figure 15-1 Certificate of Formation of Limited Partnership

The undersigned, being desirous of forming a limited partnership under the Act of ________ entitled The Uniform Limited Partnership Act, hereby make and sign the following certificate for that purpose:

I. The name under which the partnership is to be conducted is "SUNLAND FARMS."

II. The partnership shall engage in general farming, together with all other business necessary and related thereto including the cultivation and sale of crops, the production, processing and distribution of milk and milk products, the breeding, feeding and sale of livestock, and any and all agricultural activities.

III. The location of the principal place of business of the partnership is

________________________.

IV. The names and places of resident of the general and limited partners are:

A. General Partners

Name	Address
____________________	____________________
____________________	____________________

Figure 15-1 Cont.

B. Limited Partners

____________________ ____________________

____________________ ____________________

V. The partnership shall continue for an indefinite term.

VI. The limited partners have contributed the following cash to the partnership:

Limited	Cash Contribution
____________________	$____________________
____________________	$____________________

VII. Each limited partner may make additional contributions to the capital of the partnership in such amounts as may from time to time be agreed upon by the general partners.

VIII. Each limited partner may make those withdrawals from his capital account that may from time to time be agreed upon by the general partners.

IX. By reason of their contributions, the limited partners shall receive the following percentage of the net profits of the partnership:

Limited Partner	Net Profits Percentage Share
____________________	__________%
____________________	__________%

X. In the event of the retirement, death, or insanity of a general partner the remaining partners shall have the right to continue the business of the partnership under the same name by themselves or in conjunction with any other person or persons they may select.

IN WITNESS WHEREOF, we have hereunto set our hands and seals this __________ day of ____________ 197___.

__________________ L.S.
General Partner

__________________ L.S.
General Partner

__________________ O.S.
Limited Partner

__________________ L.S.
General Partner

[¶1503.9] Moving from General to Limited Partnership

When a general partnership moves into a limited partnership, the agreement is often introduced by a recital such as:

Figure 15-2 Recital

Recital

1. ____________ and ____________ have been conducting a general partnership under a written agreement dated ____________ 19 ______

2. It is the mutual desire of the parties hereto that the farming business be continued and that ____________ and ____________ be admitted as limited partners.

NOW THEREFORE, it is mutually agreed by and between the parties hereto as follows:

(This recital precedes the limited partnership agreement.)

[¶1503.10] Limited Partnership Agreement

The limited partnership agreement must incorporate the general principles of the certificate but does not need to be filed with the state. Figure 15-3 gives guidance in drafting a limited partnership agreement.

Figure 15-3 Limited Partnership Agreement Form

AGREEMENT OF LIMITED PARTNERSHIP made this

____________ day of ______________________,

19____, by and among ____________________ and

________________ both of whom are hereinafter sometimes referred to as "General Partners" and

____________________ and ____________________
both of whom are hereinafter referred to as "Limited Partners."

ARTICLE I

Formation of Limited Partnership

1. The parties hereto form a limited partnership pursuant to the laws of the State of ____________,
   Title ____________ enacted on ____________
   and known as the Uniform Limited Partnership Act.
2. The parties hereto shall forthwith execute:
   (a) A certificate and a affidavit thereto, and cause the same to be filed in the corporate office of the Recorder of Deeds in the County of __________ in accordance with the provisions of the Uniform Limited Partnership Act of the State of
   ____________.
   (b) A certificate and cause the same to be filed with the corporate office of the Secretary of State
   of ____________ and the clerk of the County
   of ____________, together with proof of publication as required by the Fictitious Names
   SCT of __________________ as amended.

Notes

These paragraphs are usually inserted to show compliance with state statutory requirements and to make a record when the name differs from that of the partners.

ARTICLE II

Name, Character, Place of Business, and Term of Partnership

1. The business of the partnership shall be conducted under the firm name of SUNLAND FARMS.
2. The partnership shall engage in general farming, together with all other business necessary and related thereto including the cultivation and sale of crops, the production and distribution of milk and milk products and other commodities usually distributed by milk routes, the breeding, feeding, and sale of

Figure 15-3 Cont.

livestock, and any other and all agricultural activities incident to the conduct of the enterprise.

3. The principal place of business of the partnership shall be at ________________, but additional places of business may be conducted at locations that from time to time may be approved by the general partners.
4. The partnership shall commence on the 1st day of the month of ______________, 19____, and shall continue for an indefinite term.

Notes

Since the purpose serves public notice concerning the scope of the business, it is desirable to make the statement broad enough to include all contemplates possible activities.

The name of a limited partnership must not include the surname of a limited partner unless it is also the surname of a general partner or was in the firm name prior to the formation of the limited partnership.

ARTICLE III

Capital Contributions, Accounts and Withdrawals

1. ______________ and ______________ shall be the general partners. ______________ and ______________ shall be the limited partners.
   (a) The general partners shall contribute as their shares of the capital the amount credited respectively to them in the balance sheet, dated ____________ 19____, of the general partnership business heretofore conducted by them under the name of Sunnyside Dairy Company, a copy of which balance sheet is attached hereto as Exhibit "A".
   (b) Each of the limited partners shall make the following contributions in cash to the capital of the partnership:

   ________________ $________________

   ________________ $________________
2. Each partners, general or limited, may make additional contributions to the capital of the partnership in such amounts as may from time to time be agreed upon by the general partners.
3. Each partner, general or limited, may make withdrawals from his capital account as may from time to time to be agreed upon by the general partners.

Figure 15-3 Cont.

Notes

4. An individual capital account shall be maintained for each partner, to which shall be credited his contributions or withdrawals, as the case may be.

ARTICLE IV

Duties, Powers, and Salaries of Partners

1. Each general partner shall have an equal voice in the management and conduct of the partnership business.
   (a) The general partners shall devote their full time and best efforts to the conduct of the partnership business.
   (b) Checks shall be drawn on the partnership bank account or bank accounts and shall be signed by any general partner or partners who may be designated by the general partners.
2. The general partners shall receive such salaries as may from time to time be agreed upon by them. Payment of salaries shall be an obligation of the partnership only to the extent that partnership assets are available, and shall not be an obligation of the individual partners. In determining the net profit or loss of the partnership in any fiscal year, as provided in Article V, each salary payment shall be treated as an expense of the partnership.
3. An individual withdrawal account shall be maintained for each general partner, to which his salary shall be credited. Any general partner may withdraw such portion of his salary as he may desire from time to time, with the amount being charged to his withdrawal account.
   Portions of salaries not withdrawn by a general partner by the close of a fiscal year shall be credited to his capital account.
4. The limited partners shall not take part in the management of the business or transact any business for the partnership and they shall have no power to sign for or to bind the partnership. No salary shall be paid to any limited partner.
5. Proper and complete books of account of the business of the partnership shall be kept by and under the supervision of the general partners at the principal place of business of the partnership and shall be open to inspection by any of the partners, general,or limited, or by their accredited representatives, at any reasonable time during business hours. The books and records of accounts shall be examined and reviewed as of the close of each fiscal year by an independent certified public accountant, acceptable to the general partners, who shall make a report thereon.

Figure 15-3 Cont.

Notes

ARTICLE V

Profits and Losses

1. The fiscal year of the partnership shall be the calendar year. The net profit or net loss of the partnership shall be determined in accordance with approved and accepted accounting practice as soon as possible after the close of each fiscal year.
2. The net profits earned by the partnership during each fiscal year shall be credited as of the close thereof to the capital accounts of the partners in the following proportions:

General Partners

______________________	40%
______________________	40%

Limited Partners

______________________	10%
______________________	10%

3. The net loss incurred by the partnership during any fiscal year shall be debited as of the close thereof to the capital accounts of the partners in the same proportions to which the partners are entitled to share profits pursuant to Paragraph 2 of this Article.
4. No limited partner shall be personally liable for any of the debts of the partnership or any of its losses to the capital of the partnership, anything to the contrary herein inferable notwithstanding.

ARTICLE VI

Termination of Partnership, Changes in Membership

1. A general partner may retire from the partnership by giving at least ninety (90) days notice in writing to all the partners.
2. Retirement, death, or insanity of a general partner shall work an immediate dissolution of the partnership.
3. In the event of the dissolution of the partnership by retirement death or insanity of a general partner, a proper accounting shall be made on the capital and withdrawal accounts of each partner and of the net profit or net loss of the partnership from the date of the last previous accounting to the date of dissolution.

Figure 15-3 Cont.

Notes

4. Upon the dissolution of the partnership business by agreements of the partners or for any other reason, its liabilities and obligations to creditors shall be paid and its assets, or the proceeds of its sales, shall then be distributed in the following order:
   (a) to the limited partners in proportion to their share of the profits;
   (b) to the limited partners in proportion to their capital contributions;
   (c) to the general partners in proportion to their share of the profits;
   (d) to the general partners in proportion to their capital contributions.
5. In the event of the retirement, death, or insanity of a general partner, the remaining partners shall have the right to continue the business of the partnership under its present name by themselves, or in conjunction with any other person or persons they may select, but they shall pay to the retiring partner, or to the legal representatives of the deceased or insane partner, as the case may be, the value of his interest in the partnership, as provided in Paragraph 6 of this Article. If the remaining partners exercise the right given them in this paragraph, the provisions of Paragraph 4 of this Article shall not be applicable.
6. The value of the interest of the reitiring, deceased, or insane partner, as of the exercise of his option given in Paragraph 5 of this Article, shall be the sum of:
   (a) his capital account
   (b) his withdrawal account; and
   (c) his proportionate share of accured net profits.

   If a net loss has been incurred to the date of dissolution, his share of such loss shall be deducted.

   The assets of the partnership shall be valued at book value for purposes of this Paragraph 6. In computing the value of the interest of a retiring, deceased, or insane partner under Paragraph 6, no value shall be attributed to good will.

ARTICLE VII

The General Partners

1. A general partner may not, without the consent of the other partners:
   (a) assign, transfer or pledge any of the claims or debts due to the partnership except upon payment in full, or arbitrate or consent to the arbitration of any disputes or controversies of the partnership.

Figure 15-3 Cont.

Notes

(b) make execute, or deliver any assignment for the benefit of creditors or any bond, confession of judgment, chattel mortgage, deed, guarantee, indemnity bond, surety bond, or contract to sell or contract for sale of all or substantially all of the property of the partnership.
(c) lease or mortgage any partnership real estate or any interest therein or enter into any contract for any such purpose.
(d) pledge or hypothecate or in any manner transfer his interests in the partnership, except to parties to this agreement.
(e) become a surety, guarantor, or accomodation party to any obligation except for partnership business.

ARTICLE VIII

Any matter not specifically covered by a provision of this agreement shall be governed by the applicable provisions of the Uniform Limited Partnership Act of the State of

______________________________.

STATE OF ______________________________

COUNTY OF ____________________________

_____________________ and _____________________, being duly sworn according to law, depose and certify that they are the general partners named in the foregoing certificate and that the facts set forth therein are true and correct.

_____________________ L.S.

_____________________ L.S.

Jurat

Figure 15-3 Cont.

STATE OF________________________________

COUNTY OF______________________________

____________________ and ____________________, being duly sworn according to the law, depose and certify that they are the limited partners named in the foregoing certificate and that the facts set forth therein are true and correct.

____________________ L.S.

____________________ L.S.

Jurat

WITNESSES:

____

____

____

____

16

Joint Venture

[¶1600] DEFINITION

A *JOINT VENTURE* is a short-term, specific-purpose association of two or more persons engaged in an enterprise to make and share profits and losses. The joint venture generally terminates at a specific time/or the accomplishment of the purpose for which it was formed. The joint venture is very similar to a partnership. The agreement by which the joint venture is undertaken should be written in clear, precise, and unambiguous language.

The joint venture bears no partnership designation. Being a temporary combination without any partnership designation and without an intent to pursue a general or continuing business, it is nevertheless encompassed within the income tax definition of a partnership. A joint venturer must file a partnership tax return.

Joint ventures associate themselves together to exploit what seems to be a temporary opportunity to them.

[¶1601] FORM OF JOINT VENTURE AGREEMENT

Below is a suggested form for a joint venture agreement.

JOINT VENTURE AGREEMENT

Heifer Heaven Associates

[A Joint Venture]

THIS AGREEMENT, made this ____ day of __________, 19__ by and between __________, a farmer hereinafter called "Manager" and the second party hereinafter called "Venturer"

WITNESSETH

WHEREAS, the Manager contemplates an enterprise on lands located on Route ___, County of ________, State of __________ and known as the Frank Wright Farm; and

WHEREAS, the Venturer has agreed to join together with others to form a joint venture called "Heifer Heaven" for the purpose of buying calves, raising them, and selling bred heifers; and

WHEREAS, the Manager has demonstrated experience in the field of this joint venture;

NOW THEREFORE, in consideration of the sum of money paid by the Venturer to the Manager as set opposite the Venturer's name and address, receipt whereof is hereby acknowledged, and in further consideration of the mutual agreements, covenants, and provisions herein contained, the Manager and Venturer agree as follows:

1. Venturer, upon the execution of this Agreement, will deposit with the Manager the sum of money set opposite his name and the Manager shall be free to expend the same for the purchase of purebred calves, feed, supplies, labor, and veterinarian care.

2. The Venturer, along with other Venturers, hereby forms the joint venture called "Heifer Heaven" with Elmer Eks as the Manager. Venturers will raise and provide equity capital. Elmer Eks is appointed as the exclusive and sole attorney-in-fact of the joint venture.

3. The Manager shall have unrestricted discretion to buy and pay for calves; to sell bred heifers; and to perform such acts as he may deem necessary or expedient to accomplish the purposes for which this joint venture is created.

4. It is mutually understood and agreed that this joint venture is only for the purpose of raising equity capital and turning it over to the Manager as an investment. It is further understood and agreed by the Venturer that the "Heifer Heaven" is a speculative undertaking.

5. Upon the death of a Venturer, his interest shall terminate. The Manager or someone else selected by the Manager, by returning the principal paid by the Venturer together with interest at the rate of 8½% per annum for the period of time from the investment to the date of death, shall terminate the obligation of the Manager and Joint Venturer to the estate of the Venturer.

6. This joint venture shall commence upon the execution of this agreement and automatically shall terminate at the end of three years without further notice between the Manager and Venturer.

7. Unless otherwise specified in writing, the address of each party hereto for all purposes shall be that set forth next to the signature of that party at the end of this agreement.

8. In the event that the project is terminated for any reason whatever by the Manager, the assets that the Manager may have shall be liquidated as promptly as possible and the proceeds shall be applied as follows:

(a) Payment of all debts, obligations, and necessary expenses of liquidation.
(b) Distribution of any remaining surplus funds pro rata to all Venturers other than the Manager.

9. The joint venture in the name of "Heifer Heaven" shall maintain an account in the First Bank & Trust Company. All moneys' received shall be deposited in this bank account. All invoices shall be submitted to the bank for payment. Each month the bank shall render an account to Venturers.

10. Legal title to the heifers shall be in the name of tenants-in-partnership. It is expressly understood and agreed that the manner of holding title to the property of the joint venture is solely for the convenience of the joint venture.

11. This agreement shall all be binding upon the parties hereto, their respective heirs, executors, administrators, successors, and permitted assigns as the case may be.

12. It is expressly understood and agreed that the manner of holding title to the property of the joint venture is solely for the convenience of the joint venture and accordingly the distributees, successors, or assigns of any Venturer shall have no right, title, or interest in any part of the joint venture property by reason of the manner in which title is held, but rather all such property shall be treated as joint venture property subject to the terms of the Agreement.

13. The respective interests of the Venturers shall not be assignable other than by the operation of law.

IN WITNESS WHEREOF, the Manager and Venturers have signed this Agreement in the State of ________ on the day and year first written above.

____
Elmer Eks, Manager

____
Address

____

SIGNATURES OF VENTURES	ADDRESS	AMOUNT
______________________/	______________________	$________
______________________/	______________________	$________

[Acknowledgment as desired]

17

The Corporation

[¶1700] REACHING BEYOND A SINGLE GENERATION

The corporation, as an artificial business entity, provides a legal vehicle for more complex and larger agricultural operations. Moreover, it endures beyond one generation. More farms are being incorporated as the corporation provides a desirable form of agricultural business organization.

Although the corporate form may require more paper work and more record keeping, it provides for more systematic management opertions. In this book only corporations that do not make public offerings of shares of stock within the meaning of the Security Act of 1933 are discussed. The concern here is with family-held corporations that are either Subchapter C or Subchapter S entities.

[¶1701] INCREASING USE OF THE CORPORATION AS A FARM BUSINESS FORM

While the individual proprietorship continues overwhelmingly to be the most general form of farm organization and the partnership provides a natural way to bring the sons and daughters into the farming operation, the corporation is becoming more common. Economic, legal, and technological circumstances combine to pin-point the corporation as a form of business organization of growing significance.

The following 25 questions raise points that should be considered when planning to incorporate a farm.

1. What is the name for the proposed farm corporation?
2. Has this corporation name been reserved according to the State Law?
3. Is the corporation to be a regular corporation or a small business corporation?
4. If the corporation is to be a small corporation, is a Sub-S election to be made?
5. Is it to exist perpetually or for a limited term?
6. What are the purposes of the corporation, and are they to be narrowly or broadly defined?
7. What classes or class of stock are authorized and how many shares of each class?
8. What are the names and addresses of the shareholders and how many shares does each stockholder own?
9. What is the date and place of the annual meeting?
10. How many directors does the corporation have?
11. Are voting requirements and quorum to be specified in the Code of Governing Rules (By-Laws)?
12. What officers are to be elected and with what authority?
13. Will the authority to sign checks be specified in the Code of Governing Rules (By-Laws)?
14. What property is to be transferred to the corporation?
15. Is the transfer tax-free or taxable?
16. What bank is to be the depository bank?
17. What method of taxation is to be followed?
18. Has application been made on Form SS 4 for an *Employer's Identification Number?*
19. What is the address of the registered office of the corporation?
20. Who is to be the registered agent of the corporation?
21. What is to be the fiscal year of the corporation?
22. Is the accounting to be on a cash or accural basis?
23. What residences and what motor vehicles are to be transferred to the corporation?
24. What fringe benefits such as health, life, and independent retirement accounts are to be provided?
25. Have memberships in cooperatives, farm organizations, and insurance been checked and arranged?

[¶1702] CONCERNING FARM INCORPORATION

The incorporation of farms falls into one of two categories. The first is known as the ordinary or Subchapter C corporation. The second is the Subchapter S corporation.

In a Subchapter C corporation, the corporation is taxed directly as an entity. In a Subchapter S corporation, the corporation itselt is not taxed; rather, its taxable income is passed through to its individual shareholders, each paying his own tax on the portion of the corporation's income allocable to him. Both forms of the corporation are discussed in more detail later on in this chapter.

Farmers seeking to determine the optimum form of business organization have misgivings and sometimes receive discouraging advice about the corporation. Why?

First of all, farmers and their wives are frightened about the alleged burden of bookkeeping, recordkeeping, and the complex record system of a corporation.

Secondly, farmers are often wary of the supposed high cost of legal and accounting services necessary to establish the corporation.

Third, social security costs will unquestionably be higher after incorporation.

Fourth, annual corporation and franchise taxes are levied against the corporation by the various states.

Fifth, individual and corporate taxes must be studied together to provide a reasoned comparison.

Sixth, the conveyance of property to the corporation requires careful treatment. It must not be treated as a sale, since such treatment would cause the owner–transferor to realize long-term capital gains.

Finally, the liquidation of the corporation—if the enterprise should fail—might be a costly operation.

Each of these potential costs and hazards can be studied and resolved—generally in favor of the corporation. Experience shows that incorporation rewards the farmer beyond these hazards and the not-so-burdensome task of recordkeeping. The corporation involves the whole family in farm policy, planning, operations, and activities; it generates family interest and ties family members more fully into the enterprise.

Farmers considering incorporation should carefully weigh the advantages and disadvantages of corporate form discussed below. In addition, farmers contemplating incorporation should give special attention to the effective corporate tax rate, which was greatly reduced under the Revenue Act of 1978. A corporate tax planning table is provided in Figure 17-1.

[¶1703] ADVANTAGES OF CORPORATE FORM

The advantages of the corporate form of farm organization are legal, economic, operational, and it provides convenience in estate planning.

Figure 17-1 Corporate Tax Planning Table

Taxable income	*Tax under TRA 76*	*Effective rate (%)*	*Tax under RA 78*	*Effective rate (%)*	*Percentage change*
25,000	5,000	20.00	4,250	17.00	−15.00
30,000	6,100	20.33	5,250	17.50	−13.93
35,000	7,200	20.57	6,250	17.86	−13.19
40,000	8,300	20.75	7,250	18.13	−12.65
45,000	9,400	20.89	8,250	18.33	−12.23
50,000	10,500	21.00	9,250	18.50	−11.90
55,000	12,900	23.45	10,750	19.54	−16.67
60,000	15,300	25.50	12,250	20.42	−19.93
65,000	17,700	27.23	13,750	21.15	−22.32
70,000	20,100	28.71	15,250	21.79	−24.13
75,000	22,500	30.00	16,750	22.33	−25.56
80,000	24,900	31.13	18,750	23.44	−24.70
85,000	27,300	32.11	20,750	24.41	−23.99
90,000	29,700	33.00	22,750	25.28	−23.40
95,000	32,100	33.79	24,750	26.05	−22.90
100,000	34,500	34.50	26,750	26.75	−22.46
105,000	36,900	35.14	29,050	27.67	−21.27
110,000	39,300	35.73	32,350	28.50	−20.23
115,000	41,700	36.26	33,650	29.26	−19.30
120,000	44,100	36.75	35,950	29.96	−18.48
125,000	46,500	37.20	38,250	30.60	−17.74
130,000	48,900	37.62	40,550	31.19	−17.08
135,000	51,300	38.00	42,850	31.74	−16.47
140,000	53,700	38.36	45,150	32.25	−15.92
145,000	56,100	38.69	47,450	32.72	−15.42
150,000	58,500	39.00	49,750	33.17	−14.96

Legally, the corporation provides a vehicle that has durability beyond the lives of the present owners. This durability is often described as "perpetual." What that means is that as an entity, the corporation survives the death of the individual owners or partners.

In the second place, the corporation generally limits the financial liability of the individuals to the amount of money invested in the corporation.

From the standpoint of economics, the corporation provides more tax options, more methods of financing pensions, more opportunities for profit-sharing, and more stock options.

Operationally, the corporation provides an orderly and systematic method of record-keeping, planning, and control. By its meetings and procedures the family is regularly and continually involved.

From the point of view of this book, however, the corporation provides an instrument for the orderly and systematic transfer of farm ownership from one generation to another by the transfer of stock. Stock certificates can be given to sons and daughters by the farmer *and* his wife in non-taxable amounts of $6,000.00 annually. Step-by-step the farmer and his wife can divest their ownership, maintain corporate control by holding fifty-one per cent of the stock, and shift increasing control to the younger generation. The stock transfer further provides a convenient way in which off-the-farm heirs can maintain an economic interest in the family farm and preserve a sentimental and historical affection in the land. In estate planning, the corporate farm is a workable and valuable instrument. It deserves the thoughtful attention of farm families.

[¶1704] DISADVANTAGES OF CORPORATE FORM

Because of their general unfamiliarity with the corporate form, many farmers shy away from the move from individual ownership and partnership into incorporation. Some county extension agents openly advise against incorporation. They cite initial costs, involvement in state laws, red-tape, extensive paper work, endless reports, hamstringing of individual initiative, complications in decision-making, and corporate taxes.

[¶1704.1] The Anguish of Decision-making

Both within the mind of the individual proprietor and the discussions in the family circle, debate develops in moving from an individual proprietorship to a partnership and much more so from a partnership to a corporation.

When discussion around the dinner table turns to incorporation, there is real anguish. Incorporation is unfamiliar. It may be thorny. It demands greater legal detail. It costs money. The decision to incorporate is arrived at only by a careful weighing of benefits.

[¶1704.2] Operational Enjoyment

Once the decision to incorporate has been made, however, the farm family discovers that the corporation becomes an enjoyable and precise form of business organization. There are regular meetings. Policies are formulated by family discussion. Management becomes more considered and responsible. There is less off-the-cuff and individual planning. Retirement plans can be projected. Some farmers who incorporate may find the new form strange and often exasperating. In the end, nevertheless, it becomes enjoyable in the context of decision-making, planning, economic returns, and estate-planning strategy.

[¶1704.3] Costs of Incorporation

In the folklore of farmer discussion—and too often among county agents—objections to incorporation most commonly recite the red tape, the complexity introduced into management, excessive costs, and steep tax burdens.

As a matter of fact, none of these objections have much validity. The so-called "red tape" is a red herring trotted out by those who resist the corporate form of doing business in a systematic way. The tax burden is a factor to be thought through with the accountant on the estate planning team. Minimum small business corporate farm taxes run upward from $50.00 in Vermont to $250.00 in New York. The cost of incorporating may be a minimum of $300.00 and run upwards toward $1,000.00.

[¶1704.4] Nature of a Corporation

A corporation is simply a collection of natural persons, joined together by their voluntary action under state law and under a common name as a form of farming economic organization. The corporation comes to life as an artificial entity by virtue of the act of the incorporation under state law. It is not the frightening form of business organization that Chief Justice John Marshall once described in the Dartmouth College case as an "artificial being, invisible, intangible, and existing only in the contemplation of the law."

[¶1705] STEPS NECESSARY TO INCORPORATE

The steps necessary to incorporate are simple. Once the decision is made and the name of the corporation is determined, a petition is made to the state for a charter that certifies the act of incorporation (Figure 17-2).

[¶1705.1] Reservation of a Name

Once the family has made the decision to incorporate, the family group selects a name for the corporation. To be sure that the name selected is not held by some other corporation, the proposed name is checked with the state corporate office (Figure 17-3). If the name is clear, then the name is reserved by the payment of a fee, which is generally $10.00.

[¶1705.2] Obtaining the Charter

The next step in the organization of a corporation is a petition for a charter.

The request for a charter is generally made on standard forms supplied by the corporate state office. A draft charter is delivered with fee for filing. While state laws vary as to the number of natural persons necessary to joining in the petition, the number varies from one—as in the State of Tennessee—upward.

[¶1705.3] Content of the Charter

The information required in the application for a charter is fairly standard in all the states. Here are some of the questions that must be answered.

1. What is to be the name of the corporation?
2. What is to be the duration of the corporation? Usually it is perpetual.
3. What is the address of the principal office of the corporation?
4. Who is the registered agent?
5. What are the purposes for which the corporation is organized?
6. What is the maximum number of shares with par value and what are the various classes of stock authorized?

When the proposed draft is satisfactory, the state issues a certificate of incorporation. Once a charter has been issued, the corporation as a business entity is in operation. (See Figure 17-4.)

Figure 17-2 Filing Receipt

STATE OF NEW YORK ——— DEPARTMENT OF STATE
DIVISION OF CORPORATIONS AND STATE RECORDS
ALBANY

FILING RECEIPT

TYPE OF CERTIFICATE
Incorporation (Business) S

CORPORATION NAME	DATE FILED
PAR Farm, Inc.	9/17/74
DURATION & CO. CODE	FILM NO.
P 58	A 182128-4

NO. AND KIND OF SHARES
180 pv $1,000. each

LOCATION OF PRIN. OFFICE	COMMENT
GRANVILLE WASHINGTON CO	RES 9/5/74 A 179765-1

ADDRESS FOR SERVICE OF PROCESS
PAUL F DOUGLASS ROUTE 2 GRANVILLE NY 12832

REGISTERED AGENT, IF ANY

FILER AND ADDRESS
PAUL F DOUGLASS
ROUTE 2
GRANVILLE NY 12832

6 DOLLAR FEE TO COUNTY
FEES AND/OR TAX PAID AS FOLLOWS:
☐ CHK. ☒ M.O. ☐ CASH $ 140

$ 50 FILING
$ 90 TAX
$ CERTIFIED COPY
$ CERTIFICATE

TOTAL $ 140
REFUND OF $

TO FOLLOW

JOHN J. GHEZZI
ACTING SECRETARY OF STATE

R 662-518

Figure 17-3 Receipt Reservation

STATE OF NEW YORK DEPARTMENT OF STATE
DIVISION OF CORPORATIONS AND STATE RECORDS 5290
ALBANY 12225

RECEIPT — RESERVATION

TYPE OF CERTIFICATE
RESERVATION OF NAME

CORPORATION NAME	DATE FILED
PAR FARM, Inc.	Sept. 5, 1974
	FILE NO. 279765-1

RESERVED FOR THE USE OF

Paul F. Douglass

FOR

creation of a domestic corporation

NAME AND ADDRESS OF FILER: Paul F. Douglass
Route 2
Granville, NY

$ CHK. ☐ M.O. ☐ CASH $ 10

$10.00 CERTIFICATE TOTAL $10.00
REFUND OF $ TO FOLLOW

R662-518 R ORIGINAL TO FILER Secretary of State

Figure 17-4 Certificate of Incorporation

Certificate of Incorporation

of

PAR FARM, INC.

under Section 402 of the Business Corporation Law

Filed By: Paul F. Douglass
Route 2
Granville, New York 12832

Office and Post Office Address

Figure 17-4 (Cont.)

A 234—Certificate of Incorporation.
Business Corporation Law §402.

Certificate of Incorporation of

PAR FARM, INC.

under Section 402 of the Business Corporation Law

IT IS HEREBY CERTIFIED THAT:

(1) The name of the proposed corporation is PAR Farm, Inc.

(2) The purpose or purposes for which this corporation is formed, are as follows, to wit:

(a) to operate a farm located on Route 27, Granville, New York 12832

(b) to engage in general and dairy farming, the sale of milk, and the breeding, buying, and selling of cattle

(c) the cultivation, use, and sale of farm products

(d) the investment of funds set aside by the corporation for the aforesaid corporate purposes

The corporation, in furtherance of its corporate purposes above set forth, shall have all of the powers enumerated in Section 202 of the Business Corporation Law, subject to any limitations provided in the Business Corporation Law or any other statute of the State of New York.

Figure 17-4 (Cont.)

(3) The office of the corporation is to be located in the TOWN (city) (town) (incorporated village)

of GRANVILLE *County of* WASHINGTON *State of New York.*

(4) The aggregate number of shares which the corporation shall have the authority to issue is

ONE HUNDRED EIGHTY (180) SHARES OF ONE THOUSAND DOLLARS ($1,000.00) EACH

Figure 17-4 (Cont.)

(5) The Secretary of State is designated as agent of the corporation upon whom process against it may be served. The post office address to which the Secretary of State shall mail a copy of any process against the corporation served upon him is

PAUL F. DOUGLASS

ROUTE 2

GRANVILLE, NEW YORK 12832

The undersigned incorporator, or each of them if there are more than one, is of the age of twenty-one years or over.

IN WITNESS WHEREOF, *this certificate has been subscribed this* 16th *day of* SEPTEMBER *19*74 *by the undersigned who affirm(s) that the statements made herein are true under the penalties of perjury.*

Paul F. Douglass Type name of incorporator	Paul F. Douglass Signature
Route 2, Granville, New York 12832 Address	
Anna Douglass Haldeman Type name of incorporator	Anna Douglass Haldeman Signature
Route 2, Granville, New York 12832 Address	
Ruth E. Douglass Type name of incorporator	Ruth E. Douglass Signature
Route 2, Granville, New York 12832	

[¶1705.4] Corporation Book

Once the corporation exists, the family-incorporated farm family will find it convenient to purchase a standard corporation kit that will be delivered within forty-eight hours of order.

This kit includes a substantial loose-leaf record book with the name of the corporation printed on the spine; a metal corporate seal; and lithographed and numbered stock certificates. The record book usually contains preprinted minutes and by-law forms. (See Figure 17-5.)

The corporate book can be purchased from any major legal supply company. Many lawyers order the kit from one of two specialty firms in New York. The names and addresses of these legal publishing companies are:

EXCELSION LEGAL STATIONARY COMPANY, INC.
62 White Street
New York, New York 10013

The most popular kit of the Excelsion company is called BLACK BEAUTY.

CORPEX BANKNOTE COMPANY, INC.
21 Hudson Street
New York, New York 10013

The most popular kit of the Corpex company is called the CORPEX GEM. Payments must accompany orders together with basic data:

1. State of Incorporation
2. Date of Incorporation
3. Total authorized stock issue
4. Number of shares___ Par value___ each or___ shares without par value.
5. Certificates to be signed by the President and (*secretary*).

[¶1705.5] Use of Corporate Book as a Cumulative Policy File

Some farm families block off a section of the corporate book to provide a cumulative fact and policy section that results from family discussions around the corporate table and clippings. These numbered and dated memorandums assemble for convenient reference farm facts and policy decisions developed from experience and readings of farm journals.

Figure 17-5 Table of Contents: Corporate Book

TABLE OF CONTENTS

[¶1705.6] Establishing the Assets of the Corporation

With the formation of the corporation, certain assets are plowed in to create the capital fund. At this point, the accountant on the planning team is essential. In return for values contributed, the corporation issues shares of stock, representing the value of each person's contribution and interest (Figure 17-6).

[¶1705.7] Excluding Residence

In establishing the farm corporation, special attention needs to be given to the policy of including or excluding the farm residences. When held by the farmer and his wife in their names, the spouses enjoy certain rights in selling their home, in building a new one, and utilizing benefits accorded to senior citizens.

[¶1705.8] Establishing the Corporate Bank Account

Once the corporation is formed, the board of directors, by resolution, needs to select its bank and file signature cards to identify the officers who have the right to sign checks.

1. Has an inventory been prepared for the property of each person transferring assets to the corporation?
2. What is the income tax basis of each asset so transferred?
3. What is the fair market value of each asset so transferred?
4. Do any debts lie against the property being transferred?
5. How long has the property being transferred been owned by the transferror?
6. What does the accountant on the team say about possible gift taxes?
7. Is any insurance on the property being transferred?
8. Is the transfer of property a tax-free exchange?
9. How are the assets to be valued when transferred?
10. Have property taxes been paid on the property being transferred?
11. How are the assets being transferred valued in the capital structure of the corporation?
12. Are any property leases inventoried, described, and accompanied by rental rates and lease documents?
13. Are resolutions for the bank adopted and filed with the bank to authorize signing of checks and documents borrowing money?

Figure 17-6 Specimen Stock Certificate

NUMBER

SHARES

INCORPORATED UNDER THE LAWS OF THE STATE OF NEW YORK

PAR Farm, Inc.

Authorized Capital Stock $180,000 — Par Value $1,000 Per Share

This Certifies that ______ is the owner of ______ fully paid and non-assessable Shares of the above Corporation transferable only on the books of the Corporation by the holder hereof in person or by duly authorized Attorney upon surrender of this Certificate properly endorsed.

In Witness Whereof the said Corporation has caused this Certificate to be signed by its duly authorized officers and to be sealed with the Seal of the Corporation.

Dated ______________________

SECRETARY

PRESIDENT

EXCELSIOR-LEGAL STATIONERY CO., INC., 62 WHITE STREET, NEW YORK

14. Have income tax choices been elected, i.e. regular filed on Form 1120 and Sub-Chapter S FORM 2553?
15. Have consents to Sub-Chapter S option been signed by each shareholder?
16. Has an identification number been requested on IRS Form SS 4?
17. Have income tax bases been computed for the corporation and each stockholder? Also what is the fiscal year to be?
18. Will cash or accrual accounting be employed?
19. Are residences transferred?
20. Are residences reserved for farm employees charged rent or non-taxable if employee is required to live on the farm?
21. Are motor vehicles transferred, with debts specified, ownership clarified, insurance reviewed, and terms of farm use described?
22. Has the accountant recommended depreciation reporting and investment credit recapture?
23. What employee benefits are provided?
24. Have wills been restudied in the light of incorporation?
25. To whom will various organizational memberships be given and who will pay the bills for such memberships?
26. Have all forms of insurances been reviewed, including workmen's compensation and automobile liability?
27. What will be the effect of incorporation on shareholders in so far as their personal income tax returns are concerned?
28. Has a due date for various tax returns been prepared and inserted in the corporate book as a tickler calendar?
29. Have retirement plans and fringe benefits been included in the corporate structure?
30. Has thoughtful provision been made for optimum financing such as stock, debentures, and gifts of stock?

[¶1706] TAX CONSIDERATIONS OF INCORPORATION

Probably the most serious consideration to be weighed in a decision to incorporate comes to focus directly in the subject of taxation. Every farmer should have at his elbow IRS Publication 334 *TAX GUIDE FOR SMALL BUSINESS* and IRS Publication 225 *FARMERS TAX GUIDE.* Nevertheless, the farm family should seek expert advice from an accountant specialized in farm taxation or from the IRS.

In general, the issues in corporate taxation relate to the choice of the kind of corporation to be selected, and the way in which the corporation type selected can best achieve the objective of the farm family.

Some options are available. One is a regular corporation. Choice two is a small business corporation. A third, if the small business corporation is chosen, is this: Shall the stockholders elect the tax option of operating as a pseudocorporation, otherwise known as a Sub S corporation.

[¶1707] REGULAR CORPORATION SUBCHAPTER C

If the farm family decides to operate as a regular corporation—and there are circumstances in which this choice will be necessary—a graduated rate schedule has been adopted under the Revenue Act of 1978. The graduated rates eliminate the two-tier normal and surtax structure provided for under prior law. Like personal income tax rates, the corporate tax structure strikes a farmer as shocking until his accountant advisor begins to put comparative figures down on paper. When the accountant comes out with his comparative figures, however, the farmer may find the computations are favorable to him.

One consideration, nevertheless, is important. In either a regular or small business corporation, the farm income is taxed twice. The corporation pays first on its income. The stockholder—less of course his exemption—pays on his dividends.

Except for very large corporate farming operations, farm families have found the pseudocorporation or Sub S corporation most to their liking. By proper election and filing of forms, the Sub S corporation provides a conduit like that of a partnership for tax purposes. The corporation files an informational return but pays no tax as a corporation. The stockholders receive a dividend, report the income, and pay the tax on their personal IRS Form 1040.

In selecting the kind of corporation, the farm family, with income varying from year to year, will consider certain additional items such as fringe benefits, group life insurance premiums, ease in splitting income, flexibility in ownership resulting from giving of shares of stock, depreciation schedules, tax preference opportunities, medical expenses related to the executive-stockholder, and capital gain in selling and liquidation.

Once again in moving into corporation, the estate planning team of the lawyer, accountant specializing in farm taxes, the insurance underwriter, and the trust officer are invaluable. Whenever a farmer on the verge of incorporating shies away from what he imagines to be the high cost of sound professional advice, he finds his economy most expensive in the end.

[¶1708] SUBCHAPTER S CORPORATION

A Subchapter S corporation is a hybrid form of business organization. Like other corporations, it is chartered by the state under procedures established by the general corporation law. However, the incorporators may elect to qualify under the Internal Revenue Code as if they were partners so that the income is reported by the stockholders. The Subchapter S corporation is an increasingly useful form of business organization for family and closely held corporations. It avoids double taxation under which both the corporation and the stockholders pay a tax on dividends.

Aside from its beneficial tax characteristics, the Sub S corporation provides a positive form of ownership, a corporate type of management, and a flexible means of gift and estate taxation made possible by the distribution of shares of ownership in the corporation.

[¶1708.1] History of the Sub S Corporation

Subchapter S corporations are referred to by a variety of names such as small business corporations, tax-option corporation, and pseudocorporations.

The Sub S corporation emerged from the Technical Amendments Act of 1958. This act permitted a corporation to elect to be taxed like a partnership.

For family farms with moderate assets and earnings, the Sub S corporation is rapidly becoming one of the most useful and productive forms of agricultural organization. The Congress studied this form of business organization for more than two years. Thus, on September 2, 1958, President Dwight Eisenhower signed the bill and Subchapter S became law.

[¶1708.2] Basic Requirements for a Sub S Corporation

While a Subchapter S corporation is glibly spoken of as being taxed like a partnership, this curbstone generalization is not quite accurate. Taxation of a Sub S corporation differs from that of a partnership in several ways. For example, its net capital gain passes through it, but not net capital loss.

The rules for establishing a Sub S corporation, chartered by the state, are specific and rigid:

1. The S Corporation must be a domestic corporation, i.e., created under laws of the United States or of any state.
2. The Revenue Act of 1978 increases from 10 to 15 the maximum number of shareholders a Subchapter S corporation may have at any time during its existence. Under prior law, a Sub S Corporation was generally limited to 10 shareholders until after 5 years when the number could increase to 15; or, if after being organized with not more than 10 stockholders additional stockholders acquire stock by inheritance.

Each tenant in common or joint tenant (except husband and wife) is counted as a stockholder. Stock held by a husband and wife is treated as owned by only one stockholder.

3. All shareholders must be individuals, estates of deceased individuals, or grantor, voting, or testamentary trusts. There are several regulations concerning beneficiaries that need to be reviewed by the lawyer establishing the corporation.
4. No stockholder may be a nonresident alien.
5. It must have only one class of stock issued and outstanding.

[¶1708.3] Changes Made to Subchapter S Corporations by the Revenue Act of 1978*

The Revenue Act of 1978, in addition to increasing the number of permitted shareholders, broadens the limitation on the number of shareholders by declaring that a husband and wife (and their estates) will be counted as one shareholder regardless of how they hold their stock. Husband and wife are treated as the shareholder only for the number-of-shareholders requirement, not for other Sub S purposes.

Under prior law, Subchapter S stock held by husband and wife was treated as owned by only one shareholder if the stock was community property or held by the couple as joint tenants, tenants in common, or tenants by the entirety.

Grantor trusts have been permissible shareholders since the Tax Reform Act of 1976, but the death of the grantor could expose a corporation to the loss of its Subchapter S status. Under the Revenue Act of 1978, however, a grantor trust may continue to hold stock in a Subchapter S corporation for two years after the death of the grantor if the entire trust corpus is included in the grantor's estate. If the entire corpus is not included, the trust may continue as a shareholder for 60 days—the same period that applies to testamentary trusts.

The Revenue Act further makes it clear that the grantor, not the trust, is counted in determining the number of shareholders.

[¶1708.4] Method of Election

To qualify as a Sub S corporation, all the stockholders must consent to the election. The election is made by filing Form 2552, together with

*Portions of this section were adapted from *Summary and Explanation of the Revenue Act of 1978 and the Energy Tax Act of 1978,* published by the Institute for Business Planning, IBP Plaza, Englewood Cliffs, N.J. 07632.

the consents of all the stockholders. Once made, the election continues until revoked or terminated. The election should be made and filed immediately upon incorporation.

Under prior law, a Subchapter S election had to be made during the one month preceding the start of a taxable year or the first month of a taxable year in order for the election to be valid. An early or late election had no effect on the corporation, and the corporation was treated as if an election had never been filed.

The Revenue Act of 1978, however, provides that a corporation may file an election for a taxable year at any time during the preceding year or within the first 75 days of the year to which the election applies. An election filed after the first 75 days of the year is automatically treated as an election for the following year.

In addition, a new shareholder who desires to terminate the corporation's Subchapter S status must affirmatively refuse to consent to the election within 60 days after he acquires stock in the corporation.

[¶1708.5] Subchapter S Annual Checklist

The following 20 questions should be useful as an annual checklist:

1. Are there no more than 15 stockholders? (Husband and wife being treated as only one stockholder?)
2. Does no nonresident alien hold stock?
3. Is there no more than one class of stock?
4. Has election of Subchapter S been elected on form 2553 and timely filed? And has it been further determined to qualify by filing under 1244?
5. Has each shareholder consented to election as of the day the election was made?
6. Has the taxable year been checked for the corporation and the shareholders?
7. Have Sections 1371, 1372, 1374, 1375, 1376, 1377, 1378 of the Internal Revenue Code, including 1978 amendments, been reviewed and complied with?
8. Does the corporation distribute all earnings to each stockholder pro rata each year?
9. Has the information return (IRS Form 1120-S) been filed with the IRS on or before the fifteenth day of the third month following the close of the tax year?
10. Have the wills of shareholders been reviewed to make sure that the distribution of a deceased stockholder estate does not result in creating more than 15 stockholders?
11. Has a shareholder acquiring stock through inheritance sold his stock to a third party? (Such a sale does not jeopardize Subchapter S status.)
12. Does the review of the wills of shareholders show that such wills do not

contain marital trust clauses or other arrangements typically used for estate planning purposes?

13. Have trusts—grantor, voting, and testamentary—been reviewed to appraise the circumstances under which such trusts may own Subchapter S shares?
14. Have any new shareholders refused to continue Subchapter S status within 60 days after acquiring stock?
15. In postmortem estate planning, has the executor reviewed all options related to the Subchapter S corporation to determine whether continuation of the corporation is desirable and financially wise?
16. Have tax consequences of a buy–sell agreement been studied in relation to the contract?
17. Have shareholders been warned to include Subchapter S income in their tax return?
18. A shareholder or officer of the Subchapter S corporation is paid a salary for performing substantial services to the corporation and thus is considered an employee. Are proper withholdings made? (Such a shareholder may not avoid employee status by electing to receive compensation in the form of profits rather than an actual salary.)
19. Do the wills of shareholders contain instructions concerning Subchapter S stock?
20. Are computations for distributions made on a pro rata basis in accordance with the number of outstanding shares of stock?

[¶1709] FLEXIBILITY OF CORPORATION STRUCTURE IN ESTATE PLANNING

By the corporate structure, the farm property is transformed into shares that can be held or given away within the farm family. Thus, for example, assume that a farm has a corporate stock value of $200,000, representing 200 thousand-dollar shares. The farmer could begin to introduce his children into management and ownership by a gift program. He *and* his wife could give tax free $6,000 each calendar year. Assuming that the farmer had three sons or daughters interested in the farm, he could make $18,000 in tax free gifts each year as he desired. If the children were married, he could double the amount by giving $3,000, or with his wife $6,000, each calendar year to each child and his or her spouse. By the giving program, the farmer could retain majority control, but still encourage participation by the family stockholders. To maintain a 51 per cent stock control, the farmer would need to continue to hold $102,000 in stock. He could thus give away $98,000. By giving $3,000 a year, he could reduce his taxable estate by that sum in some 32.6 years.

The corporation, moreover, provides a way in which off-the-farm heirs may continue their interests in the family farm by participation in stockholder meetings and income.

[¶1709.1] Example of Control by Annual Giving

What is an example of stock-giving within the family in terms of owners and control?

Assuming a $200,000 corporation with annual giving of $3,000 to each of three children—a total of $9,000 a year—the corporate structure would involve a stock transfer as shown in Figure 17-7.

[¶1710] CASE HISTORY: EVOLUTION OF FORMS OF FARM BUSINESS ORGANIZATION

In thinking about the optimum form of business organization, it is of interest to study in detail the economic history of a family farm.

George and Olive Wright bought Green Acres Farm in 1945. At the time of purchase, Green Acres was a one-man operation with twenty milking cows. After thirty years, George and Olive sold the farm to their son and daughter-in-law.

A calendarized profile of the farm's growth is shown on page 318.

Figure 17-7 Corporate Control By Stock Transfer Tax-Free Gift of $3,000 Annually to 3 Children

Year	*Farmers' Stock*	*% Owned by Farmers*	*Owned by Son X*	*%*	*Owned by Son Y*	*%*	*Owned by Son Z*	*%*
1981	$200,000	100	0	0	0	0	0	0
1982	191,000	95	$ 3,000	1.57	$ 3,000	1.57	$ 3,000	1.57
1983	182,000	91.0	6,000	3.0	6,000	3.0	6,000	3.0
1984	173,000	86.5	9,000	4.5	9.000	4.5	9,000	4.5
1985	164,000	85.0	12,000	5.0	12,000	5.0	12,000	5.0
1986	155,000	77.5	15,000	7.5	15,000	7.5	15,000	7.5
1987	146,000	73.0	18,000	9.0	18,000	9.0	18,000	9.0
1988	137,000	68.5	21,000	10.5	21,000	10.5	21,000	10.5
1989	126,000	64.0	24,000	12.0	24,000	12.0	24,000	12.0
1990	119,000	59.5	27,000	13.5	27,000	13.5	27,000	13.5
1991	110,000	55.0	30,000	15.0	30,000	15.0	30,000	15.0
1992	101,000	50.5	33,000	16.5	33,000	16.5	33,000	16.5

1945	Father George buys the farm	175 acres 20 milkers
1960	Herd increased	=60 milkers
1965	Milking parlor built	
1966	Adjoining farm purchased	+280 acres Farm now = 455 acres
1971	100-cow free-stall barn built	
1973	Farm buildings destroyed by fire	New hay and young stock barn built—20′ × 80′
1975	John and Marianne Wright buy farm from parents	Harvestor silo added Price = $210,000.
1976	John and Marianne rent 190 acres	455 acres + 190 (rented) = 645 acres
	Son, Donald, graduates from agricultural school and Financing = son assumes $140,000 existing mortgage and notes; agrees to pay father $70,000 during the next 20 years. Father enjoys steady annual income	
1977	Joins father with father-and-son agreement as partners.	
	Ralph graduates from agricultural college and joins father and brother	
	Family forms Subchapter S farm corporation.	

Here is the way the farm accounts looked in 1976:

Milk check—calendar year 1976 = $134,389.00

Monthly payments:	
Production Credit	$ 950.00
[payments on cattle and machinery]	
Federal Land Bank	634.00
Annuity to father	540.00
Fuel	1,300.00
Electricity	400.00
Wages	1,183.00
Annual payments:	
Feed grain	$3,000.00
Fertilizer	7,044.00
Seed	2,997.00
Weed and insect control	250.00
Repairs	1,325.00
Workmen's compensation + taxes	1,200.00

Green Acres net profit = $14,000.00

THE LANGUAGE OF CORPORATIONS

Annual Meetings Assembly of voting stockholders for plenary decision-making.

Board of Directors The persons elected by the stockholders to formulate policy and exercise oversight over operations.

Buy-Sell Agreement An understanding that restricts transfer of shares of stock until first offered to fellow stockholders.

By-Laws Internal rules adopted by stockholders to govern the corporate activities within the scope of its charter.

Capital Stock The amount of money, property, or other things of value constituting the financial base of a corporation.

Certificate of Incorporation The official document issued by the state that recognizes the creation of the business entity.

Chairman The presiding officer of a corporate board.

Charter The documentary authority of the state which creates the corporation and defines its scope.

Closely Held Corporation A corporation in which clear voting control is with a relatively small percentage of all stockholders. Rarely is the stock of such a corporation offered for public sale. Shareholders frequently exercise the Subchapter S election.

Common Stock The kind of shares ordinarily issued by a corporation without extraordinary rights and privileges, and that in the absence of other classes of stock, has superior rights in the ultimate ownership.

Corporation An association of individuals with limited liability who create an artificial entity for doing business under a state charter with an existence apart from that of its members.

Debentures A certificate of unsecured indebtedness of the corporation calling for the payment of a fixed sum at a fixed rate at a fixed time, especially useful in family corporations to provide retirement income to parents or income participation for off-the-farm heirs.

Director One of a group of persons entrusted with the overall responsibility of a corporation acting according to their best judgment as the mind and soul of the corporation.

Dividends A sum of money paid to shareholders out of corporate earnings.

Executive Officer A manager of a corporation who operates under the policies set by the board of directors.

Liquidation Winding up the affairs of a corporation.

Minutes A record of the proceeding of the corporation, entered in the corporate book by the secretary.

No-Par Value Stock A share with no stated value, merely indicating the number of shares held, its value being dependent upon what an investor is willing to pay in terms of his estimate of the overall worth of the corporation.

Officers Persons filling positions of responsibility created by charter or by-laws of the corporation generally a president, vice-president, secretary, and treasurer, and often an executive officer or manager.

Par Value The value established on a stock certificate describing the amount of ownership in the corporation.

Par Value Stock A share that has a stated value on its face, yet fluctuates according to the overall worth of the corporation.

Preferred Stock A part of the capital stock entitling the shareholder to priority over other shareholders in the distribution of dividends.

Promissory Note A promise to pay a specified sum of money to a designated person or to his order at a fixed time or on demand.

Proxy An authorization, usually in writing, under which one person acts for another.

Registered Agent The person to whom legal papers addressed to the corporation are delivered and answerable.

Reservation of Name Request for search and approval of proposed name of corporation.

Share of Stock Certificate of ownership in a corporation, entitling the holder to dividends and other rights.

Shareholder Holder of stock in a corporation.

Stock Certificate An instrument evidencing one or more shares of stock in a corporation.

Stockholder The owner of one or more shares of stock in a corporation.

Subchapter C Corporation A regular corporation under which any income generated by the corporation in excess of all allowable business deductions is taxed to the corporation. It often results in "double taxation," once to the corporation and once to the shareholder on dividends paid to him.

Subchapter S Corporation A small business corporation that elects to be taxed in a manner similar to a partnership under provisions of §1371–1397 of the Internal Revenue Code.

Transfer The passing of title of ownership by delivery of a stock certificate from one owner to another.

Voting The right of shareholders to express a choice in proportion to their ownership interest, generally a right attached to the ownership of common stock.

PART FOUR

Tools

Planning an estate is like building a house:
It requires tools.

18

Making and Probating the Will

[¶1800] THE WILL AS THE FUNDAMENTAL ESTATE PLANNING INSTRUMENT

Of all the tools in the kit of those who plan estates, the WILL stands as the primary and fundamental tool. Simply defined, the will is a written and witnessed directive, made by a competent person according to the laws of the state of his residence, specifically describing how his property is to be disposed of after his death. This book does not deal with oral or handwritten wills. A WILL needs to be drafted and executed early in life and kept current as the testator moves forward in his life course.

[¶1801] PROBATE AS THE COURT-SUPERVISED EXECUTION OF THE ESTATE

Probate is the legal procedure by which the property of a deceased person is transferred to survivors. It is a judicial process by which property passes to survivors with valid and legal title.

The word "probate" comes from the Latin *probatum.* This is a term taken from Roman Law. It means "to examine or to prove." In the probate process, a court determines what is to be done with the property of the deceased. The process begins with the application of a qualified heir for appointment as a personal representative to settle the estate. It ends with a court order distributing property and establishing legal title to it.

[¶1802] PERSONAL REPRESENTATIVES: TESTATE AND INTESTATE

A person who dies with a will spells out the way he wants his property to be distributed. Further, he names the person in whom he has confidence to settle his estate according to the directions he gives in the will. A person, so named, is the testator's personal representative. Depending on sex, this personal representative is called an executor or executrix. If a person dies without a will, his property is distributed according to the laws of the state in which he lived. Thus, a person who fails to make a will of his own authorizes the state to dispose of his property according to general laws. The result may or may not be what a decedent wanted. In any case, the state appoints the personal representative. Such personal representative, according to sex, is known as an administrator or administratrix.

[¶1803] DRAFTING THE WILL

Legal language commonly refers to the *LAST WILL AND TESTAMENT*. In everyday usage the terms are synonymous. Historically, however, the "testament" bequeathed personal property and the "will" devised real property. Below are 8 basic questions to be answered in any will.

1. What is the domicile of the decedent? (His principal home; jurisdiction where he votes; facility where he banks).
2. Who is to be the personal representative of the testator? What provision is made for a successor personal representative?
3. How are debts and taxes to be paid? What provisions are made to assure liquidity?
4. What provisions are to be made for the distribution of property? Who is to get what?
5. What rule is to govern what are alternative plans for distribution in the case of death by common accident?
6. What powers are to be given to the personal representative?
7. What provision is to be made for the guardianship of minor children?
8. What trusts are to be established?

[¶1804] WHO CAN MAKE A WILL?

Generally, any person eighteen years of age or over, who is of sound mind and memory, can make a will to dispose of real and personal property and exercise a power to appoint such property. Continually updated to keep current with the life course, the will is one of the most important legal documents that a farmer and his wife execute during their lifetime. Dying without a will rarely, if ever, provides a satisfactory substitute for making a will. By his will, the maker can choose the persons to receive his property and in what proportions. He can name his personal representative to administer his estate, the guardians and trustees for his minor children, and he can provide ways to save taxes and transmit maximum assets to survivors. By his will the farmer saves his family time, worry, and court appearances. At the same time, he gives his family the assurance that he has planned for their continued well-being.

The process of will-making proceeds through several stages. First of all, the farmer has to decide that he wants to make a will. Often he thinks of doing this, but even more often he never sets times and dates to get on with the work.

Once he has made a decision to make a will, however, the farmer thinks about what obligations he has to his family and how he would like his property to be distributed if he should die. He makes oral or written notes. Likewise, he thinks about what person or persons would best settle his estate as his personal representative. Then he makes an appointment with a lawyer in whom he has special confidence. Together the farmer and the lawyer go over his plan and discuss the various problems. Then the lawyer drafts the proposed will. He submits this draft to the farmer for his review and approval. When the farmer is satisfied that the document represents what he wants at that time, he arranges with the lawyer for the execution of the will.

The lawyer's fee will range for a short will from $25.00 to $50.00 and for a longer and more involved will upward from $100.00. Whatever the charge may be, the cost is really an investment. A farmer can ill afford to economize on the drafting of his will.

[¶1805] EXECUTION OF THE WILL

The execution of a will is a formal process that should proceed with dignity. While the maker does not read his will publicly before his witnesses, he must in their presence declare that this instrument is his last will and testament and that the will is made by his own free will. Thereupon he asks the witnesses to observe him as he signs the document. The witnesses, having observed the testator as he signs the will and having heard the maker's request for their signatures, sign in the presence of the maker and in the presence of each other. After their names they write their residence.

While state laws differ in the number of witnesses required—some two and some three—it is generally wise to have three witnesses. These witnesses can be friends or neighbors, although lawyers often scurry around and grab some available persons to act as witnesses. A beneficiary should never serve as a witness.

[¶1805.1] Margin Signatures

In long wills that have a text which runs beyond one page, it is desirable to have the testator sign his name vertically in the left margin of each sheet.

The pages of the will are often numbered like this: Page 3 of 10 pages.

I. INTRODUCTION [Exordium]
II. GENERAL DIRECTIONS
  Payment of Debts and Funeral Expenses
III. DISPOSITION OF HOUSEHOLD GOODS AND PERSONAL EFFECTS
IV. BEQUESTS
  A. Personal
  B. Institutional
V. MARITAL DISPOSITIONS
  A. Marital Deductions
  B. Marital Trust
VI. ESTABLISHMENT OF TRUSTS
VII. RESIDUAL AND REMAINDER ESTATE
VIII. PROVISIONS CONCERNING SIMULTANEOUS DEATH
IX. POWER OF APPOINTMENT
X. PROVISIONS CONCERNING GUARDIANSHIP OF MINORS
XI. INSTRUCTIONS CONCERNING TAXES
XII. APPOINTMENT OF PERSONAL REPRESENTATIVE
XIII. TESTIMONIUM CLAUSE
XIV. ATTESTATION CLAUSE
XV. CODICILS
XVI. AFFIDAVIT OF SUBSCRIBING WITNESSES
XVII. ABSTRACT OF WILL
XVIII. LETTER OF LAST INSTRUCTION
XIX. DRAFT OBITUARY

[¶1805.2] Will Paragraphs

A will generally follows a fairly standardized outline. No two wills, however, are exactly alike. Each deals with special and unique circumstances of human relationships and the disposition of property. Nevertheless, the above outline is a guide.

The *INTRODUCTION* to the will historically was called the *exordium.* Generally it reads like this:

Last Will and Testament

I, ______________________________ of the _____ of _________ in the County of ______________ and State of ______________ being of sound mind and memory, do make, publish and declare this my last WILL and TESTAMENT, in manner following, that is to say:

This paragraph is often shortened to read:

"I hereby make, publish, and declare this to be my last WILL and TESTAMENT."

To this introduction a phrase is often included:

"hereby revoking any other former wills and codicils made by me at any time."

This phrase is sometimes included at the end of the will.

GENERAL DIRECTIONS give instructions to the personal representative. These are often included in a letter of last instructions.

An abstract of the will should be made and filed among the very personal papers.

Unless included in the personal letter of last instructions, provisions for the disposition of the body may be made in language like this:

"I direct that I be buried next to my wife, ______________, in the Sunland Hill Cemetery."

or

"I direct that upon my death my body shall be cremated, and that my ashes shall be preserved in a suitable receptacle and interred in the family lot" or "scattered to the winds upon the acres of Sunland Farm."

or

"I give my body to the ______________ Medical School of the University of ______________ for anatomical and scientific purposes and direct that immediately upon my death my body shall be transported to such medical school."

The Uniform Anatomical Law provides for such disposition of the body.

By extensive public relations, especially among service clubs, thousands of people have donated specific parts of their body for surgical and medical transplant.

In the absence of instructions concerning burial and the disposition of the body, the first paragraph usually reads like this:

"I direct that all my just debts and funeral expenses be paid as soon as practicable after my death."

While this paragraph is generally included in the will, it is really unnecessary since such performance is now required by law.

BEQUESTS OF PERSONAL ITEMS, household goods, and personal effects are covered by a general paragraph:

"I give and bequeath to my wife, ______________________________, all my clothing and personal effects, all my furniture, furnishings, silverware, jewelry, pictures and portraits, automobiles, and all other items of tangible personal property—except cash—which may be owned by me at the time of my death and wheresoever situated; but if my wife, ________________, shall not survive me, then to my sons, ________, and ________, in equal shares to be divided between them as they shall agree or in the event of disagreement as my personal representative shall determine, or to the survivor of them, if either of them shall survive me."

If particular items are to be given to particular persons, then the language may read:

"I give and bequeath to my grandson, ____________________, my box of carpenter tools, my coin collection, and the violin which my father bequeathed to me and which is kept in the cabinet next to the piano in the house where I reside. "I give and bequeath my Hamilton watch given to me on my 65th birthday by the Farm Bureau to my brother, ____________, who has been my partner in farming during my lifetime."

PERSONAL BEQUESTS may read as follows:

"I give and bequeath to ______________________________, who has worked side by side with me on Sundale Farm for two dozen years the sum of Two Thousand Dollars ($2,000.00), if he shall survive me."
"I give and bequeath to ______________________________, the faithful assistant to my wife over many years the sum of One Thousand Dollars ($1,000.00), if she shall survive me."

INSTITUTIONAL BEQUESTS may read:

"I give and bequeath the following sums to these institutions:

"Five Hundred Dollars ($500.00) to the Shriners Hospital for Crippled Children, a wholly charitable corporation organized under the laws of the State of Colorado, for the use and benefit of the unit operated in Springfield, Massachusetts."

"Two Thousand Dollars ($2,000.00) to my Alma Mater, Class of _____, College of Agriculture and Life Sciences, Cornell University, an educational institution located in Ithaca, State of New York."

"One Thousand Dollars ($1,000.00) to the trustees of the church to which I have belonged since my confirmation in _____.

Sometimes bequests are made in factions of the estate, thus guarding against inflation.

The *MARITAL DEDUCTION* discussion is probably the most important paragraph in the whole will from a tax point of view. Since the Tax Reform Act of 1976, the paragraph may read:

> "I give to my wife, ______________________________, if she shall survive me, a sum which together with the total of any other amounts allowed as a marital deduction in the Federal estate tax proceedings relating to my estate shall equal the maximum allowable marital deduction as finally determined in such proceedings; provided that this sum shall be reduced by an amount, if any, needed to increase my taxable estate to the largest amount which after allowing for the unified credit which has not been claimed by me for transfers made during my life, and any other allowable credits, will result in no Federal estate tax being imposed on my estate."

This paragraph provides a sheltering exemption equivalent to the Federal tax credit. It is useful in estates under $500,000.00.

[¶1806] TWO DESIGNS RELATING TO MARITAL DEDUCTIONS

In qualifying for the marital deduction, two designs are helpful to the draftsman to provide optimum estate tax savings. Both designs divide the estate assets into two parts.

Design X

Under Design X, one spouse leaves his or her estate divided into two parts. Part I can be defined as a marital deduction equal to $250,000 or ½ of the adjusted gross estate. This design qualifies for the marital deduction if the property is willed to the wife outright or at least with a life estate plus a general power of appointment. This Part I of the estate plan is so set that it equals the desired marital deduction. The rest of the estate as Part II is left to the surviving spouse as an estate for life—with the remainder interest passing to the children. Part I achieves the marital deduction and, as said above, is set to equal the maximum possible marital deduction. Part II does not qualify for a marital deduction because it is a terminable interest.

Under this design, the surviving spouse, during the remaining years of life, receives an income from Part I and an income from Part II. Further, such spouse can draw on the corpus of the first Part I. Under carefully limited rights, the surviving spouse may invade the corpus of the second trust as needed for care, support and maintenance.

By the use of Design X, an imaginative estate planner can eliminate entirely any Federal tax on an estate of perhaps $350,000.

Design Y

The second plan may be called Design Y. Design Y proposes to equalize the property ownership between the two spouses by using the tool of tenancy in common. Here the objective is to balance assets so that each spouse owns property in approximately equal portions. As an alternative, each spouse may own specific assets in such proportions as to maintain a balance between husband and wife.

Thus, for example, each spouse wills his or her property to the other for life with a remainder interest to the children. Under this Design Y, the surviving spouse in each case becomes entitled to the income from the corpus of the property left by the deceased spouse as well as to the income from his or her own property. Upon the death of the surviving spouse, the gross estate includes only the property owned by that spouse. The property received from the spouse who died first and held in a life estate would not be included in the gross estate of the surviving spouse for tax purposes. That property would pass to the children or to others entitled to the remainder interest without further federal estate tax. In this Design Y, qualifying property for marital deduction is advised.

Assuming equal ownership, Design Y works equally well as Design X, no matter which spouse survives. Since Design Y assumes equal ownership of the property by the spouses, the wife often finds it more acceptable.

In the drafting of the marital deduction paragraphs, the testator, the lawyer, and the accountant must sharpen their pencils and do careful arithmetic. The team must spell out the language which gives the optimum result.

When the estate is divided into two parts, trusts may be established with language such as:

> "I dispose of the two funds as TRUSTS NEVERTHELESS——
> "To administer these trusts, as herein established by me, I hereby nominate, constitute, and appoint the First Bank and Trust Company of ____________ to act as my trustee."

A spouse or member of the family may be named as trustee or as co-trustee.

> "I authorize and empower my Trustee fully to act in my stead—and as fully and prudently as if I were living—to receive, hold, manage, invest and reinvest the funds so held in trust to them; to collect, receive, and invest the monies and principal such sums as are provided for hereinafter."
>
> "I direct that my Trustee be permitted to qualify and act in any jurisdiction without bond or security."
>
> I direct my Trustee to have and to hold the first fund during the life of my spouse, ____________, and to pay to or apply to the use of such spouse,

__________, all the net income therefrom in quarterly or more frequent installments during her life, of such spouse, __________, and upon the death of such spouse to pay, transfer, and set over the then trust fund to such persons as my surviving spouse may appoint by LAST WILL AND TESTAMENT, which WILL shall specifically refer to this power of appointment as herein granted, including an appointment in whole or in part to the estate of my surviving spouse, __________, free of trust or in further trust as my surviving spouse, __________, may determine, but in default of a valid appointment in whole or in part, to add so much of this FIRST TRUST as shall not have been so appointed to the Second Fund which then shall be administered and distributed pursuant to the provisions hereunder as applicable to the Second Trust upon the death of my surviving spouse, and me.

"FOR MY SURVIVING SPOUSE, I direct my Trustee to act generously in the care and protection of my surviving spouse, __________. To that end I direct and authorize my trustee—to pay or apply to the use of my surviving spouse, out of the principal of the part of the fund created for the benefit such part or the whole of such trust fund as my surviving spouse, __________, shall request in writing, or in the absence of such request, such sum or sums as my Trustee shall determine to be necessary or advisable, without limitation, for the comfortable support and maintenance of such surviving spouse or to meet any emergency of illness or accident which should befall such spouse.

"I further direct and authorize my Trustee to pay or apply to the use of my surviving spouse, __________, out the principal of the Second Trust Fund, such sum or sums, not exceeding Five Thousand Dollars ($5,000.00) or five percent (5%), whichever is greater, in any calendar year in which my death shall occur, to be determined at the end of each such calendar year, as my surviving spouse may request in writing, or in the absence of such request, as my Trustee deems such spouse shall determine to be necessary or advisable, for support and maintenance to meet any emergency of illness or accident which may befall my surviving spouse.

"In exercising the powers to pay to or apply principal to the use of my surviving spouse __________, my Trustee shall first make payments or applications from the trust principal held in the First Trust Fund shall have been exhausted.

"In determining what amounts of principal are in the discretion of my Trustee to be paid to or applied to the use of any of the beneficiaries of any trusts created by this WILL, I direct that my Trustee shall not be required to take into consideration any other funds or income of any such beneficiaries."

The *POWER OF APPOINTMENT* is one of the most important and delicate clauses of a will. It needs to be drafted by a skillful and experienced lawyer. Here is a clause for consideration:

"I give to my surviving spouse, __________, the power—and such power to such spouse alone—and in all events by such spouse's LAST WILL AND TESTAMENT to appoint all the property subject to such spouses's power of appointment as constituted at the time of death free of trust to the estate of such spouse or to such person or persons in such shares and proportions as such spouse alone shall determine or in trust as such spouse alone may deem proper and as aforesaid in the Paragraph next preceeding so much of the principal thereof as shall not have been effectively so appointed shall be added to FUND NUMBER TWO and shall be administered and distributed pursuant to the provisions of the Second Trust applicable upon the death of the survivor of my spouse and me.

"I hereby exercise the power of appointment established pursuant to the LAST WILL AND TESTAMENT of my spouse, deceased, and heretofore admitted to probate in the Surrogate's Court of ________ County, State of ________, and do hereby give, bequeath, and appoint all the property subject to my power of appointment under such LAST WILL AND TESTAMENT to my sons in equal shares."

[¶1807] SIMULTANEOUS DEATH IN COMMON DISASTER DESERVES ATTENTION

A farmer and his wife took off in their private plane to visit the state fair. In flight, the weather closed in. When they did not arrive on schedule, search began. Two days later the wrecked plane and bodies were found on the side of the mountain. The husband and his wife had died in a common disaster, and possibly simultaneously.

[¶1807.1] The Uniform Simultaneous Death Act Provides for Such Events

The various states have enacted the uniform simultaneous death statute. According to the provisions of this law, each spouse is presumed to have survived the other. As a result of this provision, no marital deduction is allowable in the estate of either the husband or wife, inasmuch as neither of the decedents is a surviving spouse, as regarded by tax law.

[¶1808] OVERCOMING THE FORFEITURE OF MARITAL DEDUCTION BY WILL OR TRUST

To preserve the marital deduction it is necessary to provide for a presumption of survivorship by a clear statement in the will or trust agreement.

The marital deduction is saved by what is known as a reverse simultaneous death clause. The clause depends upon the answer to two questions:

1. Does the husband propose to establish the marital deduction in his estate?
2. Will the marital deduction amass a larger corpus in the estate of his wife who may have considerable wealth in her own right?

In such cases the wife should be presumed to have survived the husband. If on the other hand, evidence can be developed to prove that the wife had in fact predeceased her husband even by seconds, the provision in the will or trust would not be operative.

Generally, sound estate draftsmanship utilizes the reverse simultaneous death clause to equalize the gross estates of the husband and wife. For equal estates, the presumption of non-survivorship should be elected for both as a general rule. Why? Because in this way each estate is paying tax on roughly half the total, and the minimum overall tax is paid.

When, however, the estates of the husband and wife are significantly unequal, the presumption of survivorship creates a serious tax burden since the wealthier survivor is placed in a much higher bracket, hence the progressive tax bites off a bigger chunk of the assets.

In cases of common disaster and simultaneous death, therefore, estate planners have to sharpen their pencils and calculate. There may also be factors such as probate fees, administrative expenses, and state death taxes when property will pass through two estates.

[¶1809] THE SIX-MONTH SURVIVAL CLAUSE PROVIDES ANOTHER CONSIDERATION

As a matter of fact, the marital deduction may be saved by a clause that conditions survival of a spouse for a period of six months after the decedent's death. If the surviving spouse dies within six months after the death of the decedent, the estate may not qualify for a marital deduction. If the spouse survives the decedent by more than six months, the spouse takes the property.

Here are some guidelines:

1. Do not presume the survivorship of the wealthier spouse.
2. Include the six-month time clause.
3. In cases where the two estates are approximately equal in size:
   (a) Do not presume the survivorship of one spouse.
   (b) Include a six month time clause in each will. Why? Because the purpose for marital deduction lies in the initial tax saving to the surviving spouse and his or her enjoyment of the property with a power to dispose of it and spend the principal during his or her life.

Suggested clauses

Three clauses may be helpful.

COMMON DISASTER

"If my wife, __________ should predecease me, or if we should die as a result of a common disaster, I give, devise, and bequeath all my property in equal shares to my children

Names	Addresses
__________	__________
__________	__________
__________	__________

REVERSE SIMULTANEOUS DEATH CLAUSE

"If my wife, __________ and I should die under such circumstances that the order of our deaths cannot be established by proof, then it shall be presumed that she survived me, and my estate shall be administered and distributed, in all respects, in accordance with this presumption."

TIME CLAUSE 6 MONTHS

"If my wife, __________ and I should die under such circumstances that there is not sufficient evidence to determine the order of our deaths, or if she should die within a period of six months after the date of my death, then all devises, bequests, and provisions made in this will to or for her benefit shall be void, and my estate shall be administered and distributed, in all respects, as though my wife, __________ had not survived me."

CONCLUDING CLAUSE ON TAXES

"I direct that all estate, inheritance, succession, transfer or other death taxes imposed as a result of my death upon any property forming any part of my gross estate for such tax purposes, whether passing under this, my WILL, or otherwise, including interest or penalties thereon, if any, shall be charged against and paid out of the share of my residuary estate that is not intended by me to qualify for the federal estate tax marital deduction if my spouse survives me, or if such spouse does not survive me then the same shall be charged against and paid out of my residuary estate. The provisions of any statute or rule of law directing tax apportionment shall not apply."

The will concludes with the appointment of the personal representative, the signature of the testator, and the signatures of the witnesses.

Appointment of Personal Representative

"LASTLY, I hereby appoint __________ executor of this, my last Will and Testament: hereby revoking all former wills by me made."

Attestation Clause

"IN WITNESS WHEREOF, I have hereunto subscribed my name the ____ day of ________ in the year Nineteen Hundred and ____________.

____________________________L.S."
(Signature of Testator)

Affidavit of Subscribing Witnesses

"We, whose names are hereto subscribed, DO CERTIFY that on the ____ day of ________, 19__, ____________, the testator above named, subscribed his name to this instrument in our presence and in the presence of each of us, and at the same time, in our presence and hearing, declared the same to be his last WILL AND TESTAMENT, and requested us and each of us, to sign our names thereto as witnesses to the execution thereof, which we hereby do in the presence of the testator and of each other, on the day of the date of the said Will, and write opposite our names our respective places of residence.

________________________ residing at ________________________
________________________ residing at ________________________
________________________ residing at ________________________."

[¶1810] CODICIL TO A WILL

As life situations change, it often becomes necessary to rewrite the will. When, however, a complete rewriting is perhaps undesirable and unnecessary, changes may be made by a codicil. A CODICIL is a supplement to a will. It adds to, takes away from, or alters the provisions of the original will. It may confirm the will in whole or in part by republication, but no codicil totally rovokes the original will. Thus a codicil makes it possible for a farmer to bring his will up to date as life circumstances change. In such cases a redrafting and execution of the whole will is not needed. Figure 18-1 gives the form of codicil.

[¶1811] FOUR DESIRABLE DOCUMENTS

In completing the formalities that execute the will, four additional documents—none of them a part of the will but helpful in probate and estate settlement—are generally helpful, but all too commonly excluded from the will package. These are the (1) Affidavit of Subscribing Witnesses, (2) the Will Abstract, (3) a Letter of Instructions, and (4) a draft obituary.

Figure 18-1 Codicil to Last Will and Testatment

Douglass - ESTATE

FORM 9 7 4 - Codicil to Last Will and Testament

TUTBLANX REGISTERED U S PAT OFFICE
Tuttle Law Print Publishers Rutland, Vt.

Codicil to Last Will and Testament

- of -

I, *, of the of*

, in the County of and State of

, being of sound mind and memory, do make, publish and declare this Codicil to my Last Will and Testament dated the day of

Nineteen Hundred and

First:

Figure 18-1 Cont.

Lastly. *I hereby ratify and confirm my aforesaid Will and Testament in all other respects.*

In Witness Whereof, *I have hereunto set my hand and seal this day of , 19*

__________________________________ L.S.

We, whose names are hereto subscribed, **Do Certify** *that on the day of , 19 the testat above named, subscribed h name to this instrument in our presence and in the presence of each of us, and at the same time, in our presence and hearing, declared the same to be a Codicil to h Last Will and Testament, and requested us and each of us, to sign our names thereto as witnesses to the execution thereof, which we hereby do in the presence of the testat and of each other, on the day of the date of the said Codicil, and write opposite our names our respective places of residence.*

________________________________ *residing at* ________________________________

________________________________ *residing at* ________________________________

________________________________ *residing at* ________________________________

[¶1811.1] Affidavit of Subscribing Witnesses

It sometimes proves convenient to attach to the WILL an affidavit of subscribing witnesses. When such an affidavit is acceptable to the court, the presence of witnesses may be avoided.

[¶1811.2] Will Abstract

Because the time span between death and burial is short and eventful, the executed will may not be found—especially if it is filed in a safe deposit box or a vault. For that reason, an abstract of the will, kept handy in the personal desk file, may be of extreme helpfulness. Figure 18-2 gives a simple form for the abstract.

[¶1811.3] Letter of Last Instructions

The will is a formal legal document. The testator, however, may have a lot more to say in a personal way. The usual name for this informal communication to the living is a *LETTER OF LAST INSTRUCTIONS.* This can be of any length and contain any suggestion not made legally binding by the text of the will.

Figure 18-3 gives a working form for such a letter of last instructions. The final Section [8] often runs to great length.

[¶1811.4] Draft Obituary

Brief death notices are inserted in the press by morticians. Local correspondents write stories. But only the testator knows his own life and what he would like to be remembered for. Therefore it is helpful when the testator drafts his own obituary at substantial length to tell the story of his life. Form this text, surviving relations and the press can have essential data at hand. A well-written obituary becomes a part of local history.

[¶1812] PROBATE OF THE WILL

The probate of the will begins when the will is delivered to the proper Court with a petition for the issuance of letters to the personal representative. Forms for such a petition are generally available from Courts exercising jurisdiction over probate. From this beginning, the probate process moves forward step by step.

While a lawyer generally handles the probate details for the personal

Figure 18-2 Abstract of Last Will and Testament

HERE IS THE ABSTRACT OF MY LAST WILL AND TESTAMENT:

I. *DATE OF EXECUTION:* My will was executed by me on the ______ day of ______________, 19____.

II. *MY WITNESSES WERE:*

	Name		*Residence*
1.	______________________	/	______________________
2.	______________________	/	______________________
3.	______________________	/	______________________

III. *MY ATTORNEY WAS:* ______________________________ Esq.

whose office is located at ______________________________

____

Telephone: ______________________________

IV: *MY EXECUTOR (EXECUTRIX) IS:* ______________________________

WHOSE ADDRESS IS: ______________________________

Telephone: ______________________________

V. *MY EXECUTED LAST WILL AND TESTAMENT WILL BE FOUND:*____

____

VI: *SUMMARY OF PROVISIONS:*

A. *DEVISE OF REAL ESTATE* *LOCATION* *RELATIONSHIP TO ME*

Descriptions: ______________________________

____

B. *BEQUESTS OF PERSONAL PROPERTY:*

1. Personal Effects: ______________________________

____

2. Intangibles: ______________________________

____

3. Livestock: ______________________________

____

Figure 18-2 Cont.

4. Machinery: ______________________________

____

5. Tools: ______________________________

____

6. Miscellaneous: ______________________________

____

C. *BEQUESTS OF PARTICULAR ITEMS:* ______________________________

____

D. *TRUSTS:* *Description*

1. For my spouse: ______________________________

____

2. For my children: ______________________________

____

3. For my grandchildren: ______________________________

____

E. *GUARDIAN OF MY MINOR CHILDREN:* ______________________________

Whose address is: ______________________________

F. *SUCCESSORS AS NECESSARY:*

1. As executor (executrix): ______________________________

Address: ______________________________

2. As guardian: ______________________________

Address: ______________________________

3. As trustees: ______________________________

Address: ______________________________

G. *REMAINDER:* ______________________________

____

H. *MY LETTER OF LAST INSTRUCTIONS IS LOCATED:* ______________________________

____

Figure 18-3 Letter of Last Instructions

For the guidance of my survivors and my personal representative, I have written you this letter of last instructions,

VITAL STATISTICS: Date of birth ______________________

Place of birth ______________________

Father's name ______________________

born ______________ died ______________

Mother's name ______________ (Maiden) ______________

born ______________ died ______________

MARRIAGE AND FAMILY: On______________
Month day ______________ year______

I married ______________________

at ______________________

The names of my children and dates of their birth are:

Name	Dates of Birth	Present Residence
______________	______________	______________
______________	______________	______________
______________	______________	______________
______________	______________	______________
______________	______________	______________
______________	______________	______________

Brothers	*Sisters*	*Residence*
______________	______________	______________
______________	______________	______________
______________	______________	______________

ESTATE RECORDS: The details of my estate are written down in my lifetime cumulative estate record which is located in______________

____

Figure 18-3 Cont.

SUGGESTED OBITUARY NOTICE: How I should like to have my life described. For the use of the press, I attach to this letter a news story of my life, together with my most recent photograph.

FUNERAL SUGGESTIONS:

☐ I wish to be buried in the family lot in ______________________ Cemetary.

☐ I ask that my body be cremated and that my ashes be disposed of as follows:

☐ I ask that my body be given to the ______________________ Medical School of ______________________ for scientific purposes including transplants.

☐ I should prefer as undertaker ______________________

☐ I should prefer as officiating clergyman the Rev. ______________________

FATERNAL ORDERS AND PROFESSIONAL SOCIETIES:

I am a member of the following fraternal orders and professional societies:

PERSONAL REPRESENTATIVE AND TRUSTEE:

My executor is ______________________

My trustee is ______________________

ADDITIONAL INFORMATION AND INSTRUCTIONS:

____

representative, there are instances when the personal representative or family handle the probate successfully.

[¶1812.1] Importance of Taxes

In the settlement of any estate, the determination of federal and state taxes is a complex problem. Here an accountant is both helpful and necessary.

Figure 18-4 Particular Courts That Handle Estate Administration

The various states administer estates through courts which have different titles. Here is a citation of the courts by state.

PROBATE COURT

Alabama
Arkansas
Connecticut
Kansas
Maine
Missouri
New Hampshire
New Mexico
Ohio
Rhode Island
South Carolina
Vermont

DISTRICT COURT

Colorado
District of Columbia
Idaho
Iowa
Louisiana
Montana
Nevada
Oklahoma
South Carolina
Wyoming

ORPHAN'S COURT

Maryland
Pennsylvania (division of court of common pleas)

COUNTY COURT

Kentucky
Nebraska
New Jersey
North Dakota
Tennessee
Texas
West Virginia
Wisconsin

SUPERIOR COURT

Alaska
Arizona
California
North Carolina
Washington

CIRCUIT COURT

Hawaii
Illinois
Indiana
Oregon

REGISTER'S COURT

Delaware

SURROGATE'S COURT

New York

Figure 18-5 Flow Chart of the Probate Process

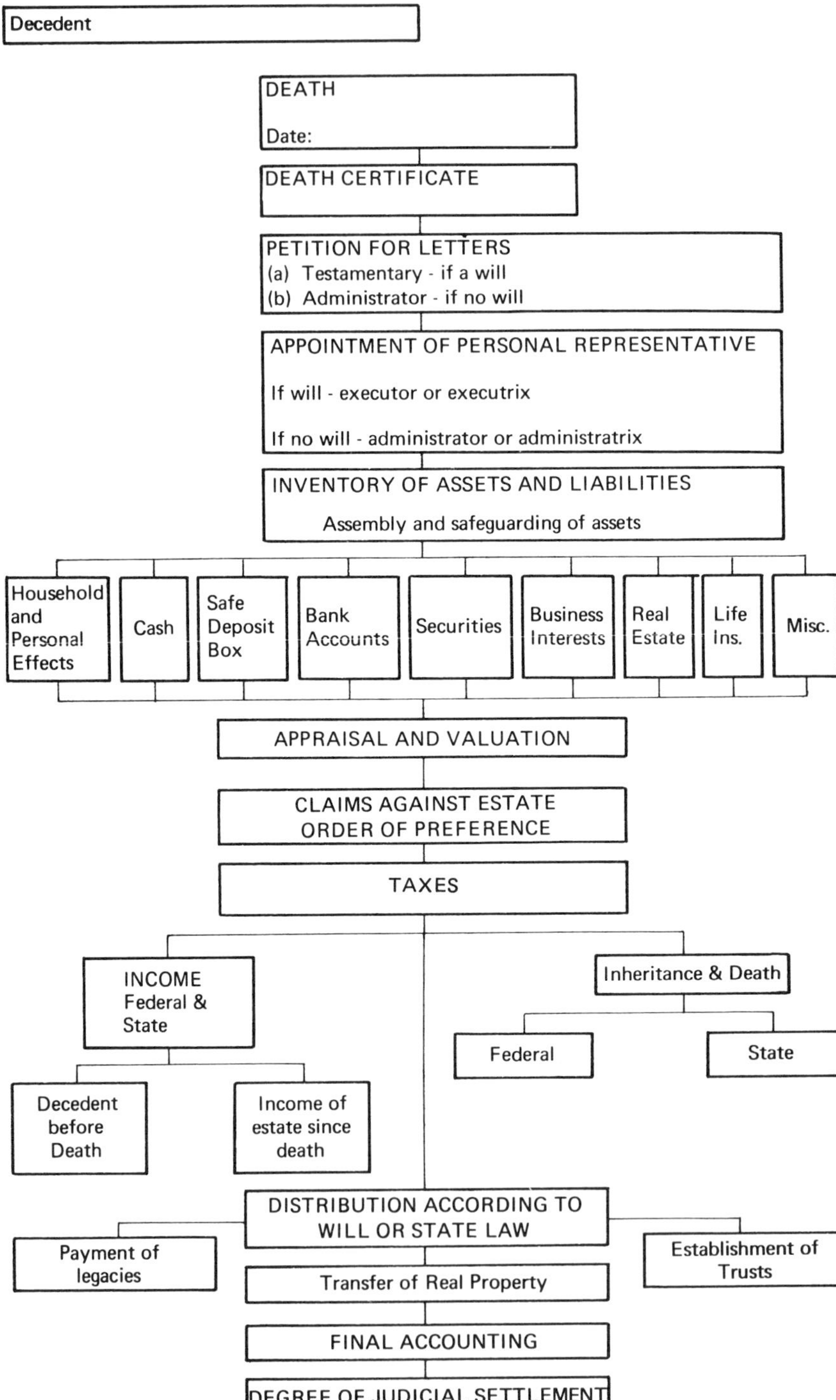

The following steps along with figure 18.5 give a general overview of the probate process.

1. Find the will, read it, and confer with an attorney who is to handle the legal details.
2. Arrange with the court for a convenient time to submit the will for probate and issuance of letters—Form ______.
3. Schedule the witnesses to the will to appear.
4. Arrange for bond as required.
5. Advise post office to forward mail.
6. Open an estate checking account.
7. Have unneeded utilities such as telephone and electricity discontinued. Be sure to protect the home from winter weather.
8. Arrange for examination of safe deposit box, preferably with attorney and state tax authority.
9. Make a search for all valuable documents.
10. Provide notice to creditors. Inform persons named in the will of the provisions made for them.
11. Inventory all assets, including real estate, intangibles, leases, and contracts. Find and study all insurance policies.
12. List all debts, including mortgages.
13. Find and review federal and state tax returns for the last five years.
14. Record closing prices of securities as of the date of death.

THE LANGUAGE OF PROBATE

Administration The management of the estate of a decedent by a fiduciary according to the provisions of a will—or if no will, then according to the laws of the state governing intestacy.

Administrator A man appointed by a court to settle an estate in the absence of a will.

Administratrix A woman appointed by a court to settle the estate of a decedent in the absence of a will.

Administrator De Bonis Non A personal representative appointed by the court upon the refusal of an executor named in the will to act or to fill a vacancy in the office of an appointed executor or administrator.

Ancillary Administration A proceeding instituted to settle a part of an estate in a state or jurisdiction other than that of the domicile of the decedent.

Appraisal An estimate of the value and worth of any item of real or personal property in the estate of a decedent.

Beneficiary A person entitled to receive something in the settlement of an estate of a decedent.

Bequeath The verb used in a will which gives or leaves something of value to a beneficiary. It generally relates to personal property.

Bequest Something of value given to a beneficiary under the provisions of a will.

Bond A security produced by an executor or administrator to guarantee the performance of the fiduciary. It is usually issued by a bonding company.

Charity A recognized, non-profit activity organized and operated exclusively for religious, charitable, scientific, literary, or educational purposes or for the prevention of cruelty to children or animals and such organizations as are provided for under the Internal Revenue Code.

Chattel Property which is moveable and not so connected with the ground as to become a part of the real estate.

Community Property A system of property rights of husband and wife, derived from Spanish, Mexican and French influences, under which in the states of Arizona, California, Idaho, Louisiana, Nevada, New Mexico, Texas and Washington earnings of either husband or wife from their own productive performance belong to the entity of the husband and wife called "the community", each spouse being entitled to one half of the property.

Decedent The hereditary transmission of property rights, particularly referring to real property.

Devise A Gift (noun) of real estate to a beneficiary as specified in a will. As a verb it means the making of such gift to a beneficiary.

Devisee The beneficiary named in a devise. The term generally refers to a beneficiary of real estate.

Disposition The process of the transfer of property in the settlement of an estate.

Distributee The person identified as a beneficiary.

Distribution The transference of property in a decedent's estate to the persons entitled thereto.

Donee The person to whom a gift is made.

Donor A person who makes a gift.

Estate The property left by a decedent.

Executor The man named as the personal representative in a will to carry out the directions of the deceased.

Executrix The woman named as the personal representative in a will to carry out the directions of the deceased.

Fiduciary The personal representative in whom the decedent has reposed a special confidence and who is bound to perform his office of trust in good faith and prudence.

Grantor The person who conveys land or makes a gift.

Grantee The person who received land conveyed or transferred as a gift.

Gross Estate The value of all property left by a decedent.

Guardianship The office of a person (guardian) to whom the law entrusts the custody and control of a person. The term especially pertains to minor children whose parents are deceased.

Heir A person who succeeds to real and personal property of a decedent who dies intestate.

Intestate A person who dies without leaving a valid and operative will.

Inventory An itemized list of articles prepared in the process of settling an estate.

Legacy A gift of personal property by virtue of a will.

Legatee A person who takes personal property as a beneficiary under a will.

Letters of Administration An instrument granted by a court to appoint a personal representative to serve as the administrator of a decedent who died without a valid will.

Letters Testamentary An instrument issued by a court to a person who has proved his designation to serve as the executor of a decedent's estate when so named in a valid will.

Life Estate An estate to be held by the grantee or devisee for the term of his own life, or for that of another, or for more lives than one.

Liquidity The term used to describe the availability of funds to pay taxes in the settlement of an estate.

Personal Representative A term used to describe the executor or administrator of the estate of the decedent.

Net Taxable Estate The value of the estate of a decedent, less all deductible items and allowances, on which a tax is levied.

Personal Property All objects and rights which are capable of ownership except freeholds in lands.

Probate The judicial proceeding which validates a will and takes jurisdiction of the settlement of an estate of a decedent.

Per Capita The distribution of an estate share and share alike throughout an entire class.

Per Stirpes The distribution of an estate according to the share which a deceased ancestor would have taken had he survived the intestate.

Personal Property Any rights to intangible or tangible objects other than land or interests in land.

Qualification Taking an oath to empower a personal representative to proceed with the settlement of an estate of a decedent.

Small Estate An estate of limited value for which statutary law provides simplified procedures for quick settlement.

Testator A man who died leaving a valid will.

Testatrix A woman who died leaving a valid will.

Testamentary Power The entitlement to make a valid will under provisions of the laws of the state.

Trust The legal relationship between one person (beneficiary) having the equitable ownership in property (trust) and another person (trustee) owning the legal title to such property for the benefit of such party.

Will An instrument executed by a competent person in a manner prescribed by the statutes of the state of domicile by which the testator directs the disposition of his property after his death.

Witness Any person who was present when the testator declared signed his will.

Ward A person whose affairs are administered by a guardian.

19

Co-ownership

[¶1900] PATTERNS OF HOLDING TITLE TO PROPERTY

Co-ownership is a legal definition describing title to property held by two or more persons. It is one of the most common forms of farm ownership, and one to be used with care. Forms of co-ownership are (1) tenancy in common, (2) joint tenancy, (3) tenancy by the entirety, and (4) community ownership.

[¶1901] ALLEGED ADVANTAGES OF CO-OWNERSHIP

In the folklore of farmers, there exists a reverential respect for co-ownership. The advantages are recited from neighbor to neighbor. What are these alleged advantages of co-ownership in estate planning?

1. co-ownership avoids probate and the delay involved in the process. When one co-owner dies, his title passes with his last breath to the surviving co-owners.
2. co-ownership may achieve some dollar economy in the avoidance of the probate process.
3. passage of title by co-ownership may avoid publicity.
4. title to property held in more than one state may allow title to pass at once upon death to the survivor without cumbersome ancillary proceedings.

To these advantages, farmer folklore quite generally attaches the fact that co-ownership avoids taxes. No myth can be more erroneous!

As a general rule, it may be said that the larger and more complex the estate, the less advantages accrue from co-ownership.

[¶1902] DISADVANTAGES OF CO-OWNERSHIP

Some distinguished attorneys flatly refuse to convey property in co-ownership, believing that co-ownership is not a satisfactory way of passing title. Why? What are the disadvantages of co-ownership?

1. joint tenancy or tenancy by the entirety remove the property from testamentary disposition by means of a will. The farmer surrenders his right to dispose of his property by will.
2. loss of testamentary control has consequences. The spouse who survives becomes the owner of the whole property held by joint tenancy or tenancy by the entirety. This ownership may have results that a farmer did not anticipate and would not want. Thus, a farmer dies and his wife becomes the owner of the property. She then remarries. She now may will the property to her new husband. The farmer's children, i.e. those of the first husband, thus lose any rights to the farm. The second husband, succeeding to the property by will from his wife, might will the property to a hospital, thus terminating all personal inheritances.
3. assume a joint tenancy created between a father and son. The son may be working side by side with his dad. He expects to become the owner of the farm upon the death of his father. Disappointment, however, may lie ahead. If the son dies first, the ownership moves back into ownership by the father. The father might marry again and leave the property to his second family. In this event, the family of the deceased son would be left without inheritance rights in the farm and possibly any investment in property that developed during the joint tenancy.
4. in the event that ownership is joint with minor children, and the children become joint owners under the right of survivorship, administrative difficulties arise under both personal relationships and state law.
5. for tax purposes, the value of property held in joint tenancy or tenancy by the entirety may be included in the estate of the first tenant to die. In large estates this situation may create undesired tax burdens.
6. trust arrangements become more complicated since most trust arrangements are established by the will.
7. if the spouses should die simultaneously, their estate becomes subject to the Uniform Simultaneous Death Act so that the property becomes subject to probate and distribution by halves, unless provisions of a will explicitly directed otherwise.
8. in some states joint tenants might be liable for debts or judgments directed toward the interests of a joint tenant.
9. joint tenancy at best is a fragile device. In some states, one joint tenant may move to sever the joint tenancy. Then the owners hold the property by tenancy in common.

[¶1903] APPRAISAL OF CO-OWNERSHIP ALTERNATIVES

In planning their estates, farmers should examine the various title alternatives, and the respective consequences of each to satisfy themselves that the joint tenancy is the most desirable form, no matter which spouse dies first.

[¶1904] WORDING OF A DEED

In establishing a joint tenancy, the lawyer must be precise in his draftsmanship. The clause most commonly and correctly used in conveyance is to "X and Y as joint tenants with the right of survivorship and not as tenants in common."

Joint tenancy is perhaps the most common form of co-ownership of land. Perhaps four out of five farm deeds establish joint tenancy or tenancy by the entirety.

[¶1905] HUSBAND AND WIFE AS TENANTS BY THE ENTIRETY

Tenancy by the entirety with right of survivorship exists only between husband and wife. The clause most commonly and correctly used is conveyance to "X and Y, husband and wife, as tenants by the entirety with right of survivorship." Tenancy by the entirety clamps the ownership into a tight vise. Neither the husband nor the wife can sever the tenancy without the consent of the other. The same binding situation may also exist when the husband and wife hold by regular joint tenancy arrangement, although joint tenancy gives more leeway.

[¶1906] TENANCY IN COMMON

While tenancy in common is a form of co-ownership, no right of survivorship exists. Each tenant can sell, divide, or transfer his interest. Likewise, the share in common passes in the estate of a deceased tenant in common. Property held by tenants in common is just a part of the deceased person's estate.

Tenancy in common has a useful function under certain circumstances, but the need for this kind of tenancy should be carefully reviewed with the attorney.

[¶1907] COMMUNITY PROPERTY

The eight states that are referred to as "community property states" provide rules governing the ownership of property by husband and wife. These rules vary somewhat from state to state, and need to be reviewed and explained by the attorney drafting the instruments.

What community ownership really means is that each spouse owns an equal undivided portion of all property acquired during the marriage. Complex problems arise when one spouse dies without a will, but in general, each spouse may dispose of his or her property or interest therein by will.

In computing community property, however, an estate owned by either spouse prior to marriage or acquired during marriage by gift, inheritance, or the terms of a will is not included in the estate valuation.

[¶1908] USEFULNESS OF CO-OWNERSHIP

Despite the foregoing caveats, co-ownership continues to be the general pattern in ordinary estates. Since personal property as well as land can be owned jointly, most families use a joint tenancy or tenancy by the entirety for bank accounts, motor vehicle titles, stocks, and bonds.

[¶1909] LIFE ESTATE AS A PLANNING INSTRUMENT

The life estate is a further form of co-ownership. The title is transferred, but the right to use, enjoy or receive income from the property transferred is retained. Thus, a farmer might convey his farm by gift to his son, yet retain the right to its sole use during his lifetime. While advantages may exist in such an arrangement, the device as a vehicle for avoiding taxes is dubious. The IRS may include the value of the life tenancy in the father's estate.

Further, a transfer from one spouse to another with the establishment of a life estate does not qualify for a marital deduction. Hence, its establishment may produce a burdensome tax liability.

Once again this caveat is in order: an examination of the tax consequences should be made before a decision is made on what is to be done with the property.

20

Trusts

[¶2000] THE TRUST AS A TOOL

In the employment of what is known as a trust, the farmer has a remarkable adaptive instrument by which he can shape his estate plan to achieve some of his goals. Legal skill, imagination, and ingenuity can draft a trust document to accomplish an infinite spectrum of purposes.

[¶2001] DEFINITION OF A TRUST

Simply described, a trust establishes a confidential relationship by which the owner of assets [grantor or settlor] conveys title to a responsible person [trustee] who undertakes the duty to manage the property, perform certain special obligations, and exercise certain powers specified in the trust document [indenture] for the benefit of a person or institution [beneficiary].

[¶2002] ELEMENTS OF A TRUST

The trust consists of four elements:

1. the corpus (the assets)
2. the grantor or settlor
3. the trustee
4. the beneficiary

Thus, for example, A [the grantor, settlor, donor, owner] conveys legal title of his assets to B [trustee] for the benefit of C [beneficiary] by means of a written document [indenture or trust instrument] that spells out the terms of the trust.

In engineering language, a trust builds a pipeline for the distribution of a flow of benefits. In a diagram, a trust looks like this:

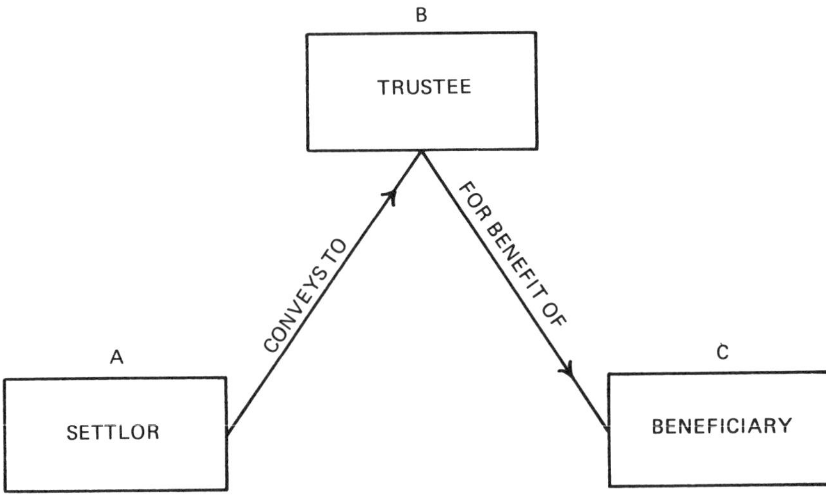

In estate planning, a trust builds a bridge through life to death. It may exist as long as the law allows. Generally, this time element is determined not to exceed the life of the beneficiary named in the indenture plus twenty-one years.

Below are ten questions that the trust draftsman must direct to himself and to the farmer.

1. Have you defined the purpose of the trust with clarity?
2. Have you provided for all possible occurrences in both the disposition of the income and corpus?
3. Have you provided for successor trustees?
4. Does your draft comply with state laws, especially in regard to perpetuities and accumulations?
5. Are resources available to fund the trust in the manner directed in the trust document?
6. Are the administrative provisions broad enough to permit the trustee to act to accomplish the goals directed in the trust instrument?
7. Are the provisions of the trust consistent with the availability of marital or charitable deductions?
8. Has the trust agreement been carefully studied to assure there are no tricky tax problems created?

9. Have you provided for the financial needs of each beneficiary both for the short-run and long-run?
10. Are the relationships between the grantor, beneficiary, and trustee cordial and understanding?

[¶2002.1] Importance of Teamwork in Trust Construction

Despite the tremendous usefulness of the trust, its drafting is fraught with innumerable technical traps that may result in high tax costs. A farmer contemplating the use of trusts should seek the advice of his lawyer, his accountant, the bank trust officer, and often his insurance underwriter.

[¶2002.2] Importance of the Bank as Trustee

In establishing his trust, a farmer must give careful attention to the selection of his trustee or trustees. Because trust departments of banks have wide experience, a farmer should think kindly toward naming a bank as trustee or co-trustee. While he can name any competent member of his family or knowledgeable friend as trustee, he will even then find the bank services useful. While a beneficiary alone cannot serve as a trustee, a beneficiary may serve along with the bank as trustee.

[¶2002.3] Cost of Bank Trustee

While costs of trust department services vary and are dependent upon what duties the trustee is expected to perform, a general ballpark figure is something like ½ of 1% of the corpus annually. The farmer, as a matter of actual experience, may find that the investment skill of the trust officer will increase both the income and sometimes the corpus by more than the bank charge.

In some cases, banks as trustees are called upon to manage farms. They do so reluctantly. The bank's management fees depend upon the amount of work required. A ballpark figure is something like 15% of the gross annual income.

[¶2003] USES OF TRUSTS

A trust can perform a variety of services. It may provide for the welfare of a wife unversed in business affairs. It may be designed to protect the well-being of a minor, a disabled person, or a special child.

It may be drafted to aid relatives who may be old, ill, disabled, or needy. It can look forward to new generations. It can assure the education of children and guide them toward vocations. It can plan annuity income. It can contribute toward the support of a religious, educational, or charitable institution. It can designate funds to carry on a special life interest. It can preserve the corpus during a lifetime, direct income to a beneficiary, and designate a remainderman. It can arrange for the unified control of a farm and estate. Expertly designed, it can sometime—and often does—minimize taxes.

[¶2004] CLASSIFICATION OF TRUSTS

Trusts can be classified in numerous ways. The basic forms, however, are (1) simple and (2) complex. They are further classified as (1) living or *inter vivos* and (2) testamentary. Trusts may still further be classified as (1) revocable and (2) irrevocable.

A "simple" trust requires the trustee to distribute all the current income from the corpus under local law and the governing instrument. All other types of trusts are complex.

[¶2004.1] Revocable and Irrevocable Trusts

The most common and useful classification of trusts is revocable and irrevocable. In a revocable trust, the settlor retains the power to revoke the instrument. In an irrevocable trust, the settlor has no right to rescind or alter the trust once established.

[¶2004.2] Living Trust

A living trust, often called an *inter vivos* trust, is set up by the settlor during his lifetime. It may be (1) revocable, (2) irrevocable, or revocable during life but irrevocable upon death.

If it is revocable, the settlor reserves the right to amend or revoke the trust at any time. He can see during his lifetime how the trust works out.

If, however, the trust is irrevocable during life, it is fixed and final—once and for all.

[¶2004.3] Index Schedule of Revocable Living Trust

A distinguished Tampa, Florida, estate planner has designed a comprehensive revocable trust schedule from extensive practice that becomes irrevocable upon death. The outline below reviews the schedule of a huge living trust that becomes irrevocable upon death. It deserves careful study.

I. 1. Declaration and publication by grantor
2. Consideration for and transfer of assets to use trust
3. Right to transfer additional securities and properties to the trust
4. Right reserved to withdraw assets by grantor during his lifetime
5. Right reserved to revoke, modify, or amend

II. 6. Dispositive provisions during grantor's lifetime
a. Accumulations of net income
b. In event of incapacity of grantor
c. Payment of expenses of last illness and death of grantor
7. Rights reserved by grantor during his lifetime with respect to investment changes and other major decisions
8. Reservation of life estate in interest owned in real property now occupied as a home, more particularly described in Schedule "A" hereof, during lifetime of grantor
9. Re: Trustees, bank accounts, withdrawals therefrom and safety deposit box during lifetime of grantor
10. Time when trust becomes irrevocable

III. 11. Dispositive provisions effective after death of grantor
1. Re: Expenses and/or taxes which may be due in settling of grantor's estate after his death whether in connection with assets in this trust or on assets passing outside of it; and dealings between trustees hereunder and executors of grantor's probate estate
PART ONE: Disposition of net trust assets, if grantor's wife survives him
1. All of net trust assets to grantor's wife, in fee simple, if she survives him
2. Re: Claiming the marital deduction upon all assets that qualify therefore of his wife's share of his adjusted gross taxable estate, whether qualifying under this trust, under grantor's will, outside of both, by operation of law or otherwise
3. Application of any provisions hereunder to said marital assets, or share of grantor's wife
4. In the event, grantor's wife predeceases him

IV. PART TWO: Contingent beneficiaries of the net trust assets if grantor's said wife predeceases him
1. To sons of grantor, in manner provided below
2. In event of death of sons of grantor, or either of them, prior to receiving actual distribution in full
3. Shares of any minor beneficiaries to be held in trust hereunder until they attain 25 years of age respectively, but with authority given trustees to make advances from net income, or principal prior to final distributions
4. Re: Exercise of power to make advances to, or for benefit of any minor beneficiaries hereunder
12. Adjustment of net income distributions on death of any beneficiary, with remainder over
13. Re: Determination of values of assets in making divisions and distributions; and Re: Establishment of separate trusts
14. Termination of trusts hereunder, respectively

15. Re: Limitation of liability of trustees
16. Re: Simultaneous death, by common disaster or otherwise of grantor and any other beneficiary hereunder
17. Protection against perpetuities
18. Spendthrift clause
19. Incapacity clause
20. Protection of third parties dealing with trustees
21. Successor trustee, or trustees, in the event of wife's death, incapacity, inability, or any other reason, to serve as a trustee hereunder
22. Powers of trustees
    1. General
    2. (a) Re: Taxes, tax returns, payment of taxes and expenses, including services of others
       (b) Allocation of receipts and disbursements for income tax purposes
       (c) Payment of other administration expenses, including those for services of others
       (d) Above expenses to be pro rated between trusts, or shares, after death of grantor
       (e) Re: Compromise of taxes
       (f) Authority to trustees to join with grantor's said wife, after his death in filing joint income tax returns if necessary
       (g) Re: Administrative expenses as income or estate tax deduction
       (h) All inclusive clause safeguarding tax beneifts
23. Arbitration
24. Trust agreement executed in State of Florida
25. Validity of provisions hereunder
26. Powers herein not intended to limit or restrict
27. Re: Any attack, or contest on any provision of this trust indenture
28. Construction of terms used herein
29. Trust indenture executed in triplicate, each of which is an original and deemed as one instrument
30. Execution by grantor and trustees respectively
31. Sworn acknowledgments of execution by grantor and trustees
32. Schedule "A," listing assets transferred to trust

THE LANGUAGE OF TRUSTS

Accumulation Trust A trust in which the income is not paid to a beneficiary, but rather accumulates within the trust, and in which the money received from the trust is taxed to the beneficiary at his bracket.

Cestui Que Trust The person for whose benefit the property is held in trust by a trustee.

Clifford Trust A trust, beneficial to high-bracket settlors, in which the income is taxed to the beneficiary who receives it or to the trust if it is accumulated. The trust must last ten years or more or for the life of the beneficiary. At the end of the trust term the property itself, together with any capital appreciation, is returned to the settlor and the accumulated income, if any, is paid to the beneficiary. The settlor must give up rights of control and enjoyment over the trust property during the term of the trust period. In general, the settlor cannot use the income of the trust to support someone whom the law says he is legally obligated to support anyway.

Complex Trust All trusts other than those falling within the definition of a simple trust.

Contingent Beneficiary A recipient of a trust which vests only in the event of a happening dependent on chance.

Corpus The capital or principal of a fund as distinguished from the income from it.

Custodian A person who bears the duty to watch, guard, administer, and account for property held for the benefit of a minor.

Dacey Trust An arrangement that combines the service of a local bank as trustee and a mutual fund as investor-manager in a plan that embraces one's entire estate, including the proceeds of one's life insurance.

Declaration of Trust The instrument by which the owner of property defines the purpose of the trust and states directions that govern the trustee in the administration of the property placed in trust.

Donor The person who establishes the trust, generally called the settlor.

Grantor The person who establishes the trust, sometimes called a settlor or donor.

Inter Vivos Trust A voluntary transfer of property in trust between living persons.

Irrevocable Life Insurance Trust A trust created by life insurance. If funded, it lessens income taxes and is not included in the estate of the settlor when he dies. A funded life insurance trust is a means of saving estate taxes in successive generations.

Irrevocable Trust A trust so established that the settlor has no right to revoke it.

Legals Investments which a trustee by state law is allowed to make when the trust indenture fails to set forth the investment power of the trustee.

Living Trust An inter vivos trust which becomes effective during the life of the settlor.

Power of Appointment Authority enabling one person to dispose of an interest that is vested in another. The power is general when it is exercised without limitation and does not limit the persons who may be chosen to recieve distributions. It is special when the donee of the power is restricted to passing on the property to certain individuals designated or described in the instrument which creates the power.

Prudent Man Rule A guideline that restricts a trustee's power to investments which provide a maximum income with maximum of probable safety.

Remainder An estate effective and enjoyable only after the determination of another estate.

Remainderman The ultimate beneficiary.

Res The subject matter of a trust.

Revocable Trust A trust so established that the settlor retains the power to rescind.

Settlor The creator of a trust who transfers property to another to hold as trustee for the benefit of a third person.

Simple Trust A trust that requires the trustee to distribute all the current income from the corpus under local law and the governing instrument.

Sprinkling Trust A trust that authorizes the trustee to pay the trust income—and principal if so desired—to those who need it most in the future.

Testamentary Trust A trust created by a will.

Totten Trust A trust created by a deposit made in a bank by one person of his own money and in his own name, however, as trustee for another, such trust being revocable at will until the depositor dies or completes the gift in his lifetime by some unequivocable act.

Trust A confidential legal relationship by which the owner (settlor) of property conveys title to a responsible person (trustee) with the duty to manage it, perform certain specified duties and exercise certain specified power trust indenture for the use and benefit of a person or institution (beneficiary) as spelled out in the instrument creating the trust which establishes the purposes, terms, and conditions of the trust.

Trust Indenture The document that spells out the terms of a trust.

21

The Marital Deduction

[¶2100] THE MAJOR TOOL

Probably the most important tax-saving tool in the kit of the estate planner is the marital deduction. This subject has been discussed earlier in this book in ¶1207. It is the pivot around which the estate plan revolves.

[¶2101] GENERAL FEATURES OF MARITAL DEDUCTION

While this paragraph is a restatement of previous material, the principles are reviewed to emphasize its use as a tool.

The Tax Reform Act of 1976 provides a more generous allowance for the estate tax marital deduction than heretofore enjoyed. It can be computed in one of two ways. The deduction allowance has a ceiling of either $250,000.00 or 50 per cent of the adjusted gross estate. Thus, in an estate of $500,000.00 the deduction would be $250,000.00. If the adjusted gross estate should be $300,000.00, then the maximum deduction would be the greater alternative figure of $250,000.00. On the other hand, if the estate were $1,000,000.00 the deduction would be 50 per cent of the adjusted gross estate, or $500,000.

The new limits benefit medium-sized estates but leave the larger estates under the same 50% deduction that existed before 1977.

[¶2101.1] Effect of Interspousal Gifts

What is the effect of interspousal gifts? One spouse is entitled to an unlimited gift tax marital deduction for the first $100,000.00 of cumulative gifts to the other spouse. For the next $100,000.00 in gifts there is no marital deduction. When cumulative gifts exceed $200,000.00, there is a 50 per cent deduction.

[¶2102] HOW RULES APPLY TO SPECIFIC TRANSFERS

Certain types of property transfers clearly *qualify* for the marital deduction. These include: (1) interests passing by bequest or devise under the will, directly or in trust; (2) property passing by inheritance or intestacy (including property received through renunciation and election to take against the will); (3) life insurance proceeds if includable in the gross estate; (4) joint ownership interests with right of survivorship (except to the extent excluded from the estate because all or part of the consideration for their acquisition was furnished by the survivor, or the interests were acquired jointly by gift or inheritance); (5) property received by the survivor through exercise or nonexercise of the decedent's taxable power of appointment; (6) property received by inter vivos transfer, but included in decedent's gross estate because the transfer was made in contemplation of death or because reservation of powers or interests by the decedent made the transfer ineffective before his death.

[¶2103] HOW MUCH MARITAL DEDUCTION?

Despite its power to reduce estate taxes, use of the marital deduction demands mathematical judgment. The savings may not always be what they seem!

Properly used, the marital deduction will reduce the estate tax liability upon the death of the first spouse. If the surviving spouse had property of his or her own, however, the full use of the marital deduction may escalate such survivor's estate tax to a level where the survivor's tax, combined with the decedent's estate, may generate an enormous tax. Mathematical judgment might well have dictated a smaller deduction calculated in terms of the combined assets.

In the author's view, the estate planner will want to make full use of the marital deduction because:

1. The tax saving on the first death will ease the liquidity problem in meeting estate tax payments.

2. The opportunity to derive income from that additional capital remaining at work for the surviving spouse will more than offset any increase in the total death taxes, particularly if the survivor has a long life expectancy over which to collect the added income.

3. The surviving spouse will have an opportunity during survivorship to dispose of property by consumption so that the apparent and presently calculated increase in combined death taxes may never mature.

In short, we will usually want to take advantage of the marital deduction on the simple precept that a bird in the hand is worth two in the bush. Moreover, in many cases where the use of the marital deduction on the first death results in an overall increase in death tax liability over the two lives, the amount of the increase will be small. The federal estate tax rates rise steeply from 18% on a taxable estate (after all deductions) of not over $10,000, to 30% on taxable values in excess of $100,000, then go into a long plateau and increase to only 41% on taxable amounts over $1,000,000, 49% on amounts over $2,000,000, and ultimately to 70% on amounts over $5,000,000. Thus between $100,000 and $1,000,000 there is an increase of only 11% in the estate tax rates. The increase in the rate brackets may normally be offset by a few years' income on the extra capital which has become available to the surviving spouse.

Keep this caveat in mind, however: *exercise mathematical judgment in the use of the marital deduction* as a tool in shaving estate taxes. Generally it works—but not always. It is not an automatic tax-saver.

[¶2104] HOW TO CHOOSE THE MARITAL DEDUCTION

There are three distinct methods of qualifying property for the marital deduction. Up to 50% of a person's adjusted gross estate will be exempt from estate tax under the marital deduction if it is bequeathed in one of these three ways:

1. outright to his surviving spouse; or
2. to a so-called estate trust, that is, to a trust in which the trustee has power to distribute or accumulate and the corpus becomes part of the survivor's estate on the survivor's death; or
3. to a power-of-appointment trust, that is, one in which the survivor receives the income for life, payable no less frequently than annually, and in which the survivor has the power exercisable during life or on death in favor of the survivor or of the survivor's estate to appoint the entire corpus free of the trust.

The latter two have the advantage of not burdening the usually inexperienced widow with the cares of managing a large estate. The experience of a professional trustee should also help conserve the estate for the remaindermen.

Sometimes a fourth method of qualifying property for the marital deduction particularly in the case of real estate, is the use of a legal life estate with certain additional powers granted to the survivor during lifetime. However, as the First National Trust & Savings Bank of San Diego illustrated, a life estate even with power to sell does not qualify for the marital deduction. The 9th Circuit Court of Appeals held that the widow who had received the life estate in two residences with a power to sell them and purchase a new home of her own choice had received nothing more than a terminable interest which did not qualify for the marital deduction. The power which the widow had was not a power of appointment exercisable "in all events." This was true even though she could, under the state law (California) consume the entire corpus. It was immaterial that she could have repurchased a new home in her own name and obtained a fee simple title. A power is always viewed at the time of the decedent's death and therefore the surviving spouse should always be given a general power to appoint the property by her will.

[¶2105] THE POWER-OF-APPOINTMENT OR MARITAL DEDUCTION TRUST AND ITS ADVANTAGES

A bequest in trust will qualify for the marital deduction if these five conditions are met:

1. The surviving spouse must be entitled to income from the trust for life.
2. This income must be payable annually or at more frequent intervals.
3. The surviving spouse must have the power, exercisable in favor of herself or her estate, to appoint the entire corpus free of the trust.
4. This power must be exercisable by the surviving spouse alone, either by will or by deed during life, and it must be exercisable in all events.
5. The corpus of the trust must not be subject to a power in any other person to appoint any part of the trust to any person other than the surviving spouse.

One of the advantages of the power-of-appointment trust is that it affords the testator the opportunity to specify in his own will the ultimate beneficiaries of the trust corpus in the event that his wife fails to exercise her power to appoint. He can thus indicate his wishes and make it easy for his spouse to abide by them just by doing nothing.

He may give the survivor power to appoint by deed of trust during life. The power to appoint by deed during life is necessary if the survivor is to have the opportunity to minimize estate tax on death by making lifetime gifts. It gives the survivor full control unless the survivor is restricted to appointing to a particular group which does not include the survivor.

The testator can limit the survivor to appointing the trust corpus by will, which will conserve it for the survivor's use during life. But he has only inadequate protection against the possibility that the survivor will appoint the property to someone other than his children or others whom he thinks should be the ultimate beneficiaries.

The power-of-appointment trust prevents the trust property from becoming part of the survivor's probate estate on death so as to make it subject to the claims of creditors. Thus, it frees the trust property from the claims of the survivor's creditors and any dower or similar claim which may arise from the survivor's second marriage.

It also prevents the corpus from being subjected to a new set of probate expenses, attorney's fees, and other administration costs. In some states, the power-of-appointment trust may escape state death taxes on the survivor's death.

[¶2106] MARITAL DEDUCTION CLAUSES

Regardless of how much marital deduction you want your estate to take, your will must include a clause that will accurately reflect your wishes. Generally speaking, there are four basic approaches to obtaining the marital deduction: (1) A simple division of the property by estimation with specific assets being qualified for the marital deduction by bequest either outright or in trust to the surviving spouse; (2) Pecuniary legacy, where we determine the exact amount of the marital deduction and allocate at date of distribution values of property in satisfaction of it; (3) Fraction of the residue formula clause, through which we concentrate on obtaining the maximum marital deduction by means of a fixed fraction of the residue the value of which may fluctuate after the marital deduction is determined; and (4) Hybrid or combination pecuniary-fraction of the residue type clauses, where the value of the pecuniary bequest is fixed but the value of property used to satisfy the bequest at the time of distribution is dependent upon the appreciation or depreciation of assets in the estate subsequent to the date that the estate is evaluated for tax purposes.

[¶2107] COMMUNITY PROPERTY

The tax law requires the adjustment of the estates of spouses in community property states. The deduction is computed as follows:

First, if the decedent and the surviving spouse at any time held property as community property under the law of any state, United States possession, or foreign country, a special rule is applied under Code

Section 2056(c)(2) to compute the adjusted gross estate for purposes of calculating the marital deduction.

From the entire value of the gross estate, the following sum is subtracted:

1. the value of property held as community property at the time of death; plus
2. the value of property transferred by the decedent during his or her life, if the property was held as community property at the time of the transfer; plus
3. the amount receivable as insurance under policies on the decedent's life, to the extent purchased with premiums or other consideration paid out of community property; plus
4. the amount determined by this calculation:

$$\frac{\text{Gross estate minus community property}}{\text{Entire gross estate}} \times (\S 2053 \text{ and } \S 2054 \text{ deductions})$$

Prior to TRA 76, no marital deduction was allowed for estates consisting solely of community property. A new adjustment introduced by the act makes a partial marital deduction available to estates consisting partially or wholly of community property.

After calculating the reduced adjusted gross estate by using steps (1) through (4) of the "basic rules," the adjustment to the alternative $250,000 ceiling must be determined. The marital deduction ceiling is the greater of the reduced alternative ceiling or 50% of the reduced adjusted gross estate.

To make the adjustment: Start with $250,000. From it subtract the sum of items (1) through (3); then subtract the deductions under Code Sections 2053 and 2054 attributable to community property. [The last figure is determined by subtracting the result in the original step (4) from the total of the deductions attributable to both kinds of property.]

The following example illustrates how the marital deduction is computed for post-1976 estates:

At Ed Green's death in 1977, his gross estate is valued at $400,000, including separate property valued at $300,000 and a one-half interest in community property valued at $100,000. Administrative expenses, debts, taxes, and losses total $40,000. Under the basic rules, the marital deduction is calculated as follows:

Value of gross estate	$400,000
Reduction under (1)	(100,000)
Reduction under (4):	
[(400,000—100,000) ÷ 400,000] × 40,000	(30,000)
Adjusted gross estate	$270,000

Under the percentage limitations, Green's estate could take a deduction of $135,000. To determine if it is to the estate's advantage to take the alternate adjustment:

Start with	$250,000
Basic rule reductions (1) through (3) minus expenses, etc., attributable to community property	(90,000)
Alternative marital deduction	$160,000

By using the alternate adjustment, Green's estate can increase its marital deduction by $25,000.

[¶2108] EXPLAINING THE MARITAL DEDUCTION

The average client knows that the marital deduction is an important tool in estate planning. Generally, however, an explanation of the angles of the law seems abstract and confusing. Here the estate planner needs to sharpen his pencil and demonstrate what dollars are at issue.

[¶2109] RESEARCH ON RIGHTS UNDER LOCAL LAW

While the discussion has centered on federal marital deduction rules, it becomes necessary to point out that most of the states have laws that protect the surviving spouses. Suppose, for example, that a marital deduction formula might make it possible for a widow to elect against the will when a large amount of intestate property shrinks the amount to pass by marital deduction? There are other issues that a careful lawyer must analyze before making a final conclusion on the size and scope of the federal marital deduction.

Parts of this chapter were adapted from *ESTATE PLANNING,* a loose-leaf service published by the Institute for Business Planning, IBP Plaza, Englewood Cliffs, N.J. 07632.

22

Exempt Investments

[¶2200] THEORY AND PRACTICE OF EXEMPT SECURITIES

A farmer in the higher income brackets may increase his income during his active career and especially upon retirement by investment in tax-exempt securities. Tax exempt securities in general are either (a) general obligation bonds or (b) revenue bonds of public instrumentalities. Income from securities of these types are generally exempt from general taxation and from state and general taxes when the bonds are issued within the state where the farmer resides.

As inflation pushes farm families toward the 35 per cent tax bracket and beyond, tax exempt securities offer substantial income benefits, especially since the tax on unearned income can range up to 70 per cent, and on long term capital gains as high as 28 per cent.

[¶2201] RETURN ON THE TAX EXEMPTS

With the caveat that tax exempt securities may not provide for growth and may not always provide liquidity in estate settlement, a little arithmetic may show that a tax-free yield of 6 per cent may provide a yield equivalent to something like 8.82 per cent for a married couple in the 32 per cent tax bracket.

The beneficial yield tends to increase with the tax bracket. Thus, a farmer and his wife in the 50 per cent bracket, i.e., $60,000.00 of taxable income would have a yield equivalent to 12.00 per cent.

[¶2201.1] Ratings of Tax Exempts

Tax exempt securities have Standard & Poor ratings. Figure 22-1 gives an overview of tax-exempt securities generally. Even bearing in mind these ratings, tax exempt investments should be bought carefully with the advice of the whole estate planning team, and should be purchased through responsible and established investment counselors with specialized knowledge of the field.

There are over 30,000 different tax-exempt issues on the market. They vary in yield, series, maturity, and risk ratings.

Figure 22-1 The Language of Tax Exempt Securities

Type of bond	*Description*	*Sampling of recent issues* *Security*	*S&P rating*	*Recent price*	*Yield to maturity Percent*
General obligation	Known as GOs, these bonds were long considered the best credit risks because they are secured by the cities' and the states' unlimited authority to tax. But since New York City's near-default, many GOs, especially in the Northeast, have lost their allure. Investors fear that community debt loads are becoming too huge, and there are practical limits to taxing powers. Also, information about municipal finances has often proved both scanty and unreliable.	Illinois 5s due 1977	AAA	99	5.1%
		New York State 5½s due 1977	AA	97	5.75
Revenue	These bonds are secured by particular sources of income, from cigarette taxes to rental payments. "Revs" have become popular with investors because yields are usually fatter than on the GOs and because financial statements are more complete. But investors must worry about what could go awry with the flow of income available to pay interest and principal. Some examples:				
Water and power	These are usually backed by long-term leases or contracts with utility companies. Revenues could suffer if a utility cannot get rate increases from its power commission.	Washington Public Power Supply System Nuclear Project No. 2 5.70s due 2012	AAA	Par	5.7

Figure 22-1 Cont.

Type of bond	Description	Sampling of recent issues Security	S&P rating	Recent price	Yield to maturity Percent
Turnpike bridge, and tunnel	These are secured by tolls. Two roads, the West Virginia Turnpike and Chicago's Calumet Skyway, have been in default because of insufficient traffic. Toll-related bonds suffered when investors feared that rising gasoline prices would restrict auto travel.	New Jersey Turnpike Authority 6s due 2014	A	Par	6.0
Hospital	These are popular with many investors because more than 90% of the revenues usually comes from medicare and medicaid payments. Other investors worry about hospital management and about malpractice suits. Thus, hospital bonds have a slightly higher yield.	Tulsa Industrial Authority First Mortgage Hospital 6½s due 2007	A	Par	6.5
Housing finance authority	These are issued by local agencies, principally to build middle-income housing but sometimes college dormitories, mental health facilities, and nursing homes as well. Security is usually rental payments, but deals can vary widely. HFA bonds are not to be confused with public housing authority bonds, which are all rated AAA because they are federally guaranteed.	Minnesota Housing Finance Authority 6¼s due 2020	AA	Par	6.25
Airport	These are secured largely by leases to airlines. As with toll road bonds, these dropped during the energy crisis, when investors feared that fuel costs would jeopardize the airlines' ability to meet lease payments.	Atlanta Airport Series 1977 6.3s due 2007	BBB+	Par	6.3

Figure 22-1 Cont.

Type of bond	Description	Sampling of recent issues: Security	S&P rating	Recent price	Yield to maturity Percent
Sports complex	These are secured largely by income from athletic teams and other sports events, but ticket sales might decline dramatically in poor seasons.	New Jersey Sports & Exposition Authority 7½s due 2009	BBB	108	6.88
Industrial revenue	A hybrid of corporate and municipal bonds, these bonds are issued by a municipality or authority to build facilities for a company whose lease payments cover payments of interest and principal. In effect, the corporation puts its credit behind the deal and gets financing at tax-exempt rates, which are lower than taxable corporate rates. A few years ago Congress limited such issues to $5 million, except in the case of port facilities and pollution control facilities, which now account for the bulk of the new issues. Highly popular with investors who find corporations easier to analyze than municipalities.	Valdez (Alaska) Marine Terminal (Sohio and British Petroleum) 6s due 2007	AA	Par	6.0
		River Rouge (Mich.) Pollution Control (Detroit Edison) 6 5/8s due 1997	BBB	101½	6.4

By special permission, from *Business Week* (July 25, 1977). Chart based on data of Standard & Poors.

23

Personal Life Insurance Trusts

[¶2300] THE NATURE OF A PERSONAL LIFE INSURANCE TRUST

For the last half century, personal life insurance trusts have become increasingly important in estate planning. A personal life insurance trust is an arrangement whereby the proceeds of life insurance are held, invested, and administered by a trustee for the benefit of the family or other beneficiaries. Some estate planners find that a personal life insurance trust can be used as a vehicle for handling the entire assets of an insured decedent. By the use of such an insurance trust, the assets of the decedent are poured over from the decedent's estate into a personal life insurance trust to be administered as one unified fund.

[¶2301] ANOTHER TOOL

The personal life insurance trust is thus one more tool in the kit of the farmer as he works out his estate plan. Its use results from a decision based on the whole context of his estate. What, for example, are his objectives? What are his plans for his survivors? What funds are available to carry out his wishes? When are his objectives to become operative? How are his directions to be carried out? As a distinguished New York authority put the question: *Who? What? When? How?*

[¶2302] IMPLEMENTATION OF THE DECISION

Once the decision has been made to use a personal life insurance trust, there are certain technical legal questions to be determined. For example: shall the policies be assigned to the trustee? Shall a living (inter vivos) or testamentary trust be the operating vehicle? What rights might creditors have in respect to the insurance proceeds payable to the trustee? Is there any question about the insurance interests? Is there assurance that no provisions for the beneficiaries violate the rules against perpetuities? Are there any state statutes that relate to the intended trust? Is there any possibility that the trust might be invalidated as violating the Stature of Wills? Do laws of other states have a bearing on the plan?

There are substantial reasons to feel that a separate living (inter vivos) trust has advantages over a testamentary trust.

[¶2302.1] The Trust and Marital Deduction

The terms of the marital deduction can be established in the personal life insurance trust. Then probate assets may be poured over into the trust and the marital deduction may be described in the trust instrument.

[¶2302.2] Tax Problems

As in all other situations, the tax expert is essential. Two principles exist in the federal jurisdiction. First, an unfunded personal life insurance trust does not involve the payment of federal income taxes until the death of the insured. Insurance dividends, even though paid to the trustee of a personal life insurance trust during the lifetime of the insured, do not constitute taxable income. The income from a funded revocable personal life insurance trust, however, is taxable to the settlor. If the personal life insurance trust is irrevocable and funded, the income is taxable to the settlor to the extent that it is, or may be, used to pay premiums of life insurance policies insuring the life of the settlor.

[¶2303] GROWTH OF PERSONAL LIFE INSURANCE TRUSTS

As a tool in estate planning, the personal life insurance trust is a relative newcomer. Before 1920, such trusts were seldom heard of. By 1927, however, life insurance trusts had come of age. Today it is hard to find a bank with a trust department that has not been named as the beneficiary of large amounts of life insurance proceeds.

Below are 8 good reasons for a personal life insurance trust.

1. The principal fund tends to have a greater security because of the breadth of the company's investment portfolio and the strict government regulations under which insurance companies operate.

2. By the availability of settlement options the estate has greater flexibility and the trustee can act to meet future contingencies.
3. Funds can be paid according to the annunity principles.
4. The insurance contract can be keyed to the tax laws, thereby assuring maximum tax advantages.
5. The personal life insurance trust may be a hedge against inflation when insurance funding is converted into equity securities.
6. By the power of appointment the trustees may be endowed with broad powers of appointment.
7. The trustee may consult with trust beneficiaries, guide them financially, and be authorized to use directions to meet individual needs.
8. Life insurance often provides the major liquid asset of a decedent. When the trust expressly so provides, the trust may purchase assets from the estate, thus making available liquidity as the terms of the insurance trust are integrated with the will.

24

Power of Appointment

[¶2400] NATURE OF THE POWER

The power of appointment is another tool in estate planning. A famous legal scholar called this power the most efficient device for the transfer of property that "the ingenuity of Anglo-American lawyers have ever worked out." What does a "power" mean?

A power is an authority that empowers a person to dispose of property for his own benefit or for the benefit of others. *The Restatement of Property* defines it as a "power created or reserved by a person (the donor) having property subject to his disposition enabling the donee of the power, within such limits as the donor may prescribe, to designate the transferees of the property or the shares in which the property shall be received." Technically it is not a form of ownership; rather it is a right affecting ownership. It is created by a legal instrument such as a will, a deed, or a contract. To be valid, it must be executed according to the same procedures by which the instrument that creates it was executed, i.e., in the same manner a will or a deed might be executed. The establishment of a power needs no special language, but the words that create it must clearly indicate the intention of the donor, the specific property that is in disposition, and the donee.

While the law of the several states establishes particular rules concerning the power, the Internal Revenue Code [Section 2514] gives a particular definition that concerns every farmer. The exercise of the power of appointment must make specific reference to the language in the instrument that creates the power.

[¶2401] REASONS FOR THE USE OF POWER OF APPOINTMENT

Why is the power a useful tool to the estate planner? Here are some of the reasons.

In the first place, the power provides an element of elasticity in the settlement of the average estate. While an estate plan looks into the future, the future at best is an opaque mirror with uncertain vision ahead and reflections of the past behind. Many persons have misgivings about family behavior in the future. A power projects an element of discretion and judgment. As the family patterns change, a current appraisal of the situation of beneficiaries may need reconsideration. There exists a need to equip a knowledgeable and fair-minded person with authority to distribute property equitably as time moves on.

In the second place, a power introduces a human element into the estate that testifies to the concern of the donor and the situation of the donee.

In the third place, a power avoids the expense, delay, and uncertainty incident to the probate of a will at the time of the death of a life tenant.

In the fourth place, a power may avoid the claims of the donees' creditors. A general power is a blank check executed by the donor for the conveyance of the property. It awaits only the filling in of the name.

In the fifth place, the power avoids the marital property rights of the donee's spouse.

[¶2402] EXERCISE OF POWERS OF APPOINTMENT

Three factors must coexist for the valid exercise of a power:

1. The transaction must meet formal legal requirements.
2. The donee must explicitly state the exercise of the power.
3. The power must be exercised carefully within the scope of the authority.

[¶2403] TYPES OF POWER: GENERAL AND SPECIAL

A power is general if it can be exercised wholly in favor of the donee or his estate. It is special if it can be exercised only in favor of a limited class of persons other than the donee if the donor has not manifested an intent to create or reserve the power primarily for the donee's benefit. Insofar as federal law is concerned, definitions are given in Section 2514 of the

Internal Revenue Code. Thus, a general power, with certain exceptions, means a power that is exercisable in favor of the individual possessing the power, his estate, his creditors, or the creditors of his estate.

THE LANGUAGE OF THE POWER OF APPOINTMENT

Appointee Person for whom the appointment is made.

Appointive Property The property subject to appointment.

Default Failure of donee to exercise the power.

Donee Recipient of the power created by the donor.

Donor Creator of the power by valid legal instrument.

Exercise The act of making an appointment by the donor to the appointee.

General Power Power which can be exercised wholly in favor of the donee or his estate.

Special Power Power which can be exercised only in favor of persons other than donee.

Trinity of Power Questions What? Why? How? (1) What the power is. (2) Why it was set up to use. (3) How it is to be exercised.

25

Taxmanship Through the Economic Life Cycle

[¶2500] THE ECONOMIC LIFE CYCLE

In the beginning of his economic life cycle, the young farmer struggles to produce gross income which becomes exposed to taxation. In the next stage of the cycle, he scouts ways and means of minimizing taxes that will enable him to retain and accumulate as much of his income as possible. In the third stage—and especially as his farm grows in magnitude and complexity—he wisely hunts for tax avenues by which he can utilize deductions in such a way as to increase his productivity and his assets. Finally, as his estate matures, he asks himself how he can best transmit his wealth and affluence with least shrinkage, with maximum fairness and harmony, and to provide for the support and encouragement of his special lifetime interests and philanthropies.

[¶2501] VALUE OF AN EXPERIENCED C.P.A. IN TAXMANSHIP

In each of the stages of the economic cycle of the farmer, there exists a need for the advice of the certified accountant on his team to guide him in the performance of taxmanship.

Taxmanship is the process by which the farmer utilizes tax laws to leave him with maximum funds to employ in his farm enterprise and to increase his wealth.

Tax legislation, rulings, and decisions move with such rapidity and complexity that only the C.P.A. can provide the immediate knowledge that the farmer needs. The size of his fees, which may seem at first to be alarming, in the end will be economy.

[¶2502] THE BASIC DECISION

Sooner or later—and preferably sooner—the farmer and his wife face this fundamental decision: What shall they do with the farm? The problem is quite different from that faced by Americans in other occupations for the reason that the operating farm generally comprises the farmer's principle asset. The farmer and his spouse, by hard work, clear-headed taxmanship, and sound estate planning, have devoted their lives to its profitable growth. They have plowed much of their disposable income into the growth of the farm. The farm is both their wealth and the product of their life. They have an emotional attachment to it because they have "lived the farm" during the life course.

[¶2503] OPTIONS

The farmer and his wife begin to explore options.

Option One—Continuance of Family Operation

If there are children who have interest and the capability to carry on the family farm, the option is clear: Transfer the farm to the younger generation in ways that will encourage family teamwork and harmony. Then the road is clear to work out the necessary legal and economic solutions.

Option Two—Leasing the Farm

By a careful lease the farmer and his wife, if they have no children, may continue to live right along on the farm for the rest of their days, receiving rental and sharing their experience with the young farmer. There are numerous historic situations in which a childless farmer and his wife have willed the farm to the renters.

Option Three—Selling the Farm

As farmers face retirement, they may explore how much money they would derive from the outright sale of the farm. Assume that the sale would produce $300,000 in cash that could be safely invested at 7 per cent. The income would be something like $21,000 annually! Twenty-one thousand dollars a year or $1,750 a month. With no worry about taxes, insurance, veterinarian expenses, repairs, grain bills, fertilizer, and labor problems, the temptation to sell may be great.

This option could include their life tenancy on the farm.

Option Four—Life Annuity

The sale, especially if it is made within the family, can be designed to pay a life annuity preferably with life residency. The farmer has a calculated income, and he has provided for the transfer of the farm to his successor while maintaining his place to live.

Option Five—The Speculative Investment

It sometimes happens that a farmer just goes out of business, holding his farm lands for appreciation and selling his acres in units that may provide the most advantageous return to him. Take the case of a farm of 400 acres of varying quality—fertile fields, woodlots, pasture, and meadows watered by a small river. The farmer just stopped farming, called in realtors, and proceeded to divide up the property for various uses. He had the parcels surveyed and put the land packages up for sale. He did very well. He invested his money, and prudently acquired a new residence in Clearwater, Florida, with all the tax benefits available to a couple over sixty-five.

Option Six—Living Trusts

Finally, it may be that the farmer and his spouse may benefit from the establishment of a living trust—revocable during life but irrevocable upon death. This kind of trust can be tailored to fit an infinite variety of needs and purposes.

[¶2504] TAXMANSHIP IN RETIREMENT PLANNING

Early in his career, a farmer may plan a retirement program to become effective when he comes to the point in his life course when he is ready to take things easier.

A young farmer, wise in taxmanship, should carefully consider one or two major retirement programs. Because of the complex requirements of a qualified plan, the farmer should sit down with the officer of his bank and discuss his participation in a plan. Or he may prefer to discuss participation in a plan with an insurance underwriter.

[¶2505] THE TWO PRINCIPAL PLANS

The two principal plans available to farmers or self-employed persons are known by the names of the legislative acts. HR-10 means the same as the Keogh Act. Both names refer to the same basic legislation: the Self-Employed Individuals' Tax Retirement Act. Here we refer to HR-10 or the SEITRA by the simple title of KEOGH.

KEOGH, first enacted by Congress in 1962, has been amended and extended over the years. It enables a farmer to set aside a certain amount of his annual income up to $7,500 or 15 per cent of his earned income, whichever is less, for investment in qualified and approved investment retirement programs. The attraction of KEOGH is this: funds contributed to KEOGH are fully and completely deductible! Likewise, the income earned by the invested KEOGH funds are free from any tax during the active income earning years of contribution. The principal and income thereon are taxable as income when the cash is withdrawn from KEOGH upon retirement or disability.

KEOGH provides that a farmer may begin to receive retirement benefits at age 59½, with benefits payable at death or in case of permanent disability regardless of age.

Under KEOGH, all fulltime employees with a record of three years employment must be included in the plan. Moreover, the farmer's wife may be entered as an employee of the farm enterprise and placed on the payroll. She must, however, actually do work for her husband.

Once again, it needs to be pointed out that contributions made by the employer are deductible as a farm business expense.

J. W. Looney, of the Department of Agriculture Economics, Virginia Polytechnic Institute and State University, has ingeniously produced a classic example of the operation of KEOGH:

1. Husband with assistance of his wife drawing no salary had a 1977 earned income of $37,500.
2. After conference with his trust officer, he enters his wife on the farm payroll at $7,500.
3. By participating in KEOGH he reduces his earned income to $28,875.
4. The wife's basic contribution in KEOGH at 15% of $7,500 = $1,125.
5. The husband's basic contribution at 15% of $28,875 = $4,331
   The husband takes a business deduction for $5,456, i.e., $4,331 for himself plus $1,125 for his wife. This is a tax-free investment.
6. Because both the husband and wife are employees, KEOGH qualifies them for further voluntary contributions. The husband can increase his contribu-

tions under the KEOGH voluntary provision by a further 10 per cent (maximum of $2,500) of earned income. Likewise, his wife could make a voluntary contribution of 10 per cent of her $7,500 salary. Thus the husband plus the wife would be making contributions of $8,706, i.e., husband = $6,831 and wife = $1,875. These amounts are dollar for dollar deductible in computing the federal income tax. Thus under KEOGH husband and wife have an annual tax shelter in their sizable contribution toward retirement.

The voluntary additional contributions of husband and wife are not tax deductible. The earnings from these investments, however, remain tax-free during the accumulation period.

Figure 25-1, prepared by an insurance representative, is a KEOGH plan analysis for a fictitious individual.

[¶2506] IRA—INDIVIDUAL RETIREMENT ACCOUNT

KEOGH continues to be a group program. In 1974, the Congress enacted a program for farmers to establish their own individual plan. The program is called Individual Retirement Account. The plan is available only for individuals not covered by some other type of group plan. Once again, the farmer should sit down with the trust officer of his bank or his insurance underwriter and work his own plan through.

A farmer in the 20 per cent bracket placing $1,500 in the IRA would have a deductible item which would save him $300 a year. The money would be put to work at compound interest. After 15 years, the farmer's account would be worth more than $43,000 and provide him with several payment options for his retirement.

IRA differs from KEOGH, among other ways, in this: KEOGH requires the farmer plus his full-time employees with three or more years of service to be included in the plan. Under IRA, the farmer may include all of his full-time employees, some of them, or none of them, as he chooses. He can include himself alone or his wife. He may include employees and all contributions made on their behalf as a deductible business expense for the farmer. Figure 25-2 is a report prepared for a fictitious individual by an insurance representative. It shows how an individual retirement account can be prepared.

[¶2507] ACCUMULATIONS UNDER THE PLANS

Again Professor Looney has figured that an annual $7,500 KEOGH savings made regularly each year for twenty-five years, with interest accumulations at 5 per cent compounded quarterly, could total $381,115 at the end of the twenty-five year period. The contributions would total $187,500, and the compounded interest $193,615.

[¶2508] EXAMINATION OF RETIREMENT PLANS

Before a farmer enters into any kind of retirement plan—KEOGH, IRA, insurance, mutual funds, personal savings—he should carefully explore all possible options and select the one which best fits his needs, and pays off to his best advantage.

[¶2509] RETIREMENT HOUSING

Farmers planning retirement will find that provisions under the Revenue Act of 1978 are helpful to them in housing. The Revenue Act provides a once-in-a-lifetime exclusion from funds derived from the sale of a farmer's principal residence. He must have reached the age of 55 before the sale and must have owned and occupied the home as his principal residence for at least three years during the five-year period ending on the date of the sale. All gain, but not more than $100,000 is excluded.

Thus, for example, a farmer born in 1922 built a farm residence in 1948 at a cost of $48,000. With appreciation over a third of a century, he sold his house in 1981 for $198,000. What would be the farmer's taxable gain?

Sale price		$198,000
Selling expenses	$14,000	
Cost of home	48,000	
Exclusion	100,000	
Taxable gain		$ 36,000

Figure 25-1

GEORGE GALLAGHER

KEOGH PLAN

FLEXIBLE PREMIUM ANNUITY WITH
INITIAL DEATH BENEFIT[1]
AGE 35 M

By putting $2,000 per year into your Keogh it is projected that you will receive:

Tax benefits	
Total contributions to age 65	$60,000.00
Less: Total "PS-58" insurance cost to 65	−.00
Net deductible contributions to 65	$60,000.00
Estimated tax saving to age 65[2]	$13,200.00
Retirement benefits at age 65	
1. Lifetime monthly income (with 120 payments certain)[4,5]	$1,694.36
Estimated Social Security[3]	+477.00
Total lifetime monthly income[4,5]	$2,171.36
or	
2. Cash retirement fund[4]	$217,784.60
Your estimated gain to age 65	
Total contributions	$60,000.00
Less: Estimated tax saving[2]	-13,200.00
Net contributions	$46,800.00
Cash retirement fund[4]	$217,784.60
Estimated gain	$170,984.60

[1]The death benefit is equal to the larger of the premiums paid or the cash value, plus any accumulated excess interest.
[2]Assuming 22% tax bracket and no change in present tax structure.
[3]Benefits are for demonstration purposes only. Full Social Security may range from $114.00 to $1,475.00 based upon income and years of qualification based upon the 1978 Social Security amendments.
[4]Based on guaranteed cash value and additional interest on the current scale; payment of additional interest is not guaranteed. Since the interest rate may vary to reflect changes in the economy, the projected benefits currently based on 8% cannot be guaranteed but in no event will the rate of interest go below the guaranteed minimum of 4% per year.
[5]Based on current annuity purchase rates which cannot be guaranteed.

AY31YA-IRA PAGE 1 OF 2 03/02/79

Figure 25-1 Cont.

ANNUAL PREMIUM OF $2,000.00

FLEXIBLE PREMIUM ANNUITY
AGE 35 M

	First 5 Years Cash Value of the Annuity	
End of year	*Guaranteed 4%*	*Current 8%*[4]
1	$1,040.00	$1,080.00
2	$3,005.60	$3,164.40
3	$5,049.80	$5,415.60
4	$7,175.80	$7,846.80
5	$9,386.80	$10,472.60

	Lump Sum Cash Values	
	Guaranteed 4%	*Current 8%*[4]
At age 60	$77,860.80	$140,243.20
At age 65	$105,150.60	$217,784.60
At age 70	$138,352.80	$331,718.60

	Lifetime Monthly Income[5] *(10 years certain)*	
	Guaranteed 4%	*Current 8%*[4]
At age 60	$557.48	$1,004.14
At age 65	$818.07	$1,694.36
At age 70	$1,182.92	$2,836.19

[4]Based on guaranteed cash value and additional interest on the current scale; payment of additional interest is not guaranteed. Since the interest rate may vary to reflect changes in the economy, the projected benefits currently based on 8% cannot be guaranteed but in no event will the rate of interest go below the guaranteed minimum of 4% per year.

[5]Based on current annuity purchase rates, which cannot be guaranteed. "The cost of this policy over a period of years cannot be appreciated without considering interest that could have been earned on premiums and the amount and timing of any payments by the company."

AY31YA-IRA PAGE 2 OF 2 03/02/79

Prepared by the International Life Insurance Company of Buffalo, Buffalo, New York.

Figure 25-2

GEORGE GALLAGHER

INDIVIDUAL RETIREMENT ACCOUNT

FLEXIBLE PREMIUM ANNUITY WITH
INITIAL DEATH BENEFIT[1]
AGE 35 M

By putting $1,500 per year into your IRA it is projected that you will receive:

Tax benefits	
Total contributions to age 65	$45,000.00
Less: Total "PS-58" insurance cost to 65	–.00
Net deductible contributions to 65	$45,000.00
Estimated tax saving to age 65[2]	$9,900.00
Retirement benefits at age 65	
1. Lifetime monthly income (with 120 payments certain)[4,5]	$1,270.77
Estimated Social Security[3]	+477.00
Total lifetime monthly income[4,5]	$1,747.77
or	
2. Cash retirement fund[4]	$163,338.45
Your estimated gain to age 65	
Total contributions	$45,000.00
Less: Estimated tax saving[2]	–9,900.00
Net contributions	$35,100.00
Cash retirement fund[4]	$163,338.45
Estimated gain	$128,238.45

---

[1]The death benefit is equal to the larger of the premiums paid or the cash value, plus any accumulated excess interest.

[2]Assuming 22% tax bracket and no change in present tax structure.

[3]**Benefits are for demonstration purposes only. Full Social Security may range from $114.00 to $1,475.00 based upon income and years of qualification based upon the 1978 Social Security amendments.**

[4]Based on guaranteed cash value and additional interest on the current scale; payment of additional interest is not guaranteed. Since the interest rate may vary to reflect changes in the economy, the projected benefits currently based on 8% cannot be guaranteed but in no event will the rate of interest go below the guaranteed minimum of 4% per year.

[5]Based on current annuity purchase rates which cannot be guaranteed.

AY31YA-IRA PAGE 1 OF 2 03/02/79

Figure 25-2 Cont.

ANNUAL PREMIUM OF $1,500.00

FLEXIBLE PREMIUM ANNUITY
AGE 35 M

End of Year	*First 5 Years Cash Value of the Annuity*		*Guaranteed Cash Surrender Value per $1,000 Contribution*
	Guaranteed 4%	*Current 8%*[4]	
1	$780.00	$810.00	$520.00
2	$2,254.20	$2,373.30	$1,502.80
3	$3,787.35	$4,061.70	$2,524.90
4	$5,381.85	$5,885.10	$3,587.90
5	$7,040.10	$7,854.45	$4,693.40
	Lump Sum Cash Values		
At age 60	$58,395.60	$105,182.40	$38,930.40
At age 65	$78,862.95	$163,338.45	$52,575.30
At age 70	$103,764.60	$248,788.95	$69,176.40
	Lifetime Monthly Income[5] *(10 years certain)*		
At age 60	$418.11	$753.11	
At age 65	$613.55	$1,270.77	
At age 70	$887.19	$2,127.15	

[4]Based on guaranteed cash value and additional interest on the current scale; payment of additional interest is not guaranteed. Since the interest rate may vary to reflect changes in the economy, the projected benefits currently based on 8% cannot be guaranteed but in no event will the rate of interest go below the guaranteed minimum of 4% per year.

[5]Based on current annuity purchase rates which cannot be guaranteed. "The cost of this policy over a period of years cannot be appreciated without considering interest that could have been earned on premiums and the amount and timing of any payments by the company."

AY31YA-IRA PAGE 2 OF 2 03/02/79

Prepared by International Life Insurance Company of Buffalo, Buffalo, New York.

26

Buying and Selling a Farm

[¶2600] TAX PROBLEMS

Rarely does a farmer buy or sell a farm more than once or twice in a lifetime. His land and going farm enterprise constitute—in most cases—his principal assets. Today the sale of a farm—or the buying of one—is the single most massive tax problem in the farmer's career.

In a good many cases, the land may have been in the family for years and perhaps for generations. Land values have soared. The selling farmer may have added improvements, erected silos, modified the farm house, built barns, irrigated fields, and engaged in soil conservation practice. His over-the-years valuation of the farm is a complicated problem in tax mathematics that only the certified accountant can work out. For the buyer of the farm—for farming purposes—the question is at what bargained price will the farm purchase pay out? When should the conveyance be made in terms of the calendar year? Should it be paid for in installments? What about growing crops and what about harvested crops?

[¶2601] EARLY QUESTIONS

What is the farm worth—to sell or to buy? Here are fundamental questions that require answers.

1. What was the beginning cost to the present owner? This may develop from an estate settlement years before or from the purchase price at which the present farmer derived his conveyance.
2. What has been the cost of the farm residence with improvements over the years?

3. What have been the capital improvement costs and depreciation taken, and what is the recapture on each item at sale time?
4. What has been the stable income for the last five years?
5. What are the estimated current income sources; what is the prediction for the future years over which the payments are expected to be made?
6. How much investment credit may be recaptured when the sale is completed?
7. What return may the farmer expect when he reinvests the proceeds derived from the sale of his farm? In short, what will be his alternative opportunity earnings?
8. At what time will the farmer find it to his advantage to divest himself of the various classes of assets that receive different tax treatment? What is the most beneficial tax year?
9. At what time of the year will it be to his advantage to sell. Growing crops can be sold with the real estate with the proceeds eligible for capital gain and installment sale treatment, while harvested crops produce ordinary income.
10. Can the sale in two or more years level the effect on the farmer's income? Can property on which investment credit has been taken but not yet earned be leased at the time of the farm sale and sold at a later time to avoid credit recapture? Can soil and water conservation expenses taken be recaptured as capital gain by holding up the sale of the lands until some future year?

[¶2602] PULLING TOGETHER THE VALUATION DETAILS: A.T.B.

On the basis of these and other questions, the farmer pulls together the data that will determine the A.T.B. These alphabetical letters mean "Adjusted Tax Basis." The A.T.B. expresses the farmer's unrecovered cost. If farm records are completed—which they rarely are—the basic data are available. If not so available, then the data must be searched out, put in order, and refined. The Adjusted Tax Basis for chattels is simpler than that for real estate.

[¶2603] TIMING THE SALE

The timing of the sale has substantial consequences. For one thing, the disposal of a farm enterprise as a whole includes different classes of assets that require different tax treatment.

If the farmer is not pushed to sell by creditors or otherwise, he has considerable freedom to schedule his sale in a tax year most beneficial to him. Here are some questions to be asked:

1. What has been the taxable income experience?
2. What future income expectations are to be considered in electing the sale year?

3. How can a sale year be scheduled to avoid unusually large sums of other taxable income?
4. What time in the crop cycle will be most advantageous since growing crops can be sold with the real estate with income normally eligible for capital gain treatment.
5. What has been the farmer's taxable income for the last four years? This information has possible use for income averaging.
6. What amount of income from other sources may be established for the current year?
7. What income from other sources may be projected over the years for which payment on the sale is expected?
8. How much investment tax credit may be recaptured upon the sale of the farm property?
9. What is an estimate of the rate of return when the selling farmer invests the proceeds from the sale?
10. Will a çash sale be more beneficial to the selling of the farm over the alternative financing of the buyer by a mortgage?

[¶2604] DIFFERENT PREMISES OF BUYER AND SELLER

In negotiations over a farm, the buyer and seller may be acting on different premises. Thus for example, the seller may want to allocate a maximum amount to land and farm house, which is taxed as capital gain. The buyer, on the other hand, would tend to gain by a lower basis on the real estate and a higher basis in those assets that are subject to depreciation and investment credit. In any case, the sales contract should identify the different classes of assets, and spell them out so that the Internal Revenue Service can have a clear-cut tax report.

The careful buyer needs to give attention to the various classes of assets before he really knows what he can afford to pay for the property.

[¶2605] BUYING A FARM ON THE INSTALLMENT PLAN

The ways a farmer conveys his property as well, as the method by which the buyer acquires the property, deserves careful consideration. Should the transaction be for cash? Or shall payments be spread over two or more tax years.*

For the farmer who wants to get out of the farming business once and for all, he has only one choice: a cash sale. Often tax benefits may be

*Farmers involved in buying and selling a farm will benefit by studying *Taxmanship in Buying and Selling a Farm* by R. N. Weigle, University of Wisconsin, and Ralph S. Smith, Cornell University, Ithaca: Department of Agricultural Economics, New York State College of Agriculture and Life Sciences.

achieved when the device of income averaging is used, especially when the gains from selling capital assets are included.

If the sale is by the installment method, then the selling farmer can't receive over 30 per cent of the gross sales price. Installment payments must be spread over two or more tax years. A reasonable rate of interest must be charged on the outstanding principal. The method of sale must be elected and shown on the tax return in the year of the sale.

[¶2605.1] Benefits of Installment Sale

Here are some questions that a farmer needs to ask himself in weighing installment against cash sale:

1. Will the installment sale command a higher selling price? Especially since the seller may help the buyer to finance the sale and the better price may outweigh tax considerations?
2. By refusing cash, does the seller risk default on future payments?
3. How does the interest on the installment contract compare with what the selling farmer could realize on investing the proceeds of the sale elsewhere?
4. Will the farmer find the installment payments beneficial in his retirement budgeting?
5. Does the farmer need more liquidity in his investments than is provided by the proposed installment contract?

While the installment sale helps to lessen the income tax impact in the sale of large farms, its benefit on smaller farms may be less.

PART FIVE

Case Histories

27

Case Histories Through the Life Course: Representative Situations

[¶2700] VALUE OF CASE HISTORIES

In thinking about planning estates, farmers benefit by studying representative case histories dealing with the several stages of the life course.

CASE A: IN THE BEGINNING— THE YOUNG FARM FAMILY

[¶2700.1] The Data Sheet

The first case history describes the economic situation of a farmer, age 41, with three small children.

As in any estate planning situation, the first step is to prepare the basic data sheet, such as, for example, the one given in Figure 27-1.

[¶2700.2] Request for Simple Wills

When the husband and wife first visited the lawyer, they wanted "simple wills." That was all. At their request the "simple will" of the husband is given in Figure 27-2. After the conferences on the wills and a discussion of estate planning in which the Will is only one tool, the lawyer wrote to the couple in a preliminary way as follows:

Figure 27-1 Basic Data Sheet

NAME:	RICHARD J. HULETT and	JENNIFER M. HULETT
OCCUPATION:	Farmer	School Teacher
ADDRESS:	R. F. D., West Pawlet, Vermont 05775	
DATE OF BIRTH:	August 21, 1938	May 14, 1941
MARRIAGE:	June 24, 1960	
CHILDREN:	1. Bruce R. Hulett—born August 19, 1970 2. Tammy L. Hulett—born August 4, 1971 3. Joshua P. Hulett—born April 10, 1977	
EXPECTED LEGACIES:	Richard—possible \$2,000	Jennifer—possible \$25,000
WILL:	Neither spouse has Will	
LIFE INSURANCE:	Prudential—\$30,000 straight life Credit Insurance—\$50,000 decreasing to cover Production Credit Loan	
DEED:	Located in Factory Point Bank, Manchester, Vermont	
REAL ESTATE:	300 acres, bottom land—Fair Market Value = \$250,000	
CATTLE:	110 Holsteins—Fair Market Value = \$40,000	
MACHINERY:	Fair Market Value = \$35,000	
CAR AND TRUCK:	Fair Market Value = \$10,000	
RESIDENCE:	Dwelling house on farm—\$40,000	
CHILDREN'S BANK ACCOUNTS:	About \$200 currently in account—parents can withdraw	
CHECKING ACCTS:	And/or	
SAVINGS ACCTS:	And/or	
PERSONAL REPRESENTATIVE:	Jennifer for Richard	Richard for Jennifer
ALTERNATE PERS. REPRESENTATIVE:	Nadine Hayes [sister of Jennifer], R.F.D., Manchester Center, Vermont	
ALTERNATE GUARDIAN:	Nadine Hayes	
NET INCOME:	Income tax shows depreciation—\$14,000 Net income—\$4,000	

Figure 27-2 Last Will and Testament

FORM 922 WILL (Short Form)

TUTBLANX REGISTERED U. S. PAT. OFFICE
TUTTLE LAW PRINT PUBLISHERS, RUTLAND, VT. 05701

Last Will and Testament

I, RICHARD J. HULETT *of the* TOWN *of* PAWLET *in the County of* RUTLAND *and State of* VERMONT *being of sound mind and memory, do make, publish and declare this my last* Will and Testament, *in manner following, that is to say:*

First; I direct my executrix, hereinafter named, to pay any expenses of my last illness, my funeral costs, all my just debts, and the administrative expenses of my estate, inclusive of federal and state taxes, which may be occasioned by the passage or succession to any interest in my estate under the terms of this instrument.

SECOND; I give, devise, and bequeath to my wife, JENNIFER M. HULETT, all the rest, residue, and remainder of my estate, both real, personal, or mixed of whatsoever kind or character and wheresoever situated, to have and to hold as her property absolutely.

THIRD; In the event that my wife, JENNIFER M. HULETT, should predecease me, I give, devise, and bequeath all the rest, residue, and remainder of my estate to my three children, BRUCE R. HULETT, TAMMY L. HULETT, and JOSHUA P. HULETT, to have and to hold as their property absolutely, share and share alike; or if any children should be born after the date of this instrument, then share and share alike among such children.

FOURTH; In the event of my death and that of my wife, JENNIFER M. HULETT, and in the event our children, BRUCE R. HULETT, TAMMY L. HULETT, and JOSHUA P. HULETT, or any children born after the date of this instrument, have not arrived at legal age, then I appoint NADINE HAYES, R. F. D., Manchester Center, Vermont 05255, as guardian of my children during their minority, instructing such guardian to have due concern for their comfort, welfare, upbringing, and education with authority to draw upon the real and personal property as need and welfare may require.

FIFTH; Should my wife and I die in a common accident or disaster or under such circumstances that it is doubtful who died first, my wife shall be deemed to have survived me.

SIXTH; I hereby direct that my executrix, hereinafter named, or her successor serve in this capacity without being required to give any bond or other security for the faithful performance of her duties.

Figure 27-2 Cont.

Lastly, *I hereby appoint* my wife, JENNIFER M. HULETT,

execut rix

of this, my last Will and Testament: hereby revoking all former wills by me made. If my wife does not survive me, then I appoint NADINE HAYES, R. F. D. Manchester Center, Vermont to succeed her as my personal representative.

In Witness Whereof, *I have hereunto subscribed my name the*

day of *in the year Nineteen Hundred and* SEVENTY-SEVEN.

RICHARD J. HULETT L.S.

We, whose names are hereto subscribed, **Do Certify** *that on the*

day of *19* 77, RICHARD J. HULETT,

the testat or *above named, subscribed* his *name to this instrument in our presence and in the presence of each of us, and at the same time, in our presence and hearing, declared the same to be* his *last* **Will and Testament,** *and requested us and each of us, to sign our names thereto as witnesses to the execution thereof, which we hereby do in the presence of the testat* or *and of each other, on the day of the date of the said Will, and write opposite our names our respective places of residence.*

________________ *residing at* ________________

________________ *residing at* ________________

________________ *residing at* ________________

Dear Dick and Jennifer:

What a pleasant visit we had the day you were in after you had finished planting your crops!

Here for your record is a rough draft of the data we worked out.

When you have studied it, revised it to your satisfaction, and made some family decisions, perhaps we can get together in the office for a further visit.

In the meantime, I thought you might be interested in a few observations from an old hand.

Let's begin with your ages in 1979. You are 41, Jennifer 38. To Social Security eligibility at age 65, you have twenty-four years. While almost a quarter century seems like a long time as it reaches over into the third millennium and the year 2003 A.D., Bruce will be 33, Tammy 32, and Joshua 26—all adults and in the prime of life. By 1987, your children will be of college age. By 1991 Bruce will be out of college and hopefully your partner or corporate co-workman on the farm.

While you have been taking heavy depreciation, your net income has been smaller but will presently increase. It is my guess that your net worth at the present time would be something like $300,000. In the next 24 years I would guess that your net worth—with added land and income—will climb to ¾ million dollars.

Assuming these facts, a simple will should probably be only a part of a comprehensive estate plan, looking forward to the time when Bruce, Tammy, and Joshua will be—hopefully—associated with you in the family enterprise.

While your momentary expense in debt liquidation and machinery investment is heavy, your net income is bound to grow.

INSURANCE—Probably you will want to consider additional insurance protection. Straight life probably will give the most protection for the smallest premium.

In the course of shaping up your estate plan—if you decide to make one—you will want the help and advice of an insurance underwriter.

RETIREMENT FUND—For your pure protection under present laws, you can set aside—income tax free—a retirement fund—let us say of $1,500 a year. When you become eligible for retirement you have to pay on the gain, but then your income will probably be less.

For pure protection straight life probably gives the most protection for the least cost premium.

U.S. BONDS—By regular investment in U.S. bonds, you will have money for college bills or for investment in the business. It would be your money—and if you didn't use it for the children you could use it as you wished. Investment in U.S. bonds is a sound estate builder.

APPRECIATION—Values of your land holdings will probably increase at about 5 to 7 per cent a year.

FUTURE HOUSING—Looking forward to the time your children may join in the farming enterprise, you may wish to do a little planning for their future housing.

As you know, you could sell to Bruce, for example, your present house. You could build a new one for yourself without paying a tax on capital gains. You could sell your new home when and as you wished to Tammy and build a new one. By systematic planning you could end up with a winter home in Florida or Arizona, in both of which states farming is a booming business.

INCORPORATION—In view of the new tax laws, you might want to incorporate your farm. By reducing ownership to shares, both you and Jennifer would have your own holdings. As the children come along, you could involve them fairly by gifts of shares.

Under present tax laws, you can give away tax-free $3,000 a year each to as many children as you wish. You can also give to Jennifer $100,000, tax-free. While an estate by the entirety vests all the estate in the surviving spouse, you will probably be in a bracket where you may have a tax problem. Together, you and Jennifer could give $6,000 annually to each of your children.

MARITAL DEDUCTION—If your net adjusted estate should come out at $600,000, your marital deduction would be $300,000. By a two-trust plan you could pay on $150,000 in Trust I and leave $150,000 in Trust II on which the surviving spouse would pay upon death.

I mention these facts merely to show that your conventional Will needs to be studied in larger framework.

1. Do you feel that you should have—and can afford—more insurance for pure protection?
2. Do you feel a U.S. bond program would produce a growing equity which will be beneficial both to you and your children?
3. Do you feel that you would like to study what an S-type farm corporation would do for you?

CASE B: IN MIDDLE LIFE

[¶2701] THE COMPLEXITY OF INTESTACY

A lawyer living on an historic family farm that dated back to 1778 practiced law, but lived on and operated the farm. Strange as the fact may seem, he died without a Will at age 48. Because of his college and law school work and for other reasons, he married in 1910 at age 36. His bride, ten years his junior, moved into the farmstead home with the lawyer's mother. The bride proceeded to have five children, pretty evenly spaced over two-year periods. The first, a son, was born in 1912. The second, a daughter, was born in 1914. The third, a son, was born in 1916. The fourth, a daughter, was born in 1918. And, the fifth, a son, was born in 1920.

The husband of the lawyer's mother, had also died intestate. The mother herself had no Will. The estate dragged along without any definitive settlement. The mother died in 1937 at the age of 83.

Under state law, the surviving widow of an intestate husband was entitled to \$2,000 and 1/3 of the remaining estate. This estate was never probated. The lawyer-son and his wife and children continued to live in the manor house with the normal unhappiness of a three-generation family and an unsettled estate.

In 1924 the lawyer-son committed suicide, leaving a widow, five children, a confused estate, no Will, and no life insurance. The oldest boy, age 12, who had grown up for a dozen years on the farm and had the skills to keep the farm going, took over. He had no other choice and in a time capitulated to his desire to go to college and become a dentist. He worked the farm, went on through high school, transporting the milk to the creamery en route. The mother, however, continued to handle the accounts and really to boss the farm with penurious interest. In time the second son joined his older brother. And so did the third son. All the children forewent higher education. In 1937 the oldest brother married and proceeded to have two daughters and one son. The son at the age of 20 joined the farming operation and married. The second brother married in 1939 and proceeded to have two sons.

Drifting without a legal framework arrangement with their mother, the boys continued to farm, meanwhile extending a small milk route into the dominant firm in the region. By purchase and lease, they increased their acreage from 510 to 1,860. Much of the land was rented from a New York psychiatrist and a banker, both of whom wanted second homes in the country, the quiet of unspoiled acres, and no trouble with farm problems.

The two sisters married at a time when land values were low. By a family conference the farm—stock excluded—was valued at $12,000 with whatever nebulous title went with it. The two brothers estimated the interest of each of the daughters at $3,000. They took their shares as represented by two small houses.

[¶2701.1] The Informal Partnership

For years the two brothers operated the farm under an unwritten, informal partnership. The herd of cows grew. The milk route turned out to be a gold mine. The farm prospered. The milk business boomed. The second brother by this time had two sons, the oldest of whom joined the informal farm partnership. The oldest son of this Brother Number 2 married a banker's daughter, an attractive young woman with a business head and a bent for accounting.

The children of the brothers loved their historic hillside farm, and built stylish houses along the roadway, each having a magnificent valley view. By 1977 the hill had become a grand residential unit of five homes of children and each drove a Cadillac or motor car of equal style. Each had a patio with swimming pool.

In 1956, however, a third son of the deceased lawyer-farmer wanted out. He had worked along with his two brothers.

[¶2701.2] The Formal Partnership

He moved to Arizona. In a tight-fisted negotiation, he demanded $70,000 in settlement of his share in the farm now grown to substantial magnitude.

The two remaining brothers confirmed their informal partnership agreement. The son of one brother who married the banker's daughter and lived in a beautiful hilltop home which his wife had designed, joined the farm enterprise in 1965.

In 1977 the son of one brother built a new house on the family farm and the one son of the second brother first moved from the historic farm manor house. Meanwhile, an offer was made to the brothers to sell the whole operation for $1,000,000. They refused the offer but took steps to incorporate as a regular small business corporation.

[¶2701.3] Incorporation

In the carefully designed corporate structure, the banker-daughter wife became the treasurer and accountant with close control of cash flow, maximum fringe benefits, and proper Wills.

She led the way to the establishment of genuine estate plans for the benefit of all concerned—plans which reached into the future with children coming along, all determined to keep the farm as a going concern and their way of home life with a majestic mountain view.

CASE C: IN SENIOR YEARS

[¶2702] SALE TO SON

Two brothers succeeded to a farm that had been in the family since the nation was formed in 1789. Their acres were fertile. Their fields were level and well watered. The brothers farmed together in informal association until one was 72 and the other was 69. Both children of the older brother moved to the city. The only son of the younger brother married an industrious ethnic and year by year assumed increasing managerial control.

[¶2702.1] Scouting Alternatives

What were the brothers to do? They both continued to live on the farm as they had done during most of their lives. The off-the-farm heirs wanted money, not acres. The brothers scouted possible alternative solutions to their problem. One solution, of course, was incorporation with ownership transformed into flexible shares of stock. By this process the brothers could retain an interest in the farm operation and the off-the-farm heirs could be given debentures for their share.

[¶2702.2] Opting to Sell

After belabored consideration of alternatives, the brothers opted to sell outright to the son of the younger brother. They felt that this option would be quickest and cost the least money.

Thus, the off-the-farm heirs saw their interest in the historic family farm dissolved. Their ultimate equity was defined by their father's cash sale of the father's share and the provisions of his Will. However, the older brother had no intention of ending his interest in the farm. He invested the installment payments—beyond what was necessary to augment his living expenses—in a testamentary trust fund that was to go to the younger brother's son upon the death of himself and his wife. Both brothers had reserved a life tenancy as a condition of the sale to the son and nephew. They continued to live in their farm houses. When the Will was probated, it became clear that the older brother's love of the acres exceeded the disinterest of the off-the-farm heirs. Under the trust, the older brother's share went to the son. When the younger brother died, probate showed that he too had set up a trust. The off-the-farm heirs won their point—they wanted money, not historic affection for the family farm. They won their point but lost their acres.

CASE D: BRINGING IN THE NEW GENERATION

[¶2703] BRINGING A SON INTO THE FARM BUSINESS

How does a father bring his son into the farm business? On the basis of the data in the FACT SHEET at Figure 27-3, a father and son drew up a partnership agreement. This document includes:

1. Date of initiation.
2. Provision for annual review.
3. Stipulation that both partners shall contribute full-time to the business.
4. Nature of joint ownership of property initially contributed and subsequently acquired.
5. Clarification of partnership vs. personal income and expenses.
6. General restrictions on management decision which can be made individually.
7. Responsibility for keeping accounts and banking.
8. Provision for salaries and draws to partners.
9. Buy-sell option in event of death or dissolution for other reasons.
10. Provision for arbitration.

Figure 27-3 Fact Sheet

Family

Father	age 48
Wife	age 45
Married Son	age 23
Daughter in college	age 20

Son Situation Gradute of College of Agriculture and Life Sciences, Cornell University; married at age 22; bought mobile home and located it on father's FARM: BEGAN WORK WITH FATHER UNDER ORAL AGREEMENT at $125 a month.

Farm Property 500 acres total; 350 tillable; free stall barn constructed for 80 cows just after son went to college; expanded to 100 cows when son came home from college; silo with capacity of 1500 tons + Harvestor for soft corn.

Figure 27-3 Cont.

Ownership All real estate held by father and mother as tenants by the entirety with right of survivorship; farm family home in excellent condition.

Son's Property Son owns pick-up used in farm business - estimated value $1500; twelve head of livestock valued at $3,500.

Finance	Father's mortgage to Federal Land Bank-		$60,000
	Monthly payments +	$450	
	Father's chattel mortgage to Production Credit Association.		$40,000
	Monthly payments +	$800	
	Father's non-farm assets		$20,000
	Son's equity in mobile home		$ 2,000
	No other debts.		
Insurance	Father		$50,000
	($10,000 whole life + $40,000 term)		
	Wife beneficiary		
	Son - no insurance.		

Tax Situation:	Father files on cash basis-calendar year.	
	Adjusted Tax Basis	
	Real estate	$50,000
	Equipment	$40,000
	Livestock	0
	Father's adjusted gross income	$20,000
	Taxable income	$18,000
	Federal income tax (personal)	$ 3,800
	28% bracket	

Health Father in prime of life and best of health; plans to share ownership and management with son.

Options Father and son discuss partnership and incorporation; evaluate advantages and disadvantages of each.

Results Father and son have $40,500 equity; each owes 1/2 Production Credit loan of $40,000; son owes father $35,500 on personal note.

In addition to the partnership contract, a second document was necessary, i.e., a rental agreement between the partnership and father and mother with the inclusion of an option for the partnership to buy at a fixed dollar value. If it became necessary for the partnership to make capital improvements on the leased real estate, then it becomes imperative to provide protection for the partnership in the event of a dissolution prior to full depreciation of such capital improvements.

[¶2703.1] Project: Toward Retirement

As father moves toward retirement he begins to calculate retirement finances. The son, now at age 40, has expanded the productivity of the farm. He proposes to buy the father's share of the partnership. By the time father retires, father has built a second house and made substantial capital improvements. Here is the way the financial situation looked as projected toward 1992 upon the assessed appraisal of two outside parties:

Value of real estate	$300,000
Personal property	$300,000
Real estate mortgage	$100,000
PCA loan	$ 80,000
Son's note to father	$ 30,000

In summary the financial situation looked like this:

Item	*Father*	*Son*
Real estate	$200,000	$100,000
Personal	$150,000	$150,000
Total Assets	$350,000	$250,000
Partnership Debts	$ 90,000	$ 90,000
	$260,000	$160,000
Son's note to father	$ 30,000	$ 30,000
Net worth	$290,000	$130,000

[¶2703.2] Financing the Transfer

The schedule for financing the transfer from father to son looked like this:

Son owes father	$290,000
Son owes creditors	$180,000
Son's equity estimate	$130,000

with the son's debt to the father bearing a nominal interest of 5% as specified in the buy-sell option.

Father's Retirement Money. Father estimated that he will need an annual income of $20,000 to live comfortably in retirement and pay his taxes. At the time of transfer he will need $70,000 in cash for the purchase of a retirement home, taxes, and legal fees associated with the transfer. He proposes to provide $20,000 of permanent capital at 9% secured by a second mortgage, and to amortize the balance over a 20-year period.

Father projected his retirement income like this:	*Annually*
Estimated Social Security	$ 6,000
Interest on $120,000 @ 9%	$10,800
Amortization payments on $100,000 @ 9%	$ 9,000
TOTAL projected income	$25,800

By this arithmetic father can expect a monthly income of something like $2150—a comfortable figure!

[¶2703.3] Tax Problems

The sale of the farm by father to son, however, involved substantial tax problems. For example:

Livestock $\frac{67,000}{2}$ = $33,500—a major tax problem.

Equipment $\frac{40,000}{2}$ = $20,000—no tax problem; Basis = sale price, but investment recapture.

Cash and accounts receivable
$\frac{\$9,000}{2}$ = $4,500—no tax problem; basis = sale price.

In figuring the tax problem, it became necessary to divide the livestock into two classes.*

Class 1 = cattle over two years of age. Assumed value = $60,000
Class 2 = heifers under two years of age. Assumed value = $ 7,000

The gain on Class 1 would be $30,000; on Class 2 $3,500, for a total taxable gain of $18,500.

Since there is zero basis for both classes of livestock, reporting is relatively simple, since for each year the amount received on principal of the son's Note paid to his father is allocated to:

1. Cash and accounts receivable.
2. Young stock purchased.

*It might be argued that the debt assumed represents a claim against equipment, not livestock. Otherwise, the livestock sale will not qualify for capital gain. Such argument might or might not be successful.

3. Older cattle purchased.
4. Equipment purchased.

The payments on principal are first allocated to those items that would result in ordinary gain. Assuming further that $500 is recaptured on equipment sold by father to son, then father must report this figure on his tax return.

CASE E: IN SENIOR YEARS—ANOTHER EXAMPLE

[¶2704] PROTECTING THE HERITAGE

A historic family farm was bought by an off- the-farm husband, age 49, of a daughter-heir. The grantee looked forward to the enjoyment of farming in retirement some sixteen years hence. He died at the age of 63; his wife at age 73.

There were three children to the marriage—two daughters and one son. The second daughter had one son, the only one of the three children to marry, who grew up in Philadelphia and Washington. Every summer he worked on the farm. He knew every inch of the land. He could perform every farm task and run every farm machine. Graduating from an Ivy League engineering institution, he continued on the faculty, soon marrying the daughter of a Philadelphia lawyer, the girl being a graduate of an Ivy League College who had spent her summers in summer camps and at summer resorts and abroad. Their two very competent and athletic sons spent summers in camp and on the ocean rather than in the hay fields, without the opportunity their father had enjoyed to master farming.

Both the unmarried son and daughter developed substantial estates and the son of the married daughter—who was the sole heir by respective Wills—began to worry about the problem of liquidity. Could he afford to hold the farm which he loved?

By proper Wills, the mother and uncle and aunt—now all retired and living together on the farm—assured succession during their lifetimes.

[¶2704.1] Incorporation

Their solution was incorporation of the farm. By a process of giving shares of stock up to $3,000 a year to the son and nephew and each of his two sons, the farm ownership through stock sharing was transferred over a period of years to the nephew and grand-nephews. Nevertheless, the unmarried brother and sister feared that the daughter-in-law might want the sizeable amount of cash that would come from selling the farm. However, there was a feeling that the grandnephews in time might want the farm to operate because of affection for it, in order to produce income, or as a summer or retirement place. Wishing to maintain the historic family farm, what protection could be taken to delay liquidation by the heirs?

[¶2704.2] Trust

Upon the deaths of the last of the three, the farm by testamentary trust would vest in a bank trustee with the income therefrom designed for scholarships for youths who plan careers in farming, such awards to be made at the annual local high school commencement. The Trust, however, provided that if the son, grandsons, and nephews should continue with the farm, then the trust would terminate and the property would vest in the three descendants.

One grandson was graduated from Harvard Medical and took an active interest in the farm. The other grandson was graduated from M.I.T. in architecture. He too loved the farm and respected the traditions. The farm corporation continued—as a profitable enterprise and haven for the succeeding generation.

28

A Hypothetical Farm Estate Plan

There are many considerations essential to the estate planning process. The individual circumstances and aspirations of every farm family will of course have a direct bearing on how the estate plan is prepared.

The hypothetical plan outlined below was developed for a fictitious farm family, and it is tailored to meet the family's particular needs. However, this individual plan is designed to demonstrate how careful estate planning can help all farm families build their wealth and provide comfort and security for the future.

Three young brothers—Patrick, Michael, and Thomas O'Leary—own and operate a 320-acre dairy farm in Eire, Vermont, under a partnership agreement. Michael and Thomas are presently unmarried; their mother, Nora, lives with them in the farmhouse. Patrick and his wife, Theresa, live in an adjacent farmhouse with their two children, Patrick Jr. and Colleen.

Their farm, including the farmhouse, adjacent dwelling house, milking barn, and three storage barns, has a fair market value of $160,000. Value of the farm machinery, fully owned by the brothers, is $40,000. Livestock, including 150 milking cows, 50 bred heifers, and 40 calves, is also fully owned by the brothers and valued at $147,000. The farm is currently producing an annual gross income of $312,000.

Neither the sons nor their mother have wills; nor do they have any present insurance coverage. Until recently, Patrick, Michael, and Thomas have not given any thought to estate planning. Now, however, Patrick desires to ensure his wife's comfort and provide for the education and upbringing of their children. It is likely that Michael and Thomas will marry, too, and raise families of their own. All three brothers are looking ahead to expanding—and profiting from—their farm operation.

ESTATE PLANNING REPORT
CONFIDENTIAL

for
PATRICK O'LEARY
MICHAEL O'LEARY
THOMAS O'LEARY

DATA SHEET

PARTNERSHIP:	O'LEARY BROTHERS
PARTNERS:	Patrick O'Leary — Birth Dates: May 30, 1944 Michael O'Leary — July 4, 1949 Thomas O'Leary — October 30, 1954
OCCUPATION:	Farmers
ADDRESS:	Killarney Acres Rupert Road, Route 1 P.O. Box 199 Eire, Vermont 05775
TELEPHONE:	802-645-0043
MARITAL SITUATION:	Patrick O'Leary is married to Theresa (Kelly) O'Leary. Date of Marriage: June 10, 1974 Children: Patrick O'Leary, Jr.—born May 3, 1976 Colleen O'Leary—born February 15, 1978 Michael O'Leary and Thomas O'Leary are presently unmarried.
GENERATION SITUATION:	Mother: Nora (Sweeney) O'Leary, born March 17, 1907, lives in the farmhouse with sons Michael and Thomas. Patrick and his family live in an adjacent farmhouse on Killarney Acres.
EXPECTED LEGACIES:	Mother has $60,000 invested in certificates of deposit.
WILLS:	Neither mother nor any of the three sons have wills.
INSURANCE:	No present coverage.
DEED:	Three brothers are grantees in joint tenancy with survivorship.
PARTNERSHIP AGREEMENT:	Dated March 1, 1979.
REAL ESTATE:	Killarney Acres 320 acres—bottom land and pasture Master farmhouse—adjacent dwelling house Milking barn plus three storage barns Fair market value—$160,000.00

CATTLE:	150 milking cows at $800 = $120,000 (market value) 50 bred heifers at $500 = 15,000 40 calves at $300 = 12,000 Fair market value of livestock totals $147,000. Livestock is fully owned by the brothers.
MACHINERY:	Fair Market Value = $40,000,000. Machinery is fully owned by the brothers.
MOTOR VEHICLES:	Chrysler 4-door (1979) $7,600.00 Dodge ¾-ton pickup $4,000.00
BANK ACCOUNTS:	Mechanics Point National Bank Partnership Checking Account: O'Leary Brothers Savings Account: Patrick, Michael, and Thomas O'Leary as joint tenants with survivorship
GROSS ANNUAL FARM INCOME:	$312,000

I. FINANCING THE PURCHASE OF KILLARNEY ACRES

Estimates of the gross annual income of Killarney Acres as operated by the O'Leary Brothers partnership show the expectation of $312,000, or $26,000 a month in the year 1979.

The monthly payment to the Federal Land Bank on the 15-year first 8½% mortgage is $1,378.64, or $16,543.68 a year.

For the record, attached to this Estate Plan is an amortization schedule so that the brothers can tell at any month where they stand.

While this monthly payment is high because of the short term of 15 years, it means that by 1994 the O'Leary Brothers will own Killarney Acres in fee without mortgage debt. As inflation skyrockets land values, each brother, without adjustment for inflation, will hold a one-third share of the $160,000 paid for the farm, i.e., downpayment plus mortgage equal to $53,000+. With soaring land values, the equity of each of the O'Leary Brothers might grow so that each brother would have something like $100,000 equity.

If the mother should die and will her $60,000 in assets equally to the brothers, the legacy could be used to accelerate the payment of the mortgage.

Hence, this estate plan assumes that for 15 years the brothers will be pinched as a first charge on the mortgage payments, but they will be building up an equity in land, cattle, and equipment. Productive land is probably the safest asset in these inflationary and uncertain times.

II. PRUDENT GROSS INCOME ESTIMATE

Because the brothers own their cattle and machinery, they have a substantial asset and equity. They probably will not need this equity in financing future operations—seeds, fertilizers, maintenance, taxes, and insurance.

The prudent gross annual income estimate on which this estate plan is based recognizes the dairy expertise of the O'Leary Brothers—high test, high production, low grain costs. The calculation is based on 150 milking cows giving an annual average production of 16,000 pounds of milk with a 3.8% butterfat test; the sale of bull calves; the replacement of 20% of the herd annually; 50 bred heifers; 40 calves; and the mixing of their own grain.

Assuming that the farm operating expenses, inclusive of grain, veterinary fees, insemination utilities, cultivation costs, taxes, and assessments will run about 60% of the gross income, thus subtracting mortgage payments and a 60% operating cost, or $187,200, the brothers have a probable net monthly income of $9,000. Thus there would be a possible sum of $3,000 a month for each brother, or $36,000 annual income.

Nevertheless, since the O'Leary Brothers, as partners, operate in an unusual pattern by drawing no salaries beyond living expenses, preferring to enhance their equity until the mortgage is paid off, and assuming a drawing account for living expenses of $100 a week, the three-way division would be roughly $30,000 a year for each O'Leary brother.

To this possible income this estate report now addresses itself.

III. INSURANCE CONSIDERATIONS

Because of the ages of the O'Leary brothers and their closely knit family partnership, insurance takes an unusual pattern also.

Since the ownership of the farm in increasing equity becomes a prime asset, there is little advantage in insurance other than group term life insurance on each of the brothers. Carried in the amount of $100,000, at an annual cost of approximately $810, the brothers would provide security in their operation and security for themselves and the families involved, with sufficient liquidity to handle any estate taxes, should misfortune overtake any of the brothers.

No real need for credit insurance exists if term insurance is carried.

They do, however, need to have medical and hospital insurance with major medical. For Patrick and his family the cost will be around $500 a year. For Michael and Thomas the cost will be approximately $200 a year each. Thus adequate health and hospitalization for the whole partnership will total around $900 a year.

To the extent that any of the brothers desire more insurance as family responsibilities increase, they may find that straight life provides the most protection for the dollar premium. The purpose of insurance is to provide for risk.

Since it is quite improbable that all brothers would be deceased at the same time in active life, the provision for their respective families is carried adequately by respective equities in the farm operation.

IV. MOTHER'S ASSETS

Mother O'Leary has assets of $60,000. She has no will and no other personal property which she is now disposing of by gift not exceeding $3,000 a year.

Her certificates of deposit amount to $20,000 for each brother. By dividing her certificates into three equal parts—one third for each brother—she could establish certificates in joint tenancy with survivorship, reserving the life income to herself. Under such a provision Mother O'Leary would need no will and there would not necessarily be any probate.

The case of each brother requires separate treatment.

V. PATRICK O'LEARY

Patrick is the oldest brother. As the senior in the family, he is 35 years of age at the time of this report, has a congenial wife interested in farming and helpful in all of its operations.

By the year 1994 Patrick, Jr., will be graduating from high school and by 1998, from agricultural school. It is expected that he will be joining the farm operation. Colleen will graduate from high school in 1996 and from college in the year 2000.

It will be necessary to make early provision for their college expenses. Assuming that state university costs will run close to $4,000 a year, or $16,000 for four years, a kitty of about $900 a year must be set aside to draw interest. If Patrick should have an understanding with Patrick, Jr., and Colleen that he will match the college fund dollar for dollar with them as they earn it, he will find the arrangement rewarding.

Certainly Patrick would want to have at least half of the account in high-interest certificates of deposit. It is recommended, however, that he establish an account with a brokerage firm. It is also recommended that he watch the market for good value buys in common stocks and purchase such together with Patrick, Jr., and Colleen, respectively, to enhance their assets. In times like these, such an operation could be highly rewarding and provide a project between his generation and theirs for action together.

VI. MICHAEL O'LEARY

Michael, at the time of this report, is age 30 and an eligible bachelor. Within the next few years it is a reasonable guess that he will marry a woman who believes in farming. He will need to give the same consideration to the care and education of his children as Patrick is about to do.

Upon his marriage, Michael will need his own home on Killarney Acres. At present costs let us assume the building and furnishings would amount to $70,000. On a 15-year mortgage, this original cost would take monthly payments of about $700, or $8,400 a year.

Because the brothers operate as a total partnership, the amortization would be paid from the farm income. Over the period of amortization—given a reasonable inflation figure—this home of Michael's would have a value of perhaps $100,000.

VII. THOMAS O'LEARY

Thomas is now age 25. Assuming that he marries before he is 30, he will undertake the same family obligations as Patrick and Michael and another $70,000 home will be added to Killarney Acres.

VIII. BUY–SELL AGREEMENT

While it is hoped that all the families will remain congenial and join in the operation of Killarney Acres, there exists the possibility that one or more brothers may want out.

That out is provided for in the buy–sell clause in the partnership agreement. The buy–sell agreement is an instrument that defines the conditions upon which one or more of the family members of the farm can acquire the farm and the conditions under which such family members will sell.

IX. INDIVIDUAL RETIREMENT ACCOUNTS

Since the younger families will be assuming greater responsibilities for the growing operation, Patrick, Michael, and Thomas may well consider individual retirement accounts which provide certain tax advantages, but at age 59½ enable any of the brothers to project retirement income.

X. OCEAN-FRONT FAMILY VILLA IN THE SUNBELT

As a common family amenity it is suggested that the farming operation acquire an ocean villa with citrus groves at some spot where a good opportunity opens up. This villa will become a priceless amenity for time sharing in vacation periods. Let us assume that the cost of this villa will approximate $100,000.

XI. INCORPORATION OF KILLARNEY ACRES

Let us assume that by agricultural education, wise and congenial marriages, and thrifty and cooperative families, all the married children of all three brothers propose to carry on farming in the family context of Killarney Acres.

It is obvious that the income from Killarney Acres, adequate to provide generous living for three brothers and their children, is not enough for six additional families plus those of the three brothers.

In looking forward to such a growth in the O'Leary clan, two steps are recommended.

1. Incorporation, so that Killarney Acres, Ltd., becomes a family enterprise with shares of stock so prudently distributed that all the family feels a part of the enterprise and that each child and his subsequent family knows exactly how and where they stand.
2. Expansion of the farming enterprise so that the income keeps pace with the size and needs of the O'Leary clan.

This expansion of the farming operation can take place with sound judgment at decreasing costs of operation as land—when opportunity arises—is acquired. This development could assume growth by 50-cow units in the O'Leary family's own large-scale scientific farming enterprise. The original 320 acres will have increased year by year by prudent purchase and leasing to something like 2000 acres. The cattle will have increased to 500 head. The family corporation will own perhaps nine residences now worth $100,000 each plus the sunbelt villa. Taking into consideration a reasonable inflationary rate, the acres will have a value of $2,000,000. The milking herd—without counting calves and bred heifers—will have a value of $600,000, and the sunbelt villa will have doubled in value to $200,000. Thus, without counting machinery, which is acquired as investment credit and fast depreciation, Killarney Acres, Ltd.—the O'Learys as a family—will have a net worth exceeding $3,500,000. The family through shared stock ownership in the corporation will operate a big business. The family members will have lifelong employment on their farm. They will enjoy their work as together they establish a large productive farming enterprise.

XII. WILLS

After the O'Leary brothers have studied this plan, each of them and their wives should execute wills. Their wills will have to be drawn to incorporate the ramifications of the O'Leary clan in addition to usual testamentary clauses. The drafting of these wills is a further task in the completion of the comprehensive estate plan.

XIII. THE FINANCIAL FEASIBILITY OF THIS PLAN

The ongoing economic productivity of this harmonious family enterprise is financially feasible, beginning with the present initial partnership of the O'Leary Brothers on Killarney Acres.

The O'Learys have ample funds to initiate this estate plan. It is recommended that they direct their certified public accountant to prepare an initial financing schedule of the whole package as of the present date. As the family enterprise enlarges from year to year, the accountant should make schedules which describe in detail the sums involved in taking each new step.

Figure 28-1

Schedule of Direct Reduction Loan

FINANCIAL PUBLISHING COMPANY
82 Brookline Avenue
Boston, Massachusetts 02215
(617) 262-4040

ANNUAL % RATE	PAYMENT $	LOAN $	TERM: YEARS	MONTHS	PERIODS
8.500	1,378.64	140,000.00	15		180

PAY'T NO.	INTEREST PAYMENT	PRINCIPAL PAYMENT	BALANCE OF LOAN	PAY'T NO.	INTEREST PAYMENT	PRINCIPAL PAYMENT	BALANCE OF LOAN
1	991.67	386.97	139,613.03	61	787.62	591.02	110,601.77
2	988.93	389.71	139,223.32	62	783.43	595.21	110,006.56
3	986.17	392.47	138,830.85	63	779.21	599.43	109,407.13
4	983.39	395.25	138,435.60	64	774.97	603.67	108,803.46
5	980.59	398.05	138,037.55	65	770.69	607.95	108,195.51
6	977.77	400.87	137,636.68	66	766.38	612.26	107,583.25
7	974.93	403.71	137,232.97	67	762.05	616.59	106,966.66
8	972.07	406.57	136,826.40	68	757.68	620.96	106,345.70
9	969.19	409.45	136,416.95	69	753.28	625.36	105,720.34
10	966.29	412.35	136,004.60	70	748.85	629.79	105,090.55
11	963.37	415.27	135,589.33	71	744.39	634.25	104,456.30
12	960.42	418.22	135,171.11	72	739.90	638.74	103,817.56
13	957.46	421.18	134,749.93	73	735.37	643.27	103,174.29
14	954.48	424.16	134,325.77	74	730.82	647.82	102,526.47
15	951.47	427.17	133,898.60	75	726.23	652.41	101,874.06
16	948.45	430.19	133,468.41	76	721.61	657.03	101,217.03
17	945.40	433.24	133,035.17	77	716.95	661.69	100,555.34
18	942.33	436.31	132,598.86	78	712.27	666.37	99,888.97
19	939.24	439.40	132,159.46	79	707.55	671.09	99,217.88
20	936.13	442.51	131,716.95	80	702.79	675.85	98,542.03
21	933.00	445.64	131,271.31	81	698.01	680.63	97,861.40
22	929.84	448.80	130,822.51	82	693.18	685.46	97,175.94
23	926.66	451.98	130,370.53	83	688.33	690.31	96,485.63
24	923.46	455.18	129,915.35	84	683.44	695.20	95,790.43
25	920.23	458.41	129,456.94	85	678.52	700.12	95,090.31
26	916.99	461.65	128,995.29	86	673.56	705.08	94,385.23
27	913.72	464.92	128,530.37	87	668.56	710.08	93,675.15
28	910.42	468.22	128,062.15	88	663.53	715.11	92,960.04
29	907.11	471.53	127,590.62	89	658.47	720.17	92,239.87
30	903.77	474.87	127,115.75	90	653.37	725.27	91,514.60
31	900.40	478.24	126,637.51	91	648.23	730.41	90,784.19
32	897.02	481.62	126,155.89	92	643.05	735.59	90,048.60
33	893.60	485.04	125,670.85	93	637.84	740.80	89,307.80
34	890.17	488.47	125,182.38	94	632.60	746.04	88,561.76
35	886.71	491.93	124,690.45	95	627.31	751.33	87,810.43
36	883.22	495.42	124,195.03	96	621.99	756.65	87,053.78
37	879.71	498.93	123,696.10	97	616.63	762.01	86,291.77
38	876.18	502.46	123,193.64	98	611.23	767.41	85,524.36
39	872.62	506.02	122,687.62	99	605.80	772.84	84,751.52
40	869.04	509.60	122,178.02	100	600.32	778.32	83,973.20
41	865.43	513.21	121,664.81	101	594.81	783.83	83,189.37
42	861.79	516.85	121,147.96	102	589.26	789.38	82,399.99
43	858.13	520.51	120,627.45	103	583.67	794.97	81,605.02
44	854.44	524.20	120,103.25	104	578.04	800.60	80,804.42
45	850.73	527.91	119,575.34	105	572.36	806.28	79,998.14
46	846.99	531.65	119,043.69	106	566.65	811.99	79,186.15
47	843.23	535.41	118,508.28	107	560.90	817.74	78,368.41
48	839.43	539.21	117,969.07	108	555.11	823.53	77,544.88
49	835.61	543.03	117,426.04	109	549.28	829.36	76,715.52
50	831.77	546.87	116,879.17	110	543.40	835.24	75,880.28
51	827.89	550.75	116,328.42	111	537.49	841.15	75,039.13
52	823.99	554.65	115,773.77	112	531.53	847.11	74,192.02
53	820.06	558.58	115,215.19	113	525.53	853.11	73,338.91
54	816.11	562.53	114,652.66	114	519.48	859.16	72,479.75
55	812.12	566.52	114,086.14	115	513.40	865.24	71,614.51
56	808.11	570.53	113,515.61	116	507.27	871.37	70,743.14
57	804.07	574.57	112,941.04	117	501.10	877.54	69,865.60
58	800.00	578.64	112,362.40	118	494.88	883.76	68,981.84
59	795.90	582.74	111,779.66	119	488.62	890.02	68,091.82
60	791.77	586.87	111,192.79	120	482.32	896.32	67,195.50

Figure 28-1 Cont.

Schedule of Direct Reduction Loan

FINANCIAL PUBLISHING COMPANY
82 Brookline Avenue
Boston, Massachusetts 02215
(617) 262-4040

ANNUAL % RATE	PAYMENT $	LOAN $	TERM: YEARS	MONTHS	PERIODS
8.500	1,378.64	140,000.00	15		180

PAY'T NO.	INTEREST PAYMENT	PRINCIPAL PAYMENT	BALANCE OF LOAN	PAY'T NO.	INTEREST PAYMENT	PRINCIPAL PAYMENT	BALANCE OF LOAN
121	475.97	902.67	66,292.83				
122	469.57	909.07	65,383.76				
123	463.13	915.51	64,468.25				
124	456.65	921.99	63,546.26				
125	450.12	928.52	62,617.74				
126	443.54	935.10	61,682.64				
127	436.92	941.72	60,740.92				
128	430.25	948.39	59,792.53				
129	423.53	955.11	58,837.42				
130	416.77	961.87	57,875.55				
131	409.95	968.69	56,906.86				
132	403.09	975.55	55,931.31				
133	396.18	982.46	54,948.85				
134	389.22	989.42	53,959.43				
135	382.21	996.43	52,963.00				
136	375.15	1,003.49	51,959.51				
137	368.05	1,010.59	50,948.92				
138	360.89	1,017.75	49,931.17				
139	353.68	1,024.96	48,906.21				
140	346.42	1,032.22	47,873.99				
141	339.11	1,039.53	46,834.46				
142	331.74	1,046.90	45,787.56				
143	324.33	1,054.31	44,733.25				
144	316.86	1,061.78	43,671.47				
145	309.34	1,069.30	42,602.17				
146	301.77	1,076.87	41,525.30				
147	294.14	1,084.50	40,440.80				
148	286.46	1,092.18	39,348.62				
149	278.72	1,099.92	38,248.70				
150	270.93	1,107.71	37,140.99				
151	263.08	1,115.56	36,025.43				
152	255.18	1,123.46	34,901.97				
153	247.22	1,131.42	33,770.55				
154	239.21	1,139.43	32,631.12				
155	231.14	1,147.50	31,483.62				
156	223.01	1,155.63	30,327.99				
157	214.82	1,163.82	29,164.17				
158	206.58	1,172.06	27,992.11				
159	198.28	1,180.36	26,811.75				
160	189.92	1,188.72	25,623.03				
161	181.50	1,197.14	24,425.89				
162	173.02	1,205.62	23,220.27				
163	164.48	1,214.16	22,006.11				
164	155.88	1,222.76	20,783.35				
165	147.22	1,231.42	19,551.93				
166	138.49	1,240.15	18,311.78				
167	129.71	1,248.93	17,062.85				
168	120.86	1,257.78	15,805.07				
169	111.95	1,266.69	14,538.38				
170	102.98	1,275.66	13,262.72				
171	93.94	1,284.70	11,978.02				
172	84.84	1,293.80	10,684.22				
173	75.68	1,302.96	9,381.26				
174	66.45	1,312.19	8,069.07				
175	57.16	1,321.48	6,747.59				
176	47.80	1,330.84	5,416.75				
177	38.37	1,340.27	4,076.48				
178	28.88	1,349.76	2,726.72				
179	19.31	1,359.33	1,367.39				
180	9.69	1,367.39	.00				
FINAL PAYMENT:		1,377.08					

TOTAL INTEREST: 108153.64 TOTAL PRINCIPAL: 140000.00
SUM OF BALANCES: 15268741.92 24

Appendix A

DIRECTORY OF LAND GRANT COLLEGES

The United States Department of Agriculture, agricultural colleges in land grant universities, and county extension services can provide a wealth of valuable information for all aspects of farm operation. Local extension services are listed in most telephone directories under the county name. The following directory lists, by state, the addresses and telephone numbers of land grant colleges and extension services. The map depicts the regional pattern by which states are grouped.

ALABAMA	School of Agriculture Auburn University Auburn, Alabama 36830 205-826-4000
ALASKA	School of Agriculture & Land Resources Management University of Alaska Fairbanks, Alaska 99701 907-479-7311
ARIZONA	College of Agriculture University of Arizona Tucson, Arizona 85721 602 884-2751
ARKANSAS	Division of Agriculture University of Arkansas Fayetteville, Arkansas 72701 501-575-2000
CALIFORNIA	College of Agricultural Sciences University of California Berkeley, California 94720 415-642-7171
COLORADO	College of Agricultural Sciences Colorado State University Fort Collins, Colorado 80523 303-491-1101

CONNECTICUT	College of Agriculture & Natural Resources University of Connecticut Storrs, Connecticut 06268 203-486-2000
DELAWARE	College of Agricultural Sciences University of Delaware Newark, Delaware 19711 302-738-2000
FLORIDA	College of Agriculture University of Florida Gainesville, Florida 32611 904-392-3261
GEORGIA	College of Agriculture University of Georgia Athens, Georgia 30602 404-542-3030
GUAM	College of Agriculture & Life Sciences University of Guam Agana, Guam 96910 749-2921
HAWAII	College of Tropical Agriculture University of Hawaii Honolulu, Hawaii 96822 808-948-8111
IDAHO	College of Agriculture University of Idaho Moscow, Idaho 83843 208-885-6111
ILLINOIS	College of Agriculture University of Illinois Urbana, Illinois 61801 217-333-1000
INDIANA	School of Agriculture Purdue University West Lafayette, Indiana 47907 317-749-6092
IOWA	College of Agriculture Iowa State University Ames, Iowa 50011 515-294-4111

KANSAS	College of Agriculture Kansas State University Manhattan, Kansas 66506 913-532-6011
KENTUCKY	College of Agriculture University of Kentucky Lexington, Kentucky 40506 606-258-9000
LOUISIANA	Louisiana State University and Agricultural and Mechanical College Baton Rouge, Louisiana 70893 504-388-5011
MAINE	College of Live Sciences and Agriculture University of Maine Orono, Maine 04473 207-581-1110
MARYLAND	College of Agriculture University of Maryland College Park, Maryland 20742 301-454-0100
MASSACHUSETTS	College of Food and Natural Resources University of Massachusetts Amherst, Massachusetts 01002 413-545-0111
MICHIGAN	College of Agriculture Michigan State University East Lansing, Michigan 48824 517-355-1855
MINNESOTA	College of Agriculture University of Minnesota St. Paul, Minnesota 55101 612-373-2851
MISSISSIPPI	College of Agriculture Mississippi State University of Applied Arts and Sciences Mississippi State, Mississippi 39762 601-325-2131
MISSOURI	College of Agriculture University of Missouri Columbia, Missouri 65201 314-882-2121

MONTANA	College of Agriculture Montana State University Bozeman, Montana 59717 406-994-0211
NEBRASKA	Institute of Agriculture and Natural Resources University of Nebraska Lincoln, Nebraska 68503 402-472-7211
NEVADA	Max C. Fleischmann College of Agriculture University of Nevada Reno, Nevada 89507 702-784-1110
NEW HAMPSHIRE	College of Life Science and Agriculture University of New Hampshire Durham, New Hampshire 03824 603-862-1234
NEW JERSEY	Cook College State University of New Jersey New Brunswick, New Jersey 08903 201-932-1766
NEW MEXICO	College of Agriculture and Home Economics New Mexico State University Las Cruces 88003 505-646-0111
NEW YORK	New York State College of Agriculture and Life Sciences Cornell University Ithaca, New York 14853 607-256-1000
NORTH CAROLINA	School of Agriculture North Carolina State University Raleigh, North Carolina 27607 919-737-2011
NORTH DAKOTA	College of Agriculture North Dakota State University Fargo, North Dakota 58102 701-237-8011
OHIO	College of Agriculture and Home Economics Ohio State University Columbus, Ohio 43210 614-422-6446

OKLAHOMA	Oklahoma State University of Agriculture and Applied Science Oklahoma State University Stillwater, Oklahoma 74074 405-372-6211
OREGON	School of Agriculture Oregon State University Corvallis, Oregon 97331 503-754-0123
PENNSYLVANIA	College of Agriculture Pennsylvania State University University Park, Pennsylvania 16802 814-865-4700
PUERTO RICO	College of Agricultural Sciences University of Puerto Rico Mayagüez, Puerto Rico 00708 809-832-4040
RHODE ISLAND	Colleges of Resource Development and Home Economics University of Rhode Island Kingston, Rhode Island 02881 401-792-1000
SOUTH CAROLINA	College of Agricultural Sciences Clemson University Clemson, South Carolina 29631 803-656-3311
SOUTH DAKOTA	College of Agricultural and Biological Sciences South Dakota State University Brookings, South Dakota 57007 605-688-4151
TENNESSEE	College of Agriculture University of Tennessee P.O. Box 1071 Knoxville, Tennessee 37901 615-974-0111
TEXAS	College of Agriculture Texas A&M University System College Station, Texas 77843 713-845-2217
UTAH	College of Agriculture Utah State University of Agriculture and Applied Sciences Logan, Utah 84322 801-752-4100

VERMONT	College of Agriculture University of Vermont Burlington, Vermont 05401 802-656-3131
VIRGIN ISLANDS	College of Virgin Islands P.O. Box L Kingshill, St. Croix, Virgin Islands 00850 809-778-0246
VIRGINIA	College of Agriculture and Life Sciences Virginia Polytechnic and State University Blacksburg, Virginia 24061 703-951-6000
WASHINGTON	College of Agriculture Washington State University Pullman, Washington 99164 509-335-3564
WEST VIRGINIA	College of Agriculture and Forestry West Virginia University Morgantown, West Virginia 26506 304-293-0111
WISCONSIN	College of Agricultural and Life Sciences University of Wisconsin Madison, Wisconsin 53706 608-262-1234
WYOMING	College of Agriculture University of Wyoming P.O. Box 3354 Laramie, Wyoming 82071 307-766-1121

THE UNITED STATES DEPARTMENT OF AGRICULTURE

The United States Department of Agriculture (USDA), 14th Street and Independence Avenue S.W., Washington, D.C. 20250, Telephone: 202-655-4000, is directed by law to acquire and diffuse useful information on agricultural subjects.

The Extension Service is the educational agency of the department. It works in a three-way partnership with state governments, land grant universities, and county governments.

The Extension Service provides information, advice, and help on agricultural problems.

Appendix B

ESTATE ANALYSIS

Forward-thinking farm families look to estate planning to help build and preserve their wealth and provide comfort and security for the future. The following hypothetical estate analysis, prepared for a client farm family, is intended to determine the need, if any, for additional estate liquidity as well as serve as an aid to the client's legal advisers in preparing wills and trusts appropriate to the client's current estate size and composition.

AN ESTATE ANALYSIS PREPARED FOR FRANK AND JANET NYE FEBRUARY, 1979

Summary of Capital Needs

If Frank dies first, payment of estate settlement costs will require additional liquid assets of . . . . $ 0
The additional capital needed to produce income sufficient to maintain the desired standard of living for the family is $251,173
At Janet's subsequent death, estate settlement costs will require additional liquid assets of . . . . $ 29,034

If Janet dies first, payment of estate settlement costs will require additional liquid assets of . . . . $ 0
The additional capital needed to produce income sufficient to maintain the desired standard of living for the family is . . . . $ 0
At Frank's subsequent death, estate settlement costs will require additional liquid assets of . . . . $ 89,789

These needs can be satisfied by creating new capital at the deaths of Frank and Janet. Life insurance will create the necessary capital at the precise moment of need.

To satisfy all capital needs at the death of Frank, regardless of the order of deaths, additional life insurance is needed on his life in the amount of $251,173

To satisfy all capital needs at the death of Janet, regardless of the order of deaths, additional life insurance is needed on her life in the amount of . . . . $ 29,034

Feb. 1, 1979

Prologue: The Beginning of Estate Conservation

Thoughtful people have a genuine concern for their family's welfare. They want to leave an estate which is adequate to provide a certain standard of living for their family.

To reach these objectives, these questions must be answered:

How large an estate will my family receive?
Will that estate be adequate to maintain their way of life?
How should my estate be transferred?

The purpose of the prologue report is to help you arrive at realistic answers to the first two questions and to describe, generally, ideas that many people are using to answer the third question.

It must be noted, however, that many of the ideas mentioned are of a legal nature. Only your attorney can determine whether they are suited to your specific needs.

An estate consists of real estate, securities, savings, business interests, life insurance, and a great variety of other personal property.

Before an estate can be passed on to the heirs, settlement costs must be paid. Settlement costs consist of taxes, debts, and probate expenses. Recent studies indicate that these costs may vary from 14 to 74 percent of the estate depending upon its size, the nature of the assets, and its disposition. Furthermore, at the subsequent death of the surviving spouse the process is repeated, and taxes, debts, and expenses must be paid again, resulting in an additional drain upon the family assets (see Figure A-1).

Your prologue report shows what it may cost to pass on your estate and the estate of your spouse. It also puts you in a position to take steps to minimize the taxes and expenses imposed upon your combined estates and to arrange in advance for the prompt and efficient settlement of your combined estates.

Expenses and taxes associated with death often can be reduced. For example, the federal estate tax law through the Tax Reform Act of 1976 provides a unified credit and a marital deduction. The unified credit permits the estate of each decedent an estate tax credit of up to $47,000 by 1981, which means that approximately $175,000 may be passed by the decedent free of estate taxation. In addition, the marital deduction permits the larger of $250,000 or half of the adjusted gross estate (assets minus liabilities and expenses) to be passed to the surviving spouse free of estate taxation. As a result, only that portion of the estate which exceeds $425,000 (the amount necessary to maximize the unified credit and the maximum marital deduction) will be subject to estate taxation if properly planned.

In most cases, there will be administration expenses and possibly estate taxation upon the death of the first to die. Passing all of the estate to the spouse can result in a portion of the first estate being again subjected to these death related expenses when the surviving spouse dies.

Estate Inventory*

	Frank	*Janet*	*Joint*
General assets			
Farm reality (35%)	$300,000	$	$
Household articles			5,000
Personal articles			5,000
Unmarketable securities	70,000		
Farm partnership	150,000		
Savings accounts (L)			5,000
Marketable securities (L)	4,000	4,000	
Estate taxable value	$524,000	$ 4,000	$15,000
Life insurance (net)			
On life of Frank	$ 52,500	$20,000	
(cash value)		(4,103)	
On life of Janet		5,364	
Estate taxable value	$ 52,500	$25,364	
Employee death benefits			
Pension plan (1)	$ 780	per year	
Estate taxable value	$ 0		
Liquid assets owned by children			
Savings accounts (2)	$ 3,000		
Securities (2)	4,000		
Estate taxable value	$ 0		
Liabilities			
Funeral and last illness	$ 3,000	$ 3,000	$
	$ 3,000	$ 3,000	$ 0
Total liabilities	$ 6,000		
Total estate assets	$620,864		

*Notes:
(L) = liquid.
(1) = $68 per month for life to Janet. Proceeds are not estate taxable.
(2) = Not included in the estate for federal estate tax purposes.

This double subjection to both administration expenses and estate taxation can be avoided by the use of a trust (Figure A-2). That portion of the estate subject to taxation at the first death can be left in trust for the benefit of the surviving spouse. Upon the subsequent death of the surviving spouse, the trust assets can escape taxation and administration expenses in the estate of the surviving spouse. The trust can continue for the benefit of the heirs, or it can terminate upon the death of the surviving spouse.

Figure A-1 Frank Dies First—Entire Estate to Janet

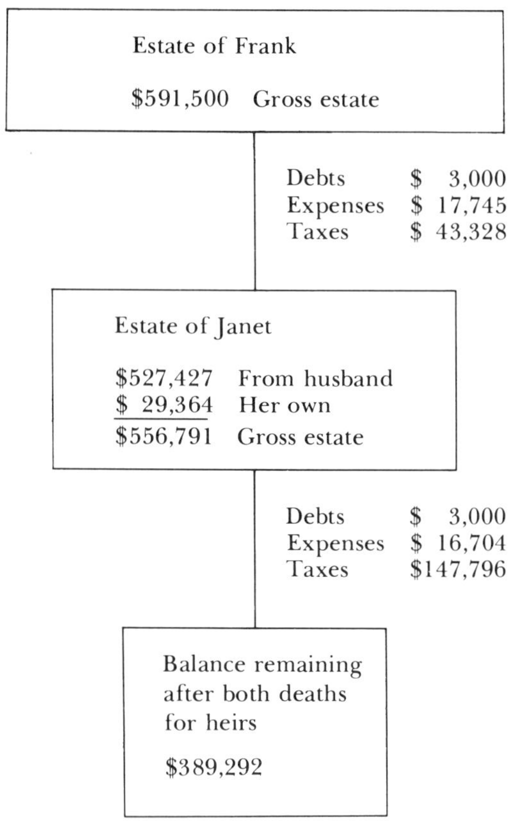

Figure A-2 Frank Dies First—Marital Share to Janet

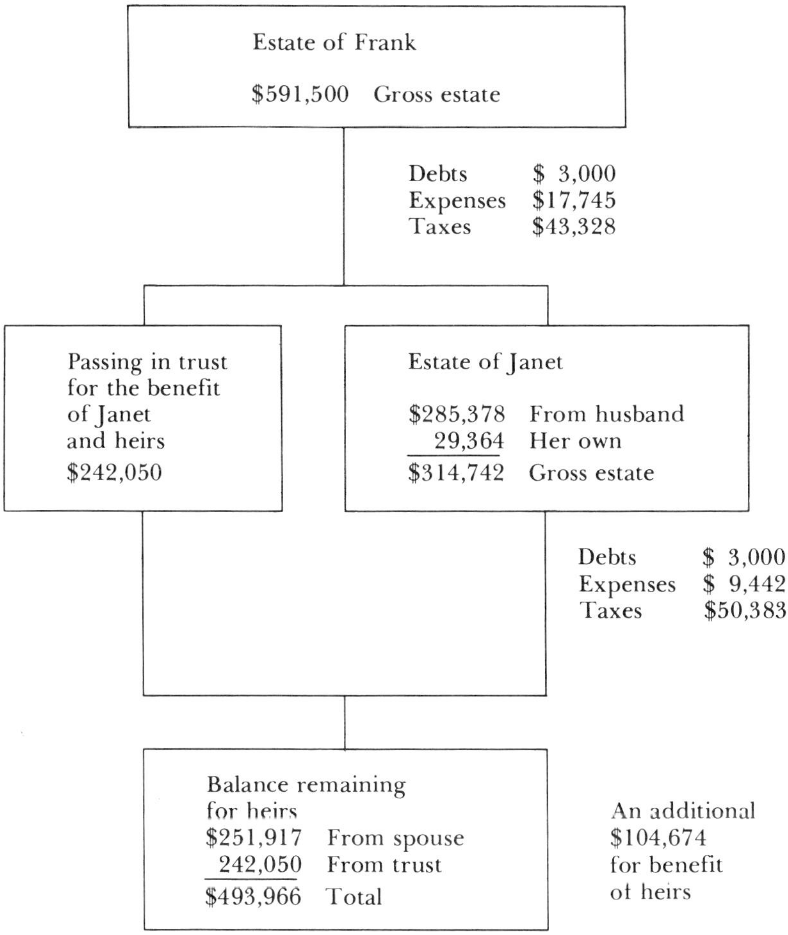

Estate settlement costs, consisting of taxes, debts, and expenses, must be paid in cash. Unfortunately, recent studies reveal that three out of four estates lack of sufficient cash to pay the settlement costs (Figure A-3). As a result, most executors and administrators are forced to liquidate estate assets. Such forced sales may result in heavy losses as well as capital gains taxation.

By providing your estate and the estate of your spouse with the necessary liquidity, you can avoid the forced sale of your assets and the associated delays in the probate of your estates.

The assets that remain after paying the estate settlement costs must be sufficient to provide an income which will permit the surviving family to continue their way of life.

It has been estimated that most surviving families require from 50 to 70 percent of the income they were receiving before the death of the principal breadwinner (see Figure A-4).

Figure A-3 Settlement Costs and Liquidity Needs at the Prior Death of Frank

	Frank Dies		Janet Dies
Settlement costs			
Debts	$ 3,000		$ 3,000
Mortgage	0		0
Administration (3.00%)	17,745		9,442
Estimated federal tax	32,579		37,908
Estimated state tax	10,749		12,475
Total costs	$64,073		$62,825
Your family must be prepared to pay costs of at the death of Frank.		$ 64,073	
Additional funds are needed to pay costs of at the subsequent death of Janet.		$ 62,825	
The settlement costs to both estates will be		$126,898	
Liquidity needs			
Liquid assets available (from entire family)	$92,500		$33,791
Liquid assets required for settlement costs	−64,073		−62,825
Education reserve	− 0		0
Liquidity shortage	$ 0		$29,034

Unless these liquidity needs are satisfied, your executors will be forced to sell estate assets for the best available price.

Figure A-4 Income Analysis at the Prior Death of Frank

Once the liquidity needs of Frank's estate have been satisfied, the family income situation will be as follows:

Family income desired		$14,760
Family income available		
From liquid assets at 5.00%	$1,421	
From nonliquid assets at 5.00%	0	
Estimated social security benefits	0	
From all other sources	780	
Total income available		2,201
Family income shortage		$12,559

The family income shortage can be eliminated by adding capital of $251,173, yielding a 5.00% return.

The previous pages have assumed a particular order of death. However, estate conservation requires that a husband and wife be prepared for a reversal in the order of their deaths (Figures A-5, A-6, and A-7).

If a husband has most of the family assets in his name, his estate can be subject to higher taxes in the event his wife predeceases him. In the absence of a surviving wife, the husband's estate receives no marital deduction and the loss of that marital deduction to his estate may substantially increase the tax payable.

In addition, the estate of either spouse may be much greater than initially anticipated. For example, if a husband and wife hold property as joint tenants, all of that property may be taxed in the estate of the wife if she dies first except to the extent that the husband can produce convincing proof that he contributed to the purchase of those assets; such proof is often difficult or impossible to produce.

Finally, the death of either spouse can cause financial hardship. In the event the chief breadwinner dies, the economic loss is clearly apparent. However, to an increasing extent today, both the husband and wife work and bring home incomes. The death of either may result in a loss of income to the family. Even if the spouse is not employed outside the home, a substantial economic loss, such as additional expenses for child care and housekeeping, may be incurred (see Figure A-8).

Figure A-5 Janet Dies First—Entire Estate to Frank

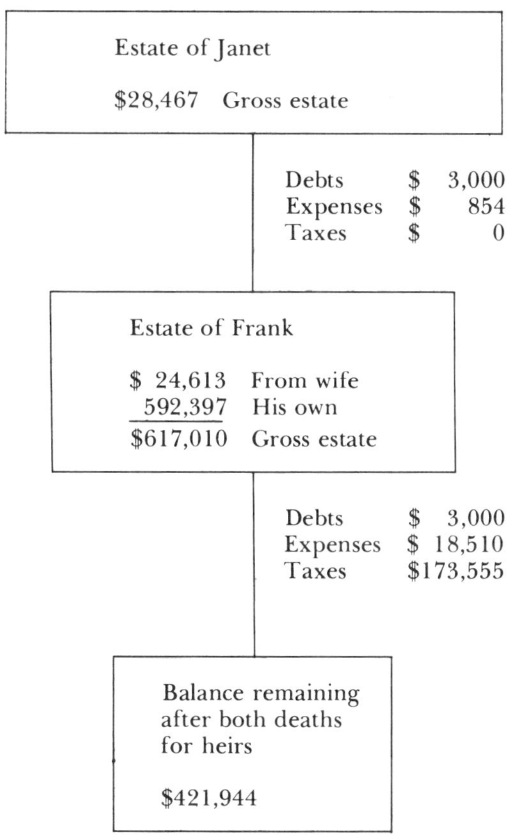

Figure A-6 Janet Dies First—Marital Share to Frank

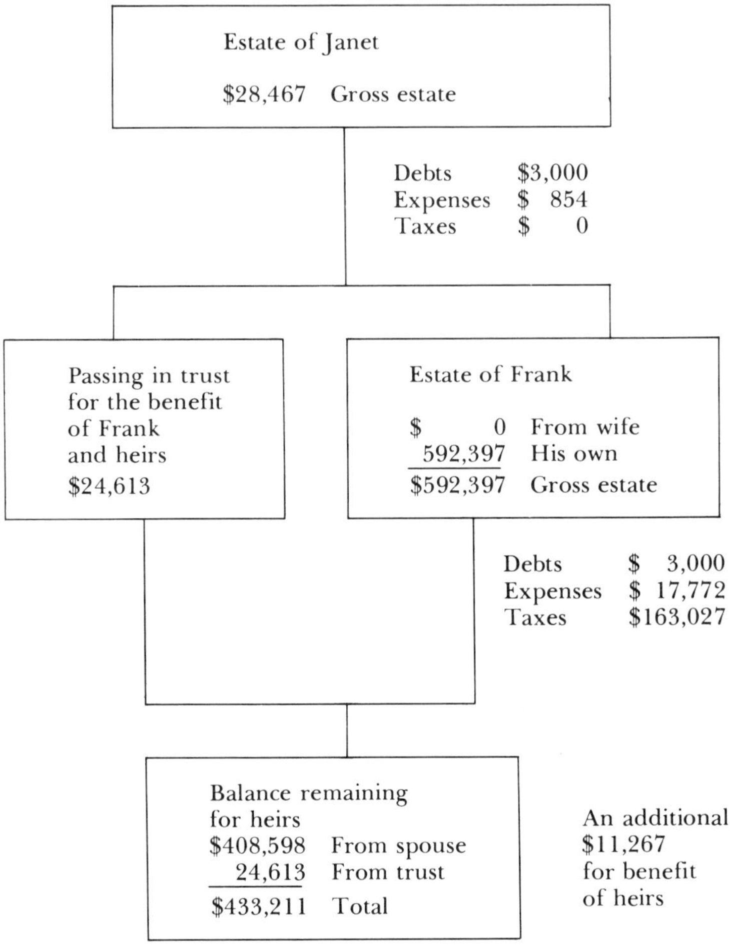

Figure A-7 Settlement Costs and Liquidity Needs at the Prior Death of Janet

	Janet Dies	Frank Dies
Settlement costs		
Debts	$ 3,000	$ 3,000
Mortgage	0	0
Administration (3.00%)	854	17,772
Estimated federal tax	0	122,436
Estimated state tax	0	40,590
Total costs	$ 3,854	$183,799

Your family must be prepared to pay costs of at the death of Janet.	$ 3,854
Additional funds are needed to pay costs of at the subsequent death of Frank.	$183,799
The settlement costs to both estates will be	$187,653

	Janet Dies	Frank Dies
Liquidity needs		
Liquid assets available (from entire family)	$25,364	$ 94,010
Liquid assets required for settlement costs	− 3,854	−183,799
Education reserve	0	− 0
Liquidity shortage	$ 0	$ 89,789

Unless these liquidity needs are satisfied, your executors will be forced to sell estate assets for the best available price.

Figure A-8 Income Analysis at the Prior Death of Janet

Once the liquidity needs of Janet's estate have been satisfied, the family income situation will be as follows:

Family income available		
From earnings of Frank	$24,600	
From liquid assets at 5.00%	1,075	
From nonliquid assets at 5.00%	0	
Estimated social security benefits	0	
From all other sources	0	
Total income available		$25,675

APPENDIX: ESTATE GROWTH

Your capital needs will increase in the future as your estate continues to grow (see Figure A-9).

The present value of your combined estates is $620,864. Assuming a growth rate of 5.00%, your estates will be worth:

in 5 years . . . .$ 770,885
in 10 years . . . .$ 962,354
in 20 years $1,518,605

Your estimated settlement costs will increase as your estates grow. Assuming Frank dies first, the total estate settlement costs in both estates will be:

in 5 years . . . .$ 139,502
in 10 years . . . .$ 200,556
in 20 years . . . .$ 388,281

Figure A-9 Estate Tax Calculations

	Frank Dies First	*At Death of Janet*
Assets		
Separate	$591,500	$ 29,364
Received from spouse	0	285,378
Gross estate	$591,500	$314,742
Expenses		
Administration costs (3.00%)	$ 17,745	$ 9,442
Liabilities	3,000	3,000
Total deductible expenses	$ 20,745	$ 12,442
Marital deduction		
Gross estate	$591,500	
Less expenses	– 20,745	
Adjusted gross estate	$570,755	
Marital deduction available	$285,378	
Tax calculations		
Gross estate	$591,500	$314,742
Deductible expenses	– 20,745	– 12,442
Marital deduction taken	–285,378	0
Orphan's exclusion	– 0	– 0
Federal taxable estate	$285,378	$302,299
Aggregate taxable gifts	0	0
Tentative taxable estate	$285,378	$302,299
Tentative tax	$ 82,828	$ 88,582
Aggregate gift tax	– 0	– 0
Unified credit	– 47,000	– 47,000
State tax credit	– 3,249	– 3,674
Estimated federal tax	$ 32,579	$ 37,908
Estimated state tax	10,749	12,475
Total estimated taxes	$ 43,328	$ 50,383

Figure A-10 Estate Tax Calculations

	Janet Dies First	At Death of Frank
Assets		
Separate	$28,467	$592,397
Received from spouse	0	0
Gross estate	$28,467	$592,397
Expenses		
Administration costs (3.00%)	854	17,772
Liabilities	3,000	3,000
Total deductible expenses	$ 3,854	$ 20,772
Marital deduction		
Gross estate	$28,467	
Less expenses	− 3,854	
Adjusted gross estate	$24,613	
Marital deduction available	$24,613	
Tax calculations		
Gross estate	$28,467	$592,397
Deductible expenses	− 3,854	− 20,772
Marital deduction taken	− 0	0
Orphan's exclusion	− 0	− 0
Federal taxable estate	$24,613	$571,625
Aggregate taxable gifts	0	0
Tentative taxable estate	$24,613	$571,625
Tentative tax	$ 4,815	$182,301
Aggregate gift tax	− 0	− 0
Unified credit	− 4,815	− 47,000
State tax credit	− 0	− 12,865
Estimated federal tax	$ 0	$122,436
Estimated state tax	0	40,590
Total estimated taxes	$ 0	$163,027

NOTES

The information contained in this report is not intended to be legal in nature. It is intended only to provide an estimate of personal needs for life insurance.

Based on the tax reform act of 1976, the estimates of capital needs are calculated on the assumption that the estate has been divided into marital and trust portions. The marital portion is assumed to be no higher than the maximum marital deduction allowable under federal estate tax law and may be less than the maximum in order to fully utilize the unified credit. The trust portion is assumed not to be includable in the gross estate of the surviving spouse for purposes of the federal estate tax. The orphan's exclusion, if any, is based on the family's current composition.

It is assumed that all family liquid assets are available to pay settlement costs, either because the assets are owned by the estate or because the owner of the liquid asset has exchanged it for other assets of the estate.

The values shown for federal and state taxes are estimates only and are based on an approximation of the size of the taxable estate and the most common distribution patterns of estate assets.

If an education reserve is established for the benefit of the children, it is assumed the fund is a separate account in which all income is accumulated to offset the effects of inflation and rising education costs.

All liquid assets remaining after the payment of estate settlement costs are assumed to be available to produce income for the family at the stated rate of return.

It is assumed that the estate has or will obtain sufficient liquidity to avoid the necessity of liquidating nonliquid assets. Nonliquid income producing assets are considered to be available for family income purposes at the amount specified.

The estate growth computations are made by applying the growth rate, compounded, to the present value of all estate assets except life insurance. The liabilities and the amount of life insurance included in the taxable estates remains constant. The unified credit and orphan's exclusion are adjusted to reflect their projected value in the years specified. It is assumed that all future life insurance policies will be held in a manner to eliminate estate taxation.

Case history prepared courtesy of the National Life Insurance Company, Montpelier, Vermont 05602.

Appendix C

SUMMARY OF STATE DEATH TAXES

The chart that follows gives capsule descriptions of the death taxes levied by the various states. Where the type of tax is listed as "credit estate tax," the tax levied is the maximum federal credit for state death taxes. Where the tax is an inheritance tax, the exemptions and tax rates listed are the maximum and minimum amounts (e.g., in California a spouse receives a $60,000 exemption and the tax rate is 6 to 14 percent, depending on the size of the distribution; a nonrelative receives a $300 exemption and the tax is between 10 and 24 percent). Where both an inheritance or estate tax and a credit estate tax are listed, the credit estate tax is payable only if the tax under the basic state death tax is less than the maximum federal credit. "Payment" indicates the time after death when the state tax is due (unless an extension is granted and payable without penalty). "Assessed on" indicates whether the tax is payable from the residuary estate or is paid proportionately by the beneficiaries (unless the will provides otherwise).

Local law should always be checked for recent changes enacted by state legislatures.

Alabama
Type: Credit estate tax
Payment due: 15 months
Assessed on: Residuary estate

Alaska
Type: Credit estate tax
Payment due: 15 months
Assessed on: Pro rata

Arizona
Type: Estate tax and credit estate tax
Exemption: $100,000
Rates: 0.8%–16%
Payment due: 9 months
Assessed on: Residuary estate

Arkansas
Type: Credit estate tax
Payment due: 9 months
Assessed on: Pro rata

California
Type: Inheritance tax and credit estate tax
Exemptions:
Class A: Spouse: $60,000
Minor child: $12,000
Lineal ancestors: $5,000
ClassB: Sibling: $2,000
Class C: Others: $300

California (Cont.)
Rates:
Class A: Spouse: 6%–14%
Minor child, lineal ancestor: 3%–14%
Class B: 6%–20%
Class C: 10%–24%
Payment due: 9 months
Assessed on: Pro rata

Colorado
Type: Inheritance tax and credit estate tax
Exemptions:
Class A: Spouse: $75,000
Minor child: $37,500
Parent and others: $25,000
Class B: Siblings, grandparents: $3,000
Class C: Aunt, uncle, nephew, niece: $500
Class D: Others: $500
Rates:
Class A: 3%–9%
Class B: 4%–11%
Class C: 7%–17%
Class D: 11%–20%
Payment due: 9 months
Assessed on: Pro rata

Connecticut
Type: Inheritance tax and credit estate tax
Exemptions:
Class AA: Spouse: $100,000
Class A: Parent, child, grandparent: $20,000
Class B: Sibling, spouse of adopted or natural child: $6,000
Class C: Others: $1,000
Rates:
Class AA: 3%–8%
Class A: 2%–8%
Class B: 4%–10%
Class C: 8%–14%
Payment due: 9 months
Assessed on: Pro rata

Delaware
Type: Inheritance tax and credit estate tax

Delaware (Cont.)
Exemptions:
Class A: Spouse: $70,000
Class B: Child, parent, grandparent: $3,000
Class C: Sibling: $1,000
Class D: Others: none
Rates:
Class A: 2%– 4%
Class B: 1%– 6%
Class C: 5%–10%
Class D: 10%–16%
Payment due: 9 months
Assessed on: Pro rata

District of Columbia
Type: Inheritance tax and credit estate tax
Exemptions:
Class A: Spouse, parent, child, lineal descendant: $5,000
Class B: Repealed 12/15/71
Class C: Others: $1,000
Rates:
Class A: 1%– 8%
Class C: 5%–23%
Payment due: 18 months
Assessed on: Pro rata

Florida
Type: Credit estate tax
Payment due: 9 months
Assessed on: Residuary estate

Georgia
Type: Credit estate tax
Payment due: On or before date of filing of the duplicate federal estate tax return
Assessed on: Residuary estate

Hawaii
Type: Inheritance tax and credit estate tax
Exemptions:
Class A: Spouse: $100,000
Class B: Parent, child: $50,000
Class C: Others: $5,000
Rates:
Class A: 2%– 7%
Class B: 3%– 8%
Class C: 3%–10%

Hawaii (Cont.)
Payment due: 18 months
Assessed on: Pro rata

Idaho
Type: Inheritance tax and credit estate tax
Exemptions:
Class 1: Spouse, child: $30,000
Others: $15,000
Class 2: Sibling: $10,000
Class 3: Aunt, uncle: $10,000
Class 4: Others: $10,000
Rates:
Class 1: 2%–15%
Class 2: 4%–20%
Class 3: 6%–25%
Class 4: 8%–30%
Payment due: 9 months
Assessed on: Pro rata

Illinois
Type: Inheritance tax and credit estate tax
Exemptions:
Class A: Spouse, child: $20,000 plus the lesser of: $20,000 or the sum which, deducted from the gross value of the transfers, reduces the tax by $1,200
Parent, lineal ancestor: $20,000
Sibling: $10,000
Class B: Uncle, aunt, niece, nephew: $500
Class C: Others: $100
Rates:
Class A: 2%–14%
Class B: 6%–16%
Class C: 10%–30%
Payment due: At death of decedent or, if assessed or appraised by order, 10 months to pay
Assessed on: Pro rata

Indiana
Type: Inheritance tax and credit estate tax
Exemptions:
Class A: Spouse: $60,000
Minor child: $5,000
Others: $2,000

Indiana (Cont.)
Class B: Sibling: $500
Class C: Others: $100
Rates:
Class A: 1%–10%
Class B: 7%–15%
Class C: 10%–20%
Payment due: 18 months
Assessed on: Pro rata

Iowa
Type: Inheritance tax and credit estate tax
Exemptions:
Class A: Spouse: $80,000
Child: $30,000
Parent, other lineal descendant: $10,000
Class B: Sibling: none
Class C: Others: none
Class D: Societies, institutions, or associations organized under law, for charitable, educational or religious purposes: none
Class E: Firm, or corporation for profit: none
Rates:
Class A: 1%– 8%
Class B: 5%–10%
Class C: 10%–15%
Class D: Flat 10%
Class E: Flat 15%
Payment due: 12 months
Assessed on: Pro rata

Kansas
Type: Inheritance tax and credit estate tax
Exemptions:
Class A: Spouse: $250,000 (available to estates of decedents dying after 12/31/78)
Lineal descendants and ancestors: $30,000
Class B: Sibling: $5,000
Class C: Others: none (unless the share is less than $200, in which case the entire amount is exempt)

Kansas (Cont.)
Rates:
Class A: Spouse: 0.5%–2.5%
Lineal descendants and ancestors: 1%–5%
Class B: 3%–12.5%
Class C: 10%–15%
Payment due: 9 months
Assessed on: Pro rata

Kentucky
Type: Inheritance tax and credit estate tax
Exemptions:
Class A: Spouse: $50,000
Minor child: $20,000
Parent, grandchild: $5,000
Class B: Sibling, aunt, uncle, niece, nephew: $1,000
Class C: Others: $500
Rates:
Class A: 2%–10%
Class B: 4%–16%
Class C: 6%–16%
Payment due: 18 months
Assessed on: Pro rata

Louisiana
Type: Inheritance tax and credit estate tax
Exemptions:
Class A: Spouse, direct descendant: $5,000
Class B: Sibling: $1,000
Class C: Others: $500
Rates:
Class A: 2%–13%
Class B: 5%– 7%
Class C: 5%–10%
Payment due: 9 months
Assessed on: Pro rata

Maine
Type: Inheritance tax and credit estate tax
Exemptions:
Class A: Spouse: $50,000
Parent, child, grandchild: $25,000 (if more than one grandchild, the total exemption is $25,000)
Grandparents: $2,000

Maine (Cont.)
Class B: Sibling: $1,000
Class C: Others: $1,000
Rates:
Class A: 5%–10%
Class B: 8%–14%
Class C: 14%–18%
Payment due: 12 months
Assessed on: Pro rata

Maryland
Type: Inheritance tax and credit estate tax
Exemptions:
Class A: Spouse, parent, children, lineal descendant or any joint savings account of less than an aggregate of $2,000 of any spouse of a lineal descendant of decedent: $150
Surviving spouse: additional $1,000
Unmarried child (under age 18): $500
Class B: Others: $150
Rates:
Class A: Flat 1%
Class B: Flat 10%
Payment due: Within 30 days after the time of the accounting for its distribution
Assessed on: Pro rata

Massachusetts
Type: Estate tax and credit estate tax
Exemption: $30,000 unless the Massachusetts net estate is $60,000 or less, in which case the exemption is equal to the Massachusetts net estate
Rates: 5%–16%
Payment due: 9 months
Assessed on: Pro rata

Michigan
Type: Inheritance tax and credit estate tax
Exemptions:

Michigan (Cont.)
Class A: Spouse $30,000 (additional $5,000 exemption for each minor child to whom no property is transferred)
Parent, child, sibling, grandchildren: $5,000
Class B: Others: none
Rates:
Class A: 2%–10%
Class B: 10%–17%
Payment due: 9 months
Assessed on: Pro rata

Minnesota
Type: Inheritance tax and credit estate tax
Exemptions:
Class 1: Spouse: $60,000
Minor child: $30,000
Class 2: Adult child or lineal descendant: $6,000
Class 3: Sibling or descendant of sibling: $1,500
Class 4: Others: $500
Rates:
Class 1: 1.5%–10%
Class 2: 2%–10%
Class 3: 6%–25%
Class 4: 8%–30%
(In lieu of the inheritance tax rates, there is the marital exemption tax, which can be used if it is less than the inheritance tax rates on property passing to the surviving spouse. The marital exemption is 50%, but not more than $250,000, of the net taxable value passing to the surviving spouse.)
Payment due: 12 months
Assessed on: Pro rata

Mississippi
Type: Estate tax
Exemption: The value of the taxable estate is determined by deducting the following sums from the gross estate: 1978—$120,666; 1979—$134,000; 1980—$147,333;

Mississippi (Cont.)
1981—$161,563; 1982—or thereafter, $175,625
Rates: 1%–16%
Payment due: 9 months
Assessed on: Residuary estate

Missouri
Type: Inheritance tax and credit estate tax
Exemptions:
Class A: Spouse: $20,000
Insane, blind: $15,000
Lineal descendant: $5,000
(in addition, an exemption is allowed for the clear market value of one-half of the decedent's estate or one-third if the decedent is survived by lineal descendants)
Class B: Sibling: $500
Aunt, uncle: $250
Class C: Great-aunt and great-uncle: $100
Class D: Others: if less than $100, not taxed
Rates:
Class A: 1%– 6%
Class B: 3%–18%
Class C: 4%–24%
Class D: 5%–30%
Payment due: 9 months
Assessed on: Pro rata

Montana
Type: Inheritance tax and credit estate tax
Exemptions:
Class 1: Spouse: $40,000
Minor child: $15,000
Lineal ancestor: $7,000
Class 2: Sibling: $1,000
Class 3: Aunt, uncle, or first cousin: none
Class 4: Others: none
Rates:
Class 1: 2%– 8%
Class 2: 4%–16%
Class 3: 6%–24%
Class 4: 8%–32%

Montana (Cont.)
Payment due: 18 months
Assessed on: Pro rata

Nebraska
Type: Inheritance tax and credit estate tax
Exemptions:
Class A: Spouse, parent, child, sibling, lineal descendant: $10,000
Class B: Uncle, aunt, niece, nephew: $2,000
Class C: Others: $500
Rates:
Class A: Flat 1%
Class B: 6%– 9%
Class C: 6%–18%
Payment due: 10 months
Assessed on: Pro rata

Nevada
No state death tax

New Hampshire
Type: Inheritance tax and credit estate tax
Exemptions: No tax on spouse, children and parents
Rates: All (except spouse, children, and parents) are taxed at a flat 15%
Payment due: 12 months
Assessed on: Pro rata

New Jersey
Type: Inheritance tax and credit estate tax
Exemptions:
Class A: Spouse, parent, grandparent, child: $15,000
Class B: Repealed 7/1/63
Class C: Sibling: if share is less than $500, there is no tax; otherwise there is no exemption
Class D: Others: Same as Class C
Rates:
Class A: 2%–16%
Class C: 11%–16%
Class D: 15%–16%
Payment due: 8 months
Assessed on: Pro rata

New Mexico
Type: Credit estate tax
Payment due: 9 months
Assessed on: Pro rata

New York
Type: Estate tax and credit estate tax
Credits: If tax is $2,750 or less: full amount of tax
If tax is between $2,750 and $5,000: difference between tax and $5,500
If tax is more than $5,000: $500
Other credits: see statute
Rates: 2%–21%
Payment due: At time of decedent's death, but interest does not accrue until 6 months after death
Assessed on: Pro rata

North Carolina
Type: Inheritance tax and credit estate tax
Exemptions:
Class A: Spouse: $20,000
Minor child, or child over age of 18 who is physically or mentally disabled: $5,000
Other lineal ancestors: $2,000
(see statute for exceptions)
Class B: Sibling, aunt, uncle: none
Class C: Others: none
Rates:
Class A: 1%–12%
Class B: 4%–16%
Class C: 8%–17%
Payment due: At decedent's death, but no interest is charged if the tax is paid within 9 months of the death
Assessed on: Pro rata

North Dakota
Type: Estate tax
Exemption: $200,000
Rates: 4%–18%
Payment due: At decedent's death, but no interest is charged if the tax is paid within 15 months after death
Assessed on: Pro rata

Ohio
Type: Estate tax and credit estate tax
Exemptions: $50,000 (but $30,000 for spouse, $7,000 for child under 18, and $3,000 for child over 18)
Rates: 2%–7%
Payment due: 9 months
Assessed on: Pro rata

Oklahoma
Type: Estate tax and credit estate tax
Exemptions:
Class 1: Parent, child, and lineal descendant: aggregate of $60,000 (there is a complete exemption for spouse except for calculating credit estate tax)
Class 2: Others: none
Rates:
Class 1: 1%–10%
Class 2: 2%–15%
Payment due: 9 months
Assessed on: Pro rata

Oregon
Type: Inheritance tax and credit estate tax
Exemption: $50,000 (various credits allowed depending on the class of beneficiaries)
Rates: Flat 12%
Payment due: 9 months
Assessed on: Pro rata

Pennsylvania
Type: Inheritance tax and credit estate tax
Exemptions:
Class A: Spouse, parents, grandparents, child, lineal descendants: none (except, there is a $2,000 family exemption)
Class B: Others: none
Rates:
Class A: Flat 6%
Class B: Flat 15%
Payment due: 9 months
Assessed on: Pro rata

Puerto Rico
Type: Estate tax
Exemption: $60,000
Rates: 3%–70%
Payment due: 270 days
Assessed on: Pro rata

Rhode Island
Type: Estate tax, inheritance tax, and credit estate tax
Exemption:
Estate tax: $10,000 (plus a marital deduction of $40,000)
Inheritance tax:
Class A: $50,000
Class B: Parent, children, grandparent: $10,000
Class C: Stepchildren, stepparents, siblings: $5,000
Class D: Nieces, nephews: $3,000
Class E: Others: $1,000
Rates:
Estate Tax: Flat 1%
Inheritance tax:
Class A: 4%– 9%
Class B: 2%– 9%
Class C: 3%–10%
Class D: 4%–11%
Class E: 8%–15%
Payment due: 6 months
Assessed on: Pro rata

South Carolina
Type: Estate tax and credit estate tax
Exemption: $60,000
Rates: 4%–6%
Payment due: 9 months
Assessed on: Pro rata

South Dakota
Type: Inheritance tax
Exemptions:
Class 1: Spouse: $80,000 (effective 7/1/79, increases to $100,000)
Lineal issue: $30,000
Class 2: Lineal ancestor: $3,000
Class 3: Sibling: $500
Class 4: Aunt, uncle: $200
Class 5: Others: $100

South Dakota (Cont.)
Rates:
Class 1: 1.5%–6%
Class 2: 3%–12%
Class 3: 4%–16%
Class 4: 5%–20%
Class 5: 6%–24%
Payment due: As soon as the amount is determined, but no interest is charged if the tax is paid within 12 months of decedent's death
Assessed on: Pro rata

Tennessee
Type: Inheritance tax and credit estate tax
Exemptions:
Class A: Spouse, child, lineal ancestor: $120,000
Class B: Others: $10,000
Rates:
Class A: 6.5%–16%
Class B: 6.5%–20%
Payment due: 9 months
Assessed on: Pro rata

Texas
Type: Inheritance tax and credit estate tax
Exemptions:
Class A: Spouse, direct lineal descendant, children: $200,000 (effective 9/1/78 to 8/31/82); $250,000 (9/1/82 to 8/31/85); $300,000 (thereafter). (Exemption is divided proportionately if the value passing to the beneficiaries exceeds the amount of the exemption. However, no Class A beneficiary will receive an exemption less than $25,000.)
Class B: Passing to the United States to be used in the state: $25,000
Class C: Sibling: $10,000
Class D: Aunt, uncle: $1,000
Class E: Others: $500

Texas (Cont.)
Rates:
Class A: 1%– 6%
Class B: 1%– 6%
Class C: 3%–10%
Class D: 4%–15%
Class E: 5%–20%
Payment due: 9 months
Assessed on: Pro rata

Utah
Type: Credit estate tax
Payment due: On or before the date the federal estate tax return is due
Assessed on: Pro rata

Vermont
Type: Estate tax and credit estate tax
Exemption: $60,000
Rates: 30% of federal estate tax. (For decedents dying in 1977 and 1978, the amount of the tax is to be reduced by the percentage which $120,000 is of the amount of the federal taxable estate, but is not to be reduced by more than 100%. For decedents dying in 1979 and thereafter, the amount of tax imposed shall be reduced by the percentage which $240,000 is of the amount of the federal taxable estate, but is not to be reduced by more than $100.)
Payment due: 15 months
Assessed on: Residuary estate

Virginia
Type: Inheritance tax and credit estate tax
Exemptions:
Class A: Spouse, child, parent, grandparent, lineal ancestors: $5,000
Class B: Siblings, nieces, nephews: $2,000
Class C: Grandnephews, grandnieces, others: $1,000
Rates:
Class A: 1%– 5%
Class B: 2%–10%
Class C: 5%–15%
Payment due: 9 months
Assessed on: Pro rata

Washington
Type: Inheritance tax and credit estate tax
Exemptions:
Class A: Spouse, lineal ancestor or descendant: $5,000 plus additional $5,000 for surviving spouse and $5,000 for each child; if none survives, an overall exemption of $10,000 is allowed
Class B: Sibling: $1,000
Class C: Others: none
Rates:
Class A: 1%–10%
Class B: 3%–20%
Class C: 10%–25%
Payment due: 9 months
Assessed on: Pro rata

West Virginia
Type: Inheritance tax and credit estate tax
Exemptions:
Class A: Spouse: $30,000
Child, parent: $10,000
Grandchild: $5,000
Class B: Sibling: none (but if decedent dies unmarried, $10,000 exemption)
Class C: Persons further removed than sibling: none
Class D: Others: none
Rates:
Class A: 3%–13%
Class B: 4%–18%
Class C: 7%–25%
Class D: 10%–30%

West Virginia (Cont.)
Payment due: 11 months
Assessed on: Pro rata

Wisconsin
Type: Inheritance tax and credit estate tax
Exemptions:
Class A: Spouse: $50,000
Lineal issue: $4,000
Class B: Sibling: $1,000
Class C: Aunt, uncle: $1,000
Class D: Others: $500
Rates:
Class A: Spouse: 1.25%–6.25%
Lineal issue: 2.5%–12.5%
Class B: 5%–25%
Class C: 7.5%–30%
Class D: 10%–30%
Payment due: At time of decedent's death, but no interest is charged if tax is paid within 12 months of death
Assessed on: Pro rata

Wyoming
Type: Inheritance tax and credit estate tax
Exemptions:
Class A: Spouse: $60,000
Child, parent, sibling: $10,000
Class B: Grandparent, grandchild: $5,000
Class C: Others: none
Rates:
Class A: Flat 2%
Class B: Flat 4%
Class C: Flat 6%
Payment due: 10 months
Assessed on: Pro rata

Appendix D

LIFE EXPECTATION TABLE

Estate planners and their clients will frequently find it useful to have at hand statistical information on life expectation. The Life Table on the following pages may be used as a planning resource.

Life Table:
Expectation of Life at Single Years of Age*

AGE	TOTAL			WHITE			ALL OTHER		
	BOTH SEXES	MALE	FEMALE	BOTH SEXES	MALE	FEMALE	BOTH SEXES	MALE	FEMALE
0	71.9	68.1	75.8	72.7	68.9	76.6	67.0	62.9	71.3
1	72.1	68.4	75.9	72.8	69.1	76.5	67.7	63.6	71.9
2	71.2	67.5	75.0	71.8	68.2	75.6	66.8	62.7	71.0
3	70.3	66.6	74.1	70.9	67.2	74.7	65.9	61.8	70.0
4	69.3	65.6	73.1	69.9	66.3	73.7	64.9	60.9	69.1
5	68.3	64.7	72.1	69.0	65.3	72.7	64.0	59.9	68.2
6	67.4	63.7	71.2	68.0	64.3	71.7	63.0	59.0	67.2
7	66.4	62.7	70.2	67.0	63.4	70.8	62.1	58.0	66.2
8	65.4	61.8	69.2	66.0	62.4	69.8	61.1	57.0	65.2
9	64.4	60.8	68.2	65.1	61.4	68.8	60.1	56.1	64.3
10	63.5	59.8	67.2	64.1	60.4	67.8	59.1	55.1	63.3
11	62.5	58.8	66.3	63.1	59.5	66.8	58.2	54.1	62.3
12	61.5	57.8	65.3	62.1	58.5	65.9	57.2	53.1	61.3
13	60.5	56.9	64.3	61.1	57.5	64.9	56.2	52.2	60.3
14	59.5	55.9	63.3	60.2	56.5	63.9	55.2	51.2	59.4
15	58.6	54.9	62.3	59.2	55.6	62.9	54.3	50.2	58.4
16	57.6	54.0	61.4	58.2	54.6	61.9	53.3	49.3	57.4
17	56.7	53.1	60.4	57.3	53.7	61.0	52.4	48.4	56.4
18	55.7	52.2	59.4	56.3	52.8	60.0	51.4	47.4	55.5
19	54.8	51.3	58.5	55.4	51.9	59.0	50.5	46.6	54.5
20	53.9	50.3	57.5	54.5	51.0	58.1	49.6	45.7	53.6
21	53.0	49.4	56.5	53.5	50.1	57.1	48.7	44.8	52.6
22	52.0	48.6	55.6	52.6	49.2	56.1	47.8	44.0	51.7
23	51.1	47.7	54.6	51.7	48.3	55.2	46.9	43.1	50.8
24	50.2	46.8	53.7	50.7	47.4	54.2	46.0	42.3	49.8
25	49.2	45.9	52.7	49.8	46.4	53.2	45.1	41.5	48.9
26	48.3	45.0	51.7	48.9	45.5	52.3	44.3	40.6	48.0
27	47.4	44.0	50.8	47.9	44.6	51.3	43.4	39.8	47.0
28	46.4	43.1	49.8	47.0	43.7	50.3	42.5	39.0	46.1
29	45.5	42.2	48.8	46.0	42.7	49.4	41.6	38.1	45.2
30	44.6	41.3	47.9	45.1	41.8	48.4	40.8	37.3	44.3
31	43.6	40.4	46.9	44.1	40.9	47.4	39.9	36.5	43.3
32	42.7	39.5	46.0	43.2	39.9	46.5	39.0	35.7	42.4
33	41.8	38.5	45.0	42.2	39.0	45.5	38.2	34.8	41.5
34	40.8	37.6	44.1	41.3	38.1	44.6	37.3	34.0	40.6
35	39.9	36.7	43.1	40.4	37.2	43.6	36.4	33.2	39.7
36	39.0	35.8	42.2	39.4	36.2	42.7	35.6	32.4	38.8
37	38.1	34.9	41.2	38.5	35.3	41.7	34.7	31.6	37.9
38	37.1	34.0	40.3	37.6	34.4	40.8	33.9	30.8	37.0
39	36.2	33.1	39.4	36.6	33.5	39.8	33.1	30.0	36.2

40	35.3	32.2	38.4	35.7	32.6	38.9	32.2	29.2	35.3
41	34.4	31.3	37.5	34.8	31.7	37.9	31.4	28.4	34.4
42	33.5	30.4	36.6	33.9	30.8	37.0	30.6	27.7	33.6
43	32.6	29.6	35.7	33.0	29.9	36.1	29.8	26.9	32.8
44	31.7	28.7	34.8	32.1	29.0	35.2	29.0	26.2	31.9
45	30.9	27.8	33.9	31.2	28.1	34.3	28.2	25.4	31.1
46	30.0	27.0	33.0	30.3	27.3	33.4	27.5	24.7	30.3
47	29.1	26.2	32.1	29.4	26.4	32.5	26.7	24.0	29.5
48	28.3	25.4	31.2	28.6	25.6	31.6	26.0	23.3	28.7
49	27.5	24.5	30.4	27.7	24.8	30.7	25.2	22.6	27.9
50	26.6	23.7	29.5	26.9	24.0	29.8	24.5	21.9	27.1
51	25.8	23.0	28.6	26.1	23.2	28.9	23.8	21.2	26.4
52	25.0	22.2	27.8	25.2	22.4	28.1	23.1	20.6	25.6
53	24.2	21.4	26.9	24.4	21.6	27.2	22.4	19.9	24.9
54	23.4	20.7	26.1	23.6	20.8	26.3	21.7	19.3	24.1
55	22.6	19.9	25.3	22.8	20.1	25.5	21.1	18.7	23.4
56	21.9	19.2	24.4	22.0	19.3	24.7	20.4	18.1	22.7
57	21.1	18.5	23.6	21.3	18.6	23.8	19.8	17.5	22.0
58	20.4	17.8	22.8	20.5	17.9	23.0	19.2	17.0	21.3
59	19.6	17.1	22.0	19.8	17.2	22.2	18.5	16.4	20.6
60	18.9	16.4	21.2	19.0	16.5	21.4	17.9	15.9	19.9
61	18.2	15.8	20.5	18.3	15.9	20.6	17.4	15.4	19.3
62	17.5	15.2	19.7	17.6	15.2	19.9	16.8	14.9	18.7
63	16.9	14.6	19.0	16.9	14.6	19.1	16.2	14.4	18.1
64	16.2	14.0	18.2	16.3	14.0	18.3	15.7	13.9	17.4
65	15.5	13.4	17.5	15.6	13.4	17.6	15.1	13.4	16.8
66	14.9	12.8	16.7	14.9	12.8	16.8	14.6	12.9	16.2
67	14.3	12.2	16.0	14.3	12.2	16.1	14.0	12.4	15.5
68	13.6	11.7	15.3	13.7	11.7	15.3	13.4	11.9	14.9
69	13.0	11.2	14.6	13.0	11.2	14.6	12.9	11.4	14.3
70	12.4	10.7	13.9	12.4	10.6	13.9	12.4	11.0	13.8
71	11.9	10.2	13.2	11.9	10.1	13.2	12.0	10.6	13.3
72	11.3	9.7	12.6	11.3	9.6	12.6	11.7	10.3	12.9
73	10.8	9.2	12.0	10.7	9.2	11.9	11.4	10.0	12.6
74	10.3	8.8	11.4	10.2	8.7	11.3	11.1	9.7	12.3
75	9.8	8.4	10.8	9.7	8.3	10.7	10.8	9.5	12.0
76	9.3	8.0	10.2	9.2	7.9	10.1	10.5	9.2	11.6
77	8.8	7.6	9.7	8.7	7.5	9.6	10.2	9.0	11.2
78	8.4	7.2	9.2	8.3	7.1	9.1	9.9	8.7	10.8
79	8.0	6.9	8.7	7.8	6.8	8.6	9.6	8.5	10.5
80	7.5	6.6	8.2	7.4	6.4	8.1	9.3	8.2	10.1
81	7.2	6.2	7.7	7.0	6.1	7.6	9.0	7.9	9.7
82	6.8	5.9	7.3	6.6	5.8	7.2	8.6	7.7	9.3
83	6.4	5.6	6.9	6.3	5.5	6.8	8.3	7.4	9.0
84	6.1	5.3	6.5	5.9	5.2	6.4	7.9	7.0	8.6
85	5.7	5.0	6.1	5.6	4.9	6.0	7.4	6.5	8.1

*From *Vital Statistics of the United States,* Vol. II-5, National Center for Health Statistics, Division of Vital Statistics, U.S. Department of Health, Education, and Welfare, pp. 5–12. based on 1974 dates.

Appendix E

INTERNAL REVENUE SERVICE CENTERS

The following directory of Internal Revenue Service Centers, listing the address of each center and the area it serves, is provided for the reference of estate planners and their clients.

Area served	Address
New Jersey, New York City and counties of Nassau, Rockland, Suffolk, and Westchester	Internal Revenue Service Center 1040 Waverly Avenue Holtsville, New York 11799
New York (all other counties), Connecticut, Maine, Massachusetts, New Hampshire, Rhode Island, Vermont	Internal Revenue Service Center 310 Lowell Street Andover, Mass. 01812
Alabama, Florida, Georgia, Mississippi, South Carolina	Internal Revenue Service Center 4800 Buford Highway Chamblee, Georgia 30006
Michigan, Ohio	Internal Revenue Service Center Cincinnati, Ohio 45298
Arkansas, Kansas, Louisiana, New Mexico, Oklahoma, Texas	Internal Revenue Service Center 3651 S. Interregional Highway Austin, Texas 78740
Alaska, Arizona, Colorado, Idaho, Minnesota, Montana, Nebraska, Nevada, North Dakota, Oregon, South Dakota, Utah, Washington, Wyoming	Internal Revenue Service Center 1160 West 1200 South Street Ogden, Utah 84201
Illinois, Iowa, Missouri, Wisconsin	Internal Revenue Service Center 2306 East Bannister Road Kansas City, Missouri 64170
California, Hawaii	Internal Revenue Service Center 5045 East Butler Avenue Fresno, California 93888

Indiana, Kentucky, North Carolina, Tennessee, Virginia, West Virginia	Internal Revenue Service Center 3131 Democrat Road Memphis, Tenn. 38110
Delaware, District of Columbia, Maryland, Pennsylvania	Internal Revenue Service Center 11601 Roosevelt Boulevard Philadelphia, Pa. 19155

Index

All numerical references are to paragraph [¶] numbers.